I ESCAPED FROM AUSCHWITZ

I ESCAPED FROM AUSCHWITZ

The Shocking True Story of the World War II Hero Who Escaped the Nazis and Helped Save Over 200,000 Jews

RUDOLF VRBA AND ALAN BESTIC

Foreword by Sir Martin Gilbert

RUDOLF VRBA ARCHIVES, LLC, NEW YORK

Edited by Nikola Zimring and Robin Vrba

Racehorse Publishing

Racehorse Publishing books may be purchased in bulk at special discounts for sales promotion, corporate gifts, fund-raising, or educational purposes. Special editions can also be created to specifications. For details, contact the Special Sales Department, Skyhorse Publishing, 307 West 36th Street, 11th Floor, New York, NY 10018 or info@skyhorsepublishing.com.

Racehorse Publishing™ is a pending trademark of Skyhorse Publishing, Inc.®, a Delaware corporation.

Visit our website at www.skyhorsepublishing.com.

10 9 8 7

Library of Congress Cataloging-in-Publication Data is available on file.

Cover artwork by Getty Images

ISBN: 978-1-63158-471-8
eISBN: 978-1-63158-472-5

Printed in the United States of America

EDITOR'S NOTE FROM
ROBIN VRBA & NIKOLA ZIMRING

This version of the book underwent some editorial changes. We have decided to comply with the wishes of the author, who initiated many of these changes when he participated in the translation of the book into Czech, which was published in 1998.

In the footnotes, we have also updated information that was not available at the time the book was written.

TABLE OF CONTENTS

Foreword from Sir Martin Gilbert..*ix*
Author's Preface...*xi*

Chapter 1 A Son Like Me..*1*
Chapter 2 I Became a Wanted Man...*19*
Chapter 3 The SS in Action...*36*
Chapter 4 The Theory of the Camps.......................................*52*
Chapter 5 New Arrival..*71*
Chapter 6 Introduction to Auschwitz.....................................*89*
Chapter 7 A Naked World...*111*
Chapter 8 The Night in August...*133*
Chapter 9 "This is Not a Synagogue!"....................................*156*
Chapter 10 My Condition Improves.......................................*172*
Chapter 11 Ivan the Terrible...*189*
Chapter 12 "Gassing People is Not Easy".............................*208*
Chapter 13 "Never Trust a German".....................................*230*
Chapter 14 Escape..*254*
Chapter 15 Hiding Out...*282*
Chapter 16 We Get the Word Out..*302*

Editor's Note...*317*
Epilogue...*319*

Appendix I..*329*
    Vrba-Wetzler Report (including the Mordowicz-Rosin Report)
Appendix II...*371*
    A Tale of Darkness: Story of the Mordowicz-Rosin Report
Appendix III...*389*
    The Preparation for the Holocaust in Hungary: An Eyewitness Account

FOREWORD

IT IS AN HONOR TO BE ASKED TO WRITE A FEW WORDS ABOUT Rudolf Vrba's book. Like many people of my generation, who began reading about the holocaust in the 1960s, I feel it was a book that made an enormous impact.

Vrba was a prisoner in Auschwitz for twenty-one months and seven days. He then escaped with his fellow Slovak Alfred Wetzler. As they made their way south into Slovakia, they carried with them, seared in their immediate memory, as a matter of personal knowledge, the true story of Auschwitz, the hitherto "unknown destination" of Jewish deportees from all over Europe.

The way in which the information brought by the escapees was handled, and mishandled, provides this book—and twentieth-century history—with a terrible cry of pain. Alas, we cannot revisit or refashion the past. But through these pages, we can learn a great deal about it, and perhaps, if we have the courage of a man like Rudolf Vrba, we can do something to prevent the continual workings and spreading of evil…

There is much that Rudolf Vrba cannot forgive. In reading this book, one comes face-to-face with a reality that cannot be expunged, and with a man who deserves the thanks of his people today as much as he needed their attention and response half a century ago.

Sir Martin Gilbert
Merton College, Oxford

PREFACE

This book consists of a handful of my memories of events that took place more than fifty years ago. It is an attempt to describe (a) how the German Reich managed to get me from my native Czechoslovakia into the death camps of Majdanek and Auschwitz against my will; (b) some of my experiences as a prisoner in these death camps from June 1942 until April 1944; (c) my escape from Auschwitz on April 7, 1944, with a fellow prisoner Alfred Wetzler; and (d) some relevant events following our escape.

I think I should say something about how and why this book was written. Its writing took place in a very different environment while I was on my regular summer holidays in August 1963 in London, England.

After the war ended in 1945, I lived in Prague. This city became my real home until 1958, when I left the country. In Prague, I studied chemistry and biochemistry and began my scientific career. To this day, my livelihood is connected with the roots I established there.

I cannot recall during all the time I lived in Prague if anyone ever asked me what actually happened in Auschwitz. I do not know whether this was caused by a lack of interest or because the subject was taboo. Many events relevant to the real history of the Czech and Slovak lands are connected with Auschwitz: for example, the largest single execution of Czech citizens in the whole history of the people living in Czech lands took place there. This event, which is a part of my personal life, was perhaps for the first time described in my book written in London.

True enough, already in the fifties, the Union of Antifascist Fighters in Prague had arranged an annual Auschwitz Commemorative Evening, and on one occasion, I even went there. I heard a lot about the heroic Czech Communists there. There were dozens of them as well as hundreds of other Czech citizens (may their memory be honored) who died in Auschwitz for their resistance to the Nazis. During this commemorative occasion, nobody mentioned the murder of the many thousands of Czech-speaking Jewish children who were murdered in cold blood at Auschwitz and became national martyrs whether they wanted it or not. Nobody mentioned the fate of the Jews either. I recognized some former Jewish prisoners from Auschwitz on the podium. After the meeting, a suspiciously well-dressed gentleman approached me and asked whether I took notice that the podium was full of Jews. I did not answer. It was sometime around the anti-Semitic Slansky trials of 1952, and I did not want to provoke my fate.

Later, I worked in Israel (1958–1960), where I spent many hours in in the library of the famous Weizmann Research Institute, named after Chaim Weizmann. For decades before and during the Second World War, he had been a leading Zionist. It could be and, indeed, it was sometimes claimed that he was a leader of all Jews. Perhaps that was the reason he became the first President of Israel when the Jewish state was established in 1948. Therefore, I read with interest his account of his leadership and of his life as he described it in his modestly entitled *Trial and Error*. In the biography's index, *Rehovot* is mentioned more than a dozen times.

I wondered how many times *Auschwitz* would be mentioned considering a hundred times more Jews died there than ever lived in Rehovot. To my surprise, I found that the word *Auschwitz* did not even rate a mention in the lifetime memories of the Jewish leader. I do not know whether this reflects a lack of interest by Weizmann and his circle, or whether the word *Auschwitz* was perhaps a taboo also in Israel at that time, albeit for some other hidden reasons.

In 1960, I was invited to come to England to take up a position on the research staff of the British Medical Research Council. This was a sort of Mecca for scientists, and therefore, I was delighted to move to England. I soon acquired many English habits and became an avid drinker of tea and reader of British newspapers, favorite occupations of the English, particularly on Sundays.

In 1960, Adolf Eichmann was arrested. Suddenly, in almost all the Sunday papers, the Holocaust was discussed, and the word *Auschwitz* was frequently mentioned. It had almost become a household word. One of my new friends, Alan Perry, a journalist at BBC, liked to discuss this subject with me, particularly when he noticed I knew more about the subject than he had ever read in the newspapers. He told me that one of the important British newspapers of that time, the Trade Unions paper the *Daily Herald*, had not yet carried a major report on the subject of Eichmann's activities. Alan Perry suggested that the *Daily Herald* might be interested in publishing an article by me in light of my intimate knowledge of the subject.

"Go and talk to them," he said.

I listened to his advice and soon afterward, one late morning, I visited the headquarters of the *Daily Herald*. I found out it is not so easy to talk to an editor. Fleet Street, then the center of British journalism, had its own rules. Due to some wrong directions, I had to mill around in a room full of journalists who were having their tea around an enormous oak table loaded with papers, teacups, ashtrays, and milk bottles. Telephones rang incessantly. The room was filled with a thick cloud of cigarette smoke. One of the journalists approached me, a man of about forty, with his teacup in one hand and a cigarette in the other. He looked at me (an intruder!) with great interest. He studied my rimless Trotsky-style glasses. (I had them made years before during a lecture tour in Moscow.) He noticed my Italian raincoat I'd bought on my way from Israel. He glanced at my good old Prague shoes with their two-inch-high soles, which had been the fashion in the fifties in Prague but certainly not in London. He asked me where I was from.

When I told him "Czechoslovakia," he was amazed. There were not too many people from Czechoslovakia milling around editorial offices on Fleet Street at the height of the Cold War. He glanced once more at my outfit. He then asked me straightforwardly whether I was a spy. I said yes, but I asked him not to spread it around. It was confidential, I insisted. He assured me of his discretion and introduced himself as Alan Bestic, a freelance Irish journalist who had lived in London since the age of three.

I told him about the purpose of my visit to the offices of the *Daily Herald* and about the topic on which I hoped to write. He considered it hopeless to try to buttonhole the editor in this unconventional way. He suggested we write the article in a standard form and only thereafter offer it to the editor. We then went for a drink at the nearest pub. (There were a lot of them on Fleet Street.) I was invited to the Bestics' for the weekend in his home in Surrey to compose the article with my new friend.

That weekend, we spent much time over many cups of tea discussing how I had spent my time during my twenty-one months and seven days as a prisoner in Auschwitz. We discussed my escape (with my friend Alfred Wetzler) from Auschwitz, how we wrote the report on Auschwitz after our escape, and what happened immediately thereafter. I was pleased to see that Bestic wrote shorthand faster than I spoke. He transcribed it on his old rickety typewriter. It sounded like machine-gun fire and came out rapidly, usually without typing errors.

Bestic thought we would need more than one installment to keep the narrative alive and comprehensible. He also added with a frown that it was unusual for the *Daily Herald* to publish more than two installments on the same subject. However, he wrote three installments of a thousand words each and hoped he would be able to negotiate with the editor to settle for two installments. A week later, he phoned to tell me I should come to stay at his house for another weekend. He said the editor had read the proposed article. To Bestic's surprise, he wanted five installments from me to be printed over an entire week, Monday to Friday. So, we wrote a narrative in five installments, each about a thousand words long.

A week later, Bestic invited me to his house to celebrate the acceptance by his editor of our five-installment article of five thousand words. On that occasion, he asked me to sign a contract giving the *Daily Herald* the rights to publish the article. He also handed me a check to compensate me for my "time sacrificed on behalf of the *Daily Herald*." I glanced at the check: it was exactly equal one year of my (or anybody else's) regular salary as an independent research worker at the Medical Research Council.

Later, I heard the rumor that at a party of his peers, the editor was proudly recounting the story about an old woman who used an Old Master's painting to keep her kitchen door open. She sold the painting for almost nothing to the first bidder who understood its real value. He boasted on that occasion that he made an even better deal with a crazy doctor from Czechoslovakia. Yes, I might know something about the Holocaust but nothing about business in the English press, so he thought. The *Daily Herald's* circulation increased forty percent during the week it carried my five articles in March 1961 on the eve of the Eichmann trial.

My life and work in London continued in an agreeable way. One of my newly acquired English habits consisted of leaving an empty milk bottle by my front door every morning before I went off to work. I would leave a note in the bottle listing the amount of eggs, butter, milk, and cream I needed for that particular day. It was all there on my doorstep every evening. On Saturday mornings, when most people were home, the milk deliverer knocked at my door and opened a big book. From this, he read out what I had consumed during the past week and how much I owed him. I then gave him a check, and he returned to his little three-wheeled delivery van. He was a small man with a strong limp, but he moved fast. He was always polite and brief. During his regular Saturday morning call, shortly after my articles in the *Daily Herald* were published, he hesitated a few seconds after I gave him my check. He said almost apologetically, "Excuse me, sir, do you think you could spare a few minutes? I would like to discuss a private matter with you."

"Of course, please come in," I said.

We sat down in my dining room, and he immediately proceeded to tell me his problem. "It is about your articles in this week's *Daily Herald*." He continued: "I have been a member of our Trade Union for over thirty years. I have always been a subscriber to the *Daily Herald*, and I think I have got the right to say that I thoroughly disliked your articles. These articles are meant to create a hatred of Germans among us here in England. To be frank with you, I think you came to this country from Czechoslovakia with the aim of disturbing our good post-war relationship with Germany by spreading incredible lies about the Germans."

I was surprised by his straightforward and accusatory approach, but of course, I understood he had little time to spare; the dairy products had to be distributed and the checks collected. "Why do you think I lied?" I asked.

My quiet and matter-of-fact question disarmed him. Almost apologetically, he said, "Please, do not think I am one of those fascists. I am a member of the Labor Party, and I fought against the Germans when it was necessary." He tapped his right leg, the cause of his heavy limp. It was audible that he'd tapped on wood. After a short pause, he added, "I lost my leg as a British soldier during our landing in France in 1944. You could not accuse me being a pro-German. But now we have peace, and the Germans are our allies. There is no need for anti-German propaganda today. You can believe me that I had no illusions about the

Germans in Hitler's time. However, what you are saying now in your articles is just malicious and incredible."

"Why do you think it is incredible?" I asked.

He paused for a moment. "I shall tell you something about myself," he continued. "I am a married man; we have three children." I listened. He inclined himself toward me and spoke in a lower, confidential tone of voice: "Between us men, I can tell you that my wife, although a very nice person, is quite a simple woman—indeed, primitive. I dare to say she is rather dumb." He paused again. I wondered what he was trying to tell me. He saw the question mark on my face. Now he raised his voice and said in an agitated manner, "But try to tell my wife that someone is going to harm our children! She will pick up an axe she will pick up a kitchen knife, they could harm our children only over her dead body! No matter how dumb she is! And you are trying to tell me that all those clever Jews from all over Europe were taking their children by their hands and delivered them into some sordid gas chambers in Upper Silesia, hundreds of miles away! No, this I cannot believe!" he exclaimed.

I realized immediately that my articles in the *Daily Herald* had explained reasonably well what was finally done to the Jews in Auschwitz. However, I had not explained well enough how all this was arranged beforehand by the perfidious German administration of that time.

I realized then that I would have to write a book to convey to a thinking person what I had seen at Auschwitz. I would have to describe in detail the intricate German deception that, for lack of better words, some today call "the twisted road to Auschwitz." This half sentence does not do justice to the wily, treacherous, and insidious administrative methods used by the Germans to delude the Jews as well as the whole civilized world. Moreover, the German campaigns against the Jews were intertwined with the use of a fast but uninhibited violence against anyone who did not follow their rules or their order.

Furthermore, the German administration always kept at the end of the deportation lines a sufficient number of henchmen to pounce upon selected victims insidiously but expeditiously, with astonishing cruelty and without any mercy whatsoever. This was an important part of their technique of mass murder. That was obviously far beyond the experience and imagination of my milkman.

A year later, I got a letter from Germany signed by Dr. Düx, the public prosecutor in Frankfurt am Main, asking me to come to Germany to help him prepare the trial against a dozen or so SS officers accused of being the perpetrators of crimes at Auschwitz. Dr. Düx looked for me a long time to ask me to help him in his task, but he had been unable to obtain my address from the Czechoslovak authorities. However, after my articles appeared in the *Daily Herald*, the German prosecutors had found out I was living in England. They established contact with me. This was the start of a more-than-thirty-year-long cooperation with the German authorities in the prosecution of some of the German criminals who were directly connected with the Holocaust. There are still quite a few around, even while I am writing these lines.

During my first post-war visit in Germany in 1962, Dr. Düx showed me a large collection of big black volumes arranged on an enormous bookshelf in his office. "I have got here eighty big volumes of written evidence about Auschwitz, and I still do not know everything about Auschwitz," he said.

Sometime after my return from my first trip to Germany, Alan Bestic thought that during the upcoming Auschwitz trial, the British public might be interested to read about some of my experiences. After my articles were published by the *Daily Herald*, I was frequently interviewed on television and radio about problems connected with the prosecution of the SS criminals from Auschwitz. My name became known in London outside my professional circle. Alan soon found a publisher who was prepared to publish a book about my experiences on the condition that the book would be no longer than two hundred pages. During my next summer holiday in August 1963, I had the time to detach myself from work and devote myself to the writing of this book. Alan visited me every day. Each day, he took down in shorthand one chapter of the book from my dictation, retyped it overnight, and made the editorial and grammatical adjustments to the best of his knowledge and ability.

Soon, we felt that two hundred pages were too few for all the information we wished to convey. After some negotiation, we obtained the green light to go to a maximum of three hundred pages. We finished the work in eighteen days, ready for print.

Before my three-week holiday was over, we submitted the manuscript to the printer. The book appeared in the same year, and virtually all major British newspapers reviewed the book positively. It was probably the first book on this subject addressed to the general public rather than to specialists. It was also addressed to my kind milkman. He should know that the leg he lost in the fight against the rule of Nazism was not lost in vain. As we all know, much toil and sweat and tears and blood were lost to defeat the worst enemy of mankind—Nazism.

I wrote this book with gratitude to all those who contributed to the defeat of Nazism. I only hope that I, too, have contributed to this end to the best of my knowledge and abilities, and that this book will help to open the eyes of many to prevent the bestial forces, which we thought we had broken forever, from ever returning.

Rudolf Vrba
Vancouver, Canada
May 2002

CHAPTER 1

A Son Like Me

IT WAS FEBRUARY 1942 IN SLOVAKIA IN A SMALL TOWN called Trnava. I sat in the living room, ignoring the Russian grammar that lay open in front of me, for I knew it was no use trying to study anymore. I could hear my mother, stomping around in the kitchen next door, banging the saucepans about, as if she had a personal grudge against them, and that was a sure sign that there was going to be an argument.

There were, I suppose, good grounds for one. An hour earlier, I had told her I was going to England to join the Czechoslovak Army in exile, and viewed through my mother's eyes from our little town of Trnava, some thirty miles from Bratislava, England seemed as distant as the unexplored jungles of Peru.

Her voice, rancid with sarcasm, rose above the discordant kitchen orchestra and reached me, loud and clear, through the open door. "Why not slip up to the moon and cut yourself a slice of green cheese? But be back in time for supper!"

I said nothing. A delicious smell, a wonderful conglomeration of wiener schnitzel, apple strudel, and frying potatoes distracted me momentarily from the debate which I felt was only beginning anyway.

"I don't know where we got you. You're certainly not like any of my side of the family. First this business of learning English. And then, as if that wasn't bad enough, Russian, if you please!" A snort. A few more sporadic clanks. Muttering which could have been directed at me or could have been meant for the schnitzel. Then: "*Russian!* Why can't you settle down like everyone else and learn a decent trade? Where do you get these uppity ideas anyway?"

I closed the Russian grammar, went into the kitchen, and said, "Momma, I'm not going to be deported like a calf in a wagon."

The saucepans were silent. My mother wiped her hands on her ample, flowing apron; gave me a long, shrewd, penetrating look; sighed; and said, "No. I suppose you're not. I suppose you're right."

Then she sprang to the gas stove and hauled a pot off the flame, as if she were saving a child from the Danube. "Now look what you've made me do!" she snapped. "You've made me burn the potatoes!"

In our house, that was a grave crime indeed, for Momma was a proud and excellent cook.

———

ANY JEWISH MOTHER WOULD HAVE WORRIED ABOUT A SON like me; for in the independent Protectorate of Slovakia, pledged by its President Father Tiso, to fight side by side with its Nazi benefactors, Jews were not expected to get above their station. Indeed, they were forbidden to do so by law.

It was not so much the laws which worried Momma. It was more a matter of conscience, a desire to do the right thing; for her mind had been so molded by the acquiescent elders of her synagogue that she had more or less accepted the status of second-class citizen as something reasonable and proper.

When I began learning English, for instance, she clucked about me and worried, as an English parent might worry if the son of the house refused to play cricket and took up baseball. She regarded my studies as an eccentricity.

2

When I added Russian to my curriculum, however, she became so concerned about my mental stability that she took me to the doctor. Luckily, he was a student of Russian himself and was able to assure her that, while my ambitions might be unusual, they were not medically abnormal.

Looking back on my own attitude at the time, I am surprised that I, too, accepted so much so quietly. I can only conclude that it was because the laws curtailing our rights were introduced discreetly, falling almost imperceptibly around us, like gentle snow.

I became aware of them first at the age of fifteen, when my name was struck off the roll of the local high school. Private tuition was denied to me, too, and I was forbidden to study on my own, a regulation which, of course, was impossible to enforce and which I ignored. Nevertheless, as I could not go to school, I went to work as a laborer.

At work, I found there were two salary scales—a low one for Jews and a higher one for all others—and when I was out of work, I found I had to take second place in the queue at the labor exchange. Jobs went to non-Jews first, and if there were any left over, we were lucky.

Next came restrictions on movement. We were allowed to live only in certain towns and then only in certain areas of those towns, the poorer parts. Travel, too, was curtailed, and we could move only certain distances without permission, and so the ghetto system moved gradually into Slovakia.

All this, of course, I resented; yet I accepted these rulings more or less as some of the unpleasant facts of life. Even when it was decreed that Jews must wear the yellow Star of David on their jackets, I conformed and thought little about it.

It was only when the deportation laws were passed by the government that I suddenly rebelled.

What precisely triggered rebellion inside me I do not really know. Perhaps it was because I was seventeen by that time and at last my eyes were open. Perhaps it was because by state decree I became overnight a Jew, rather than a Slovak. More probably, it was because I resented being kicked out of my own country.

That was the plan. We were told calmly that all Jews were being sent to reservations in Poland where we could learn to work and build up our own communities. Young, able-bodied men would be the first to go, said the announcement, and this, in the circumstances, seemed reasonable enough. It was only later, of course, that we learned the real motive was to remove the core of potential resistance.

I did not know that the reservation was an extermination camp called Auschwitz, a place where I would be expected to die decently and quietly. I simply would not stomach the suggestion that I was no longer a member of the community and that therefore I would have to be cordoned off like a North American Indian. The only difference between us, indeed, was that the Indian was left in his own country.

———

MY MOTHER WAS A STRONG-MINDED, SELF-RELIANT WOMan who had built up a small dress-making business from more or less nothing. She liked to get her own way, but once she gave in, she accepted the new situation wholeheartedly and approached it with unrelenting logic.

She slammed a sizzling wiener schnitzel down in front of me and said, "How will you get to England?"

"Through Hungary. Then to Yugoslavia. If I find I can get no farther, I'll join the Titoists."

For a while, she was quiet. I knew she was thinking of the frontiers I would have to cross, of the black-uniformed Slovak Hlinka Guards, trying hard to ape the SS; of the trigger-happy Hungarian border patrols; of the 1,001 hazards which would face me as I made my way across the tangled boundaries of a Europe at war. Then, having digested these gray thoughts, she said calmly, "You will need clothes, and you will need money."

The clothes she managed somehow. Money was more difficult. After a few days, however, she came to me and said, "Here you are, son. It's not much, but it's the best I can do."

It was two hundred crowns.[1] My fare to England. In the meantime, I had been studying my route. I decided my best plan would be to travel to Sered on the Slovak side of the border and then to make my way across country to Galanta, about seven or eight miles away in Hungary. There, a school friend of mine had relatives who he said would help me.

The problem was to get from Trnava to Sered, which was miles away, well beyond the limits within which Jews were allowed to travel. Obviously, I could not take a train because there was a constant check on passengers and I would be arrested before I had gone more than a few miles, and walking would be even more dangerous, for I would be passing through strange country and would be a suspect immediately.

It was my mother who thought of the answer. Quite casually, for since she had made up her mind about the situation she had shown little emotion, she said, "You'll have to take a taxi. Your father knows a man who will drive you without asking too many questions."

It sounded ridiculous. Who ever heard of anyone taking a taxi ride to freedom? Yet when I thought of it, I realized my mother was right.

It was another week before I was ready to go. The taxi man, a dour, paunchy character with a droopy, tobacco-stained moustache and the doleful face of a bloodhound, was not too happy about the trip, for if he were caught carrying me, he, too, would be arrested. However, in the name of friendship, he agreed to carry me, and I knew I could trust him implicitly.

---

1   Approximately $62 in 2017 dollars. --Eds.

And so, early in March 1942, I said goodbye to my mother, thanked her for all she had done, and picked up my bag. Her face showed little emotion, and all she said was, "Take care of yourself. And don't forget to change your socks."

I did not look back as the taxi drove away, not because I was choked with emotion, but because I was too busy ripping the yellow Star of David from my shoulder.

Then I lay back in the worn leather seats, my stomach twitching with excitement. In my pocket, I had my mother's two hundred crowns, a map, and a box of matches. It was not much for the journey I was facing, but I was only a boy of seventeen and had yet to learn to calculate risks.

Half an hour later, we saw the lights of Sered, and all that time, the driver and I had exchanged only a few words. The tension was mounting in both of us now, and conversation seemed rather out of place.

It was only when we stopped in the town, indeed, and I got out to pay him that we both became a little more voluble. The fare, he told me, was four hundred crowns.

It was an embarrassing moment for us both. I hauled out my two hundred crowns and offered it to him. He gazed at it sadly for a while, scratched his head, tugged at his moustache, and then said with a monumental sigh, "You'd better keep half. You're going to need it. Give me a note to your mother, and she can settle up later."

He was not a Jew, but he was certainly a friend. I tried to thank him, but he was back in the car and driving off quickly before I could get the proper words out. His mission—and for him, it was a dangerous mission—had been completed.

I picked up my bags and looked at Sered. Warm lights and laughter beckoned from the cafés. All around me, people scurried home through a whisk of snow. At the far end of the street, I could see a gendarme idling along toward me. So, I turned my back on the lights and the laughter and kept on walking until I was out in the country again, away from the warmth that was dangerous.

There I studied my compass by match light and headed toward what I hoped was the Hungarian border and Galanta. The snow was falling heavily now, and I was not only cold, but suddenly very lonely. The excitement died in the unfriendly darkness, and something very like fear took its place.

I marched for hours, pushing my rebellious nerves back into place all the way, and at last, I saw lights ahead of me. It was Galanta. I was in Hungary.

My pace quickened, and at five o'clock in the morning, I walked into the deserted town, keeping a close watch for patrolling policemen. I found my friend's house with little difficulty and, weak with relief and fatigue, knocked on the impressive door.

For a long time, there was silence. I knocked again, more loudly this time, and after what seemed like an hour, I heard distant footsteps.

The door opened a few inches, and the frightened face of a maid peered out at me. Then the door slammed shut.

I knocked again and rang the bell, keeping my finger on it and glancing over my shoulder all the time, expecting a policeman to appear at any moment. I heard more footsteps and then a muttered conversation, so I stopped ringing and the door opened again.

A tall, attractive woman in a dressing gown stood looking down at me. I said quickly. "I'm a friend of Stefan's. He said if I called here—"

She interrupted me. Studying me meticulously, she said very slowly, "You … are a friend…of Stefan's?"

"Yes. We were at high school together." For a long time, she stood staring at me. Then, very reluctantly, she opened the door a little wider and said, "You'd better come in."

I was puzzled. Admittedly, it was half past five in the morning, but even so, I had expected a slightly warmer reception from the relatives of my old school friend. And then, as I walked awkwardly into the magnificent hall, I caught a glimpse of myself in a long wall mirror.

A dark, sallow-faced youth stared back at me. His hair was tangled and his clothes were covered in mud. His eyes were red-rimmed and slightly wild; he looked like a cross between a bandit and a tramp. Anything less like a student I could not imagine.

I turned to my hostess and said lamely, "I'm sorry. I walked from Sered. I had to go through the fields…"

Her face stiffened and she almost whispered, "You mean…you came here…illegally?"

I nodded. She raised her handsome eyes to heaven, sighed deeply, shook her head as if she were trying to flick her thoughts into place, and said, "I think you'd better have a bath. We can talk over breakfast."

The maid led me to a palatial bathroom, eyeing me all the time as if I had a bomb in my pocket. She turned on the bath and scurried away as fast as her thin little legs could carry her.

That bath was wonderful, and I wallowed in it for half an hour, my tiredness dissolving in the warm, scented water. When I came out, I found that my clothes, which I had left in a dressing room, had been neatly sponged and pressed.

I went downstairs, looking and feeling a little more civilized. My hostess and her husband, a burly, elegant man with silver hair, were waiting for me at an amply loaded breakfast table. They made small talk about Stefan while I ate, and only when I had finished did they get down to serious business.

It was serious, too. Quietly, my host said, "I suppose you know what conditions are like in Hungary?"

I drained my third cup of coffee and said cheerfully, "No." I was feeling good now, clean and well fed.

"Well, I think you should know. Here we have martial law, which is bad enough. But in addition, relations between Slovakia and Hungary at the moment could scarcely be worse. The authorities know there is a certain traffic across the border, and anyone who helps a Slovak is jailed immediately for harboring a spy."

The splendid breakfast suddenly became a weight on my stomach. I felt dirty again. "You mean…I'm a danger to you here?"

He nodded. I rose to go, but he waved me back into my seat immediately. "Don't be in such a hurry," he said. "This thing will take a bit of organization. If you go out in the street on your own, you'll be picked up in five minutes; in fact, I can't understand how you haven't been picked up already!"

He went to the phone and rang several numbers. Within half an hour, the house seemed full of people. There was a brisk conference at which it was decided that I should leave for Budapest as soon as possible.

Again, I stood up. Rather impatiently, my host said, "Where are you going?"

"To the station."

"Great God, boy," he roared, "are you mad? I told you this was going to take organization!"

It certainly did. One man went with me to the station. Another bought me a ticket—a second-class ticket because people in third-class carriages were liable to talk and ask questions, and those in first-class carriages might report me to the authorities because I had not the cut of a first-class traveler.

A third man bought me a copy of the local fascist newspaper to give me an anti-Semitic veneer, and a fourth slipped me about thirty pengoe. The ticket, the money, and the newspaper were handed to me surreptitiously as the couriers brushed by me with unseeing eyes, and by nine o'clock, four hours after my arrival in Galanta, I was on an express train drawing out of the town.

The train whistled through the countryside and I lay back, pretending to be asleep. The thirty pengoe and my mother's one hundred crowns felt good in my pocket, but in my mind, I had an even more valuable asset than money. It was the address of a socialist underground worker in Budapest, given to me by my friends in Trnava. Pista, they said, would help me on my way.

I called on his home immediately, a dingy little flat in a working-class area. A woman in black eyed me nervously and said, "He's away. Call on his brother, and he may be able to contact him for you."

She scribbled down the address, which I noticed was in a more fashionable district, and off I went, feeling that at last I was getting control of the situation. At the house, I was ushered in immediately, as if I were an old friend, and coffee and cakes were produced.

As I ate, I told them my story. The brother of the underground worker listened without comment and then gave a wry smile.

"This is a bit embarrassing," he said. "You see, I'm a member of the local fascist organization!"

I stiffened and began to feel sick. I was caught, and not only that, but I had confessed everything into the bargain, even to the extent of involving my friends in Galanta. I glanced quickly at the door and the window. Then, to my amazement, my fascist host began to roar with laughter.

"Relax!" he said. "Lots of us are in the organization now. It's good for business. And health. You stay here for a while until we see what's the best thing to do with you."

In fact, I stayed with him for ten days, by which time I felt I was abusing his hospitality. So, I went to him and said, "I must get a job. I think I'll go along to the Zionists and see if they can help me get documents and then some work."

To me it sounded a sensible idea, but my host was far from enthusiastic.

"My friend," he said, "I don't think you'll get a very warm welcome."

"Why not? They'll have to help me!"

He shrugged and went back to his party files, which were spread all over the table.

That afternoon, I went to O.M.Zs.A. House, headquarters of the Zionist organization in Budapest. There, I told my story in detail to a stern-faced man in his middle thirties.

He pondered a while before he said, "You are in Budapest illegally. Is that what you're trying to say?"

"Yes."

"Don't you know you're breaking the law?"

I nodded, wondering how a man with such a thick skull could hold down what seemed like a responsible position.

"And you expect to get work here without documents?"

"With false documents."

Had I torn up the Talmud and jumped on it, I do not think I could have shocked him more. His mouth opened once or twice and then he roared, "Don't you realize it's my duty to hand you over to the police?"

Now it was my turn to gape. A Zionist handing a Jew over to fascist police? I thought I must be going mad.

"Get out of here! Get out as fast as a bad wind!"

I left, utterly bewildered. It was nearly three years before I realized just what O.M.Zs.A. House and the men inside it represented.

My fascist friend was not surprised when I told him what had happened. He agreed, however, that it would be better if I left Budapest in case the Zionist official did report me to the police. So, once again, I became the center of a family conference.

Ultimately, it was decided that I should return to Slovakia and that there, in my hometown of Trnava, friends would wait for me with false documents which would show that I was a nice, clean Aryan.

I could see only one flaw in an otherwise excellent plan. "The journey from Galanta to Sered can be tricky," I said. "What if I'm delayed?"

"Don't worry. They understand the difficulties. They'll wait for six days."

I realized then that I was dealing with men who were not only patient but courageous, too. To hang around border towns for a week was to beg for arrest.

The machinery I had known in Galanta went into reverse. At Budapest station, I was handed my ticket, some money, and a fascist newspaper, each by a different agent. I boarded the express, and three hours later I was in the outskirts of Galanta, making for the fields and the frontier.

I was feeling quite a veteran by that time. After all, I was in familiar country, and I had learned a good deal since I had said goodbye to my mother a fortnight or so earlier. In fact, I was feeling reasonably happy as I plodded on through the mud.

Then it happened. From the darkness, a voice rasped, "*Halt!*"

I stopped and turned slowly. Dimly, I could see the outline of two Hungarian frontier guards. A wan moon glinted on the barrels of their rifles.

I whirled and began to run, plunging frantically through the heavy soil. I heard more shouts and then the shots. I stopped, panting, frightened.

Had I been a little more experienced, of course, I would have kept going, for their chances of hitting me in the dark and on the move were slight, but this piece of elementary military strategy I was to learn only later…much later.

I turned again to face them. They were plodding cautiously toward me, rifles at the ready. Then one stood back to cover me while the other came close. He reversed his rifle and clouted me quickly on the side of the head, spinning me into the soft, cloying earth.

A boot bit into my groin. I writhed as pain washed over numbness and the sky wheeled above my head. From far away, a voice rapped, "Where are you going?"

I managed to gasp, "To Budapest."

"Get up!"

I tried, but failed. They dragged me to my feet and half-marched, half-bludgeoned me to the frontier post. There were about ten other guards there. They looked at me with no more than idle curiosity, for this to them was a nightly routine. Then they began to question me in a rather bored fashion.

Again, I was asked, "Where are you going?"

"To Budapest."

A fist crunched into my mouth, flinging me against the wall.

"Who do you know in Budapest?"

"Nobody."

A corporal with a pock-marked face slowly drew his revolver, tossed it in the air, and caught it by the barrel. He hit me full in the face with the butt, and as I fell, the room filled with fireworks.

Slowly, I opened my eyes. I could see a shiny boot inches from my face. Again, the voices were far away and hands were hauling me erect.

"You're a spy! Admit it!"

I blinked at him stupidly, then shook my head. The taste of blood was in my mouth, and my lips were so swollen I could barely speak, but I managed to mutter, "Going to Budapest."

They were my last words for half an hour, for now the pattern had been established. A question. A blow. A question. A blow. Even had I been willing to speak, I could not have done so because my mind was scrambled.

I was becoming almost numb to the blows; in fact, perhaps because I was semiconscious when suddenly they stopped. Through a haze, I noticed everyone in the room standing stiffly to attention. With an effort, I turned my head and saw a smartly dressed officer standing in the door.

Now at least, I thought, there would be no more beating. No more savagery. Officers behave like gentlemen.

He was a heavy, smooth-faced man in his early thirties, and he sat down behind his table with a sad, almost self-pitying sigh. For a few minutes, he sifted through the bits and pieces the rough soldiers had taken from my pockets—a rather grubby handkerchief, some coins, a few inconsequential scraps of paper. Another deep sigh which seemed to ask the good Lord to look down kindly on all duty officers.

He looked up and gazed at me for a while. It was not an unsympathetic gaze; it indicated, rather, that we both were victims of circumstances which we found equally distasteful and that it would have been much easier for all concerned if I had not been arrested at all.

In fact, I began to relax a little. The soldiers had not found my most important possession—my money, which I had sewn into the fly of my trousers. I knew, too, that I carried no written evidence, no addresses, nothing which might betray my friends in Budapest.

His face and his voice were mild as he asked the dog-eared old question: "Where were you going?"

"To Budapest. I'm a Slovak Jew. I didn't want to be deported. I've just crossed the border."

His forehead puckered with creases, and he began to toy with one of the scraps of paper. He smoothed it out in front of him and glanced at me almost reproachfully. Something in his manner made me stare at that piece of paper, too, and my stomach twisted as I recognized it.

It was a Budapest tram ticket!

Ponderously, he came from behind the table, and skillfully, he hit me twice. Two soldiers stood respectfully behind me to prop me up for the next assault, the next question.

"Where did you live in Budapest?"

"I lived rough. In parks. Places like that."

Another blow that seemed to move slowly but rocketed me back into the arms of the soldiers.

"You're a spy. Who are your accomplices?"

"I'm not a spy. I'm a refugee. I've no accomplices."

Now I was frightened. Not for myself, but for all those who had helped me, my fascist friend and the men who had smuggled me out of the capital. I was afraid this smooth-faced man would make me talk, for obviously he was an expert at the job.

Wearily, he held out his hand. Immediately, a soldier handed him a short truncheon. The two soldiers who had been standing behind me forced me back onto a table, and then he went to work on my face with an efficiency that made the earlier efforts of his subordinates seem amateurish, wasteful.

The blows sliced into my face—short, savage blows that fell with the monotonous regularity of the questions. Names and addresses trickled to the tip of my tongue only to be sent scurrying back again by some force in my mind that I did not know existed.

"You're a spy! Who are your friends? Where do they live?"

My eyes disappeared beneath puffs of flesh, and the blood on my face began to cake. My world was encompassed by that truncheon, and though I could see no longer, I never lost consciousness. The truncheon invaded my brain, but it never managed to take over completely, despite the fact that the efficient officer worked on me for three hours.

After that, he stopped—not because he had grown weary, but because he had become convinced that I must be telling the truth. Now his only problem was to dispose of me quickly and neatly, for there was no place in his life or his barracks for minnows like me.

Dimly, I heard him say to a couple of soldiers: "Take him back to the border. The usual treatment."

The usual treatment. Battered though I was, I realized I was going to be killed and dumped in the No Man's Land of the frontier, and somehow the thought was not terribly frightening. Any emotions I had, indeed, were a blending of pride that I had not been broken and relief that my friends were safe.

They dragged me back through the fields, and the fresh air revived me a little. After a while, when I knew we must be near the frontier, we stopped and one of the soldiers said, "Give me your money."

For a moment, a foolish moment, I thought I might be able to buy my life. I ripped the money from my trousers and held it out.

"Throw it on the ground, you Slovak bastard."

I flung it on the ground. Never taking his eyes off me, he picked it up, thrust it in his pocket, and said, "Keep marching!"

I kept marching, sick at my own stupidity. Soon, however, our pace slackened again, and we made another stop. I heard one soldier mutter, "We've balled this up. I think we're in Slovakia."

The other swore quietly but viciously and grunted, "That means we can't shoot him. One shot and they'll have the dogs and machine guns on us."

"We'd better bayonet him."

I twisted fast and saw one of them coming at me with a naked bayonet. I screamed. He punched me to the ground, flung himself on top of me, and pressed his hand over my mouth. His colleague stood like a frightened cat, gazing into the darkness.

The bayonet was at my throat. I could feel it pricking my skin; then the pricking stopped and the soldier who had been sitting on me rose slowly. The pair of them stood rigid, silent, and suddenly I realized that they were much more frightened than I was.

Minutes passed. One of them whispered, "Get up. Get out of here."

I got up and began walking away from them. I walked fifteen yards, and then I ran, zig-zagging, ducking, weaving, waiting for a bullet which never came.

I ran wildly for a hundred yards before I tripped and fell. It seemed like the end of the line, the end of resistance, the end of everything. I lay, my face buried in the earth, grunting with exhaustion, beaten, semiconscious.

How long I lay there, I do not know. It may have been minutes. It may have been hours. I may have slept or I may have lost consciousness, but when at last my eyes creaked open, a dog was panting in my face. All I could see was the piercing beam of a flashlight, which cut into me like a knife.

I heard a voice say in Slovak: "Jesus, he's still alive!"

Someone lifted me to my feet. It was a Slovak frontier guard, and as he gazed at me in something like awe, he said, "You should be dead! We always find them dead!"

He shouted for another guard. Between them, they half-carried me through the fields until we came to a village. There, they kicked at the door of an inn until the owner came grumbling down to open it.

The sight of me, however, my face decorated by the Hungarians, my clothes torn and stained with mud and blood, changed his humor at once. He ushered us in, and within minutes I was lying in a huge armchair, sipping brandy. A woman appeared with a basin of warm water and gently began to bathe my face. The mists disappeared with the blood, and I realized I was back among human beings.

Still, those frontier guards had to do their job. They took me to the police station and began questioning me. I told them the truth.

The guard who had picked me out of the mud frowned and said, "So you don't want to go to a resettlement area. You don't want to work. You dirty, bloody Yid, I should beat you so your mother wouldn't recognize you. But that's been done already!"

He pushed me into a cell, locked it, and went about his business. I lay on the plank bed, aching, stiff, and began to doze.

A voice woke me. The voice of an old woman. It said: "Mr. Jew… are you asleep?"

I traced it to the bars of my cell window. Heaving myself up with an effort that hurt, I said, "No."

Through the bars fell some cigarettes and some food. News that a Jew had been picked up somewhere along the frontier, it seemed, had traveled fast through that Slovak village; and somewhere a Christian woman had thought of him lying alone and maybe hungry. That this was arranged by the local Jews for money, I learned only later, much later.

CHAPTER 2

I Became a Wanted Man

JUNE IS A BEAUTIFUL MONTH IN SLOVAKIA, AND IN 1942, IT excelled itself. The sun was warm and benign and constant. The fields were heavy with lush, amber wheat waving lazily in gentle breezes, and the birds sang as if they were cheering their heads off at the success of the whole show.

Even from behind the barbed wire of Novaky camp, the world looked lovely. Indeed, probably the only person there who did not take time off from his worries occasionally to gaze at the scenery was Mr. Jew.

They had taken me there the morning after my arrest, and now I sat on the edge of my bunk, brooding over the irony of my position and cursing quietly to myself. For weeks, I had been scampering to and fro, ducking to avoid bullets, absorbing punishment, risking my neck and the necks of others, all in a grim effort to evade being sent to a resettlement area, and all I had managed to do was land myself on the launching ramp itself.

On my arrival, they bundled me into a huge barracks that held several hundred men, most of them a good deal older than I was. I still was not quite sure why I was there or what was going to happen, but listening to the conversation all around me, I soon found out.

It was tedious, doleful, and boring, revolving endlessly around bribes that had been wasted, about promises that had been broken, about corruption and deceit and injustice, and most of all, about transports.

When would the next train come? Would there be a next train? Had the whole transportation business been called off? For hours, they kicked the dreary subject round that big wooden barracks, like kids on a rubbish dump kicking a football made of rags.

I realized then that I was in a transit camp, that the next stop was somewhere in Poland, where I would be taught to work like a civilized human being, where my Jewish vices would be purged, where I would help build a new, decent community. For a while, I cursed a little less quietly, and when I had worked the bile out of my system, I began looking around me to see what could be done about the situation.

A tall, slightly balding man on the bunk beside me was saying: "I gave him five hundred crowns, and he said I had nothing to worry about. And now—"

I interrupted him. "Tell me," I said, "what are the chances of getting out of here?"

The monologue died. I felt a dozen pairs of eyes on me. Someone laughed and said, "Listen to him! Here as long as a wet day, and now he wants to go home!"

A paunchy merchant glared at me and rapped, "Jesus, that's all we need. A bloody troublemaker!"

And the man who had lost his five hundred crowns nodded towards the door and said, "Out there are two Hlinka Guards. Try to get past them, and they'll shoot you for a rat. The only time you leave this barracks is when you want to go to the shithouse. And even then, you've a rifle at your navel."

It did not sound very encouraging, but when I investigated further, I found that the situation was not without promise. I learned that Novaky was divided into two camps: one the transit section, which held those awaiting transport to Poland, and the other a labor camp, where the more favored Jews were supposed to work for the good of the Slovak government.

Everyone looked with longing towards the labor camp. Everyone was trying to get into it, for at least it meant a reprieve from the unknown, but not everyone had the necessary qualifications, which were money, influence within the Zionist movement, or some specialist knowledge. Doctors, carpenters, and blacksmiths, for instance, had a good chance of passing that vital frontier.

That ruled me out. I had no influence, no trade, no money. Nevertheless, I had been on the road long enough by this time to realize there was always a back door, and it was not long before I found one.

The Hlinka Guards wanted someone to fetch food for the transit camp from the labor camp. I volunteered immediately, and the others let me have the job because they knew I had no food and they were still receiving parcels from home. This meant at least I could get out of the barracks without going to the lavatory.

On my very first trip, I realized here was the back door, not only to the open air and the sunshine, but to freedom. Because everyone wanted to get into the labor camp and nobody thought of getting out, it was surrounded by a pathetically inadequate barbed-wire fence, and only one Hlinka Guard patrolled this perimeter, which was about one thousand yards long.

I noticed, too, that the Hlinka Guard who escorted me was much more interested in feeding his face and drinking slivovitz in the kitchen than he was in me. Had I wished, I could have slipped away that very day and gone through the wire and nobody would have missed me for at least an hour.

Experience, however, had taught me caution. I knew by now that a man on the run needs clothes. Before I went, I would have to transfer some gear to the labor camp and find someone I could trust to hide it for me.

So, for the next few days, I studied the faces around me every time I went to the labor camp. Most of them were discouraging—the smug, flaccid faces of the rich and the wealthy. In fact, it was a week before I singled out a man I thought would be ready to help someone other than himself.

He was a stout little plumber who always seemed to be working on the taps in the kitchen. He smiled a lot and sang at his work, an optimist among a broody bunch of pessimists.

Still, I had to be sure. One day, I took off my jacket and said to him, "Would you look after this for me until tomorrow? It's too hot to wear it today."

He lowered his spanner and gave me a long, shrewd look. Then he grinned and said, "Sure. I'll put it in my locker in the barracks."

Next day, I took a pair of socks, and this was the crucial test. This time, he would know perfectly well that I was not worrying about the weather. He would know my mind was on the barbed wire.

Casually, I said, "Could you stow these away for me somewhere?"

Without a word, he took them and shoved them quickly into his pocket. I had found my man.

After that, I transported my not-very-extensive wardrobe up to the labor camp more or less sock by sock. I even managed to take my briefcase along one day, making some fatuous excuse to my rather stupid escort. All this took time, of course, but by the end of six weeks, I was ready to go.

Luck, indeed, was not just running my way. It was galloping. Before I went, I had to face up to one last problem, the old-fashioned problem of money, for my last pennies had long since disappeared down the throats of the Hungarian frontier guards—and even that was solved almost miraculously.

I had become friendly in the transit barracks with a tall, handsome lad called Josef Knapp who came from Topolcany, the town where

I was born, and who, like me, had tried unsuccessfully to escape to Britain through Hungary.

"I must be the unluckiest bastard in the world," he said to me one day. "Over in Topolcany, just a few miles away, I've got one of the loveliest girls you ever saw in your life. We were going to get married in the autumn. I've got a father with so much money that he can't count the stuff. And here am I, in bloody Novaky, waiting to be sent to God knows where in a filthy cattle truck!"

Quickly, perhaps too quickly, I said, "You've got money?"

He nodded glumly and said, "What I wouldn't give to see her for just five minutes!"

"You've got money here in the camp?"

"Sure. And as much as I want outside."

"Listen, Josef," I said. "I'm leaving here, going under the wire in a few days. How about you coming along?"

After that, it was ridiculously simple. I persuaded the Hlinka Guards that I needed an assistant on the food run because the camp was filling up. He agreed without giving the matter too much thought, and three days later, I was in the labor camp kitchen again, this time with my banker by my side.

Quietly, I said to my friend the plumber, "May I have my gear?"

He nodded and walked casually out of the kitchen. I glanced at my escort, saw he was stuck deep into a hunk of meat, and walked after the plumber, Knapp by my side.

At his barracks, my temporary valet handed me my briefcase, already packed. Then he slipped five hundred crowns[1] into my hand and said, "Good luck. God bless you."

He disappeared before I could even start thanking him.

There was no sign of the patrolling guard. Knapp and I went under the wire and three minutes later were sliding down the high banks of

---

1   Approximately $156 in 2017 dollars. --Eds.

a stream that trickled down from the nearby forests. Another ten minutes, and we were deep inside that forest, laughing our heads off.

It was the laughter of pure exhilaration. Novaky was behind us; Novaky with its long faces, its dreary defeatist talk, its moans and its whines. The sun flickered through the trees as we marched, and to me, the Slovak scene had never looked lovelier.

We had been walking for about two hours when we heard a strange sound. Right in the heart of the forest, we heard the cheers of a crowd rising and falling, lilting like music neither of us had heard for a long time.

Josef frowned for a moment and said, "I know this place. Believe it or not, there's a football stadium in this forest. I used to go there every Sunday." Then he turned to me with a grin and said, "This is Sunday. There's a match on. What are we waiting for?"

We did not wait. We almost ran to that stadium, and soon the pair of us, two fugitives from a resettlement camp, were cheering ourselves hoarse; abusing the referee, the players, the linesmen; losing ourselves utterly in an hour that seemed to have been snatched straight from the past.

At halftime, we drank beer, ate sausages, and winked at the girls. Then we plunged back into the crowd, and the cheering swept over us, washing away the memory of Novaky and all thought of the future.

It was quite a few hours before we remembered just who we were and where we were. To be precise, it was midnight.

After the match, we wandered on through the forest, still chewing sausages like a couple of trippers. When it grew dark, we lay down in a cornfield and slept immediately, still drunk on the air of freedom.

At midnight, however, we both woke up. In the distance, we could hear the low rumble of a distant train and the long, lonely sound of its whistle. We sat silently and watched until we could see its headlights splitting the darkness and the orange glow of the fire in the cabin.

Another few minutes and it was passing us, a goods train with its wagons clanking and jostling each other, and still we sat watching, silent, until the red light of the guard's van disappeared in the distance.

"Wonder what it's carrying," said Josef. "Cattle? Coal?"

I looked after the train that had come from God knows where and was going God knows where and said, "Or Jews…"

We scrambled to our feet and began walking. A distant whistle shattered the last of our football-match illusions.

We were heading, in fact, for the village of Velke Uherce, where Josef had friends. He could not go into Topolcany because he was too well known there, and so I, who had not been there since I was three years old, was going to contact his girlfriend for him.

"Just tell her the name of the village," said Josef. "She'll know which house. She'll look after you, and once I've seen her, I'll see you're fixed up with anything you need."

It sounded fine. Now I had a rich backer. We parted a couple of miles from Velke Uherce, and I set off for Batizovce, where I knew I could get a train for Topolcany.

It was still only five o'clock when I reached the outskirts of the town—a dangerous hour. If I walked into Batizovce at that hour, I was courting arrest because nobody but the police would be around. So, to kill time, I wandered into a country graveyard, sat on a tombstone, and waited. There, I felt sure I would be safe, for who would go visiting graves at five o'clock in the morning?

My theory was reasonable. In practice, it did not work out. At half past five, an old peasant woman wandered in and laid a bunch of flowers on a grave. She glanced at me and then toddled away, thinking, perhaps, how sad it was to see one so young so filled with sorrow.

By eight o'clock, I was in Batizovce station. An hour later, I was in Topolcany, sitting in the parlor of a neat little suburban house, telling my story to Zuzka, Josef's girlfriend.

She listened without a word, hardly able to believe me, for she thought he was in Hungary. Then she said, "I must go to him at once. Momma will look after you until I get back. I won't be long."

With that, she was gone, having babbled out a garbled version of my story to her parents who seemed to have mixed feelings about me.

"Any friend of Josef's is a friend of ours, of course," said Poppa with a rather shaky smile, "but it's a little difficult just now. You see, they're rounding up the…Jews in Topolcany. It makes it…rather embarrassing."

Suddenly, I realized this was not a Jewish household. If they were caught harboring me, it would be more than a little difficult. It would be downright dangerous. No wonder the poor old folk were scared out of their wits of me.

"Would you mind very much," said Poppa, his face wrinkled like a worried prune, "if we put you in the shed?"

I told them their shed would be a palace compared with Novaky, and out I went to it, followed by Momma and a huge meal. As I ate it among the spades and the forks and the rakes, I thought, Soon Zuzka will be back with some money. Then off to Trnava to collect the false documents that my Hungarian friends organized for me.

A few hours later, Momma came in with another meal. I asked whether Zuzka had returned, but she shook her head, and as meal followed meal, I began to feel worried. Velke Uherce, after all, was only half an hour away, and they both knew I was waiting.

That night, I slept in the shed. The following morning, Momma brought me my breakfast. Zuzka? There was still no sign of her, and by that time, I was not really worried anymore. I was furious. I had been left in the lurch by the man I had carried out of jail. He had got what he wanted—his girlfriend—and that made me redundant.

Still, I decided to give him another day. After all, I felt, they had not seen each other for a long time. The trouble was that Poppa was not quite so patient.

That afternoon, he came to me, his face twitching with embarrassment, making me feel almost sorry for him.

"It's all very difficult," he said, "but she hasn't come back." I said nothing. "It's so dangerous these days, what with the police and all these raids and…"

I stood up, emptied my bag, stuffed what I could into my pockets, and put on a second pair of socks, for that was the easiest way to carry them. Then, leaving my bag in the shed—people with bulging bags are always suspect—I thanked him for his hospitality and went out into Topolcany, town of my birth.

I walked with mixed feelings. I felt pleasantly nostalgic as blurred memories cleared and I recognized a building here and there. I saw middle-aged people and wondered if they remembered my father. Somehow, I felt at home in Topolcany.

On the other hand, it was an uncomfortable journey. The shoes which had carried me to and fro across the Hungarian border and in and out of jail hardly had any soles left. I was slopping along like a tramp, and though I still had the five hundred crowns my friend the plumber had given me, I knew I could not fritter it away on luxuries.

The answer to this problem came to me as I passed what I knew was a Jewish house. It had no Star of David hanging on the front door, but the signs were unmistakably there—the signs of the times.

In the front garden, there was furniture. Here were people about to be deported, and as soon as they were gone, the authorities would auction the furniture for peppercorn prices and buy another Quisling by handing over the house to him.

I walked up the path beside the neat little garden and knocked. A tall, angular man who looked like an ex-schoolteacher opened the door, and I told him my story—the whole story.

He listened without interrupting, and when I had finished, he said, "I knew your father, but I'm sorry I can't help you." He gestured vaguely in the direction of the furniture and went on: "You see the way it is. We haven't much money, and we'll need every penny of what we have for the journey."

I told him quickly that I did not want money and added tentatively: "But if you had an old pair of shoes...."

He disappeared without a word and returned with an almost new pair of brown shoes in his hand.

"Here," he said. "Take these. They belong to my son, but he won't be needing them anymore. He went two months ago."

Those shoes, owned perhaps by someone I had known in Novaky, fitted me perfectly and boosted my morale to the treetops. I went waltzing down the street now, saw a milk bar, and decided to celebrate my luck—and freedom is such a heady affair that the pint I drank had the lighthearted taste of champagne.

Even the sight of a gendarme striding into the milk bar did not depress me. He was a tall, middle-aged man with a monumental moustache, saber clanking by his side, carbine over his shoulder, revolver in its holster on his shiny belt. He greeted everybody cheerfully, smiled at me, and I smiled back quite happily. At that moment, even gendarmes, most active of all branches of the police force, could not cast a shadow over my optimism.

I finished my milk and wandered out into the sunshine. It was too early to go to the station to catch the train for Trnava, so on the spur of the moment, I decided to make a short sentimental journey—to wander by the house in which I was born.

The street was photographed on my mind. Every gate had some fragment of a memory. My mind, in fact, was miles away when I heard the squeal of bicycle brakes behind me.

It was the gendarme. He towered over me on a bike as big as a horse and said with great formality, "Good afternoon. May I see your documents, please?"

I stared at him, unable to speak. To me, at that moment, he was not just a gendarme in a country town. He was the Hungarian frontier guards with their rifle butts. He was Novaky in all its dismal squalor. He was a train that had come from God knows where and was going to God knows where.

I screamed and ran, blindly, wildly, with the creak of his bicycle lancing my nerves. I could hear the clank of his sabre and thought of his carbine, which I knew he would use as a last resort. Weaving, ducking, I reached a kiosk at the end of the street and rounded it. He lurched after me. Four times, we tore around that kiosk, and then I doubled back up the street again, sick with panic.

The bicycle strained after me, still creaking. I knew I had to stay in this one stretch, up and down the houses I knew so well, for once I left it, once I went into the wider roads beyond it, he could pick me off with his carbine.

He was abreast of me now. I stopped, turned back, and headed for the kiosk again. Over my shoulder, I could see him dismounting, lifting his bicycle around to save time, vaulting into the saddle like a cavalry man.

Up and down we went, panting, breaking, turning. How he managed to keep the sabre out of the spokes I shall never know, but manage he did, and he knew I would tire before he did.

People stopped to stare at this crazy, comical, terrible hare-and-hound chase. Crowds gathered. They cheered the pair of us, and for me that was bad, for now he had to catch me as a matter of honor or never raise his head in Topolcany again.

Desperately, I searched for a foxhole. Then fear twitched my memory into action, and I thought of a laneway that led into the freedom of the fields. I found it, ducked down it, and ran into a block of fine new buildings. The fields of my childhood had been urbanized!

I stopped, panting, sweating. I heard the bicycle clatter to the ground behind me and turned to see the gendarme standing over me, sabre held high.

He roared, "Halt or I strike!"

We were both exhausted; but I was beaten. More quietly, he said, "Are you a Jew or a thief?"

"A Jew."

Slowly, he lowered the sabre. Still gasping, he said, "You're lucky. If you'd been a thief, I'd have let you have it. I'll have you know I hurt my knee, turning that bike after you."

We studied each other in silence for a few moments while we recovered, and when he had stopped blowing at last, he told me, "I don't blame you running. I did the same when the Cossacks came at me with sabres on the Russian front!"

I realized then that I had been caught by a man of character, a man who had fought for the Habsburgs for little money, a man who had learned understanding the hard way.

Still, he had his duty to do, and he did it. He had to display me to the town, to show them all that the fugitive had not escaped the net of justice which he represented, to demonstrate that right, as usual, had triumphed. So, sabre rampant, he marched me ostentatiously through the streets, and the crowds, who a few minutes earlier had cheered me, now gazed at me fearfully, wondering whom I had murdered.

He did not speak to me again until we were near the police station. Then he said, "Do you know why I asked for your documents?"

I shook my head.

"Because when I was in the milk bar, I saw you were wearing two pairs of socks. Two pairs of socks in this weather!"

Those two pairs of socks helped me on my way to Auschwitz.

In the police station, the atmosphere was informal. They said, "Give us a thousand crowns and you can go."

To me, that seemed a reasonable offer, apart from the fact that I didn't have a thousand crowns. I gave them every penny I had, every penny that was left from the five hundred I had been given just before I ducked under the barbed wire at Novaky. It came to about four hundred crowns.

I watched them divide it carefully and fairly between them, and when they had pocketed their dividends, one of them turned to me with a smile and said, "Sorry, it's not enough. We'll have to send you back to Novaky."

This raised a big laugh, and as I glanced at the sergeant's desk, I realized why. There was the warrant for my arrest and a full description of me which had been circulated to all police stations in Slovakia. If I'd had three thousand crowns, it would have made no difference. There was nothing else they could do except send me back.

To pass the time, they questioned me casually. One of them said, "You've an aunt still living in town. Why not ask her for some money? We'll send around a message, if you like."

I told them not to bother. I had learned my lesson. So, they shrugged and began to debate what they would do with me that night, for normally the station was locked up and they all went home to bed.

At last, after a lengthy conference, the sergeant came to me and, speaking more or less man-to-man, said, "Look, we're going to lock you in the cells and leave you on your own until the morning. Don't be too downhearted about the situation because it could be worse."

He tugged at his moustaches and shot me a glance from under his shaggy eyebrows. He seemed to be searching for a phrase, trying to find a nice way to say something unpleasant, for after all, I was from Topolcany and deserved some consideration.

At last, he muttered, "Don't do anything silly. I mean, if we find you dead here in the morning, we'll only have to bury you. And that wouldn't be nice for you, a Topolcany boy, now, would it?"

I told him it would be far from nice and told him I had no intention of killing myself. He smiled, gave me some cigarettes, locked me in my cell, and left me on my own to think about the future.

Next morning, they took me to the railway station. Again, there were crowds to watch me go, and just as we were about to enter the station, a little blond-haired girl darted forward and thrust a parcel into my hands, tears streaming down her face.

It was my little cousin Lici, then only about thirteen. Years later, I learned that someone had told her that her cousin was being taken away by the police. She had dashed into a shop with her few pennies and bought me all that she could afford—cherries.

Hlinka Guards took charge of me at the station. We did not talk much on the journey back to Novaky, but they did not mind eating my cherries.

At the camp, I was not received with brass bands or garlands of flowers, for the men who should have been guarding me had gotten into trouble over my escape. The sergeant in charge of the guard room beamed at me as I was led in and said, "Good morning, sir! We've been expecting you. This is indeed a pleasure."

He gave a short little military bow and smashed his fist into my face. I flew back against a table and sent it crashing into a group of Hlinka Guards who were drinking coffee. The coffee went all over their uniforms, and that did not help much either.

Slowly, they encircled me. Methodically, they beat me with their fists, their boots, and their rifles, passing me from hand to hand so everyone would get his fair share. Then, as suddenly as it had all started, it stopped.

I saw them all staring sheepishly at the door, and my eyes followed theirs. An SS officer was standing there, surveying them superciliously.

"See that this man doesn't go back to the camp," he snapped. "He's a troublemaker. Keep him in the guardroom, and make sure he is sent away on the next transport."

He saved me from further beating, but not because he had any sympathy for me. I think he probably felt the Hlinka men might kill me; if that happened, the news might filter through to the other deportees and upset them. The SS did not want their charges upset; they wanted them to go nicely and cheerfully to the gas chambers without causing any hitch.

The Hlinka men, anyway, seemed to be impressed. They looked at me with a new interest, realizing I was more than a football to be kicked around the floor. I was important, and accordingly, I was led away to a special cell.

They pushed me in and locked the door. A huge man in the uniform of a Slovak soldier looked up. I saw it bore insignia to show that he was a Jew; I also saw that his face, like mine, was black and blue, though, unlike mine, it was creased with a wide smile of welcome.

"Good evening," he said. "Who are you?"

I introduced myself.

"From Topolcany?"

"I was born in Topolcany."

He stood up and roared with laughter. I did not see anything funny in either my name or the fact that I was born in Topolcany until he said, "Your father did business with my father. He owed us a lot of money when he died. But don't worry. You need not pay me back just now. Have some salami. Have a drink of water."

He told me his name was Fero Langer and that he was the son of a wealthy businessman in Telgart. He had been conscripted into the Jewish forced labor detachments of the Slovak Army and had used his uniform to bluff his way into Novaky to help a relative who was being transported.

"Trouble was," he said with his huge grin, "they posted me as a deserter. Have that salami, and then we'll have a game of skittles."

About a yard of salami hung on the door. I bit off a chunk of it, looked at him hard, and said, "Skittles?"

"Yes. Like this."

He took a loaf of bread and broke it in half. One half he stood at the end of the room. The other he rolled into hard, little pellets.

He rolled one at the half loaf of bread, missed by a mile, and said very seriously, "Your turn. We'll play for salami."

For four days, we played skittles for that hunk of salami on the door. Even then, there was still plenty of it left, for though we had plenty of practice, we found that bread-crumb skittles is a tricky game.

At the end of those four days, Feri lost his partner. The Hlinka Guards opened the door of the cell and took me out; my transport, they said, awaited me.

I was sad to leave that cell, but just before I did so, I had a slice of luck. A parcel arrived from my sister with clothes, cheese, a cake, and some marmalade. I offered to share it with Feri, who had been more than generous with his salami, but he refused to take anything; in fact, quite the reverse, for when I opened that parcel on the transport much later, I found he had managed to slyly slip the rest of the salami into it.

I discovered when they took me to the transport that I was being given VIP treatment. While the Hlinka Guards waded through the endless formalities before we moved off, checking and counterchecking papers and people over and over again, I stood on the platform, my parcel on one side of me and a guard with a submachine gun on the other. There was one man for me and one for several dozen others; it was quite flattering.

When at last we climbed aboard, I found that my wagon had been honored in similar fashion. All others had only one guard, but mine had two, and they took the trouble to warn me before we moved off, "Try to escape again, and you're a dead duck."

In spite of this friendly advice, I felt sure there would be some chance of a break somewhere along the line, but when we reached Zwardon on the borders of Slovakia and Poland, my faith in this theory began to wane slightly. There, the Slovak Hlinka Guards left us, and the SS took over.

Even the engine driver was an SS man. I studied them carefully, and I realized that here was real efficiency. These men with their submachine guns and impassive faces made much less noise than the Hlinka Guards, but I knew once they started shooting, it would be hard to stop them, and they would not miss, either.

The door of the wagon closed. Through the window, I could see the Hlinka Guards loitering around the station. The train moved off, and suddenly I thought, After all that. . . I'm still a calf in a truck!

CHAPTER 3
The SS in Action

IT WAS UNDERSTANDABLE, I THINK, THAT THE PEOPLE ON that sardine tin of a transport, clanking morosely north, found little time at first to sympathize with each other. They all had problems enough of their own. They all were imprisoned mentally by unanswerable questions. How had it happened? Why had it happened? What was going to happen to them and to those they had left behind? And, of course, where were they going? Snatched from civilization, yet still attached to it by the umbilical cord of domesticity, they worried, too, about trifles. Had they turned off the gas at the mains? Had they locked the back door? Had they remembered to cancel the milk and the newspapers?

In fact, that wagon of ours, into which the Hlinka Guards had managed to squeeze eighty people with their luggage, was a little world of worry, and each individual was a world unto himself. Yet in spite of it all, in spite of bewilderment, fear, and acute physical discomfort, everyone had a gentle thought for the Tomasovs.

I saw him first just after we had crossed the Slovak border: a tall, dark youngster of about twenty, struggling across the wagon toward me, towing a lovely young blond girl in his wake, and suddenly, among all those milling faces, I recognized him as a lad I had known slightly in my hometown.

We shouted greetings to each other. At last, panting and sweating, he managed to reach me, and, glancing at the girl, I said, "Your sister?"

"No," he said with a smile that was both shy and proud. "I would like to introduce you to my wife. We were married a fortnight ago because...because...well, Monsignor Tiso said families would never be separated when they were deported."

I understood. Monsignor Tiso, puppet President of Slovakia, Quisling Extraordinaire, had indeed made that promise, and as a result, there had been a rash of teenage marriages throughout the country as those in love strove to stay together. Yet as I gazed at the two youngsters in front of me, on their honeymoon in a stinking transport going God knows where, I wondered what the future held for them.

That, however, was a matter for conjecture. In the meantime, something had to be done about the present. I spread the news around, and the reaction was swift.

Immediately, they were showered with gifts—food from some, trinkets from others and, from those who had nothing else to give, congratulations. Someone produced a bottle which he had smuggled on to the train, where all alcohol was forbidden, and we had what must rank as one of the strangest wedding parties ever.

We toasted the bride. We toasted the groom. We toasted their respective parents and their future family while Tomasov and his new, young bride stood blushing in a corner.

In the circumstances, it was a good party, but when it was over, we still had a major problem to solve. A young couple, just married, had to have a bridal suite, and this was not easy because the wagon was packed so tightly that only a few could lie down to sleep at a time, while the rest stood.

Still, we managed somehow. We shifted the luggage. We reorganized ourselves. Though the Tomasovs protested vigorously, we contrived to give them very special sleeping accommodation and as much privacy as possible.

The Tomasovs, indeed, softened the shell which people had built around themselves for protection, and after the wedding party, a new, rough courtesy developed in spite of the fact that we were living under conditions liable to make tempers trigger-happy, to generate quarrels, to set neighbor against neighbor. We realized suddenly that we were all in the same mess, all Slovaks, all Jews, and all heading together into the unknown.

It showed itself in many small ways. When a man wanted to get to the lavatory, which was one small bucket in a corner, he excused himself politely as he edged his way toward it, almost as he would if he were crossing a crowded ballroom floor, and when he got there, the others discreetly turned away.

Those who had food shared with those who had been rushed on to the train with nothing. My salami, for which Fero Langer and I had played a bizarre game of skittles and which, unknown to me, he had stuffed into my rucksack before I left Novaky, did not last long, but, while it was there, it was there for everybody. When it was finished and I had nothing left but my jar of marmalade, others gave me what they had themselves.

For the old, too, there was gentle consideration. At Zilina, for instance, the doors opened and an old lady of about eighty was pushed into our wagon, a crumpled bundle of lavender and old lace. I helped her to her feet, and she thanked me with an old-world charm, as if I were assisting her out of her carriage instead of into a filthy cattle truck, and immediately space was made for her near the toilet so she would be spared a journey that was both arduous and embarrassing.

These brave, pathetic attempts to lead normal lives in what was no more than a mobile prison, of course, served a purpose. They helped to wean people's minds from those questions which were nagging them.

How? Why? What? Where?

For a long time, they remained unspoken. Then old Isaac Rabinowic, a spindly little man from Bratislava, surfaced suddenly from beneath the brim of his big, black hat and said, "It must be the will of God."

He had been tucked away in a corner of the packed wagon for hours, and these, I think, were the first words he had spoken since the journey began. They were words tinged with surprise rather than outstanding piety or resignation, as if he had discovered at last the only possible reason why he should have been uprooted from his home.

Those around him murmured polite acknowledgement of his decision, but few in that sweat-stained wagon really believed their Creator had anything to do with their journey. Most, indeed, felt they had been trapped in a net of intrigue rather than moved by Divine decree.

We had sensed that net drawing around us for some time, and many were the methods used to evade its meshes. Some, for instance, had tried bribery. And had failed.

One of them was Mrs. Polanska, a large woman, wealthy by the standards of her village in central Slovakia. She was pressed close to Isaac Rabinowic, nearly smothering him, and while she felt he was considerably below her station, this overwhelming proximity did not prevent her from telling all within earshot her troubles.

"I went along to the commander of our Hlinka Guards back home," she said. "After all, I had a right to, for his sister and I went to school together, and when his daughter married last April, I lent her all my best silver for the wedding reception. Needless to say, they still have it, but that's neither here nor there apart from the fact that my own mother gave it to me when I got married.

"What hurts me is the deceit of the man. I was terribly discreet. I just left ten thousand crowns[1] in an envelope on the table, and later he told me I had nothing to worry about. He did not exactly say as much, but he gave me the impression that all he had to do was strike my name off the list.

"And what happens? I ask you—what happens?" Her featherbed of a bust heaved with emotion, crushing poor old Isaac as she went on: "He takes my money and then forgets my name. After pretending to

---

1   Approximately $3,115 in 2017 dollars. --Eds.

be a gentleman, he turns out to be a corrupt little pipsqueak without an ounce of honesty in his miserable heart!"

Some tried denying any non-Aryan strain. And failed.

Big Janko Sokol, a lumberjack standing beside me at the window, chewing a chunk of salami, said, "I don't know what the hell I'm doing here. I'm a bloody goy![2] Yet, just because I was brought up by a Jewish family, I'm kicked out of my home and out of my country.

"I even gave them a certificate signed by a parish priest to say I'd been adopted by Jews when I was a baby. And they told me it was forged!"

"They probably looked at your paies,[3] Jacko," grinned his neighbor. "I bet you're circumcised, too, like the rest of us!"

Some tried to argue that they were essential to the life of the community. And failed.

Mr. Ringwald—everyone called him "Mister"—a wealthy businessman from Zvolen, his expensive clothes crumpled and stained now, told us: "My business benefited the whole town, and I said as much to them. So, what did they do? They took it from me and gave it to my biggest rival, an Aryan who used to be violently anti-Nazi. But you should see him now."

"A clever move that," said Mrs. Polawski. "I know the man. He's a member of the Hlinka Guard now, a dirty traitor."

We listened to these tales with interest. We did not know they were going to be repeated a million times all over Europe.

I said nothing. I had chosen none of these devious methods of escaping the net. I had no money, no business, no friends among the Zionists or rabbis, no friends among the priests who might give me a clean bill of religious or racial health. My method, indeed, was unsubtle.

I fought, and so far, I, too, had failed. Yet I intended to continue fighting, and that was why I clung grimly to my position at the window.

---

2   Non-Jew
3   Side whiskers

I was not admiring the scenery, but thinking of escape, studying the route so I would know it on the way back, for I still believed this journey was little more than an irksome delay before I made my way back to collect my documents from the underground.

As we moved deeper into Poland, however, my confidence began to sag a little. Conditions in the wagon deteriorated. The atmosphere grew more tense and courtesy more strained. Sanitary facilities were a danger to health now, and though we still had enough food, we had no more water.

People still laughed, but their laughter was brittle. Occasionally, there were bantering arguments, but the banter was growing hollow and forced.

We would see cities in the distance, and men would argue about their identity.

"That's Cracow," one would say.

"Don't be ridiculous. It's Katowice."

"You're both wrong. It's Czestochowa."

These arguments helped me ignore the discomfort to some extent. I gazed out at these towns like a tourist, for after all, I was only a boy, and this was a new country. Deep down, however, I realized they were being staged for a purpose—to draw attention from the thirst which for some was becoming a torment—and the debates died as soon as someone muttered, "When are we going to stop for water?"

There were unspoken reminders, too. When we crossed a river, those near the window gazed down at it longingly. Advertisements for beer— "Drink Seybusch…It's Healthy…It's Good!"—taunted us. After a while, indeed, the thought of water dominated us, pushing all other worries aside.

At last, the train began to slow down and stopped. We had reached Czestochowa. For the first time in twenty-four hours, the trucks were opened, and heavily armed SS men rapped, "One man out to get water. Nobody else must move!"

Our man was not quite fast enough. In fact, before he reached the head of the queue which led to the pumps, the order came: "Back to the wagons!"

He hesitated. I heard him say to an SS man, "I haven't filled my can yet."

A rifle thumped across his shoulders, and he came back to us, his can empty. The doors of the wagon slammed shut, and the chains that locked it clanked into place. There was silence, a silence induced by shock.

Still, there was hope. We found that the chains of the wagon doors were long enough to allow us to open them a few inches. We hauled them back, and there, right in front of us, was a tantalizing sight. Water, gallons of it, was being thrown about all over the place, and to us, that seemed like sacrilege.

In fact, a group of German soldiers on their way to the Russian front were washing, splashing about like seals at play. Others hung around, drinking schnapps from bottles, laughing and shouting with the brash abandon of men who knew they were about to face death. Most of them were already half drunk.

I called to them: "Hey—give us some water!"

They looked around, squinted at us for a moment, then said, "What have you got? Food? Money?"

Water, it seemed, had its price. There was a quick whip-around, and we produced some salami, which seemed to suit the soldiers.

A few of them strolled over to get our cans. Immediately, an SS man with a submachine gun bore down on them, shouting, "Get back there! Get away from that wagon! You know it's an offense to go near it."

The soldiers turned slowly and faced him. They did not move. He blustered up and snapped, "Go on! You heard what I said. Get away!"

There was no love lost between the ordinary German soldier and the SS. The Wehrmacht man let his hand hover over the butt of his service revolver and said softly, "Listen, brother. We're going out to fight. We're going to the Russian front, while you lot are safe behind the lines, wheeling a bunch of bloody Yids up and down the country. Now bugger off before I get annoyed!"

Another soldier, polishing his submachine gun with loving care, said with a grin, "Don't provoke the hero, Franz. After all, he doesn't want to share his loot with someone like you."

They were all smiling now, ostentatiously baiting the SS man. For a moment, he stood his ground, and then, through the slits in the doors, we watched him turn and walk quickly away. He had weighed up the mood and found it dangerous.

The soldiers filled our containers and took our salami. The train began to move slowly, and I saw the soldier with the submachine gun pause in his polishing and watch it go, a strange, almost cynical expression on his face. Then he turned away and spat in disgust.

I wondered, as we drew away, whether it was the sight of so many Jews that upset him or the sight of a puffed-up SS man, and then I looked at his gleaming machine gun and wished I had it in my hands.

The wagon was happier for a while, but spirits sank with the level of the water, and soon, even though we rationed ourselves, we were thirsty again.

Another station, however, brought new hope. Here, too, there were soldiers, though this time, when we tried to do business with them, we found they drove a hard bargain. They laughed when we offered them salami and instead demanded money.

There was another conference in the wagon. Money was eased from carefully concealed hiding places. One man produced a gold wedding ring, gazed at it for a while, and said with a wry smile, "Lucky I love my wife so much or this would have been sold a long time ago!"

The money and the gold passed through the gap in the doors. The containers were filled again, and the man who had given his wedding ring gazed silently out of the window, his face turned away from us.

A few more hours, and the buffeting of the wagons told me we were reaching yet another station. This time, when we stopped, I saw our wagon was right beside a locomotive which was being filled with water. It was gurgling down the vast, fat hose, slopping half into the engine, half onto the track.

I gazed at this glittering waterfall. I turned to the driver, who was leaning phlegmatically out of his cabin, ignoring this strange train from nowhere; shoved a mug through the window; and said, "Would you fill that, Mister?"

We were so close we could have shaken hands, but he did not seem inclined to do so. Instead, he continued to gaze at the horizon. I glanced down at the tracks, saw that the SS men who ringed the train were looking the other way, and said more urgently, "Come on, friend. How about some water?"

He continued to stare into the middle distance. Then, without turning his head, he said, "I'm not going to get myself shot for you bastards!"

Looking back, of course, I can understand his attitude. There was an order that any civilian who helped those on the transports would be shot, and the SS did not hesitate to carry it out. A bullet in the back is a high price to pay for filling a tin mug.

Then, however, I was not in such a tolerant mood. I saw the railway workers withdraw the big hose from the engine. I saw it empty itself on to the track. I gazed up at the huge water tank, which held God knows how many gallons, and as our wagon drew away, I cursed that engine driver for being a mean, cowardly swine.

Still, we had enough water for a while, and so the debate began again. Where were we going? What were these resettlement areas going to be like? A little girl of about nine looked up at her father and said, "Will there be schools and playgrounds there, Daddy, like there are at home? Will there be lots of other children?"

For a moment, he did not answer. For a moment, indeed, the wagon was quiet, subdued by the child's shrill voice. Then her father ruffled her hair gently and said, "Yes, darling. There'll be schools and playgrounds...everything you want. You'll like it even better than home."

She squeezed his hand and smiled. I think we were all grateful for that swift, white lie.

Nobody believed, of course, that the resettlement areas were going to be anything like home. Nevertheless, they had managed to convince themselves that there would be areas where they would be able to live and work and rear their families. Only a faint shadow clouded their conviction, a shadow cast by letters from some of those who had gone already.

Zachar, a small greengrocer from Trnava, said gloomily, "I bet they'll be labor camps or some sort of ghetto. Still, it's better than a concentration camp, and the food will be better than Novaky. It's not as if it's forever, either. The war should be over in a few months, and then we'll all be back home again."

For a while, the conversation turned to the war. Nobody doubted for a moment that Germany would be defeated, perhaps because they would not let themselves think of a German victory. The only real point at issue, they felt, was just how many months it would be before the end came, and even this was but a minor point of debate, for what was going to happen tomorrow or the next day was much more important.

Zachar's sixteen-year-old daughter, a freckled-face girl with a long plait, said, "My cousin went on the first transport, and she wrote to me the other day, saying everything was fine. The food was good, and they weren't working too hard."

She paused for a minute, a look of bewilderment on her face. Then, polishing her nails more vigorously than ever, she went on: "There was only one thing I couldn't understand. She said her mother sent me her love. And her mother died three years ago."

"There was something funny in the letter I got from my sister, too," said a plump young woman who was feeding her baby. "She told me old Jakob Rakow was in fine form. But Jakob was killed in a car crash ages ago."

A gossamer web of doubt descended on the conversation. From rucksacks, handbags, wallets, cases, crumpled letters were produced and analyzed, word by word. In some were references to people who were dead or to events which could not possibly have happened, and it was these little nonsenses that made people worry and wonder.

It was only later, of course, that I learned the answer to these riddles. The letters were written in Auschwitz at gunpoint shortly before the writers died. They were written to inspire confidence among those yet to be transported, for the Nazis knew that the slightest resistance, created by fear of what lay ahead, could ruin the whole scheme.

Sometimes, however, someone managed to slip in a concealed warning by stating the impossible, a tiny act of defiance that took courage, and the tragedy was that those who received these carefully phrased letters invariably managed to explain away discrepancies as a slip of the pen, perhaps because they wanted to believe in the resettlement areas.

So it was in our wagon. The letters were read. The flaws were found, and then they were swept away by a deluge of explanations which somehow seemed to make sense.

The doubts, of course, remained, but they sank deep into the recesses of the mind. Those who tried to dig them out and parade them were scorned or mocked or ignored completely.

In our wagon, in fact, there was only one person who foresaw the future clearly and that, I think, was by intuition rather than by reasoning. He was Izak Moskovic, an untidy, frail young man of about twenty-two.

I think, perhaps, he was frank because he was used to mockery, ever since the rabbis had plucked him from his poverty-stricken home and established him in a rabbinic school where normally only the sons of the well-to-do studied. His orthodox Jewish parents were delighted, of course, when Izak was honored in this way, but the boy himself was miserable because his brain could not cope with his studies. He became a joke among the other pupils, and when he left, a failure, the family heard echoes of the laughter.

Izak, indeed, was a stage Jew. He looked it. He sounded it, and that probably was why the Hlinka Guards arrested him and tortured him— because they simply did not like his Jewish face.

After that, he became more morose than ever, as if he was brooding over his memories, conscious of the fact that he was no more than a rather poor, tormented joke, but he roused himself when his fellow travelers in the wagon began to paint the resettlement areas in optimistic pastel shades.

Suddenly, he cut across the conversation, jarring it to a stop. In his shrill, singsong voice, he shouted, "You're fools if you think you're going to resettlement areas. We're all going to die!"

There was an awkward, embarrassed silence, as if he had shouted some obscenity. Then someone said with a rather strained laugh, "Listen to who's talking about fools!"

Another man said, "Have you been listening to the rabbis, Izak? Have they been looking into the future for you? Or did you learn to do that yourself at school?"

It was heavy, cruel humor, and it silenced Izak for the rest of the journey. Soon, in fact, he was forgotten, though later his words were remembered.

At Lublin, for instance, they suddenly made some sort of sense. The transport slowly nudged its way through the station and stopped some distance outside it. The doors were whisked open, and we saw that the entire train was surrounded by a cordon of SS men, some with rifles, some with submachine guns. Officers, Iron Crosses pinned to their elegant uniforms, moved among them, brandishing bamboo canes or horse whips.

We stared at them, wondering what was going to happen, and we were not left in doubt for long, for up and down the train the officers began to shout, "All men between sixteen and forty-five out!"

At first, nobody moved simply because they could not believe their ears. This was against the rules, contrary to the principles which Monsignor Tiso, President of Slovakia, had expounded over and over again. In the newspapers, on the radio, he had never tired of saying: "It is a basic principle of the Christian faith that families should not be separated. That principle will be observed when the Jews are sent to their new settlements."

It seemed, however, that the SS men had not been reading their President's speeches in the newspapers or listening to him on the air. They advanced grimly on the open wagons, bellowing, "Come on! You heard! All men between sixteen and forty-five out. The rest stay where they are."

Slowly, the truth was rammed home in minds that had been dulled suddenly by shock. Slowly, all able-bodied men jumped down from the trucks while their wives, their sisters, their daughters, their fathers, and their mothers gazed after them, torn by fresh doubts, new fears.

They herded us into a raggedy line beside the transport. Still, we did not realize what was happening. Even when the doors of the wagons were slammed with a terrible finality, the truth did not sink in for a moment.

Tomasov was the first to understand, Tomasov of the bridal suite. Suddenly, he leaped out of the line and dashed for the wagon, shouting, "My wife's in there! Let her out!"

A horse whip slashed across his face, spinning him into the dust. He staggered to his feet, blood oozing from his cheek, and tried again to reach the wagon. This time, the SS man went to work on him in earnest. He clouted him to the ground and for a solid minute clubbed him with an efficiency born from experience.

We watched in silence, dazed by the speed of events. Behind the closed doors of the wagons, there was silence, for the minds of those left inside were just as numb as ours. Gradually, however, we all glimpsed the truth simultaneously, grasped the fact that Tiso was a liar. From the narrow, barred windows, from the splits between the doors, hands stretched plaintively and men dashed forward to grasp them.

They never reached them. The SS men dashed up and down the line, lashing out with their whips and their canes. They beat the men, and they beat the hands too, the withered hands of the old, the pudgy hands of the very young. The train jerked forward, stopped, then slowly moved away, and above the noise of the engine, the hiss of steam, the crash of buffeting trucks, we heard the wails of the women and the cries of the children whose wrists were bruised and broken.

I was lucky. I was alone. I had no wife, no mother, no daughter on that train, but for the others it was a moment of empty despair. Their families had disappeared, and it had all happened too fast for thought, let alone for action.

I saw Tomasov stumbling to his feet. He gazed with dull, hopeless eyes after the transport, then shambled back into line. Dirt mingled with the blood on his face, and his clothes were torn. I spoke to him, but he just stared at me blankly and said nothing.

An SS officer marched once or twice up and down the line, like a farmer inspecting cattle at a fair. Then he shouted, "You have a long march ahead of you. Those who think they won't be able to carry their luggage may put them on the trucks."

We had not noticed the trucks before, but now there was quite a rush for them. I clung to my rucksack, however, for I had just remembered the words of poor, stupid Izak, the boy whom not even the rabbis could teach.

"Anyone who thinks there is a resettlement area at the end of this line is a fool. We're all going to die!"

I did not believe the last part of his statement. I had no intention of dying. The first part, however, seemed reasonable enough, for the lies were falling fast. I decided I would not let my rucksack off my back, let alone out of my sight. I made up my mind, indeed, that from that moment on, I would trust nobody.

The SS men prepared us for the march, beating our raggedy ranks into a semblance of order. Then off we went, marching, not, perhaps, with the precision of "storm troopers," but at the pace dictated by the men with the guns and the sticks and the whips.

I toyed with the idea of making a break for it, but one glance at the strength of our escort was enough to make me abandon the idea. I knew I would be shot down before I had covered more than a couple of yards.

Others, however, were braver or more foolish. A few paces ahead of me, a man suddenly ran toward the side of the road. A burst of machine-gun fire struck him in the stomach, flung him backward, and left him twitching in the dust, and after that, a new discipline entered the ranks, for we all realized that, as marksmen, the SS were a credit to their instructors.

They marched us through the back streets of Lublin, presumably because they were still trying to convey the impression that Nazis were gentlemen rather than slave merchants. With us, however, they did not need to foster any such genteel image, and once we were out on the open road, away from the city, I discovered that our captors were not merely liars, but petty thieves as well.

An SS man tramping along beside me asked me the time. I glanced at my watch and told him.

Immediately, the muzzle of his rifle pressed gently into the small of my back. Quietly, he said, "Give me that watch."

I gave it to him. There seemed to be little point in arguing. This small piece of larceny, indeed, seemed unimportant compared with the prospect that lay ahead, for we seemed to be heading for a concentration camp.

I saw watch towers and barbed wire and row upon row of ugly barracks. Huge gates swung open before us, and as we marched through them, we could see men in convicts' clothes. At first, the sight merely aroused my curiosity, but after a while it shocked me, for suddenly I began to recognize faces.

These were not criminals. Some were from my hometown. I saw businessmen I knew and shopkeepers, garage owners, schoolteachers and librarians, the billiards ace from the local pub and the lad who stole my first girlfriend, the rabbi's son, the butcher's son, the blacksmith's son who could bend a coin in his teeth. They were all there, and they all looked alike now with their ragged, striped uniforms and their shaven heads.

Soon, I knew, I would be joining them. Soon my head would be shaven. Soon I would lose my identity in this concentration camp called Majdanek, a preparatory school for the academy of Auschwitz.

It was a harsh prospect softened only by one thought. At least the women and the children and the old were not with us. For them, I felt, life would be easier. Separation, in fact, was perhaps a blessing.

I did not know that they were on their way to a place called Belzec, a crude forerunner of the streamlined Auschwitz extermination machine. There, they would be gassed with the fumes of exhaust pipes. There, their bodies would be burned in open trenches, for crematoria were still in the blueprint stage.

CHAPTER 4
The Theory of the Camps

THE THEORY OF CONCENTRATION CAMPS WAS NOT NEW TO me. For years, sinister whispers had been seeping through Czechoslovakia—through Europe, indeed—rumors of ugly, self-contained worlds where the rule of gun and club and whip prevailed, where the majority died from beating or hunger or shooting, where the emaciated survivors for a day or a week or a month gazed hopelessly at a horizon of barbed wire while flamingo-legged watch towers hovered over them.

Yet the reality, the first sight of a camp in action, shocked me, even though my mind was prepared for it. I was not afraid for myself, for I was determined to live, to get away. It was the whole, dreadful atmosphere of the place that I found nauseating, lingering as it did in my nostrils like the stench of stale blood.

As we moved from section to section, for Majdanek was divided into several watertight compartments, skeleton-thin prisoners whispered, "Any food? Anything in the pocket?"

They did not look at us as they spoke. They just kept on working, digging or sweeping or mucking about with wheelbarrows which threatened to jerk their stick-like arms from their sockets.

We tossed them what food we had, not high in the air, carelessly, but furtively with a quick flick of the wrist, and then I saw how life in a concentration camp can degrade a human being.

Like jackals, they pounced on the scraps, fighting, snarling over them, and then I saw another aspect of concentration camp life, something quite foreign to my mental picture—something quite sickening. Half a dozen quaintly garbed men fell upon them with clubs, lashing them indiscriminately. The prisoners ignored the blows, went on scrabbling in the dirt, and then at last one broke from the ruck and ran, cramming a filthy fragment of cheese into his mouth while these strange guards ran after him, beating him.

I was curious about these men and studied them closely. Obviously, they had authority, but even more obviously, they had nothing to do with the SS. They were dressed like circus clowns, yet I did not feel like laughing.

One had a green uniform jacket with gold horizontal stripes, like something a lion tamer would wear; his trousers were the riding breeches of an officer in the Austro-Hungarian Army and his headgear was a cross between a military cap and a priest's biretta.

Another had a prisoner's striped jacket, but his trousers were those of a German soldier circa 1911—black with a thick red stripe down the side. A third wore the full prison uniform, but it had been tailored to fit him splendidly, and the crease in his trousers would have made a guardsman envious.

I could see that they were prisoners and from the green triangles on their uniforms—it was clear that many were professional criminals—and then I realized that here was a new elite, a prisoners' establishment, so to speak, recruited to do the elementary dirty work with which the SS men did not wish to soil their hands. It was clear to me, too, that they were fulfilling this task with an efficiency and brutality which equaled and occasionally excelled that of their masters.

These were the infamous kapos, an essential part of the structure of every concentration camp and extermination center in Europe: men who held the power of life or death over their fellow prisoners and who did not hesitate to use it.

The idea that here big dogs ate little dogs, big prisoners beat little prisoners lower on the social scale was unpleasant. There was, however, another shock in store for me—this time, a personal shock. It came when I saw Vrbicky.

I knew him well back home. So did everyone in Trnava, for Vrbicky was a character, a man whom some liked, some despised, and some avoided, for often it spelled trouble to associate with him.

He was about twenty-six, a lorry driver with a somewhat haphazard approach to life. He had a wife and kids and an eye for every passably pretty girl in the town. The respectable Jewish community disliked him because he drank too much and was careless about his marriage vows.

The less orthodox—myself among them—could not help liking him. He was a pleasant, easygoing fellow who wielded a billiard cue in the local pub as skillfully as Yehudi Menuhin wields a bow.

And now suddenly I saw him wielding a whip with all the savage skill of an SS man. A prisoner groveled on all fours in front of him, trying to scamper away like a dog, but from Vrbicky's lash, there was no escape. It rose and fell, monotonously, regularly, accurately, and I looked in horror into the face of my old lackadaisical, lecherous, hard-drinking friend.

The lazy eyes were like little stones now. The mouth that used to smile so easily was tight. Vrbicky had been remolded, or perhaps, I thought, he had found at last his right niche, the one job he could do with efficiency and enthusiasm. Certainly, he was too busy to notice me, and I was glad. I did not want to know him anymore, for Vrbicky was a kapo in clown's clothes, a man with a bloody whip.

They marched us to a barracks which bore the sign "Left Luggage." It was so incongruous that I almost felt like laughing. It was as if we had just arrived in a railway station and were about to dump our baggage so we could go out and enjoy ourselves on the town—only this time there was no town, and soon there would be no luggage.

I handed over my rucksack which contained all my possessions—the clothes my mother had sent me in Novaky and my jar of marmalade, which somehow had survived. With punctilious efficiency, a man gave me a ticket for it, as if I were going to call back to collect it in an hour or two, and then he pitched it across the floor.

It landed with a crunch. The marmalade began seeping slowly out of the rucksack. I thought to myself, If they're going to use my shirts and socks, they'll have to have them laundered!

On they marched us from section to section. I saw others from Trnava, but I had no chance to speak to any of them until we came to the gate of section five. There we were delayed for a while, and there I saw Erwin Eisler. The long-faced Erwin, whose burly, slow-moving frame held the heart of a keen, if ponderous, student. My mind went back to Trnava, to the days when Erwin used to blush when we teased him about girls and always made excuses when we asked him to come for a drink in a café.

There were other memories, too. I remembered Erwin and myself going along to the local authority to hand in our books, for Jews were not allowed to study and were forbidden to have anything which might help them do so. I had walked away, glum and empty-handed until Erwin whispered to me, "Don't worry. I've still got that chemistry book."

After that, we studied together secretly either in his home or mine, sharing the one book left to us. Years later, after the war, those clandestine studies paid dividends for me because when I went to the Technical University in Prague, I found they were still using the same textbook.[1]

Now, however, Erwin Eisler was no longer a student. He was a prisoner, fiddling about with a wheelbarrow at the gate to section five, pretending to work and waiting to see whether the newcomers had any food.

---

1   The chemistry book was by Emil Votoček, a significant Czech chemist, whose textbooks Inorganic Chemistry and Organic Chemistry had been used for decades. --Eds.

I attracted his attention. He looked up, and his face seemed even longer because the bones jutted out and the flesh was drawn tight. Recognition flickered at once in his eyes, and then it was carefully masked. He bent over his wheelbarrow, pretending not to see me.

"How is it here?"

He glanced up very casually and pulled a skeptical face. It reflected not so much despair, for he was too kind to tell the whole truth, but rather a warning that I must expect the worst.

"Do they take everything from us?"

"Everything."

"Can a man live?"

"A short time…perhaps."

It was a weird conversation, spoken more with gesture, with expression, than with words. Yet I knew precisely what Eisler was trying to say. He was trying to tell me that all of us were going to die.

I suppose I should have accepted his verdict. After all, he knew Majdanek, and he was intelligent, but I did not believe him. The others might die. That was sure. But I was going to live.

The gate swung open. Eisler, bending over his wheelbarrow, whispered, "Anything in the pocket?"

"Sorry…all gone."

He gave me a last quizzical grin. We marched through the gate. I never saw Erwin Eisler again, and it is certain that he died in Majdanek.

Someone roared, "To the baths!" We were herded into a gloomy barracks where the smell of disinfectant rasped in our nostrils.

"*Strip!*"

We took off our clothes, and I plunged into one of the troughs. Behind me, an old man was feeling his way in gently because he was feeble.

"Faster, you old bastard!" A stick thumped on his frail, bare back, plunging him face forward into the murky water.

Out we went into the open air again in time to see them taking away our clothes. I stood there, shivering, and took a good look at my surroundings for the first time.

There were barracks all around me—squalid, wooden affairs. Barracks, barbed wire, and beyond that, nothing. Not a tree, not a shrub. Desolation. Majdanek had been set apart from civilization.

It was depressing, but not nearly so depressing as the sound effects. From the other sections, we could hear cries and the sound of beating and occasionally a shot. We could catch glimpses of prisoners scurrying about frantically, one jump ahead of a stick or a bullet, and in our shivering, naked group, morale sagged until thoughts of death began to dominate our minds.

I still felt I could win out, though I knew now that my chances were tissue-paper thin. All around me, however, I could see men who had given up, men whose spirit had left them.

And then, in that dreary, death-ridden atmosphere, came one of the most splendid examples of tragi-comic courage I have ever known.

Beside me stood Ignatz Geyer, whom I had known back home by the inappropriate nickname of "Nazi." We had chased girls together, "Nazi" with spectacular success.

He, too, was sure he was going to die and, indeed, he was right, for they killed him soon afterwards, but he was determined to die with dignity. He was not going to let them degrade him.

He looked around at us all and said with a grin, "What a lousy collection of pricks you lot have!"

The crowd stirred. Somebody laughed. The gloom lifted a couple of inches.

"Tell you what," said "Nazi". "Let's have a contest. Let's see who has the biggest!"

Maybe it was ridiculous. Maybe it was childish. Certainly, it was vulgar, but it revived humor, an emotion which was nearly dead at that moment.

"Nazi", for the record, won. He gazed down at his prize-winning property, gave a slow grin, and said, "A pity you're never going to be used again. But still, you haven't had a bad life!"

Now the kapos were shouting again, driving us on to the next operation, which was shaving. First, they sheared the hair of our heads. Then we stood on stools and they shaved the hair on our bodies. Nazi looked me over with a comically quizzical eye and said, "The girls of Trnava wouldn't recognize you now. You wouldn't get very far with them on a Saturday night!"

He was right. Now I was a convict and looked it. The girls of Trnava were very far away indeed!

They flung us some clothes. A pair of trousers. A jacket. A pair of wooden shoes. A shapeless hat. I pulled them on and then an oberkapo, a master lackey, came to lecture us.

First, he told us about the roll call.

"Every morning and every evening, you will parade outside your barracks in rows of ten to be counted. When the SS man approaches, the order will be given: 'Caps...*off*!' When he moves away, the order will be: 'Caps...*on*!'

This will be done smartly and with precision. The slovenly will be beaten. Nobody must move, and those who do will be killed immediately. Whenever you pass an SS man in the camp, you will take off your cap when you are three yards from him and keep it off until he passes you."

And so on. We were troops in an armless army, subject to discipline more severe than that known by any German soldier.

There was one point, however, that the oberkapo did not mention about the roll call. Not only were the living counted, but the dead, too. They were piled up neatly behind us, a pathetic heap of corpses, some scraggy with starvation, some bloodstained from beating, and some who had died simply because they no longer had the will to live. They were the ones who had died in the night.

Starvation was a major killer. German scientists reckoned that the rations were sufficient to keep a man alive for three months, but for once they were inaccurate. Beatings and shootings ensured that the death rate remained high, and so did dysentery. It affected many of the newcomers, and they were liquidated immediately because they could not work.

The following morning, after roll call, the kapos rounded up their cattle. Some were marched out to nearby factories, slave workers who helped swell the profits of German industrialists. Others, myself, for instance, were put to work on the camp.

We worked as builders' laborers, though at the time I was not quite sure precisely what we were building. Now, of course, I realize I was helping to extend a vast extermination machine, a machine which was to obliterate six million people, for Majdanek was a crude forerunner of Auschwitz.

As I carried around my bricks and timber, I learned unwritten concentration camp rules which the oberkapo had not mentioned. That morning, for instance, a man beside me suddenly ran for the wires. He was shot long before he reached them.

It could have been sudden madness. It could have been deliberate suicide. Who knows? It taught me, however, not to go near the wires because even to be suspected of attempting to escape meant death.

Later, I began talking to my neighbor in a normal tone of voice. A kapo's club sent me sprawling on my face. I learned to keep my mouth shut.

I saw men beaten for trivial offenses: moving too slowly, perhaps, or forgetting to take their caps off when an SS man passed. I noticed that those who stood silently got off comparatively lightly. Those who cried out were beaten more savagely because they were a nuisance. Those who ran were chased by three or four kapos, for now it was a sport. So, I learned to stand still and silent when the kapos went to work on me.

In fact, I learned the art of survival, and after that came the art of living, of making the best of appalling conditions. I discovered, for instance, the camp grapevine, which gave me a link with friends who were in other sections, and it was through this grapevine that I managed to arrange a brief, silent family reunion.

A Slovak friend of mine who had been carrying wood from section two, where we worked, to section three told me one day: "Your brother Sammy is here. In section three."

The news came as a shock to me. I had known that both my brothers were due to be deported to those mythical resettlement areas. Occasionally, I had wondered whether they might be in Majdanek, but the idea of finding them in that vast, strictly segregated camp seemed out of the question. And now I learned that Sammy was only a few yards away!

My instincts drove me toward the wire which separated the sections. My common sense held me back, for to be caught at the wire, even the internal wire, meant death. So, I decided that if we were to meet, the meeting would have to be carefully planned.

Indeed, such meetings were taking place in the evenings after roll call, when few kapos were on the prowl. My friend, my wood-carrying courier, said he would arrange for Sammy to be at a certain part of the wire at a certain time the following evening.

I turned up at the appointed time only to find that I had to take my place in the queue. Already two people were talking through the wire and a group of others were waiting around at a distance of about ten yards for them to finish. Only one could approach the wire at a time, for a crowd would be bound to attract attention.

On the other side, a similar group idled about, waiting their turn, and then, although it was nearly dusk, I recognized my brother, the tall, dark Sammy, who was ten years older than I was. He saw me almost simultaneously, and we raised our arms in brief salute.

Another two went to the wire for a brief conversation. I was next. I felt a tingle of excitement, of expectancy, and of fear, too, for we both were taking a big risk. I was not walking up and down now; I was standing, poised, almost like a runner at the start of a race. I saw the man on our side of the wire turn, and as I moved forward to take his place, I heard a roar and a clatter of boots.

The kapos swarmed on the scene, bludgeoning the man near the wire unconscious. The rest of us disappeared in the gloom.

Next day, I was told that Sammy had been moved to another section, and I never saw him again. I learned, however, that he managed to survive as long as Majdanek survived, but when Majdanek died, everyone in it, Sammy included, died with it.

———

ONCE I HAD FOUND MY FEET, ONCE I HAD LEARNED THE tricks of survival, I was able to think actively, to proceed with the plan which I had not abandoned since I had left home months earlier. I was still determined to escape, and never had the incentive been greater than it was at that time.

I was certain that the Zionist leaders in Slovakia who encouraged their people to go quietly to the resettlement areas had no idea what, in fact, lay ahead of them. I was equally certain that the people would resist, would unite and fight, if only they could be warned, and I knew, too, that the deportation of thousands would be impossible if they did not go passively. If I could escape and somehow get back across the Slovak border, I might be able to save thousands, for by this time I had realized just what sort of a place Majdanek was.

It took me some days to understand its true purpose. I had noticed that people disappeared from our section but presumed at first that they had been transferred elsewhere. I had watched the daily caravan from the hospital, a pathetic column of the sick and the old and the dying, making their stumbling way to a building some distance away, a building with a tall chimney. Some were able to walk; some had to be helped by those a little stronger; some went in wheelbarrows.

I had noticed that they never came back. I had wondered what went on in that building, but I had never asked because another unwritten law of the camp, of any camp, ruled that questions were dangerous. In fact, I learned the truth only when I overheard a kapo give a casual order to a prisoner.

He said, "Take those bricks over to the crematorium."

I watched the man wheel them away in his barrow. I saw him heading toward the building with the tall chimney, and then I knew why those fragments of humanity from the hospital never came back.

That gave me yet another imperative reason for getting out of Majdanek. If I was not shot, if I was not beaten to death, I might collapse one day from hunger, and then they would send me to the hospital, which meant that ultimately, I would burn.

Even when my circumstances improved drastically, I continued to search for a chink in the heavy armor of the camp—even when I got a job that made me the envy of all my fellow laborers.

One day, I was loading wood when I noticed a well-built, middle-aged kapo watching me. I worked a little faster, just to keep out of trouble, and after a while, he came up to me and said in Czech, "Hey, you! Come with me. I've a job for you!"[2]

I walked smartly after him, wondering what lay ahead. He led me to a huge pile of potatoes and rapped, "Bring a pile of those into the kitchens. And hurry up about it!" To add slight emphasis to his words,

---

2   Between 1918 and 1938, Czechs and Slovaks were united in Czechoslovakia. Although Czechoslovakia broke up shortly before WWII started, there was a special bond between Czechs and Slovaks; also, their languages were very similar, and they could easily understand each other. --Eds.

he gave me a clout across the back with his stick, but I did not feel it; I was still too dazed by my luck.

In Majdanek, working in the kitchens meant food. Food meant survival. Even though there was a vicious SS guard known as the Boxer at the door to see that nothing was stolen, it was usually possible to grab a cooked potato and eat it without being spotted. It was a risk, of course, for the Boxer prided himself in being able to kill a man with a blow of his fist, but it was a risk worth taking.

For an hour, I carted potatoes while the Czech kapo kept a perfunctory eye on me. Whenever the Boxer looked in our direction, the kapo gave me a few whacks on the back and swore at me a bit, but generally speaking, he was decent enough.

For this, there were a number of reasons. In the first place, I was a hard worker. Secondly, I was a Slovak who spoke his language. And thirdly, beneath his kapo's uniform there still beat a Czech heart.

He had been a member of the Sokol movement,[3] a quasi-military organization which had been violently anti-Nazi, and had been arrested in 1939. Since then, he had seen the inside of Dachau and Sachsenhausen before being sent to Majdanek as a kapo, and though he wanted to keep his soft job, there was still a bright spark of patriotism burning within him.

I ate well that day, augmenting my staple diet of anemic soup and bread with two or three potatoes which the kapo deliberately dropped from the pot; and it must have been my lucky day because that night, I heard startling news.

After roll call, one of the kapos bellowed, "Any of you bastards know anything about farm work? We're sending four hundred men to a farm, and if you think you can do the work, give in your numbers."

Farm work! A train ride! An officially blessed exit from Majdanek instead of squirming through the wire and probably collecting a bullet

---

3   Sokol was a gymnastic organization founded in Prague in 1862. Its purpose was also educational and it focused on moral strength. Sokol played an important part in the development of Czech nationalism. --Eds.

in the back! I was one of the first of about a thousand who volunteered; and I was one of the lucky four hundred chosen.

Next day, the Czech kapo again took me away from my laboring work and put me to shifting potatoes. Again, we chatted in a more or less friendly fashion, while now and again he gave me a thump or two just to show the vigilant Boxer that he was conscientious.

"You know," he said at last, "you're certainly a good worker. I could get you a permanent job in the kitchens."

Had I been given that offer a few days earlier, I would have grabbed it like a pike grabs a minnow, but now it was different. Now I had my visa to the big wide world.

"Thanks very much," I said, "but I'm leaving the camp soon."

"Where are you going?"

"To do farm work. The train's due to leave in a few days." I heaved another sack of potatoes on to my back, and automatically, he gave me a kick in the backside.

"Are you crazy? Do you know where that train's going?"

"No." I dumped the potatoes in the kitchen and went back for more. As we passed the glowering Boxer, Kapo Milan struck me a glancing blow on the back of the neck, and as soon as we were out of earshot, he snapped, "It's going to Auschwitz. I've seen the papers. If you've any sense, you'll stay right here. Stay in this kitchen, and you'll stay alive."

I could see he was angry that his generous offer had been turned down, but that I could not help, for the opportunities for escape stretching before me were much more tempting than a few potatoes.

"Anywhere's better than this dump," I told him. "Auschwitz couldn't be worse."

He gave me a vicious blow on the back, not because I was doing anything wrong, but because my stupidity irritated him. "Look, you young fool," he growled, "I've been in Dachau. That was bad. But when they wanted to punish anyone really badly there, they sent them to Auschwitz.

Go there and you'll die!"

He gave me a whack on the backside. It was a whack of exasperation.

I knew his advice was well meant. I knew he was sincere in everything he said, for here was the Sokol in him talking. Yet I decided to ignore his warning.

I was, as events turned out, right in my decision; yet broadly speaking, he was right about Auschwitz, even though he was wrong about Majdanek. Nobody who stayed in Majdanek survived. In fact, from those who went from Majdanek to Auschwitz, I am most probably the only one still alive.

The end indeed, was described with ponderous detail by an SS man called Erich Mussfeldt, who saw the last days of the camp, then was transferred to Auschwitz, and ultimately was hanged in Cracow.

He wrote: "The camp ended on November 3, 1943. The operation had the code name 'Harvest Festival.' Behind sections five and six in the camp and about fifty meters from the new crematorium which was being built, huge trenches were dug. About three hundred prisoners worked on these trenches for three days and three nights. There were three main graves, two meters deep and one hundred meters long.

"At this time Majdanek had a special detachment of prisoners from Auschwitz. The commanders of police and SS came from Cracow, Warsaw, Radom, and Lublin with about one hundred noncommissioned SS men. On the fourth day—November 3—the camp was woken at five o'clock in the morning and surrounded by armed patrols about five hundred strong.

"Opposite the crematorium at the entrance were two loud-speaker vans. Marches and dance music blared through the loudspeakers. At six o'clock in the morning, the great action began. The Jews were driven into barracks in section five and told to undress.

"Then Commandant Thumann cut the wire between the section and the graves. An avenue of armed SS men immediately formed up, and down this avenue the naked prisoners were forced to run to the ditches.

"They were pushed into the ditches and those already in were pushed to one side and made to lie down so that there would be more room. Then SS men stood on the edges of the ditches and shot into them with their machine guns. The living were piled on top of the dead until the graves were full.

"Men and women were shot separately. The whole action continued until five o'clock in the afternoon. The SS men who carried out the executions were changed frequently, and all the time the loudspeakers were playing loud dance music or marches.

"I saw the whole action from my place in the crematorium. The action was organized in military fashion. An officer watched it all and kept the various police commanders informed by radio about the situation, how many had been shot and so on.

"That day, 17,000 people of both sexes were executed at Majdanek. Only three hundred women were left to sort and dispatch the camp property, and three hundred men from Special Detachment 1005 to take the bodies from the graves and burn them.

"One SS man told me that the Jews from this detachment tried to escape, and as a result, the survivors had to work with chains on their legs.

"When the action was over, the graves were covered with a thin layer of earth. I was ordered to eliminate all traces immediately and to burn the dead. On November 4, I started to bring in the wood, and on November 5, I started cremation. On the bottom of the ditches which were not quite full we put the wood and the bodies on top of it. On this bonfire we poured methylated spirits, and thus we carried on the work in each of the mass graves.

"When the ashes had cooled down, prisoners from my Special Detachment had to clear them from the graves. From these ashes which still contained bones, a bone powder, for use as fertilizer, was prepared at a special mill, driven by an electric motor. We filled the fertilizer into sacks and took it by lorries to the SS stores.

"The work was controlled by an officer of the Security Service who made sure that all traces were eliminated. Before burning, we took the gold teeth from the dead and all valuables were dispatched regularly. This action had the code name 'Reinhardt.'"

Had I stayed at Majdanek, I surely would have ended up as fertilizer. On the other hand, Auschwitz was no farm where a lad could lead the good, clean, country life. As an extermination center, it made Majdanek seem very small beer.

Still, at the time I had no idea of what lay ahead. Nobody, indeed, had, except, of course, the SS planners, and had anybody told us, we probably would not have believed them, for our minds had yet to be conditioned to accept the existence of such enormous death factories.

The day of our departure came. I had said goodbye to Milan, who had simply shrugged and grunted, "You'll find I'm right. You'll be sorry."

Then the four hundred of us were lined up, surrounded by kapos and SS men, and for me this was a very big moment, not merely because we were leaving Majdanek, but for a less vital reason.

We were going to be given civilian clothes. Dead men's clothes from the crematorium, admittedly, but that did not worry us. We were going to be gentlemen again.

They handed me a jacket, then a pair of trousers. After that—here was real luxury—a shirt! Nor were they finished. To add a final edge to elegance, they gave me a cap. It is true that they were not thinking of the sartorial effect when they did so. They merely wished to cover our shaved heads from the rude gaze of the outside world, but their motives worried me not a bit. That cap made me feel as if I were off to a wedding!

For hours we stood while they checked and counter-checked us. In fact, it was almost evening before we saw the columns of SS men forming up on either side of us, and then we were off, just twelve days after my arrival.

To me, it was a moment of mixed emotions. I was elated, and I was sad. Somewhere in that sprawling, soulless camp that grew smaller behind me as I marched was my brother Sammy. In my heart, I knew he could never survive.

————

AT LUBLIN STATION, THE SS OFFICER IN CHARGE OF THE train guard wasted no words. He knew he was not dealing with bewildered civilians who thought they were on their way to resettlement areas. He knew we were experienced, hardened prisoners, well used to camp life and train life.

In an utterly toneless voice that reflected neither hate nor contempt, he said, "You will be given food for the journey. Save this food, for I have no idea how long we will be traveling. And remember—it is useless trying to escape."

They gave us our food—bread, marmalade and salami. The officer cracked his whip, and we climbed into the wagons. The great doors slapped shut, and the train, after a convulsive preliminary jerk, began to move slowly.

I studied the eighty men in my wagon, seeking a possible collaborator in any escape bid that might be possible. Suddenly, I spotted a familiar face—Josef Erdelyi, who had been with me in Novaky. Not only had we been friends there, but we had something else in common: I had been to school with his girlfriend.

I elbowed my way across to him and in a whisper told him I was going to try to make a break from the wagon. Immediately, he was interested, and we began to examine our traveling prison closely.

We looked closely at the small window. It was heavily barred. Josef scratched his head and said, "How about the floor? Maybe we could rip a hole in it and drop through when the train slows down."

It seemed a good idea, but there were two main snags. We did not know where the guards were, and we did not know which end the engine was because it had not been coupled to the train when they locked us in. So, we decided to wait until the first stop, when I reckoned the odds might be in our favor.

After all, it was dark now. My experience on the Hungarian border had taught me that even crack shots find it hard to hit a moving target at night, and if there were two targets, breaking in different directions, it would be almost impossible to bring them down.

However, we soon found that the SS officer in charge was no fool. After a few hours, I felt the tempo of the train slowing. It passed through a station and, when it was well outside it, jerked to a halt.

The doors grated open. SS men began bawling everyone out. Josef and I looked at the tight cordon of machine guns right around the train and felt sick to our stomachs.

Still, we felt there might be a chance, some slight loophole, but even that frail hope was soon ground into the dust. The SS officer with the whip shouted, "You are to be counted here and will be counted several times on the journey. If at any stage any man is missing, ten men in his wagon will be shot."

My hopes slumped. Beside me, Josef muttered, "Don't worry. There's still the farm ahead of us!"

It was a comforting thought. Open fields were difficult to guard. Perhaps it was best for our peace of mind that we did not know the farm was to be Auschwitz.

On we went. By the time we had been traveling twenty-four hours, all the food was gone, but that was not our main worry. All the water was gone, too, and in the stifling heat of that packed wagon, thirst became a torment—nor was there any hope of getting a drink at a station because the security precautions were so stringent that we always stopped well outside them and had to watch the SS men drinking from their water bottles as we were being counted.

In fact, the journey lasted two and a half days. At last, the train began to slow down for its final stop, and I looked out the window to see where we were.

It was a strange sight. I saw watch towers, but they were empty. I saw buildings that were solidly built of brick, a sharp contrast to the wooden shacks of Majdanek. Obviously, this was a concentration camp, but a camp that was vastly different from that which we had known.

We stopped. The doors opened, and this time the guards dragooned us into line and ordered us to march.

I was on the fringe of Auschwitz.

CHAPTER 5

New Arrival

IT WAS JUST NINE O'CLOCK IN THE EVENING OF JUNE 30, 1942, a pleasant time, for dusk was falling, cloaking the blemishes, mellowing the mundane, accentuating beauty with its gentle half-light. I could see shrubs and trees, which made a soothing contrast to the desolation, the awful nothingness which surrounded my last base, and mentally I chalked up a point in favor of Auschwitz.

My wooden shoes, which they gave me in Majdanek, were making an unfamiliar sound as I marched. I was on a concrete road again, a civilized road, away from the crumbling dust, the rubble, the decay of Majdanek. Point number two for Auschwitz.

These, of course, were only fleeting, first impressions, no more than barely conscious thoughts. My mind was focused mainly on what lay ahead, on the camp which until now had been just a dark, brooding hulk in the dusk and which, as we drew closer, was revealing some of its details.

I had seen the searchlight as soon as I had dropped from the wagon. Static, unwinking, it played on the entrance, spilling out about fifty yards around it. Now we were within its pale, in sight of the tall double gates with their fine wire mesh; of the watch tower, cradle of the searchlight; and of the SS.

It was these men in their faultless green uniforms who gave me my first inkling that Auschwitz was different from any other place I had ever known. I had seen many SS men before, but none quite like these. They were lined up on the right-hand side of the road a few yards apart, statuesque figures, holding the leashes of Alsatian dogs in their left hands, submachine guns or rifles in their right. Their faces were impassive. Their still, erect figures exuded an air of cold, bloodless efficiency, and the sight of them puzzled me.

Already, after all, we were under heavy escort as we marched. Already, there were enough guns to wipe us out in a few minutes. So why did they need more? Why did they need dogs? Did they think we were dangerous killers? Saboteurs? The cream of the Allied armies? Somehow it did not make sense.

Indeed, very little made sense on the evening of my Auschwitz debut, for black and white and gray alternated with every step I took. I looked again at the gate, for instance, and saw for the first time, right across the top, in large brass letters "*Arbeit Macht Frei.*"

"Work Brings Freedom." Soon that legend was to make a mockery of us all, like some monstrous April Fool joke. Yet that June evening I believed it and was encouraged by it. Work Brings Freedom. I was young and strong. If they wanted work from me, they would get it.

A huge red-and-white pole, somewhat similar to a continental level crossing barrier, lifted slowly in front of the gates, which swung open simultaneously. We marched through them in rows of five, and as an SS man counted us, another slide clicked into the magic lantern of my mind, another black picture which drove away the legend over the gates and all its inspiration.

Standing watching us was an SS Oberscharführer—roughly sergeant major—one of the biggest men I had ever seen, a craggy human mountain, well over six feet tall, resting both hands on a huge club that nearly reached his chin. It was not, however, merely the physical bulk of the man or his broad gangster's face, his unblinking eyes or the detached indifference with which he watched us, which set him apart, though all these made an impact. It was the aura around him, an aura of evil, of death, something which told me instinctively that in that massive frame there was not one ounce of pity or decency or good.

This time, my first impressions were accurate. Here was Jakob Fries,[1] one of the most brutal men ever spawned by Auschwitz, mother of so many murderers. For me, in fact, Fries was Auschwitz and always will be.

We passed him, and I saw an equally chilling sight. On either side of the gate was a double row of white, concrete posts, each topped with an electric bulb. In each post were a dozen or so porcelain insulators, and through these was threaded wire which presumably ringed the camp, wire charged with high voltage electricity, a double line of instant death.

At that moment, the searchlight began roving round the camp, and I saw the watch tower properly for the first time. It was a well-built affair with windows around three sides. The fourth side was open. I could see an SS man standing behind a table, and on the table a machine gun was mounted.

Here was the basis of the Auschwitz security system: high voltage fences; a ring of watch towers, and constant light so no man could move at night without being seen.

Never had I seen such precautions, and they depressed me because, after all, one of the main reasons for my journey had been to escape. Yet, even more than depression, I knew bewilderment. What were they guarding in this strange camp, with its clean, concrete roads and its uplifting slogans, its dogs and its thugs and its double lethal fences? What treasure was stored here, for surely all this vast anti-escape machinery was not designed to corral a few thousand insignificant Jews?

---

1   At Nuremberg in 1952, Jakob Fries was sentenced to fourteen years imprisonment for crimes he committed against German political prisoners in Sachsenhausen Concentration Camp. Eight years later, he was given a conditional discharge by Adenauer's Ministry of Justice. He was arrested again on June 12, 1961, in connection with far more serious crimes at Auschwitz and was allowed bail, pending his appearance before the court at Frankfurt. Early in 1963, however, the public prosecutor dropped proceedings against him because he had been sentenced already to fourteen years imprisonment on previous charges and was unlikely to have his sentence increased!

I was, of course, wrong. It is true that Auschwitz yielded its treasures—its gold, jewelry, money, clothes, artificial limbs, hair, and even ashes—all the ancillary products of its crematoria. The security precautions, however, were for us insignificant prisoners. Himmler had ruled that nobody must escape. The world must never know of this place, his most efficient death factory.

On into the camp. Still concrete beneath our feet. Neat rows of red brick barracks, for Auschwitz had been built before the war for the Polish Army, and each barrack with its well-lit number; "streets" with suburban-sounding names—Cherry Street, Camp Street, and so on—and beside each name plate, a beautiful, comical carving, showing, for instance, an SS man kicking a prisoner in the bottom, the prisoner falling and knocking over another prisoner. Crude humor, delicately depicted by the hands of a craftsman. Everywhere, I saw neatness and order and strength, the iron fist beneath the antiseptic rubber glove.

They marched us to Barrack Sixteen, a two-story building, then down into its basement. On one wall, we saw a water tap, and instinctively, we moved towards it, for we had not had a drink for two and a half days, but before we reached it, a clatter of boots came down the stairs and a voice roared, "*Quiet!*"

Standing, surveying us with the quick professional eyes of a butcher in a slaughterhouse, was a stocky man in well-creased prisoner's trousers, a blue military jacket that buttoned up to the neck, and a black biretta—a kapo, but not an undisciplined clown-kapo like those we had known in Majdanek. Here was a man of authority, an old-timer; I saw from the green triangle on his jacket, too, that he was a professional criminal—a murderer, in fact, I learned later.

Surrounding him were his satellites, other kapos lower on the social scale. He put his hands on his hips and rapped, "I am the block senior here. You're in Auschwitz concentration camp, and you'd better not forget it. It's not a sanatorium, and you're not here for a rest cure or a holiday.

"Here, everyone has a chance to survive, but there is no chance, absolutely no chance for any bastard who breaks the rules. Anyone who gets me out of bed at night by kicking up a row will be taught manners. Anyone found out of the barracks at night will be shot. Obey all orders, or you'll be sorry."

He looked us over with distaste. We had spoiled his evening by arriving at such an hour. Then he saw our eyes straying toward the tap on the wall and said more quietly, "It's not forbidden to drink that water. But anyone who does will get dysentery, and the next stop will be the crematorium. There's no room for sick weaklings around here. Drink only tea. You'll get it in the morning. And remember—here are only the healthy or the dead."

Off he clumped up the stairs, followed by his entourage, and I watched him go with mixed feelings. He was tough, obviously, and quite ruthless; yet it was decent enough of him to warn us about the water. All I had seen of Auschwitz so far, in fact, was tough but efficient, unlike the dangerous chaos of Majdanek. And...*Arbeit Macht Frei*. That was some consolation. I lay on the floor of the cellar and went to sleep.

At five o'clock the next morning, the jangle of a gong woke us, and I could hear the camp erupting to life. From everywhere came the harsh clatter of wooden shoes; looking out the window, which was at ground level, I could see them scurrying by, hundreds of pairs of legs without bodies, bustling, jostling, tripping, but always hurrying, as if in fear of their lives.

On they rattled, monotonously, endlessly, the noise punctuated here and there by sharp orders, the sickly thud of blows, a scream or a low, hopeless moan. Now I was hearing a new Auschwitz.

Our door was flung open, and a squad of prisoners carried in barrels of steaming tea. As we began to drink it greedily, the block senior came in and said, "Today you may move around the camp. There is no work for you yet."

We finished every drop of the tea and assembled, still in our civilian clothes, for roll call. For me, this was routine, for I had learned it the hard way in Majdanek, and as soon as it was over, I began wandering around the camp, like a tourist, with Ipi Müller, an elderly man who had traveled in the wagon with me from Majdanek. At least, to me he seemed elderly, but he could not have been more than forty-five, and as we walked, he said, "Maybe I'll find my son here."

I knew all about his son. He had talked a good deal about him on the journey, about how he played the violin so beautifully. I remembered thinking what a fine man Ipi was, a poor Slovak tailor who had paid for his son's violin lessons and, even in that filthy wagon, thought only of him, rather than of himself. I said, "Yes, Ipi. Maybe we'll find him here."

And at that moment, an orchestra began to play martial music. Ipi froze; his eyes glowed, and a smile spread slowly over his thin, lined face. He gripped my arm, and as we turned toward the music, we saw the orchestra by the gates of the camp on a platform.

Still gripping my arm, Ipi said in a whisper, "He'll be there. He'll be up there, playing."

We moved toward the orchestra, but we never got near enough to see whether Ipi's son was part of it, for suddenly the camp was transformed. We heard the order: "To work!" It was shouted over and over again until it sounded like an echo, bouncing from every corner. Then came the noise of the clogs again, but more rhythmical this time, and we saw thousands and thousands of men marching like ants from every section in neat rows of five. The gates swung open, and the seemingly endless lines moved out of the camp.

I studied them closely, and I was shocked. A few looked fit and strong, but the vast majority were scrawny, pallid, grotesquely angular. They marched with the jerky movement of puppets, trying to keep up with the fit, as if their lives depended upon it, as indeed they did. Those who could not work, I was soon to learn, were killed, either in the gas chamber or by an injection of phenol in the heart, an operation performed by a member of the SS Sanitary Service, Josef Klehr.

Pity, however, soon made way for a more selfish thought. Those men were marching out to the Lord knew where, but at least they were leaving behind them for a while the watch towers and the high-voltage wires. Thoughts of escape, crushed by the sights of the previous night, began to flourish again, which shows that I was still very naive.

The camp was more or less empty now, it seemed. Those left behind were not idle, however. They bustled about on mysterious tasks, moving always at the double, while the kapos shouted and the SS men watched aloofly. Those who dawdled were beaten with clubs or whips; yet I could not understand what was the need for all this terrible urgency.

A shout behind me jerked me back to reality. I jumped just in time to avoid being knocked down by a huge cart pulled by a party of Ukrainian prisoners. It drew up at the door of a large, windowless building a few yards away, and I moved toward them, mildly curious about what they were going to load.

The double doors opened, and two prisoners came out, chatting in Polish and laughing. The Ukrainians turned the truck so it was at right angles to the half-dozen steps which came down from the doors.

Then the Poles stopped their banter. They turned inward, facing one another, their arms held tense, slightly away from their sides and palms upward, like two wrestlers about to fight. I tried to see through the doors, but the entrance was dark and I was viewing it from an angle. I noticed, however, that two of the Ukrainians had climbed onto the end of the cart and were waiting, equally tense. This, I decided was going to be quite an operation.

It was. Suddenly, from the blackness of that doorway, a naked human body shot like an arrow, head first, arms stretched. The Poles caught it in midair, an ankle and a wrist each, and sped it on its way to the cart.

It crunched onto the bare wooden boards, thin, gray, twisted. The Ukrainians grabbed it and ran—yes, ran!—to the other end of the cart, stretched it out neatly, then ran back to grab yet another wasted, shapeless corpse, drag it back, and lay it on top of the first bundle.

They were coming fast now, as if they were shot from guns. Out they flew, some like birds, some like divers, but all facedown and all headfirst. The Poles rocketed them on their way, and the slap, slap, slap as they fell had a rhythm now, like some terrible metronome. The Ukrainians were sweating, stacking their cargo in piles of ten, neatly, professionally, the head of one between the legs of another to save space.

Slap, slap, slap. Another and another and another. Out they flew, pitiful clay pigeons, empty, weightless, lifeless, bones straining against taut skin. Only occasionally was the rhythm disturbed, and then when a heavier body flew from that dark door, a body with a battered head, a body thick with blood and excreta. Yet even then the Poles never wavered. Their reflexes reacted. Their muscles tensed, and their burden sped on its way to land with a heavier crunch that shook the cart.

The Ukrainians bent their backs. They grunted as they hauled the heavyweights to the top of the pile, and as they ran back, I could see the blood from open heads seeping slowly out and soiling the bodies beneath.

After ten minutes, the floor disappeared under fifteen neat piles of ten. The Ukrainians heaved themselves on top of the load and stood, ankle-deep in dead flesh. They could not run anymore now, so two more climbed up on the heap and stood at the far end of the cart, a slight change of pattern, for now the bodies were thrown from the two at the front to the two at the back, where they were piled as neatly as ever.

The music changed, too. The harsh note of flesh against wood was gone; now it was the soggy, blunt sound of flesh hitting flesh, though sometimes an arm or a leg cracked the sides of the cart, bringing discord to this dreadful symphony.

One last note from one last drab rag doll, gray, yellow, balding, mouth agape, and then it was over. The Poles closed the doors, relaxed, and continued their laughing conversation. Someone flung blankets to the men on the meat wagon, and they spread them over the top of the heap.

We newcomers, we to whom work was going to bring freedom, stared at the cart, hypnotized by what we had seen. Two hundred bodies were packed together, and the whole operation had taken no more than fifteen minutes. Yet there had been time for the blood from the battered ones to dribble through the close network of flesh, and we saw it drip monotonously from the cart to form a dark red puddle on the spotless concrete.

One of us said, "Who are they? They don't look like Jews."

"Ukrainians, maybe. They're always tough with the Ukrainians."

"Or Poles. I'd say Poles."

"They're not Slovaks anyway," said Ipi Müller. "Definitely not Slovaks."

For some ridiculous reason, it was comforting to hear someone say they were not from Slovakia. Indeed, standing there in our civilian clothes, we felt completely divorced from the scene. This was something which happened to others, to men who came from some other world. We were not hunks of meat. We were people. Our minds were on the run, scattering before a truth which had yet to catch up with us.

The four Ukrainians jumped down. A kapo moved around, giving orders quietly. Six burly Ukrainians took hold of the shafts and swiveled the cart round until it was parallel again with the door. A few more went to the rear, and one man put his shoulder to each wheel.

"Hey-up!" shouted the kapo.

"Hey-up!" echoed the cart horses, and they all heaved as one. Slowly, the cart began to move, creaking and swaying. Here and there, a neatly packed arm or leg was dislodged by the motion and flopped over the side, where it dangled, as if waving a macabre farewell to the death house.

I gazed after it as it gathered speed. The cart horses were trotting now, and the cart lurched from side to side until I thought it was going to overturn and spill its cargo, but no—these men knew what they were doing, for obviously this was not their first journey to the red brick barracks without windows.

The puddle was spreading, seeping into the concrete. Two prisoners came along with heavy brushes and began scrubbing the street clean.

I glanced at them casually, hardly seeing them indeed, for my mind was still far away, following the swaying death wagon, but when they straightened up and turned toward me, I received yet another shock. Here were two friends of mine, Otto Pressburger and Ariel Engel from Trnava, and somehow the sight of them brought me a little closer to the terrible truth of Auschwitz.

Just four months earlier, big, burly Otto, with the dark eyes and the moon face, and I had been to a dance together, competing with each other for the local girls. Now the flesh had melted from that moon face, making it seem much longer, and his massive frame was thin.

The change in Ariel Engel, however, was even more frightening. It was as if Auschwitz had carefully selected every one of his many assets and obliterated them meticulously.

Once, we had teased him about his elegant clothes. Now the zebra stripes hung loosely on him, mocking him. Once, he had been a fine athlete. Now the trim, erect figure had the sag of a hungry middle-aged man. He had been a fine musician, too, a popular man at parties, for he played the balalaika superbly. Now the music had disappeared from him, and in its place, I saw dull apathy.

I went over to them. For a moment, their faces brightened, and then the light died, for nobody wanted to see his friends in Auschwitz. Otto said with a sad smile, "I thought you were in Hungary. I thought you'd made it."

I shook my head. At that moment, Hungary seemed another world which held no interest for me. All that mattered to me was solving the secret of this strange, sinister camp.

"What's going on here, Otto?" I said. "What happened to those poor devils?"

"What poor devils?"

"The ones on the cart."

He glanced at me quickly, surprised at my ignorance, forgetting I was a new boy who knew nothing about such routine matters.

"They're today's harvest."

He could see from my face that still I did not understand. So, he explained patiently, as if he were talking to a child.

"They died during the night. Some from hunger. Some from illness. Some because they were hit a bit too hard with a club. It happens all the time."

My mind grappled with these simple, casual words but could not digest them completely. So, I changed the subject and asked him how he and Ariel had reached Auschwitz.

"We came in a batch of six hundred from Trnava," he said. "There are only ten of us left."

"And the others ? What happened to the others?"

He shrugged and said, "They got the wrong jobs. They put them to burning Russian prisoners of war who had been killed by the SS. After that, those few who did survive the job had to die because they knew too much."

"How about you? And your brothers?"

He answered me almost casually, as if he were telling me the time or reading out the football results. I knew, however, that he was not being callous but fatalistic.

"My brothers are dead. All four of them. Me—and you, for that matter? The chances are slim. It could be a question of days, weeks, or even months."

They were gloomy words, yet somehow he managed to breathe the warmth of hope into them. He was giving me a frank, factual appraisal of the situation, but I knew from his tone that he was not yet broken.

With Ariel Engel, it was different. In a voice already lifeless, he said, "Soon we're all going to fly through that door. In a few days, maybe. It's only a matter of time."

I looked at him. The eyes that once had laughed and danced to his own music looked back at me, and I saw they were dull with the shadow of death. Otto laughed, an awkward laugh, and said: "Don't mind Ariel. He's always pessimistic!"

A shouting kapo with a whip broke up the conversation. Otto and Ariel trotted off smartly on some mysterious, meaningless task, and I was left to ponder their words, to sift and examine them like a miner panning for gold. I decided at last that survival was possible for people like Otto and me, for those who had the will to live, but not for the Ariels of the camp because they had accepted death already.[2]

The next day brought a change in our status. Until then, we had worn our civilian clothes which, in a way, was a disadvantage because

---

2   Otto Pressburger indeed survived Auschwitz and moved to Israel after the war, where he worked for the military. The author met him in Tel Aviv in 1959, and they kept in touch for years. --Eds.

the other prisoners shied away from us, afraid to talk with these new, dangerous idiots whose ignorance might land them in trouble. Now, however, we were about to become fully accepted members of the Auschwitz club.

They marched us to a shower room and told us to strip. The kapos began bellowing, "Into the showers!" For a moment, we hung around the entrance, hesitating, for there were four hundred of us, and this room was designed to hold no more than thirty. It was all rather confusing.

The kapos, however, soon solved the problem for us. Swiftly, they moved among our naked bodies, lashing at us with their clubs until every one of us was crammed into the small shower room and the harsh jets of icy water were sluicing away the dirt of the transport and the blood from our newly opened wounds. Dimly, above the noise of the water and the chaos caused by something near to panic, I heard our new masters shouting, "Out! Everybody out! Faster, swine!"

We plunged toward the door, fighting to get out. They moved among us, beating and kicking our still wet bodies until at last they had marshaled us in a shivering, defenseless line out in the July sunshine, and we were still naked when they marched us fifty yards to a spot where other prisoners took down our names and places of birth, registering us as if we were entering some weird new university. That, indeed, was the last time I used my name officially for nearly two and a half years; for now I was prisoner number 44070. Nor was I allowed to forget it, for the next stage in the initiation ceremony was tattooing.

Behind a table sat two more prisoners—one, a Frenchman known throughout the camp as Leo, the tattooist; the other, a Slovak called Eisenberg. They were cheerful fellows who joked about the whole business, asking the cattle politely where they would like their numbers branded—on the left arm or the right, underneath or on top. There was something strangely comical, being given a choice in circumstances such as these; it was rather like asking a man which side he would like his hair parted before his head was cut off. Anyway, for the record, I chose the top of my left forearm and bear my brand to this day.

Next came clothes, the zebra stripes. A tunic, trousers, a floppy shapeless hat, and wooden shoes. They were degrading, certainly, but less degrading than nothing, and I pulled them on almost with a sense of relief. Now I was one of the herd, a cipher in stripes, anonymous, unknown, and, provided I moved fast, so long as I kept my nose clean, so to speak, unnoticed.

This whole procedure—the showers, the registration, the tattooing, and the clothing—took a long time, of course. It began in the morning and that evening was still going on. I was generally near the front of the queue, which meant I had to wait for the others to pass through each process, and while the clothes were still being distributed, I noticed two young Polish prisoners talking together.

It was their clothes which first attracted my attention. They looked as if they had been tailored. The caps had a definite shape and were worn at a jaunty angle. The trouser legs were impeccably creased. Their jackets fitted them perfectly, and the whole outfit was worn with an air of confidence that bordered on arrogance.

There was something else, however, which made them stand out from most of the others. They were sturdy, well fed. Their faces had no prison pallor, but were bronzed and healthy. Here, I decided, were men who knew the secret of survival—men who could help me.

I strolled over to them and introduced myself. They stopped talking and studied me for a while, puzzled frowns on their faces, and all of a sudden, I felt like a small boy at school who has been brash enough to interrupt the conversation of a couple of prefects.

Then one of them smiled and said in rather condescending tones: "I take it you're new here."

"Yes. I arrived two days ago. How long have you been here?"

They exchanged amused, tolerant smiles. The taller one said, "Two years."

Two years! I felt my heart jump. I remembered the somber words of Ariel and even Otto, my friends who spoke in terms of days and weeks and months, and quickly, gladly, I rejected them as overly pessimistic, for obviously they did not know what they were talking about.

The two Poles were still smiling quizzically at me, amused by the impertinence and the ignorance of the new boy. I smiled back and said, "Two years! That's good. That's very good. Some idiots have been telling me that you only last a few days here."

I must have sounded a trifle patronizing because the attitude of these two camp aristocrats changed quickly. Obviously, they not only resented praise from a greenhorn but were irritated by the faint suggestion that he could emulate their feats of endurance.

"Listen, friend," one of them snapped, "a thousand of us came here. Four of us are left. Do you know what I'd do if I were a Jew, like you, in Auschwitz?"

I shook my head and waited, feeling that I had been put in my place, but anxious to pick up all the advice I could from these two boys who had proved that survival was possible.

For a while, however, he did not speak but just stood there, looking at me cynically, yet pityingly through lowered lids; then his face relaxed, and he laughed quietly.

"If I were you," he said, and there was still laughter in his voice, "I'd run for that barbed wire over there. They'd shoot you long before you reached it. Take my advice, my friend, and die today!"

With that, the two of them strolled away, bored now, no longer amused by my childish prattling, my naivety. I glared after them, hurt by the snub, bitter at their condescension, and as I watched them go, I found myself saying aloud, "I'll be still alive when you two are dead!"

It was, of course, a quick judgment, made in anger, but in fact, I was right. A month later, an epidemic of spotted typhus swept the camp, and both those Poles died.

That evening, they moved us into a new barracks. This time, we were not in the basement but in the attic, the beams of the roof slanting over our heads. Most of the floor space was occupied by soiled, anemic blankets which did not look very inviting but were better than the stone floor of the cellar. As soon as we moved in, supper was served— half a pint of tea and a couple of ounces of bread for each man.

I ate mine greedily, for I was learning my Auschwitz lessons slowly but surely. Food meant strength, even if the bread contained sawdust and the tea looked like sewer water. Strength meant survival, for, as the block senior had said, there was no place in the camp for sick weaklings. As I swallowed down the lumpy piece of loaf, I thought, Maybe I'll be able to rob some vegetables when I get out to work in the fields.

I was never to see the fields. Neither, for that matter, was anybody else, though for different reasons. At that moment, a burly young kapo erupted into our attic and stood glaring at us.

We were silent at once, watching him cautiously, wondering whether this visit meant a beating, or work, or no more than a tirade of abuse, for by that time we had come to expect little else from these members of the prisoners' hierarchy. I saw a red triangle on his tunic and felt it was a good sign because it meant he was a political prisoner. Then I studied his face, trying to read this new persecutor, but I did not get very far, for it was a bewildering mixture of arrogance, slight contempt, and a new element: humor.

He put his hands on his hips, set his legs wide apart, and roared in a heavy Viennese accent, "Let's have a look at you bastards!"

We stood silently. His quick eyes flicked over our faces, and then he moved among us, swinging his club idly. He stopped in front of one prisoner, prodded him in the stomach with the end of it, then swiftly raised it above his head. The prisoner leaped backward, tripped on a mattress, and fell flat on his back, and the strange new kapo went on his way through the sullen, silent ranks, roaring with laughter.

On he came, giving a prod here, a push there, now and again aiming a mock blow that scattered the men like pigeons and brought forth that deep-throated, full-blooded laugh, and all the time I was wondering whether this was just a game, or whether there was something serious, something sinister at the other end of the joke.

Now we were face-to-face. He stopped and looked me up and down, the corners of his mouth twisted downward in a cynical half smile. I waited, determined not to move, not to be the butt of his crude humor.

A light-hearted punch in the stomach. I stood my ground, though his fist was heavy enough. He walked around me, a slight frown of interest rather than displeasure on his face, then slapped me on the shoulder.

"Strong boy, eh?"

I said nothing. A huge hand stretched forward and felt my bicep. Instinctively, I flexed it, and the kapo gave a slow, approving nod.

"Where are you from?"

"Slovakia."

Another few prods. Another thump on the shoulder. Then: "So you're a Slovak. You might do. Speak German?"

"Yes."

"Well?"

"Fluently."

He took a deep breath through uneven teeth, tapped his leg with his club, and peered hard into my face. I knew I was under examination, but I had not the faintest idea what was going to happen to me if I passed.

I soon learned, for apparently I satisfied my examiner. Giving me one last prod with the point of his club, he said, "Okay. You'll do. Come with me."

He turned and walked quickly toward the door. I followed him, apprehensive of the unknown, but glad in a way, for obviously he had singled me out for my health and strength. What I did not know as I clattered down the steps from the attic in my wooden shoes was that the new kapo with the slap-happy manner in fact was saving my life.

Neither did I know that he had bought me from my block senior for a lemon. At that time, I knew nothing of the vast black market in the camp—a market which kept some alive and led others to torture and then to death.

CHAPTER 6
Introduction to Auschwitz

I LEARNED A GOOD DEAL ABOUT AUSCHWITZ, ABOUT THE art of survival, and about life generally from my new boss. Indeed, the lessons began as soon as the door of the attic closed behind us.

First, however, I had a pleasant surprise. Waiting outside the door for us were two other new recruits, Ipi Müller and Josef Erdelyi, my old friends from the Majdanek transport. Ipi, who was still searching for his son who played the violin, and Josef, whose girlfriend had sat beside me in class an eon ago back home in Slovakia.

My first lesson taught me that Kapo Franz was a man of many aspects. As we clattered down the stairs, the bluff, almost braggart manner vanished, and in its place was a quiet, brusque friendliness which gave me confidence. He tossed brisk, terse words over his shoulder, and I knew then the fate from which he had saved me.

"You're lucky boys to be taken off that agricultural work. D'you know what it means?" He did not give us time to answer, but just rattled on: "It means digging up bodies and burning them. Most of them die on the job, get shot or beaten to death. The rest die immediately afterward. They know too much."

I thought back to the Majdanek days when first I had volunteered for this work—to the transport, where Josef and Ipi and I had talked together about escaping through the fields of corn—and I realized that the three of us were very innocent and ignorant.

Later, I was able to sketch in the details which Franz had omitted from his cryptic message on the stairs. There were 107,000 bodies buried near the camp, including 20,000 Russian prisoners of war who had been murdered. This evidence of mass murder had to be removed, not merely to cover up the crime, but because it was a danger to health, and therefore, a special labor force of 1,400 men had been collected to get rid of it.

It was a disgusting, dangerous job. When the graves were opened, the stench was sickening. The prisoners had to work, mainly with bare hands, knee-deep in decomposing flesh, heaving disintegrating bodies to the surface, while heavy, drunken SS men with whips and machine guns bullied them and harried them.

Drunkenness, mind you, was not a common crime among men of these Death's Head battalions, but in this case there was some excuse for it because the nature of the work they had to supervise was so revolting that each of them was issued with a bottle of schnapps a day to bolster their morale and, incidentally, to disinfect them internally!

They hated the work. They drove their slaves without mercy because they wanted to get the whole dirty business over fast, and as they gulped down their liquor, their anesthetic, the slender threads of their restraints snapped, and they shot or beat to death those they thought were flagging. Of the 1,400, only 300 were alive when the last body was burned, and these, too, were executed.

Out we went into the open air, and again Franz's manner changed abruptly. Back came the braggart, the exhibitionist. As we walked down Lager Strasse, the main street of Auschwitz, past other kapos and SS men, he began roaring at us, chivvying us.

"Get on there, you bloody Yids!" he yelled. "Don't you know how to march yet? You lazy pack of swine, I'll teach you to walk and work like human beings."

As he shouted, he swung at us with his club. To the passing SS men, he looked and sounded a splendid kapo, heartless, brutal, efficient, yet never once did he hit us. In fact, all the time I knew him, I never saw him strike a prisoner, and that in Auschwitz was quite a record.

I learned the reasons for his humanity later. In the first place, he was a civilized, honorable man. Secondly, he had suffered under the Nazis much longer than we had and hated them much more deeply. His battle against them had begun when he tried to reach Spain at the age of seventeen to fight against Franco. He never got further than the Austrian frontier, however, and when the Nazis took over his country, they sent him to Dachau concentration camp.

After that came a succession of concentration camps, and when war broke out, he became a kapo because experienced, hardened prisoners were needed to teach manners to the naive newcomers who were being driven behind barbed wire in hundreds of thousands from all over Europe.

"Halt, you Jewish pigs!" The club swished over my head, fanning the bristles the camp barber had left, as we slammed to a stop outside a new barracks, our new home. We trooped in, and I found I was no longer to live in a cellar or an attic, but in a vast room, like any other prisoner. There were no mattresses on the floor; instead there were rows of bunks, packed tightly together, three tiers high, yet still not enough for the lodgers, for I saw that each bunk was shared by two, three, and even four.

Josef and I were lucky. We managed to grab one for ourselves, and, as we sat on the edge of it, we studied our new surroundings. First, we noticed that the block senior and all his underlings wore the green triangles of German criminals, which was a bad omen. The barracks itself, however, seemed clean enough, and I was glad to see that Franz appeared to be on good terms with our block senior. That meant we would not be beaten too hard or too often because no kapo liked bruised and bleeding workers. In fact, that night I went to sleep more optimistic than I had been since first I had entered the camp.

The gong jangled us awake at five o'clock the next morning, and we fought our way to the washroom to dash the sleep away, for there was neither time nor space nor soap for anything more effective; out to roll call after that, and then the bellow: "To work!"

Again, I saw the columns trudging toward the gates in rows of five and blocks of a hundred. Fries, the indefatigable, monumental Fries, was there as usual, weeding out the weak and the sick with blows from his huge club, cursing and kicking occasionally at the kapos.

I watched the rejected lope back into the camp in a pathetic attempt at haste, for now they knew they had only one hope. These were the living dead, known for some strange reason as *Muselmänner*,[1] the men whose eyes were empty, whose flesh had fled, whose blood was near to water. Off they straggled to the timber yard, where some decent kapo might let them work for their lives, for they knew the alternative was hospitalization, which meant a dose of phenol in the heart and death. Even there, of course, they were not safe, for later Fries would comb the camp, weeding out those he felt made the place untidy.

Now it was our turn to march. We passed Fries and his subordinates, who were checking the numbers. We held our heads high, for we were fit and strong, and I noticed that he scarcely glanced at us. By that time, Franz had built up a reputation as an efficient kapo, which meant that the SS, even Fries, felt it unnecessary to examine the ranks of his workers.

We marched along a weaving road through trees, strange, anonymous buildings, and here and there a hut. Franz began singing a German marching song, and we all joined, like kids on a school excursion. Indeed, I had a light-headed feeling, not because of the sunshine or the trees, but because I was outside those electric wires, away from the guns and the dogs. There was not an SS man in sight, and to me

---

1   Plural form of Muselmann. --Eds.

that meant I was as good as free. As I sang, I nudged Josef beside me; he grinned back, and I knew he was thinking just as I was.

At last, we reached what seemed like a huge storeroom. A railway line ran up to it, and there was an unloading platform. We marched in, mildly curious about the work that lay ahead, but still thinking mainly of the wide, open spaces; then Franz halted us, which was just as well because the sight before me would have stopped me in my tracks anyway.

Everywhere I looked, I saw food. Mountains of it. Solid walls built from tins of ham, beef, jam, vegetables, fruit. Bottles of mineral water, neatly stacked in endless rows, a vast army of sparkling little soldiers. Acres of food and luxuries at that, drawn from all parts of the world and assembled here in the hellhole of Auschwitz.

Franz was grinning at us newcomers. In his official voice, he rapped, "This is the SS food store. Your job will be to unload the railway wagons outside and to stack the stuff neatly here. I insist upon utter cleanliness, for I am not going to have German soldiers contaminated by dirty Jewish lice. Here you will find water, soap, and towels, and see that you use them. Now get to work, you lazy brutes."

Food and then freedom! It was unbelievable. A goods train was clanking into the platform outside, and as we ran to it with the others, Josef and I were laughing.

Our wagon contained choice Hungarian gherkins. We hauled the crates off with a song still in our hearts, and I muttered to Josef, "No guards! No dogs! No guns! They must be mad. Or maybe they think we're simple."

Franz ambled up. Amiably, he said, "Come on, boys. Put your backs into it. Get those gherkins stored up on the third floor."

Josef and I picked up a crate each and stomped up to the third floor. There was nobody else there, and I took a little time off to look out the window, to gaze again, this time from a height, on that beautiful, tree lined road to freedom, and suddenly all the beauty dissolved before me.

"Josef," I said gloomily, "come here."

He came over, whistling to himself, and looked over my shoulder. The whistle faded and died. Josef was silent for a moment, and then he said softly, "The bastards! The cunning bastards."

He saw, we both saw, that the entire panorama was ringed by watch towers. In each tower were a couple of SS men, manning a machine gun mounted on a table, just as we had seen when first we had marched through the gates a few nights earlier, and we realized that the electric wires and the dogs and the guns were only the inner defenses which, of necessity, had to be strong because all prisoners had to be contained within them during the dangerous hours of darkness.

But when it was light, it was safe to let us out into those wide, open spaces. Those towers, brooding over the camp like Cyclops, could spot a small dog escaping, let alone a human zebra, and before he got within a quarter of a mile of this outer perimeter, fire from half a dozen of them would have destroyed him.

Nor was that all. From our vantage point, we could see SS men and kapos who until now had been hidden from our little world by the trees and buildings. Long before we came within range of the machine guns, we would be caught, for in Auschwitz, the paths a prisoner could tread were very narrow.

Josef sighed and muttered, "Come on. Let's get these gherkins shifted."

We soon learned, however, that we had been landed into one of the best jobs in the camp and that life under Franz was civilized, even if escape at the moment seemed out of the question. When we had finished stacking our gherkins, for instance, we moved onto another wagon which was packed high with tinned ham in wooden crates.

Josef and I were inside the wagon, manhandling the crates to the doors. Franz strolled up, watched us keenly for a moment, then muttered, "Drop it, you stupid idiots!"

For a moment we hesitated. Then we heaved. The crate splintered on the platform, and as the tins of ham rolled around his feet, he shook his head in mock anger and said, "Those bloody army clowns! Every week they send us a broken crate!" He pointed his stick at me and rapped, "You—go to the Oberscharführer and report this! Make it snappy!"

I jumped down. As I passed him, he thrust a huge tin into my hands and muttered, "Slip that between the lemonade crates."

I took the tin and ran to the SS sergeant major's office, but before I reached there, I had deposited my tin in one of the dozens of hiding places which Franz had dotted around the store.

Minutes later, I was standing before the Oberscharführer, cap by my side, face blank, saying in a monotone: "Herr Oberscharführer, the kapo reports that a crate has been delivered broken and suggests with respect that you should come and inspect."

"Another?"

"Yes, Herr Oberscharführer."

With a snort of anger, he whipped up his report book and rushed from his office with me trotting obediently at his heels. He bore down on Franz, who was gazing down on the smashed crate with impatient indignation.

He glanced up, sprang to attention, and rapped, "Another one, Herr Oberscharführer!"

"Yes. And I'll bet they did it deliberately. I bet you'll find that one of those tins is missing."

Franz sank to his haunches and began counting the tins of ham. When he had finished, he looked up, his broad, open face shining with admiration.

"Herr Oberscharführer," he said in tones that were almost reverent, "you are absolutely right. There is one missing!"

The SS man swelled slightly, turned a delicate shade of pink, and growled, "They're not going to get away with this. They're not going to make a monkey out of me. This time I'll report them!"

Off he swept. Franz looked at me solemnly and said softly, "It's a bloody disgrace, isn't it? Those dirty army crooks are trying to rob the SS?"

"Yes, Herr Kapo," I said in equally shocked tones. "It's a bloody disgrace!"

At that moment, the SS man came bustling back, his face puckered by a frown. He drew Franz aside and said so that we all could hear: "Are you sure you can trust these blasted Jews?"

Franz drew himself up and with a pained expression said, "Herr Oberscharführer, I have been a kapo for three years…"

"Of course," muttered the SS man. "I was just wondering…"

We small fry never shared in this illicit loot, for it was much too valuable. It was more than food; it was money with which the various kapos did big business, buying not only soft lives for themselves, but their safety and the safety of their friends. The block seniors swindled prisoners out of their daily rations. The men in the kitchen traded in meat. Franz, in charge of the SS stores, was a powerful man indeed, one who had been able to insure his life over and over again. Had he not slipped a lemon to my block senior, for instance, he would never have been able to whisk me out of the command for "agricultural work," for this was strictly illegal. Lemons, however, were very hard currency, for they contained a high vitamin content, and the block senior knew he could easily replace me by buying someone else for a lower price.

These kapos, in fact, were the aristocrats of the camps. They had their own rooms in each barracks, and there they entertained their friends to splendid meals. They cooked steak and chips on their stoves while the smell wafted through thin partitions to starving prisoners, and they washed it down occasionally with slivovitz stolen from victims of the gas chambers.

Franz was often a guest of honor at these intimate little gatherings. Unlike other kapos, however, he never failed to reward his workers for services rendered. Occasionally, he would kick over a jar of marmalade or gherkins and mutter, "How careless of me!"

Then he would walk away, leaving us to eat the mess off the scrupulously clean floor. He never minded us stealing a bottle of mineral water here and there, either, provided we did it reasonably intelligently without leaving any evidence for snooping SS men. In return for all this, we used to carry a lemon or two back into the camp for him. We knew we could get twenty-five lashes or be killed if we were caught, but it was worth it to be protected by such a powerful personality.

Life in the SS storeroom, indeed, was as good as it could be in Auschwitz for us run-of-the-mill prisoners until the day Franz overplayed his hand. Whether he became too confident, too arrogant, too contemptuous of the SS, or just plain careless I shall never know, though personally I think it must have been the irate letters from the Oberscharführer to the regular Army Catering Corps about the number of broken crates we received that backfired on us.

Anyway, no matter what the cause, the effect was drastic. We received a visit from a Catering Corps Oberwachtmeister called Zwingli, a thin-lipped tall man with spectacles and the narrow shoulders of a Dickensian clerk. In front of us all, he told the Oberscharführer: "I'm going to get to the bottom of this business because there's something funny going on. I'm going to put this store in order."

Franz's face was impassive. The Oberscharführer's face was purple and undulated slightly. The Oberwachtmeister's face was pernickety, petulant, and he swung into action immediately with every ounce of his tiny authority.

"I want sentries at the doors, here," he snapped, pointing to the entrance. "They will search everyone leaving. And that includes the kapo."

I saw a cloud darken Franz's eyes for a moment, but it disappeared as the little efficiency expert who, glad to have a job that would keep him away from the Russian front for a few weeks, was rattling on.

"Every item in the stores must be checked regularly, twice, three times a day, if necessary. That will be my responsibility, though, in certain circumstances, I may delegate it to others."

He bustled off, the Oberscharführer floundering furiously in his wake, to work out precise details of the great Clean-Up Franz looked at us, sighed, and said, "Boys, this Zwingli man is obviously an idiot, but even idiots can be dangerous, particularly when they are lashing all around them with a new broom. I suggest there should be an outbreak of utter honesty for a while at least."

We agreed with him thoroughly, particularly when we saw that Zwingli meant business. Every time any of us went out of the store, the sentries ran their hands over our clothes, not casually, but carefully, probing any unusual bulges. One day, indeed, I heard a shout and saw them holding Josef, who was very red in the face.

Out galloped Zwingli, like a hunter who has just heard his gin trap snap. The sentries snapped to attention and reported, "Herr Oberwachtmeister, this prisoner has something hidden in the leg of his trousers."

"Get it out."

They fumbled with the bottom of Josef's trouser leg and managed to drag out a battered brown paper parcel. I found myself cursing him for his stupidity.

"Give it to me."

A sentry handed the packet over to the Army man, who unwrapped it quickly. I strained my eyes to see whether it was bread or gherkins or maybe a piece of ham, but, as I edged closer, I saw it was none of these things. It was a bundle of well-thumbed photographs.

Immediately, the Oberwachtmeister's eyes narrowed. Documents! Illegal pictures! A saboteur, a spy perhaps! As he flicked through them quickly, however, glancing up every few seconds at Josef's beetroot face, the gleam faded from his eyes. They were photographs of Josef's girlfriend, of Josef and his girlfriend, of his girlfriend on a bicycle, his girlfriend in a swimsuit, his girlfriend in a deck chair, his girlfriend with Josef's mother, his girl sitting on a wall, looking over the wall, leaning against the wall, his girlfriend, indeed, in every possible pose that decency and modesty permitted.

Zwingli was impersonating a beetroot now. For a moment, he breathed deeply, and then he exploded. He stepped forward and began beating poor Josef over the face with his dog-eared family portrait gallery, shouting between blows: "You...dirty...swine...don't...you know...you're...not...allowed...to...have...photographs...here?"

Josef did not move. At last, Zwingli ran out of words and energy more or less simultaneously The situation, in fact, was too much for him. Suddenly, he thrust the photographs back into Josef's hand and almost ran into the safety and sanity of the Oberscharführer's office.

I felt like laughing because it was all so ridiculous and crying because it was all so moving. I did neither, however, for I was too busy wondering how the crazy idiot had managed to hang onto his photographs. How had they survived when they stripped him entering Majdanek and again when he left and a third time when he arrived in Auschwitz? What happened to those pathetic pictures when they pummeled him in and out of the showers in both camps?

I never learned the answers to these impossible questions, either. When I asked Josef, he just shrugged and said with a grin, "To tell you the truth, I've been wondering that myself!"

When the Oberscharführer and the Oberwachtmeister were chewing over this same piece of cud together, Franz gave us another lecture. Fixing Josef, who was still flicking through his pictures, with an old-fashioned look, he said, "Be careful, boys. Times are changing."

———

OUR KAPO WAS RIGHT. IN FACT, HE COULD HAVE SAID THAT the camp was changing and he would have been equally accurate. As the Gestapo net spread more and more widely throughout Europe and dropped more and more prisoners into Auschwitz, the death graph tilted upward. The young, the fit, the healthy seemed overwhelmed by the *Muselmänner* now, the wan, weary zombies who shuffled frantically about only inches away from a lethal dose of phenol. The piles of dead grew higher with every roll call, and the red brick building without windows was serviced by lorries instead of a wooden cart.

The more prisoners there were, indeed, the more there were who died, and not always by beating, starvation, or murder. Sanitary arrangements, always inadequate, became positively dangerous. Dysentery, always threatening, swept the camp, and then, even more terrifying, came spotted typhus. As the work columns shambled from the camp every morning, struggling to stay erect, the club of Oberscharführer Fries fell faster and faster.

There was, of course, a vaccine to prevent spotted typhus, discovered by Rudolf Weigl,[2] a Polish doctor during the first world war, but with the second world war at its height, supplies were scarce and there was certainly none for such outlandish spots as Auschwitz. So, the camp authorities, who knew the disease was caused by lice, decided to get to the root of the problem which, basically, was dirt. In a

2   Ironically enough, during WWII, Rudolf Weigl harbored Jews, thereby risking execution by the Germans. His vaccines were also smuggled into the Lwów Ghetto and Warsaw Ghetto, saving countless Jewish lives. In 2003, he was posthumously awarded the Righteous Among Nations of the World prize by Yad Vashem. --Eds.

camp which had little water and less soap, the unwashed were treated like murderers, not, of course, because it was feared they might infect their fellow prisoners, but because the SS themselves might be contaminated and die.

It was, in fact, a new inquisition. Men trooped back from work tired, dirty, bloodstained. The kapos snarled around them, abusing them for filthy swine, a phrase which was no longer an insult but a death sentence. The battle for soap and water became a battle for survival, and as usual, it was the weak who went to the wall as prisoners fought each other to get clean.

I was lucky. Once again, I owed my life to Franz, for had he not selected me for the food store, I would have been as dirty as the rest of them. Instead, I was able to keep myself scrupulously clean because in the store there was plenty of soap and water to ensure that hands which touched the SS food were thoroughly sterilized.

Yet, though physically I was probably fitter than most, I had to fight to keep up my morale. The smell of death, the sight of walking skeletons, the constant degradation all pressed in on me, trying to force me down, and once, these morbid allies nearly succeeded.

We were marching one morning to the storehouse when a faint, ugly smell swept over us. It became stronger and stronger, and suddenly, as a column of women prisoners rounded a corner ahead of us, we realized where it originated. Never had I seen human beings in such a condition.

Franz stopped our column to let them go by. They shuffled toward us, their clothes in rags, heads shaven, though here and there a few who still knew pride wore skimpy head scarves, but it was their faces which chilled me most—faces like skulls, with eyes that were empty and unseeing.

The dust scuffed around their wooden shoes. The women kapos, buxom, well-fed, rude with health, whips in their hands, drove them on toward us, shouting, threatening, beating, while SS women with Alsatians supervised the operation. We stood, humiliated by our own strength, almost ashamed to be healthy in the presence of these pathetic specters.

Then gradually they saw us, first one, then five, then the whole shambling column, and from somewhere they summoned up reserves of strength and spirit from God knows where. They raised their heads, these female *Muselmänner*. They tried to straighten their backs, and as they drew level, an emaciated heroine shouted, "Anyone there from Slovakia?"

Josef, Ipi, and I shouted, "Yes…we're from Slovakia!"

"Have you seen—"

We never heard the name she was trying to shout. A burly woman kapo lashed out with her whip and caught the girl full in the face. She stumbled. Her friend caught her and half-carried her past us, the blood from her wound staining the shapeless clothes of the pair of them, and we stayed quiet now, for we knew our words could only set the whips lashing.

At least I tried to keep quiet, but failed. As the tattered line marched on and on, the gray faces seemed to blur before me until suddenly one moved from the mists and was etched on my mind.

It was my cousin Eva. Eva from Topolcany.

She was about my own age, just over seventeen—not a beautiful girl ever, but strong, intelligent, full of fun, famed indeed, throughout the town for the smart clothes she wore. Eva, the intellectual who spoke English so well. Eva, the pianist, who was always going to parties. Eva who was not a *Muselmann*, for she still held her head high.

I called her name. Her head turned, and she gazed, puzzled, unbelieving, at me. I saw her frown, and then I saw her eyes flood with recognition and life flow into her taut, thin face.

She screamed my name.

A whip rose and fell, but Eva did not falter. I raised my hand, and she raised hers in a gesture of splendid defiance, and as she passed only ten yards away from me, she shouted once more. *"Goodbye. Goodbye."*

Again, the whip, but it might as well have been a fly swat, for this was no ordinary girl. Her voice was not strong, but it sang with courage. Here was no whine, no plea for pity. Here was the spirit of resistance, still smoldering on the edge of death.

"Goodbye, Eva. Good luck!"

They were foolish words. Meaningless words. Empty words, for I knew and she knew that luck could not save her now. I knew and she knew that she was going to die, and as the column disappeared behind a block of buildings, I did not look after it.

"Get on, you bastards! This isn't an excursion! *March!*"

Franz's voice was harsher than I had ever heard it before. Franz understood.

Where those Slovak girls had come from and where they were going, I never learned. A few days later, however, another batch marched past the store and were herded by their kapos into a yard which adjoined the yard at the back of our building. We knew they were starving; we would have known even if we had not seen them stretching scrawny arms through the barbed wire, scavenging empty food tins from the garbage bins and scraping them clean with their fingers.

For a while, Franz watched them, frowning, nibbling at his thumbnail. At last he said to me, "We must do something for those girls."

"What the hell can we do for them with those bloody armed monkeys guarding the door?"

"I don't know yet. But leave it to me."

I left it to him, though for once I had little faith in him. It was true that we were sitting on top of a fabulous store of food, but the place was so closely guarded that we might as well have been a million miles away. I was certain that not even the wily Franz could break the barrier around us.

He, however, was not discouraged easily. After a while, he came to me and said, "Listen, there are 1,000 boxes of marmalade on the ground floor—good Italian stuff with nuts in it—and I know there are exactly 1,000 boxes because that little rat, Zwingli, has counted them twice." He grinned at me, winked and went on: "If I know Herr Oberwachtmeister, he'll count them just once more. When he does, let me know."

He was gone before I could ask him what was in his mind, but I had to admit that he certainly knew his Zwingli, for a few minutes later, the meticulous little man trotted into the store and began to count the marmalade boxes. It took him time, but he was thorough, and when at last he had finished, I told Franz.

"Fine. I knew he'd come back for a final count. Now we can take what we like."

"But supposing he comes back again."

"He won't. Three counts…that's his ration."

"Maybe. But how the hell are you going to get the stuff past the sentries?"

Franz was in his element now. He picked up a box of marmalade, balanced it on the tips of his fingers, and said, "Just watch me, boy!"

He walked calmly to the door, carrying the marmalade high, like a waiter carries a tray through a crowded restaurant. At the door, he raised the other arm just as high and said, "Search me fast, please, gentlemen. I'm in a hurry."

The sentries swept their hands down his clothing, patting the pockets, feeling the legs of his trousers. They sent him on his way with a jerk of their heads, and Franz disappeared around the back of the building.

I ran to an upstairs window, overlooking the girls, and watched. I saw him walk calmly toward the wire, turn, and, with a backward flip of the wrist, send the marmalade flying toward a group of Slovak girls. It shattered at their feet. For a second they gazed at it in amazement, this gold that had fallen from heaven, and then they fell on their knees and ate it. That marmalade disappeared in less than a quarter of a minute.

Franz came back, whistling quietly to himself. He was delighted on two counts—first because he had fed a few of the girls and then because he had been able to fool the sentries in such an outrageous manner. I was still worried, however, and I told him so.

"How do we cover up if he counts them again?"

"He won't count them again. He never counts more than three times. He's a creature of habit, like all dogs."

For once, however, the shrewd, confident Franz was wrong. Zwingli came back and began counting those boxes of marmalade for the fourth time.

"Ein…zwei…drei…vier…fünf…"

I ran to find Franz. He swore softly and hurried back to the store-room with me. Together, we watched the human computer.

"Fünf und sechzig…sechs und sechzig…sieben und sechzig…"

Franz was looking at him almost dreamily now through lowered lids. My stomach was knotted with tension. On and on and on he droned, the numbers falling relentlessly, like grains of sand slipping through an hourglass.

On and on and on until the inevitable drew near, and I began to sweat. Yet Franz remained imperturbable.

"Neun hundert sieben und neunzig…neun hundert acht und neunzig…neun hundert neun und neunzig."

Zwingli straightened up slowly and tugged the lobe of his left ear. He had not seen Franz and me watching him from a corner of the storeroom. He had not seen anything except marmalade boxes, and at that moment, he could not believe his eyes. For what seemed like a long time, in fact, he just stood there, gazing at the rows of neatly piled boxes, and then he started all over again just to convince himself he was not going mad.

"Ein...zwei...drei...vier...fünf...sechs..."

It was a reprieve, but one of only limited duration. Men like Zwingli did not make mistakes with figures, and we knew the moment of reckoning was only a thousand seconds away. Casually, Franz said, "Come on, let's get some work done. There's no point hanging around here."

Out we went, and I began unloading a wagon automatically. Franz shouted and joked in his usual, good-humored fashion, as if Zwingli were counting stitches instead of collecting evidence which could send the kapo in charge of SS stores to the gallows.

"Come on, you Yiddisher bastards! Get moving! Shift that...!"

"Kapo!"

Franz turned slowly, almost lazily. His face was bland and respectful as he said, "Herr Oberwachtmeister?"

"One of these boxes of marmalade is missing. When I counted them this morning, there were a thousand of them. Now there are only 999!"

Franz frowned slightly and tapped his teeth. Then he glanced up and said innocently, "Perhaps, Herr Wachtmeister, you made a mistake. I've often done so myself."

It was arrogance, supreme and superb. Zwingli flushed and roared, "I don't make mistakes! One of your dirty, thieving Jews has stolen a box!"

Springing to attention, Franz rapped, "If that is so, sir, we will soon find out who is responsible."

Then turning to us, he shouted: "You heard what Herr Wachtmeister said. Now which of you is guilty? Which of you stole that box of marmalade? Confess or I'll beat the brains out of the lot of you!"

Nobody spoke. Everybody with the exception of Josef, myself, and three new French prisoners who had seen Franz walk away with the loot began to shuffle their feet and look at one another anxiously. Franz rapped, "Very well. Herr Wachtmeister and I are now going to search the entire building. If we find one splinter of that box, God help you all."

Off they went to comb the haystack for a needle that was not there. We continued to work, and it was an hour before they returned. Franz was still quite cool, but Zwingli's nerves were fraying.

"I'm holding you responsible for this, Kapo," he snapped. "I'm sending you to Block Eleven."

Block Eleven. The Punishment Block, where men were given a mockery of a trial which seldom lasted longer than three minutes, and then were sentenced to death.

Franz gave him a long look which was at the same time lofty and reproachful.

"Sir," he said softly, "I have been a kapo for a long time. I am, as you know, a German. Am I to understand that you are questioning my honesty?"

"Take him away," growled the Wachtmeister, but I could see that he was shaken. The sentries fell in either side of Franz, who tipped me the suspicion of a wink as they marched him away.

Zwingli went into his office and a few minutes later summoned the deputy kapo, a Pole called Skharzinsky who had a poor opinion of us Jews but until now had been kept well in check by Franz. Half an hour later, Skharzinsky returned and came up to Josef and me, smiling.

"Look, lads," he said, "I've a fair idea how this was done, and I know there's going to be bloody murder about it. That boy, Zwingli, means business. If you tell me exactly what happened, I think I'll be able to bluff it out."

Josef and I looked at him blankly. "We don't know a thing," I said. "I still think he must have counted them wrongly."

He turned to the Frenchmen, new boys whose Auschwitz eyes were not yet open. Speaking in fluent French, he tried the same smooth line, and this time it worked.

I could not understand what they were saying, but from the way they were holding one hand aloft and pointing toward the door, I knew they were describing in detail how Franz had made away with the marmalade. The deputy kapo nodded curtly and disappeared into the Oberwachtmeister's office. A few minutes later, the pair of them walked to the yard where the Slovak girls had been and returned with the fragments of wood, which were enough to hang Franz.

Zwingli sent for him immediately and faced him, his hands behind his back.

"You stole that marmalade. Admit it!"

"Sir, I do not mind suffering unnecessarily," said Franz, "but I must repeat that I am a German prisoner, and as such, I expect justice from a German."

Slowly, Zwingli drew the broken wood from behind his back and hit Franz across the face with it.

"You stole it," he yelled. "You carried it on the palm of your hand past the sentries. You threw it to those Jewish bitches!"

Franz looked around at us, glancing from face to face. Then he said, "Which of you dirty swine gave me away?"

For the second time, they marched him off, and I was sure I would never see him again. Soon, the news trickled back that he had not been condemned to death, but the sentence in many ways seemed worse than death.

He was sentenced to fifty lashes with the "cat," a fortnight in the standing bunker, and "life" in the Punishment Command. We all knew that anyone of these three could kill.

Many died under the cat, for instance. Most went mad or died in the standing bunker, which was a contraption like a telephone box without windows. Five prisoners under punishment were packed into it after their day's work and left there in total darkness for the night. Their shoes were taken away, and they had to stand on bare stone.

Only one man could sit down at a time, and after a few nights, fighting for this privilege usually began.

If Franz could stand both these tortures, I thought, he would be superhuman,; and, even if he did, he could never endure the Punishment Command, which was designed to kill slowly.

Its main task was digging huge ditches five yards deep and six yards wide around the perimeter of the camp to reinforce the security system. They were given no tools, which meant they dug with their hands and carried the soil away in their caps. Each morning when they went to work, they dragged a cart with them to carry back the bodies of those who died, and generally speaking, it was fairly well loaded because the kapos and the SS men in charge of this work party were chosen for their sadism.

When the prisoners carried away the earth, for instance, they had to run between lines of guards, who beat them and kicked them as they ran. If a man fell and could not get up, a kapo would say in a loud voice, "Let's see whether he's shamming or whether he really can't run."

While the others watched, he would beat the man to death, then announce with a grin, "He really can't run!"

Others had a more subtle sense of humor. There was the lazy kapo who was a virtuoso with a lasso and only came on duty in the evening.

After supper, he would look into a large box which was kept handy for the bodies of those who died in the night. If it was empty, he would gaze in amazement at his fellow kapos and say, "Something must be wrong!"

Then, grinning all over his face, he would chase prisoners with his lasso until he caught one round the neck with the noose, and after that, the guards would gather in a circle and watch this disgusting rodeo act, which always ended in strangulation. The others would cheer. The lazy kapo would yawn and announce, "I've done enough work tonight. I'm going back to my room!"

I had heard all these stories before they took Franz away. Indeed, he had told me some of them himself. As I hauled crates out of the wagon that afternoon, I hoped he would die quickly under the lash, that the first stroke would crush his kidneys.

The reasons for my death wish were good, but I underestimated the powers of Franz. I had forgotten the insurance policies he had been taking out for so long, the premiums he had been paying to influential kapos in lemons, ham, salami, and marmalade.

When he went to be flogged, a kapo went to the two prisoners who had to do the job and muttered, "Go easy with Franz. Make it look good, but go easy."

When he went to the standing bunker, the upright coffin, the kapo found that there were no other prisoners scheduled for that particular punishment. Somehow, he forgot to take away Franz's shoes, and somehow, a blanket was left lying on the floor of the standing bunker.

When he went to the Punishment Command a fortnight later, everybody shouted, "Well, look who's here! It's Franz Marmalade!"

They were all glad to see him, even the lazy kapo who normally liked new blood for his rodeo—so glad, in fact, that somehow they forgot to beat him.

He was, indeed, one of the more remarkable men I met in Auschwitz. He survived the camp and today in his native Vienna, where he owns a hotel, he is known still as Franz Marmalade.

CHAPTER 7

A Naked World

OBERSWACHTMEISTER ZWINGLI HAD THE SATISFIED AIR OF a man who had not only had a fine meal, but a successful row with the head waiter. Hands behind his back, he bounced up and down on the balls of his feet for a while, his putty-colored face almost lively with a supercilious smile. This, undoubtedly, was his moment.

"I have never liked Jews," he said mildly, as if he were lecturing a Society of Anthropologists. "Never trusted them. But I never thought I'd see even a Jew sink as low as you scum have sunk. All that can be said for you is that you may have been influenced by that vile Communist kapo.

"But don't think you will be excused because of that. You are worse than thieves. You are saboteurs, vermin, trafficking in the food of men who are fighting to save civilization. Tomorrow you will be assigned to new work, and I only hope that the Camp Commandant sends you to the Punishment Command."

Civilization! I thought of the starving Slovak girls, groping in the dustbins; of the *Muselmänner*, wrapped in an aura of death; of the shootings, the beatings, the murders. I looked almost in wonder at the greasy, twitching face in front of me, and suddenly I realized that he believed implicitly in every word he was saying.

His wish that we should be sent to the Punishment Command, however, was not granted, for Rudolf Hoess, the Camp Commandant, had other ideas.

This we discovered as soon as we returned to the camp, having taken our last look at the haven of Franz Marmalade, as he was now known by prisoners, kapos, and even the SS themselves. We trooped into our nice, clean barracks and were told abruptly, "You're being transferred to Block Eighteen. To the Buna command."

So, it was not the Punishment Block. It was Buna. Josef and I looked at each other, and we wondered which of them was worse, for this strange name had been drifting around the camp for a long time now, like an ugly, unidentifiable smell. Few knew just what it meant, but everybody knew it was a place to be avoided.

We soon learned that these rumors were accurate. At three o'clock the following morning, we were roused and paraded outside our block. Josef muttered, "At least we're going to miss roll call!"

That was about the only advantage the Buna command had over the rest of the camp. A German kapo with the green triangle of a professional criminal strutted up and down and then shouted, "Some of you are new to this command. I'm going to give you a bit of advice. When you get your bread at night, eat only half of it. Save the rest for the morning because you get nothing to eat until noon. Not only have you a heavy march ahead of you, but you're going to work harder than you've ever worked in your lives, and those who go out with empty stomachs will die."

His words were acknowledged by a rumble from my empty stomach. Tersely, he went on: "Has everybody got bread?"

Nobody spoke, least of all Josef and Ipi and me because by that time we had learned it was not wise to call attention to ourselves in any way. The kapo marched quickly over to us and said, "This is your first day with Buna, isn't it."

"Yes, Herr Kapo."

"I'll bet you've no bread."

A pause; then: "No, Herr Kapo."

He swore softly, pulled some bread from his pocket, broke it in three, and gave us each a few ounces. We took it gratefully, but at that moment all three of us knew that life was going to be tough indeed, for German criminals are not noted for their generosity.

It was, in fact, only partly an act of philanthropy. He gave us that bread not merely to help us survive what lay ahead, but because he did not want us collapsing as we marched to work. That would bring Fries's club down on his head, for the kapo was supposed to see that all men were fit to work, and if he failed, he would suffer, not merely through beating, but perhaps through being reduced to the ranks.

Somewhere, someone shouted, "March!" We began trooping toward the gates, column after column, neatly packed in blocks of a hundred. I was in the sixteenth hundred, and as we passed the SS men who were counting us, I saw Fries glowering at us over his club. The man, it seemed, never slept and never relaxed his vigilance for one moment.

We marched down the familiar concrete road, built with the blood of prisoners, down through the trees and the buildings until we came to a freight train with seventy or eighty wagons. SS men with dogs and machine guns watched us coldly, and then the kapos swung into action.

Before I realized what was happening, they were beating us into the wagons, cursing, kicking, driving us to the one escape hole that lay behind the open doors. Frantically, we hurled ourselves inside, fighting each other in our efforts to get away from the clubs, tripping over and tramping on those who fell beneath the feet of the stampede. The dazed ones were pitched in after us, and we supported them, for there was no room to sit.

There was no room to move, indeed, for the wagon had been divided into two compartments—one for one hundred and twenty prisoners and the other for the kapo and his staff. I glared at them in their first-class carriage, the professional criminal, his deputy, the clerk and his deputy, and a young, handsome, smooth-faced boy who seemed to have no official function.

I muttered to the man beside me, "Who's that blond geezer?"

"The kapo's boyfriend, of course. Who the hell did you think he was?"

After we had waited, crammed together and cramped for half an hour, the train jerked and began to rumble slowly on its way. We were off to Buna, and I realized, after what I had seen, that my attitude to Auschwitz would have to change. No longer was it simply a question of surviving. It was a question of surviving today without thinking too much about tomorrow.

The journey must have lasted about two hours, but it seemed endless. Jammed beside me was a man with dysentery, someone who would not survive the day. In a corner, another, an arm broken by a kapo's club, was retching with the pain of it. Even the fit found it difficult to breathe with the stench of sweat and blood and excreta.

At last, however, we dragged to a stop. The doors were whipped open, and the kapos fell upon us again, tearing us out of the wagons, lashing at us wildly, working at an insane speed, shouting over and over again, "Faster, you bastards! Faster!"

The SS were there in force, too, with dogs and guns. They kept glancing at their watches, growling, "Quick...we're late! Get them moving! Get them into line!"

They got us into line, and they got us moving. The long line of battered zebras plodded toward Buna to the brisk music of constant blows and sporadic gunfire.

In front of me, a man stumbled. A kapo clubbed him, and he staggered out of line. Immediately, an SS man fired at him, missed, and brought down the man beside him. Another kapo roared, "Pick up that bloody body! This is not a graveyard! Carry it with you."

The summer sun scorched the back of my neck. The Alsatian trotting beside me was panting. A man reeled from the ranks, fell, and had the top of his head blown off by an SS man who did not even bother to stop as he fired. Farther up the line, a man ran wildly into the road and was bowled over by a burst of machine-gun fire. The SS were kicking the kapos now, and all the time they were shouting, "Faster, you bastards! We're late! We're late!"

This, I thought, must be the real hell of Auschwitz. Hell on the double, and an Auschwitz that until then I had managed to avoid, but I was wrong, for it was only a mild form of purgatory, an evil aperitif, so to speak, to prepare us for Buna itself.

I saw the work site ahead: piles of wood, cement mixers, and all the paraphernalia of building. Half-built houses thrust toward the sky, and everywhere hundreds of men were scurrying, ant-like, driven on by the bellowing of the gangers. It was a grim vista even from a distance, but as we drew nearer, the entire canvas unrolled before me, revealing awful detail.

Men ran and fell, were kicked and shot. Wild-eyed kapos drove their bloodstained path through rucks of prisoners while SS men shot from the hip like television cowboys who had strayed somehow into a grotesque, endless horror film, and adding a ghastly note of incongruity to the bedlam were groups of quiet men in impeccable civilian clothes, picking their way through corpses they did not want to see, measuring timbers with bright-yellow, folding rulers, making neat little notes in black leather books, oblivious to the bloodbath.

They never spoke to the workers, these men in the quiet gray suits. They never spoke to the kapos, the gangers. Only occasionally, they murmured a few words to a senior SS NCO, words that sparked off another explosion. The SS man would kick viciously at the kapo and roar, "Get these swine moving, you lazy oaf. Don't you know that wall's to be finished by eleven o'clock?"

The kapo would scramble to his feet, pound into the prisoners, lashing them on, faster, faster, faster, for in Buna, there were only two types of workers—the quick and the dead.

They marched us to a huge store filled with sacks of cement. Our kapo bellowed, "Shift these to the site over there. Get moving! At the double! Run, you pigs, run!"

Someone dumped a bag of cement on my back. I ran. At the door, a kapo thumped me over the kidneys with his club. I stumbled but kept on running. Ten yards farther on, a deputy kapo lashed at me. Ahead of me, a man went down, and a club smashed his skull. I tripped over his body, somehow kept on my feet, and dumped my bag by a mixing machine and a bewildering network of heavy wire that soon would be covered in concrete. Josef panted behind me, and then we were running back for more cement, more abuse, more blows, in a frantic, nightmare race against a clock we could never beat.

Bag after bag I carried, always running, until the sweat stung my eyes and the dust made a desert of my mouth and my throat. For hours, how many I shall never know, I kept going to and fro, to and fro, for I knew now I was part of a machine, a cog that would be thrown away if it cracked.

At last, a whistle blew. The site ground to a stop. The rattle of the cement mixers died, and men sank to their haunches. I just stood there, numb mentally and physically, with Josef beside me; then my eyes began to focus, and I saw one of the taps where they drew water for the cement. Slowly, mechanically, I moved toward it and was about to turn it on when someone gripped my arm.

I swung around, jerking my arm free. A tall, sturdy prisoner of about thirty looked down at me and said, "Don't touch that, friend. One mouthful, and you'll get dysentery. And then you're for frying!"

I looked down at the tap and back at the prisoner. Then I thanked him and walked back to Josef and Ipi Müller, who were sitting on the ground, their heads between their knees.

Ersatz tea arrived and soup in huge urns, thin, gray gruel of un-known and probably unthinkable origin. We guzzled it greedily, but still I was thirsty, and I found my eyes straying back to the tap again. Nor was I the only one to be hypnotized by it. A scrawny Ukrainian, blood caking one side of his face, lurched suddenly to his feet and stumbled toward it. His friend yelled, "Stop, Ivan! It'll kill you! *Ivan…*"

He was too late. Water from the tap was gushing over Ivan's head now, and he was gulping down mouthfuls. His friend ran to him and pulled him away.

"You bloody fool," he snapped. "You're as good as dead."

Ivan gave him a long, slow grin; shrugged; and said, "What the hell! At least I won't die of thirst!"

I gazed around the site, around this giant anthill which for a mo-ment had died. In front of me a Pole lay full length, his eyes closed, the sun gleaming on his sweaty face. One of his countrymen dug him in the ribs with his toe, but he did not move. Another dig, and his eyes opened slowly.

"Get up, Janek. That sun will kill you. If you don't get up now, you'll never get up."

Janek closed his eyes again and mumbled, "Leave me alone. For Chrissake, leave me alone!"

His friend bent down, grabbed his arm, and heaved him to his feet. Janek blinked at him, grinned foolishly, and muttered his thanks, for now he was awake and knew he had been saved from almost certain death.

Others were less lucky. When the whistle blew again after an hour, I had to force myself upright. A few, however, did not move because they could not move, and in the moment before the machines began to clank again, the kapos went to work.

One stood over the Ukrainian who had drunk from the tap. He was lying flat on his back, his mouth open, his face gray. The kapo booted him in the ribs and grinned when he did not move.

"So, you can't get up!" he said. "Or maybe you won't get up. Let's see which it is."

A couple of other kapos gathered around for the sport. A club fell twice, splintering the Ukrainian's skull. The kapo looked around solemnly at his colleagues and said, "Well, now we know. He really can't get up!"

They laughed at this little post-lunch witticism and then went into action themselves. Clubs swinging, they swept down on us, roaring, "Back to work, you bastards! Get moving! On your feet! Run, *run, RUN!*"

Again, we ran. The cement mixers rumbled. The kapos cursed. The SS men moved ponderously, aloof, impregnable, eyes restless for any cog that failed, that was showing signs of wear. Someone slapped a bag of cement on my back, and once more I was part of the conveyor belt.

Resuming work was harder, much harder, than starting it had been. In the morning, I had been not merely fresh but innocent of what I had to do. Now my limbs ached and the prospect of humping bag after bag for hour after hour whittled away at the remnants of my willpower. Every fiber in my body screamed for rest; my throat was dust-dry again; and had it not been for the sight of the dead and the dying, I think I would have sunk back to the ground.

The afternoon session, however, turned out well, thanks to one of those slices of luck which were essential to every prisoner if he were going to survive in Auschwitz. My job was to dump my cement bags at the feet of an overalled civilian worker who was building the heavy wire pylons which were to be the basis of reinforced concrete. After I had been working for about an hour, I pitched down one of my bags and it split open.

The workman—he seemed to be a craftsman—swore in French, and Josef, who was right behind me, sympathized, again in French. The overalled man looked at him with sudden interest, and for a minute they had a rapid conversation which I could not understand.

I noticed, however, that Josef was looking very pleased with himself. At last, he turned to me and said, "We've got a new job. This gentleman says we're to stay here and help him assemble these wire contraptions."

The thought of spending the rest of the afternoon twisting pieces of wire instead of carting cement at the double and running the kapo gauntlet seemed too good to be true. I glanced around at them and to my amazement saw that neither they nor the SS men were taking any notice of us.

Our new boss grinned and said, "Don't worry about those fellows. I'll fix them."

Immediately, he walked over to an SS man and spoke to him rapidly, pointing at us. The German did not even look at us. He just nodded, and when the Frenchman returned, he gave us a brisk lecture. "This section is about forty yards square," he said. "Inside that area, I am in charge and nobody else. Stay within it, and neither the kapos nor the SS have the right to touch you. Step outside, and they'll probably shoot you because beyond it, I have no authority. Now, let's get to work."

For the rest of the afternoon, we twisted wire in our little sanctuary while outside its boundaries, the shooting and the beating and the murders went on. The ants bustled until they dropped, but for Josef and me, there was peace and comparative rest.

At five o'clock, the whistle blew again, and work stopped for the day. Our new French friend said: "See you in the morning. What group were you in?"

I told him, "The sixteenth hundred."

"See that you're in it every day, and you'll be able to work here with me."

As we marched away, Josef said to me, "Lucky I had the sense to learn French instead of Russian like you, you bloody fool!"

"Lucky?" I said. "We're more than lucky. Take a look at that column."

It was not a pretty sight. As usual, the kapos were lying about them. The SS men were on the prowl, and the Alsatians were padding at our heels, but now nobody seemed to care very much. They had not the strength to care, and if their minds were not completely numb, they were focused on the bread and tea that was waiting for us in camp.

This, in fact, was a very different column from that which had marched past Fries that morning. Then, at least we all had been alive. Now we had the dying among us and the dead, for the bodies had to be counted along with those who were still alive once we got back to the camp, and in each group of a hundred, dragging its way along that fine concrete road, there were at least ten limp, lifeless forms.

We piled into the waiting freight train and waited for another half an hour while the registrars checked and counterchecked, argued and fussed over their little pieces of paper. The kapo and his underlings climbed into their private compartment, and the journey back to Auschwitz began, with the dead and the dying held upright against the sides of the wagon by the weight of those who had survived another day in Buna.

It was about eight o'clock and getting dark by the time we reached the approaches to the camp. The usual reception committee was waiting for us: the silent SS men, the dogs, the guns, and, inevitably, the sinister bulk of Fries, alert as ever. I glanced up at the uplifting sign, *Arbeit Macht Frei*, and remembered how once it had encouraged me in the days before I had heard of Buna.

Through the gates. Past the electric wires with their bright, bare electric light bulbs. Up to Block Eighteen, where we stacked our dead neatly. The block registrar was waiting with his notebook to check them. Wearily, for it was a boring job, he lifted arm after arm, glanced at the number by the light of a match, crossed it off his list, and moved on to the next pile, and all the time, the searchlights swung right and left, sweeping away the darkness, blinding tired eyes, reminding us constantly what we were and where we were and where we were going to stay.

Josef and I collected our bread and margarine and drank our half pint of tea. With a supreme effort of will, we forced ourselves to eat only half the bread, and then we debated where we should hide what was left.

I decided I would keep mine in my hand all night. Josef's tactics were more subtle. He shoved the precious bread into the pocket of his trousers, rolled them up, and used them as a pillow. Then we lay down and, too tired to sleep immediately, listened to the noises of an Auschwitz night.

Raucous snores in a hundred different keys. Heavy, irregular breathing and the meaningless mumbles of the dreamers who even in sleep could not escape the nightmares of the day. The moans of the dying and the harsh, frightening, unreal ramblings of the delirious, rising to a shout, sinking to a whisper, calling the names of wives and children and mothers, weaving fantasies that sometimes made them laugh and sometimes made them cry. It was not exactly soothing.

Yet I must have dozed, for I remembered nothing else until I felt Josef shaking my shoulder.

"Wake up," he whispered to me. "Wake up. My trousers are gone. Someone's stolen them."

His trousers...and his bread. Somehow a thief had managed to ease them out from under his head while, like me, he dozed. Quickly, quietly, we got out of the bunk and found them a few yards away, tossed on the floor. Josef shoved his hand into the pockets, then without a word withdrew it. I could barely see his face, but I knew his bread was gone, and instinctively my fist tightened on my own breakfast, which I was still clutching. We were among wolves in Block Eighteen, a pack of starving, ruthless wolves.

We climbed back into the bunk. We were growing used to the grunts and the moans and the snores, the orchestra of hundreds of troubled sleepers. Then suddenly there was a new note…a wail of despair and a cry: *"My bread…my bread!"*

We heard the scuffle of half a dozen feet, a thud, a jumble of quiet curses, and a cry that was stifled and faded into a groan. Then…silence.

Dimly, I could see a form lying, face downward, in the narrow corridor between the bunks. In the tier below me, an older prisoner was leaning out, watching with mild curiosity. I said to him, "What's going on up there?"

"Some lousy swine stole a *Muselmann's* bread. The poor devil was too weak to get up and go after it."

"So, what happened? Did the others beat him up?"

"They killed him, of course. What's the use of beating up a bastard like that?"

That was the law in Block Eighteen. If a man stole your food, you killed him. If you were not strong enough to carry out the sentence yourself, there were other executioners; it was rough justice, but it was fair because to deprive a man of food was to murder.

At three o'clock the next morning, our block was jarred into action by the rasping of the kapos. We staggered out on parade, leaving behind only those who had died in the night or who were dying. The kapos marched up and down the still-dazed lines, here and there clouting a man out of the line and shouting, "Hospital!"

It was, of course, a death sentence. Sometimes the prisoner, who a few weeks earlier had been strong enough, just slunk away, accepting, perhaps even welcoming, his fate. Others pleaded, pathetically fervently. "Please, Herr Kapo, let me go. Just once more. I'm still strong enough…"

"I don't want *Muselmänner*!"

"Please, Herr Kapo. I'll work hard. I swear I'll work hard!"

Sometimes a decent kapo would weaken. Generally, the decision would stand, however, for Fries would not tolerate passengers on any working command. If he spotted a man unfit for work in the columns, he would attack the kapo on two counts: first, for allowing him to march from the camp and then for causing delay. The column had to stop for the weeding-out process, and that meant the counting had to be done all over again. It was irksome and uneconomic.

So, every day, old faces disappeared forever from the Buna command and new faces replaced them. At first, I found this depressing, perhaps in a selfish way, because every day brought me nearer to the hospital in spite of the fact that my job was slightly easier than many others. After a while, however, my mind, all minds, became conditioned to the appalling mortality rate. I developed a protective immunity that was shattered only when I realized Ipi Müller was dying.

His eyes were still bright, almost twinkling at times. His heart still beat strongly with courage; I think, indeed, he was kept going by one main generating force, and that was his unwavering belief that somewhere in Auschwitz he would find his son, Filip, the boy who played the violin so beautifully.

Every day, he would say to me, "I wish we could get off this Buna job. If we left for work at the normal time, the orchestra would be playing and I could have a good look for him."

His blind faith made me sad, for I felt sure that Filip must be dead. Luckily, however, I did nothing to undermine it, for after we had been working in Buna for about a week, Ipi came dashing up to me, his face brilliant with excitement.

"He's here," he gasped. "I've had a message from him. He's coming to see us on Sunday."

For a brief moment, a ludicrous thought crossed my mind. I thought of the visitors who used to come to our house in Trnava on Sundays—of their carefully correct clothes; of the cakes and the coffee and the polite conversation in the parlor, the subtle, genteel gossip. Now in Auschwitz, in Block Eighteen, we were expecting a Sunday guest, and though I was delighted for Ipi's sake, I could not help smiling, for Sunday in the camp was a little hell all of its own, different from the mundane misery we knew throughout the week, but hell nevertheless.

The one big advantage, of course, was that we did not go to work. Thus did the Nazis acknowledge their Lutheran Sabbath in this beleaguered town where half of the population were Jews. There, however, concessions to whatever God still occupied any tiny recess of their minds ended. Religious services of all kinds were forbidden. Those found celebrating them were put to death; yet, in spite of this, many brave priests, mostly Poles, held secret Masses for their faithful and never lacked a congregation.

Apart from the fact that we did not work, Sundays were dangerous days. The kapos had nothing to do except seek out our sins against the administration. They moved like weevils through every barracks, searching for a blanket that was a millimeter out of true, a few grains of dust, for anything which might offend the rigid rules.

Sunday, indeed, was punishment day, the day when trivial offenses, usually cloaked by the feverish chaos of work, were unmasked and, in the comparative quiet of inactivity, screamed a confession which could earn no absolution.

It was also "Health-Through-Joy" day, if I may borrow a phrase from the Hitlerian dictionary of slogans. Our masters, it seemed, felt that we might grow soft and flabby, lazing around in the sun, and that, of course, would never do. So, the kapos rounded us up for physical jerks which, they assured us, would do us all the good in the world.

It was quite a spectacle, this drill—this knees bend, arms stretch, mark time on the double routine—such a spectacle, indeed, that it attracted a substantial audience even from the upper echelons of the SS, who stood around, smiling tolerantly while the sick and the starving, the weak and the dying presented their grotesque pantomime in honor of physical culture.

For Ipi, however, neither punishment nor the humiliation of the drill display mattered that day. Filip was coming, and that obliterated all other thoughts, and when he came at last, a tall, dark, rangy lad of about twenty-two, I left them alone, for I knew they had not much time together. It was good, indeed, just to see them, the tough, gray-haired, sensitive tailor and the artistic son who was thin, but still vibrant with life, to watch them from a distance, sweeping away the present, delving into the past, planning a future which Filip knew his father would never see.

This, in fact, he made clear to me. I saw Ipi smiling as his son said goodbye, but Filip's face was sad as he pushed his way through the crowded barracks to shake my hand.

"My father has told me how you've helped him," he said. "I want to thank you. And I want you to do me another favor."

"Of course," I said. "Anything."

"He asked me if I was in the orchestra. I told him I was, and that was a lie." He grinned almost sardonically, the lips twisting downward in a gesture of self-depreciation. I knew he was not finding the conversation easy.

"Do you know where I work? In the crematorium and in the Punishment Block under Unterscharführer Palitzsch. I suppose you've heard of him."

I shook my head, and at first, he seemed surprised. Then, remembering that he had been longer in the camp than I had, he explained: "Every day in Block Eleven, prisoners and civilians, brought in by the Gestapo from various prisons, are tried for various crimes. These trials last about three minutes, and generally, they are condemned to death. Most of them are shot up against the wall, but some die in the building itself, and my job is to help with this little operation.

"The men are told to strip, and, one by one, they are pushed into this room that looks a bit like a doctor's consulting room. Anyway, they think they're going to have a medical check or something, and they're quiet enough. They take them over to one of those wall measures—you know the things with a wooden arm that comes down on top of your head. They stand under it. Maybe they wonder who the hell cares what height they are when they are going to die, but what they don't know is that there are holes in the wall behind that measure and that Palitzsch is looking through them, one by one, until he finds the back of their heads. When he finds it, he shoots them with an air pistol which makes no noise and causes no panic.

"Sometimes, of course, we're too busy for all this carry-on with the measure. Then he just calls them in one by one, and when they are a couple of feet away from him, he shoots them between the eyes. No matter what way it's done, my job is always the same: to get rid of the body and clean the blood off the floor before the next customer arrives. It's not a particularly nice job, but at least it has one advantage. The boys usually have some bread or something in their pocket before they get the pellet, and Palitzsch doesn't mind if I take it."

He was trying to speak casually, cynically, but all the time he was watching my face, scanning it for signs of disgust or anger or even fear. Quickly, I told him I understood, and at once, his manner changed. He was speaking gently now, and urgently, with the soft intensity of Ipi.

"Look," he said, "I'm not kidding myself about my father. I know he's going to die soon, and so do you. But I'd like him to die thinking I'm up there on that bloody platform by the gate, playing first fiddle."

"Filip," I said, "so far as I'm concerned, you are."

The tautness eased from his face, and for the first time, he seemed relaxed. He grinned, slapped me on the shoulder, and said, "Thanks, pal. I'll see you again."[1]

---

1   Filip Müller survived Auschwitz and recorded a very intense account of the events he witnessed firsthand in a book Eyewitness Auschwitz, Three Years in the Gas Chambers (Chicago: I. R. Dee, 1999). --Eds.

I saw him, in fact, half a minute later. He came hurrying back, thrust two small parcels into my hands, and disappeared again without another word. I opened them unobtrusively and found a piece of bread and a handful of sweets.

Three days later, Ipi Müller died quietly and without any fuss. He died in his bunk, and I was glad that a man of his caliber was not dispatched by beating or shooting or any of the routine degradations of Auschwitz.

Josef and I continued with our daily Buna routine. Perhaps because of our French protector, perhaps because we were strong and still living off the fat of the SS food store, we stood the pace better than most. In fact, by the fifth week, we were probably the sole survivors of the sixteenth hundred, which by chance we had joined on that first day after the fall of Franz.

Hour after hour, we twisted together our wire pylons. Day after day, we saw them covered in concrete and watched the white buildings rise and take form. Precisely what or for whom we were building, we neither knew nor cared very much. Indeed, it was only some time after the war that I learned what our function was and why thousands died in trying to fulfill it.

At that time, the Royal Air Force was stepping up their attacks on major German industrial centers. To escape these unwelcome attentions, big concerns, like Krupps and IG Farben, decided they would move farther east, and the area around Auschwitz was chosen for a number of reasons.

In the first place, the Silesian coal mines were at their disposal. Secondly, there was plenty of water, and, finally, there was a more than adequate and exceptionally cheap labor force neatly located behind the high-voltage wires of the camp.

Commandant Hoess, of course, was delighted to find industries springing up close to his domain, for at that time, he was hard-pressed for money. The budget allowed to him for running the camp was totally inadequate, and though he complained many times, even to Himmler, he was always told, "It's up to you to manage somehow."

One of the ways in which he managed was by selling cut-price labor to IG Farben, for instance, whose factories we helped to build at Buna. The money he received helped keep the camp going, and the working conditions were so bad that the vast majority of prisoners sent there exterminated themselves, all of which saved time and trouble. The fact that few of them lasted more than a month or two at the most worried neither Hoess nor the IG Farben administrators, for there were always others with a little fat left to take their places.[2]

———

THE FACT THAT JOSEF AND I MANAGED TO SURVIVE FOR SO long was not something which gave us cause for pride. On the contrary, we realized that every day brought us nearer to death in one form or another, for those who went to Buna were not meant to live. Indeed, the sands were running out for us fast, and it is ironic that we were saved only when tragedy hit the camp.

The crisis broke toward the end of August 1942. I remember it was a Wednesday, a red-letter day for the Buna boys, for on Wednesdays and Fridays, we got an extra half loaf and a piece of salami with our rations. In fact, throughout the long journey back to the camp, I could think of little else except the feast that was waiting for me.

---

2   Buna ultimately became a major industrial center for the production of ersatz rubber, and it is still the site of heavy industry operated now, of course, by the Poles. After the war, indeed, I was offered a job as an industrial chemist there, but refused because I could not forget the price in human lives which had been paid to build it. In 1961, I, with some other survivors, sued IG Farben for back wages and was awarded 2,500 marks by a West German Court. [Approximately $5,250 in 2017 dollars. --Eds.] Both the Court and IG Farben refused, however, to pay any compensation to the relatives and dependents of those who had died building these massive plants, which meant that they got 90 percent of their labor for the pennies they paid to Hoess.

As soon as we marched through the gates, however, I could see something was happening. Normally, it was quiet when we got back, for everybody else was in bed already, but this time the entire camp was alive and every prisoner in it seemed to be mustered on the main square. Day shifts and night shifts were there, zebra stripes stretching as far as I could see in every direction.

Our kapo called us to halt. I stood there, irritated, still thinking of my extra rations and cursing the bureaucrats who had dreamed up this crazy new exercise which made no sense to me. I turned to complain to Josef beside me, but the kapo barked me into silence.

Far in the distance, I could see bright lights moving about and hear brief, staccato orders, but I could not see what was happening, and I did not care. My stomach was gnawing at me; my limbs were aching; and fatigue was sweeping over me like a wave, threatening to overwhelm me.

Yet still we stood, for hour after hour. Occasionally, we moved a few paces toward the faraway lights, but it was midnight before I could distinguish figures in what seemed to be the center of this lunatic operation: kapos, prisoners, bathed in the light of portable searchlights carried by SS men with batteries on their backs; men running aimlessly to and fro; more shouts and the restless shuffle of a thousand wooden shoes. It was all too much for me. The scene blurred in front of me, and my knees suddenly gave way as I fell asleep on my feet.

Half past midnight. One o'clock. Two o'clock. Half past two. Now we were nearing the heart of the matter. Three o'clock, and I was blinking in the light of the searchlight, gazing around me at a bewildering scene.

The man in charge, as I might have guessed, had I given it any thought, was Jakob Fries. All around were kapos and SS men. Farther away to the left were a group of prisoners, surrounded by kapos, and to the right, another similar group.

A line of prisoners was parading past Fries. As each man drew level with him, he examined his legs in the light of the searchlight and then roared, "Run!"

The prisoner ran for about twenty yards and then ran back. Fries jerked his thumb and he went over to the group of prisoners on the right. Another man had his legs examined, and even at a distance, I could see they were bloated with hunger. Without another word, Fries sent him to the left-hand group. A third passed the initial leg test and was ordered to run, but all he could manage was a stumbling, swaying trot. He, too, went to the left.

Still, I had no idea what was going on, but I was disinterested no longer. I knew now, by instinct, by experience, that we all were facing something that was sinister, something dangerous, and it became even more ominous when I saw the group of men on the left being marched off into the darkness.

At last, it was my turn. Fries looked at my legs, which were slightly swollen, but not too bad. He barked, *"Run!"*

Never in my life had I felt less like running. I had been up for twenty-four hours and slaving at Buna for eight of them. For another four hours, I had been either marching or almost suffocating in an overcrowded cattle truck, and I had eaten nothing since soup had been dished out in Buna at noon.

Yet somehow, I knew that I was about to run for my life. I took a deep breath and went pounding, flat-footed, down this ghastly race course, turned and pounded back to the hulking Oberscharführer with the huge club.

He jerked his thumb to the left, where about forty others had already taken the places of those who had been marched away. I was panting, and I was frightened, though I did not know why.

Another man was running now. It was Josef. He stumbled twice, nearly fell, and Fries sent him to join our group, and as he walked, still panting, to my side, I suddenly noticed that all the others around us were trembling, not from cold, but from fever. From spotted typhus.

Quickly I told him what I had seen. He thought for a moment and said, "Christ, it must be some sort of a test. That's why he was looking at our legs—because it always shows there first. That's why he made us run. He wanted to see if they worked!"

We had not been able to run properly because we were starved and exhausted, but Jakob Fries had diagnosed spotted typhus. With a flick of his thumb, he had sentenced us both to death—and thousands of others, too.

We looked at the other group, the group with clean bills of health. It was about twenty yards away, but there were enough kapos around to stop us getting a quarter of the way if we made a break for it, and all the time, our group was growing.

"Listen, Josef," I whispered. "There are about eighty here now. When they've collected a hundred, they'll march us off. We've got to get away before that, even if they shoot us."

"Wait a while," he said. "We may get a chance to sneak away yet. Wait till we're just about to go."

Reluctantly, I took his advice, for I was too exhausted to argue, and I am happy to say that I lived to acknowledge he was right. I lived, in fact, because he was right.

Suddenly, a kapo appeared out of the gloom, a man Josef knew well. He stared at us for a moment, then hit the pair of us a couple of hard whacks over the shoulders.

"You bloody bastards!" he roared. "What the hell are you doing here! Don't you know you're supposed to be with that bunch over there? Can't you obey even the simplest order?" He pitched us out of the trembling crowd and, cursing loudly, drove us to the other group. Only when we had lost ourselves among a hundred others did he stop abusing us.

Then he whispered, "You're lucky, boys. Another few minutes, and you'd have been on your way to the ovens. Look over there."

We turned just in time to see the typhus victims we had just left, slouching away to the crematorium.

Dawn was breaking. A kapo rapped an order, and we began marching over toward the wall that divided us from the women's section. When we got there, we were told to strip, and then I noticed a large hole in the wall. Naked prisoners were passing through it, but just before they did so, two kapos examined their legs again and wiped down their bodies with a rag that reeked of disinfectant. Shivering in the cold morning air, I paused for my final inspection, waited a moment while I was swabbed down, then crawled through the hole in the wall into a new world.

It was a naked world. Even the kapos were naked. In fact, their only signs of rank were their well-fed bellies and their disinfected clubs.

CHAPTER 8

The Night in August

IT WAS ONLY BY DEGREES THAT I LEARNED THE FULL SIG-
nificance of what happened on that dismal night in late August 1942.
My eyes, my ears, my wits had been made quite sharp on the Auschwitz
flint by that time, and so, with the aid of the bush telegraph which I was
beginning to understand, I gathered that half the camp's population
had been murdered.

I had played my part, my naked role, only in the finale. The overture had been sounded, not in the mother camp of Auschwitz, as it
was called affectionately by its administrators, but in the poetically
named Birkenau—"Birch Tree Alley"—a massive subsidiary about
two miles away. Here was the extermination center proper; here were
the gas chambers and the long, deep ditches where the bodies were
burned; here was the site of the crematoria, the cradle of streamlined
mass destruction; here lived prisoners who were forced to take part in
the obliteration of thousands, then tens of thousands, and ultimately,
millions.

Here, Camp Commandant Rudolf Hoess began his major offensive against spotted typhus, which had achieved epidemic status. He
realized it was endangering not merely the lives of the worker prisoners whom he needed if he were going to run his camp efficiently, but
the lives of his SS men, too. So, he called in an expert, Doctor Kurt

Uhlenbrook,[1] an acknowledged authority on the disease, and the good doctor, having pondered the situation carefully, decided that those who were infected would have to be eliminated.

He began his task in Birkenau, where he condemned to death about fi fty percent of the prisoners, which gave him room to move, so to speak. The camp was already divided into two sections, Birkenau One and Birkenau Two, and when the ailing had been weeded out, Section One was split into Subsection A and Subsection B. Then he concentrated his skill upon the women's section of the mother camp, which was separated from our preserve by the wall through which I ultimately crawled. Here again, about half of the residents were considered redundant, owing to the state of their health, and were sent to the gas chambers. The remainder were transported to Birkenau One, Subsection A, and that left an empty, well-sterilized space for those of us who survived the diagnosis of Oberscharführer Jakob Fries, or managed to evade it.

As I have said, however, these details I learned only later. On that night, I knew merely that I was lucky to be alive and that I would have to keep my wits about me if I was going to remain in that healthy condition. So, for a while, Josef and I stood quietly amid this bedlam of naked men, trying to get our bearings, striving to set our compass with the aid of snatches of conversation which swirled in half a dozen languages around us.

Then suddenly, from this polyglot miasma of Polish, German, Ukrainian, French, and Dutch, came the dulcet tones of a Slovak. I homed in on them at once and found myself facing a small, dark man with the bright eyes of a bird. Though he was thin, I could see he was still tough and alert.

---

1   Doctor Kurt Uhlenbrook was to have faced trial at Frankfurt for participating in mass murder in Auschwitz. For reasons best known to the public prosecutor, all charges against him have been dropped, which left him free to practice medical science as skillfully and as conscientiously as he did during those last few days of August 1942. Uhlenbrook died in 1992.

I said to him, "What part do you come from?"

"Nove Mesto. And you?"

"Trnava. Nearly next door."

"I know it well. I was a dentist back home and had some patients there."

We introduced ourselves. His name was Laco Fischer, and when he told us he had been five months in Auschwitz, we looked at him with respect, for here was a man who knew how to survive, a man who could mark our cards for us. Indeed, he could see the questions in our eyes before we spoke.

"You want to know what's happening?" he said. "I'll tell you. Half the camp has been murdered, and the work commands are being reorganized. I hear they're looking for men in Canada Command."

Josef and I looked at each other quickly. We had heard of this place the prisoners had nicknamed Canada because in one way it was supposed to be a paradise, but we had heard, too, that it was a dangerous paradise where men died violently after barely sipping its nectar.

Cautiously, I asked Laco, "What's it like? Is it as good as they say? Or as bad as they say?"

"Both," he said, "I've worked there. You can get all the food you want—bread, margarine, butter even, tinned sausages, sardines, chocolate, soap, the lot. So help me, I once got bananas there!"

He smiled at the memory of it. Then suddenly he was serious again, very serious. "I'm going to try and get back there," he said. "If you want to come, stick by me because I know a few of the kapos. But remember…in Canada, you live on the edge of a precipice. And there's a bunch of thugs there just dying to push you over."

"What do you do there? What's the work like?"

"It's tough. Let's leave it at that."

Josef and I were silent for a moment. We were thinking of bread and butter, sausages and sardines, soap, bananas, and precipices, for this was no easy decision. We had to choose, it seemed between eating or dying on the one hand and eating and dying on the other.

Laco watched our faces, sensing the silent debate, and he showed no surprise when we both said more or less simultaneously, "Let's go. Where are these Canada kapo friends of yours?"

We soon discovered that Canada Command was an elite corps, a strong, healthy bunch of men surrounded by would-be recruits prepared to do anything for food. The deputy kapos—all Jews, I noted—were beating them away with casual efficiency and without showing any particular animosity.

Laco, however, had not been exaggerating his influence. He walked up to a sturdy deputy kapo who spoke German with a Yiddish accent and said, "I've got a couple of good Slovak lads for you, Isaac."

"I'm fed up with you and your bloody Slovaks, Laco," said the kapo. Then, eyeing Josef and me, he said, "Still, they don't look bad."

Turning to me, he said, "Run for that wire."

It was a tough order. I knew I could be shot by an SS man if I obeyed. Yet I wanted to show I was well disciplined, so I began to run, hoping like hell he would stop me.

He said nothing, however, and I had almost reached the wire when a German kapo, conspicuous because he was wearing clothes, grabbed my arm and roared, "Stop, you idiot! Do you want to commit suicide?"

Then he shouted to Isaac, "He's all right. So is the other one." Isaac shrugged and said, "Okay, Bruno. Have them if you want. But you know what those Slovak bastards are like!"

We fell into line with the rest, and they marched us off to the washrooms, where I suddenly realized that I now belonged to a very special command. Not only did the other kapos not beat us, but they actually turned on the showers for us, making sure they were neither too hot nor too cold. After that, they moved us to the cellar of Block Four, where an extraordinarily gentlemanly registrar entered us in his book and actually said "please" and "thank you." It was almost frightening!

The entire atmosphere, indeed, was unlike anything I had known in Auschwitz before. Though we were still naked and had not eaten for over twenty-four hours, the men of Canada seemed almost relaxed. We were hungry, certainly, but hunger was a bit of a joke instead of a knife in the belly.

A big, bronzed Pole nearby said, "Don't worry, lads. We'll get food soon enough."

Somebody else laughed and said, "That's right. A touch of starvation's good for the stomach and the soul."

I glanced from one to the other, hardly able to believe what I'd heard. Here we were in a camp where thousands were dying of starvation, and these men were talking like a bunch of overfed business executives.

Even when the block senior arrived, this tone of civilized relaxation remained. He was a Polish political prisoner whose zebra uniform had a Saville Row cut, and he said to us, "I'm very sorry you've been assigned to this cellar, but we'll soon make it reasonably inhabitable. My name is Polzakiewicz, and as your block senior, I expect order and discipline."

That was all. Looking every inch a Polish regular army officer, he gave us a hard, dignified stare, and then he was gone.

We stayed in Block Four all that day, and to my amazement, each man was given a blanket and a bunk to himself. All that worried me, in fact, was the way everyone evaded my carefully worded questions when I tried to find out what work we were going to do.

Most smiled and said, "You'll see."

A few, a young Slovak called Bock from Piestany, for instance, sneered, "Why worry? You won't survive very long!"

From what they did not say, I realized that soon I was to learn yet another of Auschwitz's secrets, and I had an uneasy feeling that somehow the knowledge was going to be dangerous. The next morning, however, when they released us from our camp, all thoughts of the future were driven temporarily out of my mind by the sight that stretched before me.

The entire face of the camp had changed. The wall had been knocked down between the two sections. There seemed to be twice as much space and half as many prisoners, which, of course was true, and there were no *Muselmänner* anymore, for they had been swept away by Fries and Doctor Uhlenbrook.

After roll call, we stood motionless in our rows while other commands marched from the camp, and I realized that every single diseased limb had been amputated from the body of Auschwitz and burned in a single night. Heads were held high, shoulders square. Nobody shuffled. Nobody drooped. For once, there was not a man who looked on the verge of death.

For an hour, we stood, and I gazed in wonder at this strange, almost exhilarating sight. The order came: *"Aufraumungskommando, antreten!"* "Clearing command—forward!"

That was Canada. We marched through the gates like the Brigade of Guards. The prisoners left behind stopped their mundane tasks to watch us go by. The SS looked at us with professional interest; even Fries, I thought, had a slight gleam in his eye as we passed him and had our numbers checked. For the first time since my arrival in the camp, I felt I was sharing in a communal pride which was slight, but evident nevertheless.

Laco Fischer, however, soon dissipated my embryonic vanity. As we marched, he muttered to me, "We're going to work on confiscated property. But for Christ's sake don't talk about it to anyone because if they catch you at that, they'll kill you. Stick close to me, and do what I do. And don't eat too much."

"Don't eat too much? Are you mad?"

"I'm very sane, boy. You'll be able to steal all the food you want here, if you're careful. But don't eat anything except dry bread for the first couple of days. Your stomach won't stand anymore."

With that, we marched into Canada, the commercial heart of Auschwitz, warehouse of the body-snatchers where hundreds of prisoners worked frantically to sort, segregate, and classify the clothes and the food and the valuables of those whose bodies were still burning, whose ashes would soon be used as fertilizer.

It was an incredible sight, an enormous rectangular yard with a watch tower at each corner and surrounded by barbed wire. There were several huge storerooms and a block of what seemed like offices with a square, open balcony at one corner. Yet what first struck me was a mountain of trunks, cases, rucksacks, kit bags, and parcels stacked in the middle of the yard.

Nearby was another mountain, of blankets this time, 50,000 of them, maybe 100,000. I was so staggered by the sight of these twin peaks of personal possessions that I never thought at that moment where their owners might be. In fact, I did not have much time to think, for every step brought some new shock.

Over to the left, I saw hundreds of prams. Shiny prams, fit for a firstborn. Battered prams of character that had been handed down and down and down and had suffered gladly on the way. Opulent, ostentatious, status-symbol prams and modest, economy prams of those who knew no status and had no money. I looked at them in awe, but still I did not wonder where the babies were.

Another mountain, this time of pots and pans from a thousand kitchens in a dozen countries. Pathetic remnants of a million meals, anonymous now, for their owners would never eat again.

Then I saw women. Real women, not the terrible, sexless skeletons whose bodies stank and whose hearts were dead and who had been the downfall of Franz Marmalade. These were young, well-dressed girls with firm, ripe figures and faces made beautiful by health alone. They were bustling everywhere, running to and fro with bundles of clothes and parcels, watched by even healthier, even more elegant women kapos.

It was all a crazy jigsaw that made no sense to me and seemed sometimes to verge on lunacy. Beside one of the storerooms, I saw a row of girls sitting astride a bench with zinc buckets on either side of them. One row of buckets was filled with tubes of toothpaste, which the girls were squeezing out onto the bench and then throwing into the other, empty buckets. To me it seemed thoroughly un-German, an appalling waste of labor and material, for I had yet to learn that perhaps one tube in ten thousand contained a diamond, a nest egg that some pathetic, trusting family had felt might buy privilege or even freedom.

We slammed to a halt outside the block of offices. Our kapo, Bruno, went to the balcony, a few steps from the ground and, cap in hand, knocked respectfully. The door opened, and a huge SS Scharführer stepped out, a man of about thirty, six feet tall and blond, with Slavic features; fresh, reddish cheeks; and piercing blue eyes that looked as if they could X-ray people. He was sturdy, too, though slightly paunchy, like an athlete out of training, and flanking him were two magnificently handsome Unterscharführers, one dark, disdainful, the other blond, pure Aryan. These three men, Scharführer Wiglep[2] and Unterscharführers Otto Graff and Hans Koenig,[3] both professional actors from Vienna, were to play a significant role in my life throughout the weeks that followed.

Wiglep, the inevitable stick in his hand, strode forward to the edge of the balcony to have a look at us. His eyes wandered up and down the ranks, scanning the newcomers, pigeonholing them in his mind as

2   Wiglep's real name was Wyklef; he was never found after the war and allegedly died on the battlefront. (According to the author, Wyklef used the name Wiglep in the camp; the author even saw his signature.) --Eds.

3   The real name of Hans Koenig was Hans Kühnemann. After the war, he returned to his native Essen in North Rhein-Westphalia and became a singer in the local opera. In 1989, the author learned about his whereabouts and started criminal proceedings against him. In the trial against Kühnemann, (1991–1993) at the Landsgericht Duisburg, the author acted as one of many witnesses for the prosecution. The trial of Kühnemann was stopped by the Supreme Court in 1993 due to the medical condition of the defendant. --Eds.

troublemakers, workers, layabouts, or potential informers. Here and there, he recognized an Unterkapo and greeted him with rough humor.

"Well, Isaac? Still alive? How do you manage it?"

Isaac grinned and shuffled.

"And you, Stefan. You still breathing, too? We'll have to do something about that!"

All good, clean fun, the master joking with the servant. Yet somehow I knew this handsome, jocular man was a merciless killer, a man to be avoided, and at that moment, as if to confirm my fears, he roared, *"Los! To work!"*

Graff and Koenig, like two graceful greyhounds in a field full of hares, leaped among us, sticks swinging, fists and boots flying.

"Los! Los! Los!" A few men fell, but I followed close to the old hands and ducked the blows. They pounced on the mountain of luggage, snatched what they could carry, and ran with it to a storeroom, with me right on their heels, two suitcases in each hand. Graff was outside the door already to thump us through, and Koenig was inside to propel us even faster.

We dumped out trunks and cases and rucksacks on a huge blanket in the store. Immediately, they were ripped open or burst open with a sledgehammer, and food, clothes, toilet equipment, valuables, documents, pathetic family pictures were emptied out. Specialists fell upon them, segregating them, pitching men's clothes to another blanket, women's to another, children's to a third, until half a dozen blankets were piled high. The suitcases and trunks were whisked away and burned with all documents. More porters descended on the blankets and carried them away to the women, who would classify them by quality and pack them away in the warehouses, and all the time, while the experts sweated and we apprentice donkeys galloped to and fro, Graff and Koenig were beating, searching, punishing and bellowing their signature tune: "Los! Los! Faster, you bastards, faster! *Karacho! Karacho!"*[4]

---

4   An SS slang word, meaning "quickly."

Only one man seldom moved. Scharführer Wiglep sat on his patio, a glass of beer by his side, taking an occasional sip, watching every move and intervening only when he spotted a serious crime.

His confidence in his two Unterscharführers was justified. They missed very little, and they did their job efficiently. On my tenth trip, I dropped a suitcase. It split open, and shirts, shoes, apples, sandwiches and salami spewed out around me. I jerked to a stop, ravenous, careless after forty-eight hours fasting, and the two SS men swept down on me, whacking me on my way, helped by half a dozen servile deputy kapos.

As I stumbled on, almost grateful to be beaten away from temptation, I saw the prisoner behind me swoop on the salami, crush it into his mouth, and swallow it on the run.

That was the first important lesson I learned with the Canada Command. Steal only what someone else drops. Snatch fast beneath the cloak of another man's beating. By noon, my hunger had gone, and somehow I had steeled myself to heed Laco's warning to eat only dry bread the first day.

There was another temptation, just as hard to resist. That was to snatch food and hide it for friends or relatives or barter back in the camp, but the three wise men, King Wiglep and his princelings, were up to all these tricks. I saw Koenig drag a man from his human conveyor belt and roar, "Dump your luggage. Don't move!"

He searched him quickly, pulled an apple and a piece of bread from his pockets. "Stealing, are you?" he bellowed so everyone could hear. "I'll teach you manners, you swine. Twenty-five lashes!"

They were delivered on the spot, and as I scampered by the victim, I learned another lesson: keep still and keep quiet under punishment.

The prisoner was a newcomer. Koenig's stick lashed across his buttocks once, twice, three times. At the fifteenth stroke, he screamed, and Koenig lashed harder, yelling, "Quiet, you sniveling bastard!"

In agony, the man jerked erect. Koenig doubled him up again with a vicious blow on the back of his neck. The prisoner clasped his backside in a futile effort to protect himself, and the SS man smashed his fingers, and these blows which did not hit the original target did not count. Seven, eight, maybe nine blows on the neck, the back, and the hands were added to the twenty-five on the buttocks because the prisoner did not behave. Because of his bad manners, in fact, he was beaten unconscious and left to die.

I grew used to the sight of these punishments that first day. I began almost to welcome them, indeed, for when Koenig or Graff were occupied, I could steal, and that meant I could survive.

These beatings by the Unterscharführers were bad enough, but could not be compared with the punishment doled out by Wiglep. Occasionally, he would rise from his chair and shout slowly, ponderously, "Come here…you…lazy swine."

A prisoner would move out of the running line and stand before him.

"So, you think you're in a sanatorium. Or on your holidays, perhaps. Or maybe you think you're a tortoise. Well, you're wrong. You're a man who can move fast, and I have a magic stick here, a miraculous stick that makes tortoises move like men."

Then quietly, expertly, without any of the hysterical fervor of his underlings, he would beat the prisoner until he crumpled, bleeding, useless.

At last, this fantastic day ended. We stood in our rows of five, ready to march back to camp, but before the gates were opened, Wiglep came down from his throne on the balcony, and moved among us, prodding a man here and there with his stick.

"You…and you…and you…*stand out!*"

About fifteen men, chosen not quite at random, for Wiglep's eyes were always active, moved from the ranks. Koenig and Graff searched them meticulously, and out of the fifteen, they found four or five smugglers.

One man had two lemons. Twenty lashes. Another a shirt. Twenty-five lashes. A third, a tin of sardines. Again, twenty-five lashes. The other two had only bread and got away with a couple of thumps and a kick. Then and only then did the Canada Command move off, and as we marched, I noticed a strange new sound. The clack of clogs was missing, and in its place was the soft pad of leather. I glanced down and saw that nearly every man was wearing shoes, some in suede, some in crocodile, and all a world away from wood.

Laco noticed the look of amazement on my face and said with a grin, "It's one of the perks. Somehow, they don't seem to mind if we lift shoes. Maybe they think it adds tone to the command—or perhaps that clogs slow us up!"

Back we went to the camp. I heard the loud, toneless voice of Fries at the gate say: "Well…here comes Canada! *Halt!*"

We stopped. Six SS men ran through the ranks, searching us quickly but without the efficiency of the two Unterscharführers. They struck lucky only once, in fact, hauling out a man who had hidden a shirt in his tunic. Almost lazily, Fries beat him to death, and we carried his body along with the others who had died back to Block Four for roll call.

Exhausted by the work and the heat, bruised by the few blows I had collected, a little dazed by the sights I had seen, I began to wonder whether Canada was worth the risk. As I looked around me at the old hands, however, my doubts vanished.

They were unloading their loot, which somehow they had managed to smuggle through a double screening. One had six tins of sardines; another, two pounds of figs. Shirts and fruit and soap, salami, sausages and ham appeared until the barracks began to look like a well-stocked grocery. Polzakiewicz, the block senior, strolled in to collect his percentage, a lemon here, a pair of crocodile-skin shoes there, meat, fruit and even aspirins to soothe the headaches that authority brings.

After that, men began drifting toward the door. I followed them, and the scene outside convinced me finally that I was going to stay in Canada.

Hanging round the block were the hungry ones. The men from Canada scanned their faces, searching for friends or relatives, singling them out and handing them scraps of food. The camp doctors, themselves prisoners, were there, too, looking for drugs, for medicines, for anything which might help them in their hopeless task. They got them because every man in the Canada Command knew that any day, he might end up in the hospital and badly need a friend.

After a while, they drifted away. Josef and I fell into our bunks. I sank back on my mattress, and before I closed my eyes, I realized I was not hungry for the first time since I had left Franz's food store, which, now that I thought back on it, was no more than a huckster's shop compared with Canada.

———

ONE WEEK IN CANADA TAUGHT ME MORE ABOUT THE REAL purpose of Auschwitz than I had learned in the three months that had passed since my initiation. It was a sickening lesson, not so much because of the sadism or the brutality or the sporadic deaths, but because of the coldblooded commercialism of the place.

Slowly, the bags and the clothes and the food and the sad, smiling photographs became people to me; the prams became babies, and the heaps of carefully segregated little shoes became children, like my cousin Lici in Topolcany. I knew that the vague suspicions I had tried without success to kill were true.

I was in a death factory, an extermination center where thousands upon thousands of men, women, and children were gassed and burned, not so much because they were Jewish, though that was the primary thought in the sick mind of the Führer, but because in death they made a contribution to Germany's war effort.

Daily, I saw the freight trains arrive. I saw them loaded with grade-A men's shirts on Monday; with minks on Tuesday; with children's underwear on Wednesday; with overcoats or general textiles, according to the edict of Wiglep. I realized they were going to a blockaded Germany to boost the morale of civilians who all the time were being asked to pull their belts just one notch tighter.

I saw the pickings which were not loaded onto these wagons by prisoners—the marks, the francs, the lira, the black-market dollars and pounds, the gold and the jewelry and the carefully secreted gems being carried into the office, the palace of Wiglep. I knew these assets were destined for the Berlin State Bank once the King of Canada had taken his percentage, though it was only later that I discovered how cleverly they were used, not only to bolster the Reich's economy, but to manipulate the foreign exchange through Swiss banks so the Allied economy would suffer.

Only later did I learn the importance of this psychological warfare on the home front. Baby needed shoes in Berlin, for instance. Hitler found shoes in Auschwitz, and Momma wrote to Poppa on the Russian front, lauding this savior with the little black moustache.

There were other, more immediate lessons to be digested, of course. I realized that there was a hierarchy who lived like aristocrats; that there was a social ladder which could be climbed; that feuds simmered, smoldered, and exploded; that love affairs flourished, were consummated, and died; that life in Canada, indeed, was similar in many ways to life in other places. It was not so important what you were, but who you knew.

I found that the longer I survived, the nearer I drew to the hard core who had learned not only to live, but to prosper. I became recognized as a semi-permanent fixture. People began calling me by my first name, and once I was accepted by the older hands, I earned a promotion.

Instead of hacking about with luggage, I was given the job of carrying blankets full of clothes from the stores where the cases were unpacked to those where the girls were sorting, and I discovered they were Slovak girls, which brought another little ray of sunshine into my life. Sometimes I could smuggle them a lemon or two, a piece of chocolate or a tin of sardines. In exchange, they gave me their smiles, a glass of lemonade, a hunk of bread and cheese, or maybe some of my sardines back to swallow down fast behind the storehouse. The work was hard, but it was rewarding, for I never went hungry or thirsty, and somehow the bitterness of the place was melted a little by this feminine warmth.

Prisoners low on the social scale, the rank and file, formed innocent friendships with these girls whom they could admire only from a distance and to whom they could seldom speak. They exchanged letters and small gifts. I carried these little tokens of affection on my journeys to and fro, not realizing at first that the higher echelons of society, the kapos, knew what I was doing.

They did nothing to stop me. On the contrary, once they had decided that my personal delivery service was reliable, they began to make use of it themselves, which, for me, was both an advantage and a danger. It brought me small rewards from the kapos, and to a certain extent, I was sheltered from unnecessary punishment by the umbrella of their protection. On the other hand, it brought heavy risks, for these aristocratic liaisons were not always so innocent, and the gifts I had to carry were not tokens, but luxuries. If I was caught, I would get at least twenty-five lashes; yet I could not refuse to act as messenger boy.

With my help, indeed, a torrid little love affair blossomed between my own kapo, Bruno, and Hermione, the kapo in charge of the Slovak girls who were sorting clothes. She was a beautiful Viennese girl of about twenty, splendidly dressed in expensive blouses and skirts from the stores and high black boots that gleamed like those of a Prussian cavalry officer. She was firm with her girls, but I never saw her beat them. Instead, she carried her whip more or less as an adornment, as if she were about to ride in a gymkhana.

She always greeted me with a smile that was half motherly, half flirtatious, when I panted up to her with my heavy blanket. She was so attractive, indeed, that I was not at all surprised when Bruno drew me aside one day and slipped me a letter for her.

Then came the gifts. First an orange or two, some butter perhaps, or a chunk of ham. As the affair developed, however, Bruno became more extravagant in his courtship, and I found myself carrying expensive toilet soaps, eau de cologne, and rare French perfumes. Hermione took them all with an enigmatic, almost majestic smile, and soon Bruno was finding constant excuses to loiter in the vicinity of the women's stores.

He was not the type of man, however, who would be content with a few smiles and a kind word in exchange for his attentions. It was not long, indeed, before this liaison lost some of its virgin purity, which illustrates, incidentally, both the power of the kapos and the desire of the pair of them to express their love in tangible fashion.

They were, of course, taking a risk which could cost them their lives at worst or, at best, their rank and the privileges which went with it. Nevertheless, this was a chance they were prepared to take, as I discovered one day when I dumped my burden with the Slovak girls and saw no sign of Hermione.

Normally, she was always there to see what the parcel held for her and to ensure that her girls did not steal too much. When I asked where she was, one of the girls grinned and jerked her head toward the storeroom.

"In there. With Bruno."

There was no time to ask any more. Back I ran for my next load, and this time I must have broken the record between the men's and women's stores, for I could not wait to hear the next installment of this tender romance.

"What are they up to? I mean…how?"

"We've built them a little love nest. It's really cozy."

Off again with my empty blanket. Back again, even faster this time.

"What do you mean…love nest?"

"We've piled up a few thousand blankets to make a wall. After all, lovers need a bit of privacy, don't they?"

She smiled at me coyly and said, "I wish I was a kapo!"

On my next trip, I saw Bruno slipping quickly out of the store. He glanced at me as he strode by, and I restrained an impulse to wink. If I had known what this affair was going to cost me later on, however, I would not have felt so cordially toward him.

The trouble began when the rent of the love nest rose. Hermione's appetite for luxuries grew. Every day now she expected an expensive present, and on top of this, the other girls had to get their percentage, for, without their cooperation, love would have withered.

As a result, my illegal loads became heavier, and so did the risk I was running. To make life even more uncomfortable, I felt sure that Wiglep was keeping a particularly close eye on me.

At first, I thought it was my imagination, my guilty conscience. Soon, however, I was certain that he suspected me of something, though precisely what it was, I did not know. It could be that he thought I was smuggling, or it could be that he had merely an uneasy feeling that here was a man who had managed to retain a spark of defiance, a prisoner who had not become a well-trained dog.

Yet there was nothing I could do about it, for by that time, I was so deeply involved in the Hermione-Bruno affair that I could not back out without creating big trouble for myself, and now Hermione, who had her boyfriend completely under her thumb, was giving me daily orders.

Sometimes she would say: "I'm short of toilet water." Or: "I'm dying for some milk chocolate. I can't stand that horrible black stuff. And try to get me some anchovies."

Back I would trot to Bruno, my shopping list in my head, and some time later, I would tell Hermione, "It's coming in the next batch."

It was, of course, a fantastic situation. There we were in the worst concentration camp the world has ever known. Yet the elite were living on a scale far higher than most people in Europe because, of course, they were living on loot that had come from all over Europe.

The longer the love affair between Bruno and Hermione lasted, of course, the greater the risk became for me. I knew my luck must run out eventually, and when at last Wiglep called me out, I was not surprised. In fact, I was rather pleased, for that time I was carrying nothing.

Slowly, deliberately, he walked down from the patio, stood before me, and growled, "Dump it!"

I dropped my blanket. It contained only clothes, for though I carried as many as three hundred blankets a day, only about five of them held contraband.

He struck me an almost friendly blow over the shoulder with his stick and said, "Carry on. And make it snappy."

Off I scampered, glad in a way that I had been caught because I felt that now he would ignore me for a while—but I was wrong.

On my very next trip, I heard the familiar roar from the balcony: "Halt, you swine! Dump it!"

Again, I had nothing. Again, he thumped me casually on my way. Again, I began to feel smug, sure now that I was immune from his attention, and again, I was wrong. On my third trip, I got my third summons in succession, which must have been a record for anyone in Canada. Once more, my hands were clean.

Bruno, of course, had been watching this cat-and-mouse game very carefully. When I went to the store for my next blanket, he was waiting for me.

"Listen," he whispered. "He's searched you three times in succession. He won't stop you for the rest of the day now, certainly not on the next trip, so take some stuff over to Hermione."

To me, that seemed logical enough, though I must say I felt a twinge of anxiety when I saw what he had dismissed so lightly as "stuff." It looked more like the result of a wild shopping spree in prewar London, Paris, or New York...eau de cologne, delicately perfumed soap, a little bottle of Chanel, a tinned chicken, the most expensive German frankfurters, and sardines from Portugal.

"Bruno," I said a little nervously, "it's quite a load!"

"Don't worry. He won't stop you. He daren't risk a fourth failure, not in front of Koenig and Graff. You should have seen them sniggering behind his back last time."

That made sense. When Wiglep descended from his throne to search a prisoner, it was an unspoken criticism of his two Unterscharführers, a sly way of telling them they were not doing their job properly; to draw a blank was to admit publicly that he had made a mistake. I picked up my blanket and started to run.

"*You...halt!*"

I could not believe it. I kept on running, careful not to quicken my pace, pretending that I thought he meant the man behind me. If only I could make it to the women's store, I'd be safe.

"*You*, you bastard! Stop foxing. Come here and drop that blanket before you're shot!"

I turned and ran over to Wiglep, the shrewdest psychologist I have ever met. He knew how my mind had been working. He knew that I thought he would never stop me a fourth time, that I felt I was safe. I dropped my blanket, which was more like a mobile delicatessen-cum-beauty-shop, and a look of exaggerated surprise spread over his face as he murmured with grinding sarcasm, "Well! What a strange collection of clothes!"

He walked around my blanket slowly, ticking off the items one by one. His voice was soft and dangerous.

"A chicken. Milk chocolate all the way from Switzerland. Eau de cologne…and Chanel! I wish I could get perfume like that for my wife. Now I wonder what lucky girl was going to get this little haul."

I said nothing. He looked at me sharply and rapped, "It was for Hermione, wasn't it?"

Still, I kept silent, and now I knew I was no longer just a prisoner who had been caught smuggling. Wiglep knew well that a new boy like me could never have stolen such luxuries. He knew they came from Bruno, and he was going to prove it, to crush this kapo who thought he could do as he wished. It was the last round, he felt, in a battle that had been going on for months, a battle to the death between Bruno, veteran of prewar prisons and half a dozen concentration camps, and Wiglep, who had won his sergeant's stripes in Dachau and Sachsenhausen.

"Kapo, come here!"

Bruno knew well what had happened. He knew the chips were down, that he and Hermione could die in the Punishment Block if Wiglep could make me talk, yet his face was innocent as he trotted up obediently and gazed at the haul.

He was a good actor. First, he registered utter amazement, then wild, mock fury. He lashed at me with his stick and bellowed, "You filthy Yiddisher swine. You stinking, thieving pig!"

He went on beating me until Wiglep said very quietly, "Leave this to me, kapo. He'll talk to me more quickly than he will to you. He's going to tell me where he got this loot, even if they're his last words."

Across the camp I could see Hermione, lovely as ever, watching. The whole working detachment, in fact, was watching as it bustled about its business, for news of big trouble traveled fast in Canada. Briskly, Wiglep called Otto Graff and Hans Koenig, who whistled their amazement when they saw the blanket and made witty remarks about the excellent taste I had shown in my selection.

Then I was bending. His stick crashed against my buttocks, jerking me forward. Koenig's boot pushed me back into place.

"Who gave it to you?"

Again, his arm rose with the easy, economical movement of the expert, the craftsman. Again, the stick fell. Again: "Who gave it to you?"

Three times. Four. Five. Unhurried, methodical blows that crushed into my flesh. And the question, not shouted, but almost whispered, the monosyllables mouthed tonelessly, monotonously.

"Who…gave…it…to…you?" Six…seven…eight. "Who…gave… it…to…you?" Dimly, I could see Bruno's boots and hear the prisoners scurrying by. Nine…ten…eleven. "Who…gave…it…to…you?" The professional beater was increasing the volume of pain with each blow now, adjusting it methodically, accurately, like a good technician. Bruno's boots swam before my eyes. The noises of the camp faded, then came roaring back into my ears. I hardly noticed the kicks of Graff and Koenig as they pushed me back into place when I lurched.

Twelve…thirteen…fourteen…fifteen. I could not see the boots anymore, just a red haze. I could not hear the prisoners or even the swish of the stick, just a dull roar. The pain was constant now and all-embracing, seeping into every living cell of me, exploding to new, unbelievable heights with every new blow.

"Who…gave…it…to…you?" I sensed the words rather than heard them, but they were meaningless. Useless. Wiglep was wasting his time because my mind was clutching at one theme alone: When would he stop? When would I die? When would it all be over? "Who gave it to you? Who gave it to you? WHO GAVE IT TO YOU?" The blows carved the question mark, and then the words were tumbling around my brain and I was floating and the lights, the red, yellow, and purple lights flickered all around me in a crazy aurora borealis. The concrete hit my face, but I never felt it.

It should have been the end. The accepted camp procedure when a prisoner became unconscious was that the beating continued until he was dead, but Wiglep was more subtle He knew he had done enough to prepare me for hospitalization and a phenol injection.

I woke up in my bunk the following morning, stabbed awake by the pain of unconscious movement. I lay very still, wondering what had happened to me, then slowly remembering. Bruno was looking down at me, his eyes carefully guarded.

"You did all right yesterday," he said. "Forty-seven blows, by Christ, and he knows how to hit, that fellow. He couldn't believe it when you wouldn't talk. He'd never known anyone like you. D'you know, I think he had a bit of admiration for you in the end."

He rambled on, like some veteran football fan recalling the greatest match he had ever seen. With an effort, I said, "How did I get here?"

"Two of the boys carried you back. The whole bloody yard knew what was going on. The boys going by, in fact, were giving a blow-by-blow commentary! I think they were taking bets on when you'd crack!"

I knew what he meant. I knew too that he and Hermione had had the biggest bet of all. They had staked their lives on my silence. They had won, and I had won as well, for the entire Canada Command would be waiting, watching, to see if Bruno would pay the debt he owed to me.

I said to him, "I can't get up. I can't work."

He understood what I was saying. Those who could not work died.

"Don't worry," he said. "I've friends in the hospital who'll look after you. That beating will give you phlegmona.[5] Your backside will

5   In English, edema, caused by malnutrition.

swell like a balloon, and they'll have to operate. But don't worry. You'll have everything you want…food and the best of attention."

He went away to round up his sheep. I lay motionless, trying to assess the situation, adding the good and subtracting the bad and each time getting a different answer. The hospital meant death, but Bruno was powerful; I had stood by him, but would he stand by me? His friends could keep me alive, but maybe he would like to see me die, for I knew too much.

Josef was beside me, holding a glass of lemonade to my dry lips. It was pure lemon juice with water and sugar. It tasted good.

CHAPTER 9

"This is Not a Synagogue!"

POISON, CAUSED BY THE BEATING, FLARED IN MY BUTTOCKS and legs. For four days, I lay in agony which was increased by the slightest touch, and all that time, Bruno; Burger, the registrar in Block Four; and the block senior managed to shield my presence from the camp authorities, a task which could have cost them their lives.

I was visited daily by a doctor prisoner whom Bruno could keep supplied with drugs, and on the fourth day I heard him say tersely, "If he doesn't have an operation soon, he'll die."

This, of course, was putting quite a strain on the organizing abilities of my more or less reluctant benefactor, but, nevertheless, he had been expecting it and was prepared. First, he had to ensure I was kept well clear of Oberscharführer Josef Klehr,[1] whose hospital job was to inject with a fatal dose of phenol those who were selected for "euthanasia" by the SS doctor.

Then he had to arrange for me to receive fairly decent rations from Canada, for my strength had to be maintained at a reasonable level if the operation was to be a success. I was, in fact, quite a little headache

---

1   Josef Klehr (1904–1988) was taken as a prisoner in Austria by the Americans in the beginning of May 1945 and was held until 1948. When released, he returned to his family in Braunschweig and resumed his profession as a cabinet maker. On August 19, 1965, the Frankfurt court convicted him of murder in at least 475 cases and also of assistance in the joint murder of at least 2,730 people. He was sentenced to life imprisonment with an additional fifteen years. On January 25, 1988, Klehr's sentence was suspended. On June 10, he was ordered to serve the remainder on probation. Klehr died at the age of eighty-three, after seven months of freedom. --Eds.

for him, yet he managed to arrange what, relatively speaking, was VIP treatment for me in the hospital.

This I learned, however, only by degrees. At first, for instance, I did not appreciate that it was a considerable advantage for me to be allocated a top bunk, when many men have weeping wounds or are suffering from dysentery and the discharges from their bodies are seeping through to those beneath them. Another little luxury was the fact that when one of the men with whom I was sharing my bunk died, he was not replaced, which gave a little more room. All these little privileges, I fear, were blotted from my mind by the utter nausea I experienced when first I became a patient at Auschwitz hospital.

The room itself was not too bad, and prisoner orderlies tried to keep it reasonably clean with carbolic, but the overcrowding was so appalling that their task was almost impossible. Bunks rose three tiers high, and there were at least three men in each of them. Poisoning, gangrene, dysentery were commonplace, and though those orderlies did their best, the stench of rotting flesh and excreta rose above the antiseptic smell of the carbolic.

I found myself sharing a bunk with a man of about forty whose right arm was slowly disintegrating and another, less than twenty, who had typhus and dysentery and twisted constantly in delirium.

Both were Polish Jews; both were dying; and both, I say with some shame now, I found completely repugnant. In the narrow confines of the bunk, I tried to shrink from them, from the entire, ghastly place; in fact. I tried to close my eyes and my ears to it, to its noises that never ceased, its pitiful, frightening moans and cries in the night, to the thud of the dead, hitting the stone floor, kicked out by the living in search of *Lebensraum*.

After a while, however, though I never got used to it all, I realized there were peaks of courage and islands of incredible dignity in this hell of sickness. Monek, the middle-aged Pole beside me, was in constant agony from his rotting arm. Yet he never mentioned it, and when his friend on the other side of me—they both came from the town of Mlawa—began shouting in his delirium, he said to me gently, "Please forgive the boy. He's very sick. But normally he's such a nice lad...."

I was less tolerant, a good deal more selfish, for I still was not quite sure whether I could trust Bruno or whether my next appointment would be with "Doctor" Klehr of phenol fame, and so, when the orderlies came to take me to the operating theatre, I knew I was facing either relief from pain or death in less than ten minutes. One point made clear to me quickly, however, was that I was in for a rough time, one way or another.

In the operating theater, half a dozen white-coated doctor prisoners were already working on a patient. They finished the job quickly, lifted him onto a stretcher, and gave a sign to the orderlies with me.

Suddenly, I felt trapped. They heaved me onto the table, face downward, and tied me there by my ankles and wrists. An assistant held an ether pad over my face, and I knew now that there was no escape.

"Start counting..."

"One...two...three..." Was it going to be the needle with phenol or the knife?

"Four...five...six..." Why the hell doesn't the stuff put me out? Why don't they give me more?

"Twenty-two...twenty-two...twenty-two..." I got stuck there somehow, and now I was really scared. Supposing they started to work on me before I was out. I tried to shout to them, but no sound came, and then I felt the knife, the searing knife, bite into my leg.

It was my last memory for some time. Whether the ether finally worked or whether I fainted, I shall never know, but when I came to my senses again, I was no longer on the table, but being held up in a corner while two Polish orderlies bandaged my legs and my bottom. Though still dazed, I could see that the doctors were at work already on the next patient, and I remember feeling not merely gratitude, but admiration for them, for even among the degradations of Auschwitz, most of them managed to retain their humanity and their professional integrity.

That night, I slept in spite of the noise because the ether fumes were still in my head. The next morning, my middle-aged friend was sitting up in the bunk, looking more composed than ever, and his young friend was quieter, too.

"How is he?" I asked. "He seems better."

The Pole smiled gently, sadly, and said, "God has helped him. He is dead."

Suddenly, I felt almost guilty. I remembered my spasms of irritation against the boy, against them both, and I said lamely, inadequately, "I'm...sorry. Really sorry."

"You mustn't be," whispered the older man. "I'm glad he's dead. I knew him when he was only a child, you see. I knew his parents. I'm glad he is out of Auschwitz and his sufferings are over."

I was silent, for there seemed little I could say. Monek from Mlawa, Monek who had suffered in silence beside me, had said it all with those strangely formal words of his.

"There's only one favor I want to ask you," he went on. "Would you mind if we left him in the bunk until the gong sounds? Would you mind...if we didn't kick him out, like the others?"

"Of course not. I wouldn't dream of it..."

When the gong finally went, we carried the boy gently from the bunk. Monek murmured a prayer in Hebrew, the first I had heard in Auschwitz, and I said "amen" in deference to the sincerity of his feelings rather than for any other reason.

A few mornings later, an orderly, one of Bruno's hired helps, detailed to look after me, came to my bunk and whispered, "There's going to be a selection. Now listen carefully. See that you're clean—in fact, go in and wash yourself now. Be very quiet and stand smartly. If anyone asks you about your health, say you're feeling fine. I'll see you're standing with your back to the wall so they won't see your wounds."

I felt a tenseness in the pit of my stomach. Here was the next hurdle, the hurdle that followed the beating in Canada and the operation. I knew it could be the most dangerous of them all, for now my life depended on the whim of an SS doctor, a man who could send me to my death if he did not like the look on my face, a judge who would order the execution of three-quarters of the prisoners in hospital.

In the washroom, I cleaned myself up thoroughly. When I came out, the orderlies were preparing their patients for the big moment, shouting, "Everybody up! Off with your shirts. Come on. Hurry up! Get into lines!"

Some just lay where they were, for they were too weak to move. They knew they were signing their own death warrants because they would be condemned automatically, but they did not care. The rest scrambled to their feet, some tottering at the effort, and I found myself lining up with a mass of naked skeletons, each of whom knew well just how heavily the dice was loaded against him. Some sagged, certain already that they were going to die, yet again I could sense their spirit, their dignity, their courage.

"*Achtung!*" The bark came from the door, the overture that always preceded the appearance of an SS officer, and the ranks shuffled as men tried to drag themselves to attention. The block senior sprang into action as the doctor, followed by his entourage, entered.

"Herr Obersturmbannführer, I report with respect that there are forty-six prisoners, members of the staff, and seven hundred and thirty four ill prisoners."

The doctor, tall, thinnish, middle-aged, nodded curtly. He had the air of one who is about to perform a distasteful task with efficiency, of a man who, because of his high calling, his medical oaths, would stoop even to examining stinking Jews. Yet we all knew and he must have known, too, that here was no noble purpose. Here was a dismal routine and nothing more.

Behind him came an SS man with a notebook, the block senior and the block registrar, and drawing up in the rear, like first-year medical students, were the doctor prisoners, among them some of the finest medical brains in Europe.

The Herr Doktor Obersturmbannführer was working fast that morning. He paused slightly before the second man in the first row and pointed his military cane at his chest.

Immediately, the block senior grabbed the man's arm and shouted out the number: "23476!" The SS man made a note of it. So did the block registrar, and number 23476, a gray, little man who had been trying so hard to stand up straight, gazed sightlessly straight ahead. He knew he had just been written off, literally and in duplicate.

"15923...9467...43188." The cane pointed, though never touched. The numbers were called, and the busy clerks scribbled. Only here and there did the SS doctor pause, presumably to show what a meticulous, conscientious man he was. He would gaze at a naked patient, stroking his chin, as if in deep thought. Then he would throw a quiet word over his shoulder, and one of the doctor prisoners would leap to his side.

"What's the matter with this man?"

"Phlegmona, Herr Oberstumbannführer. And dysentery."

Another slight pause while the Great Man pondered. Then he would record his diagnosis and the treatment to be administered with yet another stabbing movement with his cane.

He drew closer to my place in the back rows. I tried to make myself as inconspicuous as possible—not too erect, yet not slouching; not too smart, yet not sloppy; not too proud, yet not too servile—for I knew those who were different died in Auschwitz, while the anonymous, the faceless ones, survived.

The smart green uniform was in front of me, and the gray eyes were examining me with mild interest. A quiet word, and a white-coated doctor prisoner was called in for consultation.

"What's wrong with this prisoner?"

"Just an abscess, Herr Obersturmbannführer. He's going back to work tomorrow."

The scrutiny became more intense. I knew even the most cursory examination would show that the man, a friend of Bruno's, was lying, was covering something, but the entourage moved on and I held my breath in case they might hear it sighing from my lungs with relief.

At last, the play was over and the principal actors left. Now it was time for the scene shifters to get to work, though here, too, there was a careful timetable. The condemned could not be removed until their rations had been ordered, for, though they would never eat them, it would be a pity to waste good food.

So, the order went down to the central stores. At noon that day, we who had survived would get some extra soup and bread, the rations of men who already would be dead, and as soon as the order had been given, the numbers of the rejected were called out for the last time.

Those who could walk lined up. Those who could not were put on stretchers. A few lay motionless in their bunks, for they had died already and would be taken away in good time by the meat wagon.

I saw Monek from Mlawa fold his blanket neatly and gather together the few pathetic possessions he had managed to secrete, just like a man who was packing for a journey. His face was quite serene, and he took his place in the line without complaint or fuss. He did not say goodbye to me, not, I knew, because he was afraid he might break down, but because he felt it might embarrass me, and he was right, for what could I have said in reply?

A brisk order and the ghastly march to Dr. Klehr began. The shambling line, wearing just their striped shirts, some with legs like matchsticks, some whose limbs were bloated and running with pus, lurched away for their final injection, leaving a trail of blood and excreta behind them.

The next day, my friend, the orderly, came to me with serious news. "We're expecting a big batch of sick," he said. "It'd be better if you got out."

I thanked him for the information, but I was by no means happy about the situation. All prisoners discharged from the hospital were distributed to the various commands, according to the labor demands of Jakob Fries, and I knew my chances of getting back to Block Four, where I had powerful friends, were slight.

Indeed, I was right, and my posting could not have been more ominous. The Central Office had marked me down for Buna, the worst command in the camp, a place where my still-emaciated condition would ensure my death within a few days.

Still, I was not completely defenseless. I remained on the fringe of the camp hierarchy even though I was coming to the conclusion that Bruno was getting rather tired, repaying his debt. So, I decided to see what influence I could use by bluff and name-dropping.

The sight of the hospital registrar was not exactly encouraging when I went to get my card from him, for he was obviously in a sour humor. Nevertheless, I said to him more or less brightly, "I'm from Canada Command and have to go back to my block. The kapo there is a good friend of mine; do you think it can be arranged?"

It was, in fact, an outrageous request, one which normally would have earned me a blow with a stick, but everyone knew who the kapo from Canada was. Everyone knew Bruno and the power he wielded.

Instead of hitting me, he glowered and grunted, "You're for Buna. You know I daren't change you."

"I know it's difficult. But I won't forget. And neither will Bruno."

The magic name worked again, even though I had a feeling I was taking it in vain. The registrar grumbled off to have a sly word with the block senior, and when he came back, he tossed me my card for Block Four, my passport to comparative safety.

Bruno, indeed, did not exactly embrace me when I turned up. In fact, he was surprised to see me and not quite sure what to do with me now that I had landed on his doorstep.

Scratching the top of his closely shaven head, he muttered, "I can't bring you to work with me; that's for sure. If Wiglep sees you alive, he'll kill you. I tell you what—go on the ramp for a while."

The ramp, symbol of Auschwitz for millions because they saw little else except the gas chambers. A huge, bare platform that lay between Birkenau and the mother camp and to which transports rolled from all parts of Europe, bringing Jews who still believed in labor camps. Scene of the infamous selections, where a handful of workers were sent to the right, and the rest, the old, the very young, the unfit, were sent to the left, to the lorries, to the crematoria, still believing that somewhere ahead lay a resettlement area.

There I worked for eight months. There I saw three hundred transports arrive and helped to unload their bewildered cargoes. There I saw in action the greatest confidence trick the world has ever known, and there I had a profound change of thought about escaping.

I was determined to get out, but no longer because I wanted freedom for myself. I wanted to warn those yet to come what lay ahead because I knew they would rise and fight, as the Jews of the Warsaw ghetto had fought. Once they knew the truth, they would refuse to walk meekly to the slaughterhouses.

———

THE SYSTEM BEHIND THE GREAT SWINDLE WAS VERY SIMple and very effective. As soon as a transport arrived, it was surrounded by SS men with submachine guns, rifles, or heavy bamboo canes.

As the dazed victims tumbled out, they were forbidden to speak, and about twenty or thirty SS men were detailed to ensure that this rule was observed.

They ran up and down the ragged, shuffling lines, bellowing, "Silence, everybody! This is not a synagogue! Behave like civilized human beings, and you will be treated well. Behave like animals, and you will be treated like animals."

Invariably, the order was obeyed, for these were people who were thoroughly confused and already a little demoralized by the fetid squalor of their journey. They wanted no trouble, particularly because they had their families with them and partly because they saw how quickly any of the few rebels were clubbed down by the SS.

So simple, as I say, and so effective. Without speech, without a whisper to fan spirit into flame, there can be no rebellion. Those who had doubts kept them to themselves and felt a little easier in their hearts when they saw an ambulance with a big red cross go by, though they would not have been quite so comforted had they known it was filled with the chemicals which were to kill them in the gas chambers half an hour later.

The impact of this mass acquiescence did not strike me immediately. Nor did the transports themselves make much impression upon me, for I had seen it all before. I had lived, remember, in these little hells on wheels. I had seen people clubbed and killed. I had watched families being ripped apart and had heard their cries, and after my experiences in Auschwitz, I suppose I had become a little numb to suffering.

Indeed, for those first few nights on the ramp, my thoughts were selfish. I was concentrating on staying alive. True, I saw the great selections and heard the lorries revving up with their cargoes for the crematoria, but my major tasks were dodging the trigger-happy SS men who seemed to be everywhere, unloading the luggage from stinking wagons, and stealing food from it before I was spotted.

Soon, in fact, I became an adept. I could pick out the case containing food as soon as I climbed into the wagon. I could run with two heavy bags while chewing a chunk of salami and then flick it to another prisoner a yard or two away without being seen by the guards. I learned, we all learned, to identify different transports with different goods.

A train from Greece meant a feast of figs and olives; from France, sardines, perhaps; from Slovakia, salami and beautiful black home-made bread. We found tin openers on the floors of the wagons, and we learned to open tins and swallow their contents in a few seconds.

It may seem callous, inhuman almost, that we should eat while thousands were being herded to their deaths. Yet there was nothing we could do to help them, for we were bound by an even more rigid rule of silence. To break it meant instant death out of sight behind the wagons.

Very occasionally, however, somebody tried, usually a newcomer who did not realize he was sacrificing his life for nothing. There was, for instance, one young Czech boy who had been in the camp only about three months and was unloading a transport of Prague Jews.

It had been a good trip, relatively speaking, and most of the victims were in fair physical shape. One woman, in fact, was almost jaunty, bouncing along the ramp with her fur coat thrown loosely over her shoulders and her two well-dressed children by the hand.

The young Czech prisoner watched her, maybe with pity, maybe with nostalgia for the lush café society which obviously had been hers. He saw her pass an Obersturmbannführer, and he heard her say to her son in a loud, almost gay voice: "Wipe your nose, dear. That's a German officer!"

At that, his control snapped. He edged toward her and muttered, "You stupid bitch, you'll be dead in half an hour!"

She stopped and stared at him, her plump, still beautiful face sagging. Then she twirled on her heel and marched straight up to the SS man. Pointing a finger at the prisoner, she shrilled: "That...that convict says we're going to die. What does he mean? What's happening? What are you—"

The SS man interrupted her blandly, politely, almost apologetically.

"Please, madam," he said, "calm yourself. Nothing is going to happen to you. Kill you? Do you honestly believe we Germans are barbarians?"

She turned around to face the Czech prisoner, a look of smug contempt on her face, but he was no longer there. He had been taken behind the wagons by two SS men and shot with an air pistol that made no noise and disturbed nobody, except, of course, the prisoner.

My nights on the ramp rolled on remorselessly, like the trains themselves that came rumbling out of the darkness and then disappeared, and like those trains, they were jarred out of their morbid routine only when some trifle momentarily slowed the smooth machinery—some trifle like that Czech boy who could stay silent no longer.

Indeed, throughout my eight months on that job, there were only two other incidents that threatened to upset the strong, simple efficiency of the SS system. The first occurred when a transport carrying three thousand French Jews arrived.

For the SS, this was an easy load. These people knew nothing of ghettos or pogroms. They had never had their senses toughened by real persecution. They were docile to the point of apathy, in fact, and they did precisely what they were told without a murmur of protest, an utterly amenable mass of human putty in the hands of experienced artists.

Yet these were the people who nearly made the SS panic.

It happened at midnight in the cold winter of 1942. Men, women, and children were queueing obediently for selection when something went wrong.

Every night, a truck carrying a harvest of dead from Auschwitz to Birkenau passed at right angles to the head of the ramp. Normally, nobody saw what it held and it was gone before anyone could even think about it, but that night, it was overloaded. That night, it was swaying and heaving with the weight of dead flesh, and as it crawled over the railway lines, it began to bounce and buck on its tired, tortured springs.

The neatly packed bodies began to shift. A hundred, two hundred scrawny arms and legs flopped over the side, waving wildly, limply in a terrible, mocking farewell, and simultaneously from those three thousand men, women, and children rose a thin, hopeless wail that swept from one end of the orderly queue to the other, an almost inhuman cry of despair that neither threats, nor blows, nor bullets could silence.

With one, last, desperate lurch, the lorry cleared the tracks, disappearing out of the arc lights into the darkness, and then there was silence, absolute and all-embracing. For three seconds, four at the most, those French people had glimpsed the true horror of Auschwitz, but now it was gone, and they could not believe what their eyes had told them. Already, their minds, untrained to mass murder, had rejected the existence of that lorry, and with that, they marched quietly toward the gas chambers, which claimed them half an hour later.

Yet the SS realized well what could happen if mass hysteria of this nature had time to catch hold of their victims—if the lorry broke down, for instance. Every night after that, a secret signal was given when it was approaching, and all arc lights were switched off until it was safely out of sight.

It was, indeed, an unsettling incident for them. A few weeks later, however, they had something much more unnerving to handle. In January 1943, a transport with several hundred inmates from Dutch Jewish mental hospitals arrived after a ghastly twelve-day journey under unspeakable conditions. Some of them were violently mad; some only slightly so; some were the sane who had tried to evade deportation with the aid of a psychiatrist's report, and the result of it all was a nightmare that not even the most hardened SS man present could ever forget.

Apart from its cargo, there were two unusual aspects of this transport. In the first place, it arrived in daylight because Mr. Eichmann's timetables were getting overloaded. Secondly, this was the only time we prisoners were allowed to be in close contact with the victims for any length of time.

For this, the SS had sound reason. When they opened the wagons, the sight was so revolting that they could not face it. So, they whipped in the prisoners to handle some of the dirtiest work that even Auschwitz had witnessed.

In some of the trucks, nearly half the occupants were dead or dying, more than I had ever seen. Many obviously had been dead for several days, for the bodies were decomposing and the stench of disintegrating flesh gushed from the open doors.

This, however, was no novelty to me. What appalled me was the state of the living. Some were drooling, imbecilic, live people with dead minds. Some were raving, tearing at their neighbors, even at their own flesh. Some were naked, though the cold was petrifying, and above everything, above the moans of the dying or the despairing, the cries of pain, of fear, the sound of wild, frightening, lunatic laughter rose and fell.

Yet amid all this bedlam, there was one spark of splendid, unselfish sanity. Moving among the insane were nurses, young girls, their uniforms torn and grimy, but their faces calm and their hands never idle. Their medicine bags were still over their shoulders, and they had to fight sometimes to keep their feet, but all the time they were working, soothing, bandaging, giving an injection here, an aspirin there. Not one showed the slightest trace of panic.

"Get them out!" roared the SS men. "Get them out, you bastards!"

A naked girl of about twenty with red hair and a superb figure suddenly leaped from a wagon and lay, squirming, laughing at my feet.

A nurse flung me a heavy Dutch blanket, and I tried to put it round her, but she would not get up. With another prisoner, a Slovak called Vogel,[2] I managed to roll her into the blanket.

"Get them to the lorries!" roared the SS "Straight to the lorries! Get on with it, for Christ's sake!"

Somehow Vogel and I broke into a lumbering run, for this beautiful girl was heavy. The motion pleased her, and she began clapping her hands like a child. An SS club slashed across my shoulders, and the blanket slipped from my numbed fingers.

"Get on, you swine! Drag her!"

I joined Vogel at the other end of the blanket, and we dragged her, bumping her over the frozen earth for five hundred yards. Somehow, she clung to the blanket, not laughing now, but crying, as the hard ground thumped her naked flesh through the thick wool.

"Pitch her in! Get her on the lorry!" The SS men were frantic, for here was something they could not understand. Something that knew no order, no discipline, no obedience, no fear of violence or death.

We pitched her in somehow, then ran back for another crazy, pathetic bundle. Hundreds of them were out of the wagons now, herded by the prisoners who were herded by the SS, and everywhere, the nurses. Still working.

One walked slowly with an old, frail man, talking to him quietly, as if they were out in the hospital grounds. Another half-carried a screaming girl. They fought to bring order out of chaos using medicines and blankets, gentleness and quiet heroism instead of guns or sticks or snarling dogs.

Then, suddenly, it was all over. The last abject victim had been slung into one of the overloaded lorry. We stood there, panting in the chill January air, and all our eyes were on those nurses. In unemotional

---

2   Michal Vogel survived Auschwitz and settled in Indianapolis, USA, as a businessman; he and the author kept in touch. --Eds.

groups, they stood around the lorries, waiting for permission to join their patients.

The SS men were watching them, too, with a respect they seldom showed for anyone. I heard one say: "Don't say Mengele's going to send those kids off in the lorries. If he does that, he's as crazy as any of those poor, bloody sods."

Another muttered, "You're right. God knows, we could use some decent medical help around here."

Now my eyes were on Mengele, chief doctor of Auschwitz, a man who until now has escaped justice.[3] He was standing with some SS officers who seemed to be arguing with him. I saw him shake his head vigorously and hold both his hands up to end all further discussion. One of the SS officers shrugged and shouted, "Get the girls aboard! It seems they've got to go, too."

The nurses climbed up after their patients. The lorry engines roared, and off they swayed to the gas chambers.

For once, there had been no selection. For once, it had not been necessary.

---

3   Josef Mengele (1911–1979) disappeared to Argentina in July 1949. He initially lived in and around Buenos Aires, then fled to Paraguay in 1959, and to Brazil in 1960. In spite of extradition requests by the West German government and clandestine operations by the Israeli Mossad, Mengele eluded capture. He drowned while swimming off the Brazilian coast in 1979 and was buried under a false name, Wolfgang Gerhard. (His remains were disinterred and positively identified by forensic examination in 1985.) --Eds.

CHAPTER 10
My Condition Improves

I<small>F</small> D<small>R</small>. K<small>URT</small> U<small>HLENBROOK</small> <small>AND HIS ENERGETIC, IF UN-</small>
qualified deputy diagnostician, Jakob Fries, thought they had rid
Auschwitz of spotted typhus forever by their massive purge of August
1942, they were sadly mistaken. Within a few weeks, it had wormed
its way back into the camp, thanks mainly to the fact that more and
more transports were arriving and more and more workers were being
demanded by the nearby war factories.

Overcrowding, dirt, lack of decent sanitation bred the louse which
bred the fever, and with it returned the old, familiar, ugly face of Auschwitz,
the face which had been bathed clean with the blood of the thousands who
had died on that dreadful night in August. The face of the *Muselmann*.

Once more, I began to notice the staggering figures marching on
their way to work, trying to haul themselves erect as they passed the
gimlet eyes of Fries. I saw them rejected and sent back, and, even more
pathetic, I saw others, barely able to stand, begging a kapo, any kapo, to
let them go to work. Once more, "Doctor" Klehr was back in business,
his "practice" bigger than ever.

An ugly, unpredictable thing indeed is spotted typhus. It cost me
my best friend, Josef Erdelyi. It all but cost me my own fife. Yet it put
me in touch with an element in camp life which I never dreamed existed: a powerful underground movement, without whose help I could
never have escaped.

I think Josef and I must have felt ourselves immune to typhus, perhaps because we were young, strong, and well fed, he on his Canada pickings and me on the varied menu offered by the ramp. Even when we developed all the well-known and much-feared symptoms, we thought we would be well again in a couple of days.

I first noticed dizziness, then that I could not run very well. After that, there was a general loss of equilibrium which made me weave as if I were slightly drunk, and when I mentioned this to Josef, he admitted that he, too, had been feeling groggy in the same way.

We knew, of course, that we would be setting ourselves up for a swift slug of phenol if these symptoms were noted officially. So, we decided it would be best if we wangled ourselves a couple of days away from work.

This could be done in a number of ways, most of which were dangerous. Since the typhus purge, however, ambulance stations had been set up around the camp, and sometimes it was possible to persuade one of the orderlies in charge to issue a card which gave a prisoner permission to remain within his block and away from work, and this method we decided to try.

We must have been very naïve. It never dawned on us that these men, who dealt with typhus in all its stages all day and every day, would spot a couple of suspects in a few seconds, and even to be a suspect meant death.

At my ambulance station, a young Pole was on duty. He took a good look at me when I reached the top of the queue and, before I could speak, said, "Show me your tongue."

I shoved out my tongue. With a frown, he said, "It's pretty nasty. Spots and brown stripes."

"Tummy upset," I said in Polish. "I was wondering could I have a card to let me off work for a couple of days."

"Let's have your temperature." He stuck a thermometer in my mouth. After a couple of minutes, he glanced at it and said, "It's high. Too damn high."

"Look," I said. "It's just a chill. Please let me have that card."

This time, I did not like the look in his eyes, but I cheered up when he said, "Okay. I'll put your number down for one. You'll get it later."

I did not realize until much later that day that he was signing my death warrant, and that I learned only by chance and only just in time.

I was passing the station in the evening after work and went up to thank him for his kindness earlier. I honestly thought he was doing me a favor, but again he puzzled me with a long, quizzical stare.

Then suddenly, quickly, he said, "Listen, boy. You've got typhus. You're not going to get any card. When I wrote down your name, I was booking you for the hospital. For a dose of phenol."

I gazed at him, unable to believe him. After all I had weathered, I had given myself up! It simply did not seem possible.

"Now see here," he said, "I can do one favor for you. I can take your number off my list. But for God's sake, don't tell anyone you've even been here, or *I'll* get the phenol."

That, I think, must have been one of the luckiest conversations I had ever had in Auschwitz. I had never met that Pole before. I never met him again. To this day, I cannot think why he risked his own skin to save my life—unless it was because I spoke to him in Polish!

I thanked him anyway and dashed off to find Josef. He, too, had gone through the same routine that morning. He, too, had been told he would get his card later.

"Go back!" I told him. "Go back now and somehow get your number off that list. They're fooling you. They know you've typhus. Get it rubbed out or you'll die tomorrow!"

"Nonsense!" he grinned. "I knew the orderly quite well. He wouldn't pull a fast one like that on me."

"Good God, man," I whispered, "will you go back? Why chance it? What I'm telling you is true!"

This time, he laughed. "Stop worrying," he said. "I'm feeling much better already. I tell you what—you're looking pretty groggy. Get yourself lost among the night shift tomorrow. I'll go to work and bring you back some pills and something to eat—some fruit maybe—from Canada."

For at least an hour, I tried to persuade him that he was being stupid, pigheaded, but it was no use, and in the end, he had almost convinced me that I was wrong, that I had been fooled by the Pole who had been playing a rather poor practical joke on me. In fact, that night I went to bed thoroughly bemused and feeling sicker than ever.

The next morning, I had to struggle to get up, but Josef was fitter than ever. We lined up for roll call, and when it was over, Ernst Burger,[1] the quiet, gentlemanly registrar of Block Four, read out the numbers of those listed for hospitalization.

Suddenly, all my fears of the previous evening returned. Out of the corner of my eye, for nobody was allowed to move at roll call, I glanced at Josef and saw that he was quite calm, quite confident. Burger's voice, unemotional, toneless, droned on, and one by one, the condemned dropped out of line.

Still Josef remained impassive, unperturbed. Even when his own number was called out.

He did not move. It was as if he had not heard, as if the words had not sunk. I saw Burger pause and glance toward him, for he knew him well. Then he called the number again.

Josef's head jerked, and a puzzled expression spread over his face. As Burger moved toward him, he said, "There must be a mistake. I'm quite fit. I'm going to work."

Quietly, the registrar said, "Come on. Your name is on the list. You've got typhus."

---

1   Ernst Burger, a political prisoner from Vienna, was hung in Auschwitz for organizing resistance and escape. He was the last officially hanged prisoner in Auschwitz. --Eds.

Josef was angry now. "Don't be crazy," he snapped. "I'm all right, I tell you. I'm buggered if I'm going to the hospital."

Two kapos came up quickly, hauled him out of the line, thumped him over the neck and shoulders with their sticks, and drove him toward the raggedy band of doomed men. He ignored the blows, kept on protesting, and Burger said gently to himself, for Josef was not listening, "I'm sorry, boy. There's nothing I can do about it."

Powerless to help him at that moment, I watched my friend being marched off toward the hospital, still protesting, still being beaten. I caught Burger's eye, and in it I thought I detected a flicker of sympathy.

For me, that day was longer than any I had ever known. I did not dare show my face outside Block Four, for someone, probably Fries, would have spotted me and known I was dodging work. As soon as the day shifts returned, however, I dashed down to the hospital, chocolate, lemons, and cigarettes hidden under my tunic, determined to do for Josef what Bruno had done for me: to buy him better treatment, to buy his life.

I slipped the registrar of the hospital fifty cigarettes and asked about Josef. Reluctantly, he thumbed through his lists and told me, "Nobody of that number here."

"But he was sent down this morning."

A gleam of understanding came into his eyes. "This morning?" he said. "With the typhus bunch?"

I nodded. The registrar closed the heavy book in front of him with a snap and muttered, "You needn't bother about him anymore. All that lot went straight to Klehr's office!"

I left the hospital feeling sick, dazed. I had seen many die in Auschwitz, many of my friends, but Josef, somehow, was different. We had been together since Majdanek. We had planned our naïve escapes together. We had survived Buna and Canada and Fries's typhus race. Incongruously, perhaps, I thought of the pictures of his girlfriend he had smuggled all the way from Slovakia to Franz Marmalade's store, and I did not realize that many years later I was to meet her with another boyfriend outside a Prague café.

We spoke casually of our school days together then, but we did not speak of Josef or of Auschwitz because it all seemed too unreal.

When the initial shock of his swift disappearance wore off, I decided there still might be hope. Josef, I knew, was a fighter. He might have created so much trouble that he had been sent to Block Eleven—the Punishment Block, and if that had happened, there was still a slender chance.

I began subtle enquiries, for open questions were dangerous. For two days, I sought some clue about his fate, but then I gave up, for I knew that Josef Erdelyi was dead.

A hospital orderly told me, "You mean the big, blond Slovak? He fought the kapos and made a break for the wires. They shot him just as he got there."

In one way, Josef's troubles were over. Mine were just beginning, it seemed, and they were growing fast. I was now too sick to work on the ramp and had been lying low so long in Block Four that it was becoming dangerous, not only for myself, but for those who were covering up for me—people like Ernst Burger.

Drastic situations called for drastic measures, so I went to Bruno and told him frankly, "I'm in a jam. I've got typhus, and sooner or later they're going to pick me up for the hospital. Can you help me?"

"I'm sorry for you," he said, "but it's not my fault, is it?"

It was the brush-off. Bruno felt he had repaid his debt, that he owed me nothing. I knew then that I would have to rely on less powerful men, but better friends, if I were going to live.

One of the thoroughly reliable Canada men was Laco Fischer. I said to him, "Laco, I've got to get out to Canada with the command and hide there. Do you think you can help?"

It was a steep order. Nevertheless, Laco was not overawed by the size of the task. He simply thought for a while and then said, "We could hide you out there, all right, but how the hell are we going to get you past Fries? How are you going to march properly when you can barely stand?"

He was right, of course. By that time, my legs had grown really weak and I wobbled when I walked. Without much hope, I said to him, "Maybe you could prop me up?"

Laco roared with laughter. "Sure," he said. "That'd be marvelous! We hoist you on our shoulders and chair you all the way to Canada like a bloody conquering hero. And Fries could take the salute as we go by!"

For a while, we were both silent until Laco said slowly, "You never know. It might work."

"What might work?"

"We might be able to prop you up. But you'd have to walk past Fries on your own two lousy legs!"

The next morning, I marched toward the gates, Laco on one side of me and Maurice Schalefess, a Dutchman, on the other. Each had an iron grip on my arm and was lifting me so my feet barely touched the ground. We drew nearer and nearer to Fries, and I knew that any moment, I would have to walk solo for just ten paces until I was past him.

"Ready?" muttered Laco.

"Ready!"

The grips relaxed. My props were taken away. I forced my feet to do what they were told, to go forward instead of sideways, and to my amazement, they obeyed me.

"Right...*hup!*"

The props were back. For a while, I was safe.

As soon as we reached Canada, they whipped me into a familiar quarter—the women's section where the clothes were sorted—Hermione's section. I was staggering by that time with fever and exhaustion, but I did not lack for nurses.

The Slovak girls hustled around me, and I felt myself going up in the air. Suddenly, I realized I was being put to bed in the middle of Canada—right on top of a pile of old clothes where nobody could possibly see me.

Hermione, of course, knew precisely what was happening, but she, unlike Bruno, had not forgotten.

The details of that day are hazy in my mind, but I remember being visited several times. A girl would climb up the mountain of clothes with a glass of lemonade and sugar. Another girl would bring me some pills. They never left me alone for longer than half an hour, and they never came to me empty-handed, though most of them were sure I was beyond help, that I was dying.

My fever subsided a little in the evening, maybe because of the pills, maybe because of the lemonade, maybe because those Slovak girls were able to boost what little remained of my morale. At any rate, I was strong enough to march back to camp with the aid of Laco and Maurice and to give ten more or less sprightly steps past the grim, old watchdog at the gate.

The next day, the routine was the same. For three days, in fact, I was hoisted to Canada, hidden, dosed with medicine, and hoisted back again, but at the end of that third day, it was quite clear that this pick-a-back operation would have to stop. I was verging on delirium and needed injections, not pills and sympathy.

So back I went to Block Four, staying with the night shift by day again and the day shift by night. Laco got me the medicine I need-ed from Canada, but that still left the problem of finding someone who knew how to inject it. Suddenly, in one of my moments of clarity, which were becoming shorter and less frequent, I remembered a quiet little orderly from the hospital who used to visit the registrar, Ernst

Burger. I told Laco, "Ask him to help. He's a Slovak like ourselves, and he might do it."

Laco took a long look at me but said nothing. I knew he was thinking that the little Slovak orderly would have to come quickly if he was going to be in time to help.

That night, however, there was no sign of him, and that night was the worst I had ever known—worse, even, than those I had spent in the hospital. My delirium reached its peak, wafting me back to Buna, then to Wiglep and his slow, crucifying stick, then out of Auschwitz altogether. Sometimes I was at home, arguing with my mother about that Russian grammar; or walking with a girl in fields of long grass; or scurrying away from the Hungarian border patrols.

Occasionally, there were moments of lucidity, and these, perhaps, were worse. I remember crawling from my bunk and trying to find the lavatory. Then blackness, and I was lost, unable to find my bearings. I tried to head for the door and was faced by blank walls all the times, frightening, strange walls I seemed never to have seen before.

Then the noises began, the hostile noises, the shouts of abuse from strange throats, pounding in my ears, jeering me because I did not know where I was and could not find the lavatory or even the door. I tried to crawl away from them up some endless corridor, but always they were there, behind me, ahead of me, above me, all around me. Voices without bodies or heads or mouths or tongues—just voices with hands which grabbed me and flung me over on my back.

I struggled against them, weak, petrified, for hours, it seemed, until reality trickled slowly back into my burning senses.

I was in my bunk, two burly deputy kapos leaning over me. One of them growled, "You bloody bastard! For Christ's sake keep quiet and let other people sleep."

Dimly, I heard the other mutter, "He's bad, delirious. If we don't get him into hospital soon, we'll all have typhus."

I lay there, gasping, drenched in the sweat of fever, and I realized I was finished if the little Slovak did not come next day, for those deputy kapos were not merely powerful, but frightened.

I slept, I think, for what was left of the night. I must have dozed much of the next day too, for it was evening when I was woken by a voice. A Slovak voice.

It said, "I'm Josef Farber. I think you were looking for me."

I opened my eyes and saw a thin, prematurely gray man in his early thirties, and the sight of him gave me new hope immediately, for he was the hospital orderly.

He gave me the injection I needed so badly, then chatted with me for a while, asking me about my Slovak background and so on. Gradually, however, I realized his questions were becoming more and more pointed.

"Tell me," he said mildly, "how exactly did you end up in a place like this?"

It was the first time a stranger had asked me that question since my arrival in the camp, and though I had trained myself to guard my tongue, I found I was talking to him freely, telling him the whole story of my flight from home, my adventures with the Hungarian underground, my beating by the Hungarian border patrols…everything up to the moment when I first marched beneath the legend *Arbeit Macht Frei!*

He listened without interrupting. Then, very quietly, he said, "I know those Hungarian underground boys and a few more of them, too."

"You know them?"

"Yes. I worked with them. After I got back from the International Brigade in Spain. And from what you've just told me of your record, I think you'll be all right here."

"But my typhus. And those deputy kapos. They want to ship me off to the hospital. And what about Ernst Burger? He's risked enough already, hiding me here."

He smiled. "I'll cure your typhus. The deputy kapos? They're ex-Inter Brigade boys, too. And you needn't worry about Ernst. He's one of us."

One of us! It took me some time to realize just what he meant, and then I understood.

Here in Auschwitz was an underground, a network, a striking force that had even the deputy kapos on its rolls!

Josef Farber grinned at me more broadly this time and said, "Don't worry. We'll see you are all right."

He did, too. From that day on, my status changed drastically. Nobody cursed and tried to wake me if I muttered in my sleep. If I wanted to go to the lavatory, one of the deputy kapos got out of his bunk to make sure I found my way, that I was not delirious. Every day, too, one of these deputies brought my injections back from Canada, and Farber was always there to administer them.

My fever faded. Soon, I was able to eat again. My strength slowly returned, and fourteen days after my worst delirium, I managed to stagger out of my bunk on my own as far as the washroom. I cleaned myself up as best I could, then glanced at the results of my handiwork in a piece of mirror one of the other prisoners had been using.

For a full half minute, I stared into that mirror, and the face of a *Muselmann* stared back. The thin death's head of a man about to collapse.

"Christ!" I muttered out loud, "I can't go to Canada like that!"

The underground, of course, had no intention of letting me do anything of the kind. First, I had to stay in Block Four while I was built up with good food. Only when they were quite certain that I was strong enough did they allow me to march out of the camp again, and even then, I was under close security guard.

It was essential, they said, that Wiglep should not see me, for he undoubtedly would kill me. So, a sedentary task was found for me, sorting spectacles in a quiet backwater, where Wiglep and his watch-dogs would never bother going. Others went there, however, friends of mine who would scurry in with more spectacles and food or lemonade.

That was how I spent my convalescence. Soon I found I could run again and lift bags. So, another job was fixed for me, one which would keep me well away from Wiglep, yet give me enough exercise to tone up my flabby muscles. They put me to loading carpets onto the wagons which called constantly at Canada for the loads they were to bring home to the Reich.

In fact, I was reasonably happy in my work. I was fit, well fed, and satisfied I was in a job that would never bring me into contact with the man most likely to kill me. Unfortunately, I had forgotten what an unpredictable man the Scharführer was—how he delighted in doing the unexpected, in remaining one jump ahead of his work dogs—but I was reminded sharply one afternoon when I trotted up to the open wagon, my carpet on my shoulder.

Scharführer Wiglep stood at the open doors of the wagon, notebook in his hand, eyes observing every detail.

I could not run. I could not even hide behind the carpet. I simply had to move along with the queue of loaders until I drew level with him.

Inevitably, he saw me. His jaw dropped a fraction, then tightened swiftly. For at least a minute, he stared at me, his face expressionless. I stared back, carpet still on my shoulder, wondering when he would put down his notebook and reach for his stick.

Then, almost gently, he drawled in his slow, deep, menacing voice, "So it is really you! I didn't think it was possible. And just look how fit you are, you old swine!"

The words had an edge of sarcasm, but there was another element. There was a thin vestige of respect, perhaps even of admiration. I kept on staring at him, saying nothing, just waiting for a swift move, and I saw that the eyes in an otherwise grim face were laughing.

Suddenly, he glanced down again at his notebook and roared, "Come on, you bastards! This is not a holiday camp! Get loading!"

I hurled my carpet through the doors and light with triumph, ran back for the next one. Ostensibly, the incident had been closed, but in fact it was just beginning. Wiglep had acknowledged my powers of endurance, my durability, and what was good enough for him was good enough for most people in Auschwitz with the possible exception of Jacob Fries.

———

AFTER MY ENCOUNTER WITH WIGLEP, MY STATUS IMPROVED considerably, and so did my peace of mind. So long as I stayed with Canada Command, I felt, I would not go hungry, for the boss had given me a reprieve, and his underlings were not likely to reverse the decision.

Conditions in the camp generally, however, were deteriorating rapidly. The *Muselmänner* grew in number. The typhus lists grew longer, and whispers over the camp grapevine said that life in Birkenau was even more deplorable.

My knowledge of Birkenau was scanty. I had seen the fires, crude forerunners of the crematoria, reddening the sky. I had watched thousands of people climb into lorries and head toward those fires on their last journey from the ramp—their last journey anywhere. I had heard, as everyone in the mother camp had heard, that Birkenau made Auschwitz seem like a sanatorium.

These few facts together with these vague rumors should have been enough to make me anxious to stay clear of the place. Yet, for a variety of reasons, I wanted to learn more about it.

In the first place, I had already begun to compile statistics of the mass murders which were being committed daily. While on the ramp,

I had kept a careful mental note of each transport that arrived and the numbers on board in the hope that sooner or later I would be able to tell the free world about these terrible figures.

In Birkenau, however, the whole story was unfolding; the ramp was merely a long and somber preface.

Secondly, I had an idea that it might be easier to escape with these statistics from Birkenau. With the aid of a school atlas I had found while acting as a sorter during my "convalescence" in Canada, I had been able to pinpoint our geographical position fairly exactly. I knew the layout of the mother camp and the strength of its defenses, and I was determined to find out whether Birkenau was fortified equally strongly.

So, when men were needed to work for a day in Birkenau, which, apparently, was getting a little clogged, I volunteered immediately, and half an hour later, I was rolling toward the heart of Himmler's biggest extermination center, happy that I had been able to fiddle the job and quite unaware that I was about to be thoroughly sickened.

All that worried me slightly was the cold, for it was a bitter December day, but even that I was able to tolerate, for underneath my zebra shirt, I wore heavy woolen underwear and a warm sweater which I had selected carefully from Canada's vast departmental store.

As we drove slowly into Birkenau, however, all thoughts of the weather, of Auschwitz, for that matter, vanished. Suddenly, about a hundred yards away, in a wired-off section of the camp, I saw at least ten thousand naked women lined up in neat, silent rows.

Around them were dotted the green-uniformed SS men, and beyond them, forty or fifty lorries. Distance dulled the harsh outlines of the scene and killed all sound, yet it was even more eerie in its appalling silence, so grotesque that even Unterscharführer Sparsam, in the cabin below us, a man who had seen, perpetrated, and been unmoved by most cruelties, told his driver to slow down while he had a closer look.

We were nearer now and could hear the faint whiplash of commands, see a figure stirring here and there. I gripped the arm of Moses Sonenschein beside me and said, "Those poor bloody girls. They'll freeze to death. They'll die of exposure in this weather."

Moses, son of a Polish rabbi and a sincerely religious man, murmured, as he always murmured, "It is the will of God."

I hardly heard him. The full meaning of the horrible vista was slowly becoming clear to my mind, which at first had been numbed by the sight.

"Do you know what it is, Moses?" I said. "It's a typhus inspection. If they don't die of exposure, half of them will die in the gas chambers!"

"It is the will of God."

The lorry gathered speed again. The silent naked phalanx, the vast female army that was going to be cut in half, disappeared as we rounded a slight curve in the road.

"Moses," I said, "does God really…"

Then I stopped. Somehow, the question seemed pointless.

The lorry drew into a small forest, and I felt as I climbed down that at least everything I would see from now on would be an anticlimax, that we had reached our apex of horror for the day, but I was wrong, for Birkenau still had some reserves.

The air, despite the bitter frost, was slightly warm, I noticed, and it was not difficult to see why. Stretching all around us were ditches vast enough to hold a row of houses, the ditches that spawned that red glow I could see in the sky from the mother camp—great, gaping sores in the forest, not blazing now, but still smoldering.

I moved to the edge of one and gazed in. The heat struck my face, and at the bottom of this great open oven I could see bones—small bones. The bones of children.

Moses murmured, "It is the will of God."

I had no time to reply, for we were ordered to work, driven into a huge barracks about sixty yards long. Every inch of its space was packed with clothes of every size, shape, and quality, and our job, we were told, was to remove enough to give the Birkenau prisoners room to work.

I worked blindly, automatically, fast, trying to get the stench of that pit out of my nostrils, to wipe the picture of those naked girls out of my mind, but it was impossible. Every time I picked up a child's overcoat, I thought of those bones. Every time I loaded a bundle of women's clothes, I thought of those who had no clothes.

We worked for three hours in that barracks, like ants burrowing in a graveyard, and when we were finished and back on our lorry, I suddenly found myself dreading the sight of that women's camp again, yet lured by the awful fascination of it. I felt I had to know what had happened, how many were left, how many would die.

They were still standing there, naked in the frost, but this time the ranks were much thinner, and now the lorries were packed to capacity. Only the silence, the overpowering silence, was the same, but as we drew close, it was ripped to pieces.

The engines of forty lorries roared simultaneously, shaking the still air, dominating it, but they were not quite loud enough to cloak the shame of the deed.

From the throats of those thousands about to die came a banshee wail that rose shriller and shriller and became louder and louder and went on and on and on, a piercing protest that only death could stop, and then came the panic that was inevitable.

The trucks started to move. A woman flung herself over the side. Then another...and another. The SS moved in with their sticks and their whips to beat back those who were trying to follow. Those who had jumped were being beaten too and were trying to clamber back. They fell beneath the quickening wheels while this funeral for the living dead went faster and faster until we could see it no more.

Moses Sonenschein murmured, "There is no God..."

Then his voice rose to a shout: *"There is no God! And if there is, curse Him, curse Him, curse Him!"*

Again, I said nothing, for there was nothing to say. Instead, I turned my back on Birkenau and hoped I would never see it again. I am glad that at that moment I did not know I was soon to be transferred from the mother camp and was to spend a year and a half there.

CHAPTER 11

Ivan the Terrible

DECEMBER 1942 WAS A BUSY MONTH FOR THE MEN WHO administered Auschwitz. In the first place, Christmas was coming, and while the birth of the infant Jesus was scarcely an event hallowed in Nazi gospels, the SS, nevertheless, like so many who wallow in cruelty, wallowed also in sentimentality. They would burn without scruples, indeed with patriotic fervor, one thousand children, but their eyes would grow misty when they swapped pictures of their own loved ones at home.

Therefore, Christmas could not be ignored, particularly when they were surrounded by a bunch of bloody Jews who did not believe in baby Jesus and whose barbaric forefathers had crucified the Savior in the first place. The problem was how they could acknowledge the event without relaxing what they called euphemistically discipline, and this they solved simply by making it compulsory that in every barracks, prisoners should sing in chorus "Silent Night." Those who sang badly, it was decreed, were sent to bed without supper.

So, every evening after work, we men of Canada stood before Block Senior Polzakiewicz. A violinist, borrowed from the orchestra, drew gently on his bow, and we began to bawl out the words of this fine old carol. For those of us who spoke German, of course, it was not a particularly onerous duty, but those who did not, most of the Poles, for instance, had a hard time.

Polzakiewicz would tear his hair as they mangled the beautiful old German words. Then he would chum down among the ranks, trying to beat the words into their thick skulls with his club, as a result of which few of them slept, to quote the carol, in heavenly peace.

That, however, was, relatively speaking, no more than an irritation. Causing the SS far greater concern was the spread of typhus and the decision that there would have to be another selection on similar lines to that which Doctor Uhlenbrook had organized the previous August. What I had seen happening in the women's section of Birkenau was to be repeated in Auschwitz. Half the camp was going to die.

It was the routine as before, conducted this time in temperatures around the freezing mark. For me, however, there was one important difference. This time, I knew my life was not in danger, for I was a member of Canada Command, the strongest and fittest command in the camp. Fries knew that Canada men were either fit or dead, and so he did not make us run.

Nevertheless, we had to strip in the fierce cold, plunge into hot showers, then dash out into the open air again. As a result, many of those who survived the typhus test contracted pneumonia and died anyway.

For two days, we were left naked and without food, an ordeal which weeded out a few more. In fact, I found I was suffering more from cold than from hunger, and I think the most welcome Christmas present I have ever received was the zebra uniform which was issued to me on December 23.

"All is calm," sang the SS men, indeed, "all is bright. Run, you bastards, run, and there'll be no typhus for Christmas."

Unfortunately for them and for us, the caroling and the cauterizing could not remove the last and the greatest problem. For weeks, rumors had been simmering that SS men were smuggling gold, jewelry, and currency from the camp. They reached such heights ultimately that Doctor Rudolf Mildner, head of the Gestapo at nearby Katowice, arrived to investigate.

I, personally, had an inkling that the rumors were well founded, though I had no real inside information. I gathered, however, that leaders of the underground were stealing substantial quantities of gold and jewelry and considerable sums of money, not for personal gain, but so they could bribe their guards. Most of the hard core in Canada knew this, and the arrival of Mildner created an air of tension in the command. We knew the SS men would talk, if they were caught, and then heaven alone could help any prisoners involved.

Day after day, the probe went on until we grew almost accustomed to it and our nerves began to relax a little, but that was a mistake, for even this delicate sense of security was very false indeed. On St. Stephen's Day, Ernst Burger, our registrar, called out the numbers of fifteen members of Canada Command after roll call. They were marched off to Block Eleven, the Punishment Block, and among them were some members of the underground.

The situation which had been tense now became grave in the extreme. If those men cracked under torture, it would mean more than their deaths, more than fierce reprisals against the rest of us. It would mean that the underground movement, the first sign of unity, of fight I had known since the deportations had begun, would be liquidated.

The leaders of the underground were fully aware of the danger and took swift evasive action. They smuggled poison into Block Eleven, and within a few hours, the men in Block Eleven were dead. Rather than risk revealing the names of their comrades, they had committed suicide.

This act of calculated courage relieved the immediate pressure. Behind the scenes, however, fresh and even more sinister trouble was bubbling. Battle was joined between two powerful men, and on its outcome the lives of those in Canada Command depended.

While the titular administrators of Auschwitz were Commandant Rudolf Hoess and his SS officers, the ruthless day-to-day routine was in other hands. It was left to men like Oberscharführer Fries and Scharführer Wiglep, and now these two giants were locking horns.

From fragments of information which filtered through to us, we were able to piece together a fairly accurate picture of how the battle was progressing, though we were denied, naturally enough, a round-by-round description.

Fries's arguments were simple. Fifteen men from Canada Command, he said, had been found guilty of stealing valuables and currency, but how many more had escaped the net?

The only way to stamp out thieving completely, he held, was to gas the entire command and build a new one from raw material which he would supply.

Wiglep objected vehemently to this idea. It had taken him months to build up his command. He had done so by forcing the pace to such an extent that three out of four recruits died, leaving only the tough and the shrewd. He rebelled violently against going through this grueling business again.

It seemed that one of these giants would have to back down, which would mean the end of his career in Auschwitz, for such a defeat would make his position intolerable. Hoess, however, merely because he could not afford to lose either of these extremely efficient noncommissioned officers, arranged a compromise.

"We'll move them to Birkenau," he said. "Then we'll have them next-door to the gas chambers. And, at the first hint of any more trouble, we can get rid of them."

In fact, he made a serious, if forgivable, mistake. Had he adopted Fries's suggestion, he would have removed many valuable men from the underground, though not their leader, whose identity I had discovered by that time.

It was Ernst Burger, the mild-mannered, gentlemanly registrar.

When the men of Canada learned they were being transferred to Birkenau, the spirit of resistance strengthened almost imperceptibly and almost, it seemed, spontaneously. There was a new alertness in the air, an atmosphere of carefully controlled rebellion. We knew where we were going, but we were not sure why. Were we really going to work there? Or was it a trick? Were we to be marched straight to the gas chambers?

In his heart, I think, every man had decided for himself that he would not die like a sheep, that he would fight, and in the eyes of the others, he saw a similar decision reflected.

Yet it was only when we were paraded, ready for the march, that I saw the first positive signs of unity. One would nod slightly to the other. Every prisoner was as tense as a cat in the dark, and I knew I had gauged the mood correctly when deputy Kapo Shimon whispered to me, "Watch us, be alert!"

For one hour, we stood there before the gates. Two hours. Three hours. Then came Fries of the big stick, and we knew that soon we would be on our way. The gates swung open, and somewhere someone roared, *"March!"*

Out we swung with a precision that was fine even for Canada. Out under the sign *Arbeit Macht Frei*, which I felt I would never see again. Out past Fries, impassive as ever. Out onto the concrete road, flanked by the biggest, most heavily armed force of SS guards I had ever seen marshaled in Auschwitz.

If there was to be a fight, I told myself, it was going to be a short one.

———

BIRKENAU CAMP WAS DIVIDED INTO TWO MAIN SECTIONS. As we marched down the concrete road which lay between them, we could see the glow of the flaming ditches growing brighter and the clean lines of the brand-new concrete crematorium standing out starkly before us, yellow flame stabbing the sky from the top of its tall chimney.

Every step brought us nearer and nearer to these symbols of Auschwitz, and in the mind of every man of us, there was but one thought.

Was this our last road? Was this the end? In a few minutes, were we going to fling ourselves against a cluster of submachine guns? The pall of smoke hung heavy at the bottom of Birch Tree Alley, and still we did not know whether we were to add to its volume.

Suddenly, the head of the column pivoted left. We were going into the camp after all. We had been granted at least a brief reprieve, and for us that was enough because no man in Auschwitz ever thought in terms of living. He thought merely of living a little longer.

Yet our relief was quickly dispersed by the sight of our new home. As we stepped off the concrete road, heavy, remorseless mud sucked greedily at our boots, clogging our brisk footsteps, reaching up above our ankles.

In fact, we sank into a slime that seemed to permeate the atmosphere. Here, there were no neat terraces of red-brick buildings—just dark, dank wooden barracks. Here there was no antiseptic order, product of ruthless discipline. Instead, there was a brooding chaos, the smell of disintegration, a vast compost heat in which bodies and minds were rotting.

Through the mire, I began to see details. From every corner, scrawny *Muselmmäner* were dragging their dead to some central clearing house, to some ghastly rag-and-bone depot where the only customer was the furnace man, and before each barracks I could see more dead, piled in higgledy-piggledy heaps, encased in glistening mud so thickly that their stick-like limbs seemed molded together.

I looked, nauseated, then looked again. Were they dead? Did I see a movement? As I gazed at one gray-brown heap, an inert shape stirred slightly. A head rose slowly from the hillock of corpses. Then shoulders. Claws at the end of skeleton arms slapped feebly on the muddy ground until a passing kapo kicked the impertinent rebel back into place in a gesture of irritation against the dead who would not lie down.

With an effort, I closed my mind to the morass and concentrated on the immediate future. We might still be on the road to the furnaces, I felt, and then there would be the battle, but if not, there was hope, for I had not left the mother camp empty-handed. In Birkenau, too, the underground operated, and Josef Farber had given me the names of two contacts: David Schmulewski and Doctor Andreas Milar.

They marched us into a washroom, where I asked an orderly whether he knew either of them. He pointed across the room and said, "There's Doctor Milar. The one with glasses."

I saw a slim, bespectacled man of about twenty-seven with red hair and the thin, almost sharp features of the Jewish intellectual—a man I knew by repute already as the brilliant son of an extremely wealthy Jewish family. A man who could have evaded Auschwitz, had he kept his wallet open and his mouth shut.

I shouldered my way through the crowds and introduced myself. He smiled easily, the eyes behind the spectacles summing me up shrewdly but without offense. Then he said, "So Farber sent you. Did he give you any special message?"

"No. He just said I was to contact you. But tell me…what's going on? Are we washing for the gas chambers?"

"Don't worry. You'll be all right here. This is just routine delousing. I can't tell you much now, but if you want anything, let me know."

I thanked him and asked about Schmulewski. He said, "I don't know him, but you'll find him in Block Twenty-Seven. He's the deputy block senior."

That was the way of the underground. Cells were kept small. Contact between members was reduced to a minimum. The less a man knew, the less he could tell under torture.

I knew Schmulewski, too, by reputation. He was a man who had fought for his ideals all over Europe and was still fighting.

In Poland, he had known persecution because he was a Jew. He had resisted until he managed to escape and make his way to Palestine, an illegal immigrant. There, he was harried by the British and harried back until another call came, this time from Spain. He linked up with the International Brigade against Franco, and when that war was lost, he crossed into France, where he was interned. There, the Germans found him and his road to Auschwitz began, a road that was to take him through Dachau and Sachsenhausen.

Yet still he was only thirty, tall, dark-haired, strong, and remarkably unscarred for a man who had been at war all his life. As soon as he heard I was from Slovakia, he said, "Good! Maybe you know Fred Wetzler. He's a countryman of yours, and he's registrar in the mortuary next door."

Fred Wetzler! He was from my hometown, Trnava, and though I had never spoken to him, for he was six years older than I was, I had always admired him, if only for his casual bohemian manner and his easy way with girls.

"Come on," said Schmulewski. "Let's call on him. He'll give us a cup of coffee."

We went round to a wooden building behind Block Twenty-Seven. Schmulewski pushed open the door, and I followed him into a dimly lit room, and then I stopped suddenly.

Every available inch of space was occupied by bodies, all piled neatly in rows of ten. There must have been at least four hundred of them, but for all my guide seemed to care, they could have been carcasses in a butcher's shop.

He picked his way through them casually while I stumbled in his wake. Though I was used to the sight of death, I felt uneasy at the sight of so many bodies in such a small space, and then I realized that now I was inside the Birkenau equivalent of the red-brick building without windows which had given me my first insight into Auschwitz—the building from which the bodies had flown like birds.

Schmulewski knocked politely at an inner door. A cheerful voice invited him in, and there was Fred Wetzler, a little thinner, perhaps, but as jovial as ever, with his roving, laughing eyes; his expansive manner; his easy humor.

"How nice to see you!" he roared. "Come in and make yourself at home!"

Looking back, of course, I can see this remarkable scene in its true perspective. There we were, with dead bodies almost spilling over the threshold, and there was Fred, greeting me as a long-lost friend who had just called at his home in Trnava. At the time, however, it did not seem incongruous at all. I was merely pleased and flattered that the ever-popular Fred had remembered the kid from back home, someone to whom he had never spoken before.

"I'll be with you in a moment," he said. "Just wait until I get this lot shifted."

"This lot?"

"The stiffs."

I saw that a lorry had drawn up outside the outer door. Four husky Poles came in, the men who would make the birds fly, and Fred, his notebook ready, joined them.

One man glanced at an arm and called the tattooed number out to Fred, who jotted it down. Another opened the dead mouth with a pair of pliers, hauled out a few gold teeth, and dumped them with a clank into a tin can beside him. The remaining two picked up the corpse and sent it whirling through the door toward the lorry.

They worked swiftly, rhythmically, like a closely knit team. The number was called, the teeth came out, the flight began, and Fred, all business now, surveyed the operation like an experienced foreman, watching for flaws that might snaggle the smooth machinery, and I watched too, fighting down a twinge of nausea, yet morbidly fascinated.

At last, the room was empty. An SS man came to collect the tin can of gold teeth, many of which still had half a gum attached. The lorry moved away, and Fred led us into his sanctuary, grumbling all the way.

"That bloody Polak'll have to go," he said, shaking his head. "He's slowing up the whole business. Next thing they'll be onto me because the lorry isn't getting away in time, and then there'll be hell to pay!"

He closed the door behind him and suddenly beamed at us as if he had just shut out all his worries. "Right, lads," he said. "How about that coffee now?"

We sat down to our cups and our chat, wandering back through the streets of Trnava, knocking at the doors of old friends and forgetting for a moment that so many of them were dead. Slowly, the memory of the flying corpses was washed away in a flood of nostalgia, and I relaxed.

That was the first of many cups of coffee I had with Fred. Oddly enough, in fact, his little death house became almost a sanctuary for me, a place in which I could hide for a moment from the horrors outside, for it took some time to grow accustomed to Birkenau, even for one who had been to Auschwitz preparatory school.

The death rate was appalling. Many died in Birkenau, not because they had committed some minor misdemeanor which had irritated an SS man or a kapo, but merely because those with sticks wanted to amuse themselves, were seeking a diversion to break the monotony.

To them, the *Muselmmäner* were footballs. Sometimes they would find one bogged down, unable to walk because he had not the strength to drag his feet from the mud.

"Don't worry, old man," they would shout. "We'll get you out!"

They would, too. By kicking him until his inert body lay on top of the mud instead of half-submerged in it.

These, however, were casual, sporadic killings, though they happened every day. The organized murder was even more terrible. The hospital, for instance, made "Doctor" Klehr's clinic in the mother camp seem almost humane.

There was no question of a phenol injection for those patients who had been weeded out to die. A couple of green triangle kapos, professional criminals, would simply stretch the victim on the floor and put an iron bar across his neck. Then, simultaneously, each of them would jump on it, breaking his neck.

Yet even this daily slaughter paled in significance in comparison with that symbolized by the tall chimney which dominated most of the camp and most of our thoughts. Here was the heart of the factory which killed on a conveyor belt scale. Here was the real purpose of the extermination center, and now, for the first time, I was able to see what until then I had only imagined.

I was still working on the ramp, though living in Birkenau. Every night, I unloaded the wagons and watched the human cargoes line up for selection, but now, instead of going back to Canada's well-organized block with my sardines or my figs, I moved in the same direction as the victims. Often, I arrived back in camp in time to see them being herded toward the innocent gray building with its mock washrooms, all but a few still believing they were traveling another section of the road that would bring them to a new life. Here the statistics I had been gathering so carefully, the numbers I held in my head, suddenly became men, women, and children, the living, only inches away from death.

These were not pleasant sights. They served a good purpose, however, for they breathed reality into my task. Here before my eyes were the type of people who could be saved if only one man with enough knowledge could escape and give it to the world, and I was confident there would be no more sheep, queueing for the Auschwitz butcher, if only they could be warned of their fate before they were loaded onto the transports.

In Birkenau, too, I had far greater opportunities of checking, counterchecking, and amplifying my figures. Fred in the mortuary was a help. I met other registrars as well and renewed contact with Filip Müller, who became one of my most valuable sources of information. Filip stoked the furnaces in the crematorium. By the amount of fuel made available, he could reckon how many bodies were to be burned because the SS never wasted fuel by overloading their fires. Every day, in fact, my dossier grew and the more determined I became to make a break.

Nor had my chances decreased with my transfer from the mother camp. In Birkenau, the vast majority—the *Muselmmäner* and the new arrivals, fresh from the transports—were doomed, but the green triangle kapos, the killers of the camp, treated the hard core of experienced prisoners with something bordering on respect, and as my contacts with the underground developed, my position became more and more secure.

In fact, through Fred, I began to advance my social status, so to speak. He introduced me, for instance, to his kapo, Lubomir Bastar from Brno, a man who was to have some considerable influence on my life in Birkenau.

He had been arrested in 1939 and had run through the whole gamut of Nazi concentration camps before ending up in Auschwitz—an aristocrat, in fact, who treated me at first with fatherly condescension.

"Another Slovak?" he said. "I suppose you know prisoners aren't allowed in the mortuary, but that's Fred's fault. Anyway, how about some coffee?"

We sat down with him a little uneasily, and for a while he eyed me as a headmaster will eye a pupil who could be quite good if he were not so wild.

"A Slovak!" he said again. "Any good at languages?"

"Not bad."

"What do you speak?"

"German. Polish. Hungarian. Russian."

"Russian? A Slovak boy who speaks Russian? Now that's interesting!"

I knew I had gone up in his estimation and caught myself thinking back to the rows I had had with my mother over that Russian grammar. At the time, however, I did not realize how valuable those hours of illegal study were going to be.

Lubomir spread the news around. The underground, who until then had thought of me as a small if useful cog regarded me now with a new interest, and others, too, for soon I found I was being invited to Lubomir's private room, where the cream of the camp's Czech intellectuals gathered sometimes for supper.

They were simple affairs, these meals, potatoes with margarine, or some porridge, perhaps, a sharp contrast, in fact, to the lavish, ostentatious affairs enjoyed by some of the kapos in the mother camp. The austerity, however, was not compulsory, but deliberate. These men could have had almost anything they liked, for the traffic in food was brisk. It was clear to me, however, that it would go against their grain to feast while others starved outside.

Anyway, my status rose rapidly. Though I was still just an ordinary prisoner, I ate fairly frequently with the red-triangle kapos, the politicals, or with members of the underground who in some cases were the same people. When not on the ramp, I walked around the camp with comparative freedom, and gradually I became friendly with everyone who mattered—with the fighters, with the intellectuals, with the people who gave us prisoners some cohesion and guidance.

Life, in fact, was as pleasant as it could be in a place like Birkenau until June 1943, when it was shattered once again by typhus.

There was another selection, not on the grand scale which I had experienced earlier, but big enough to merit a transfer to the other section of Birkenau, which was split into seven subsections, none of which had been occupied until then.

Here again, however, I made progress. We were sent to Subsection D, where our new block senior growled at Fred, "There are going to be a few thousand new prisoners in these subsections. You'd better see that you have enough assistants."

So I became an assistant registrar. Fred, of course, could not appoint me on his own authority, which was far from substantial, but Lubomir and members of the underground saw that I got the job, not entirely because they were friends of mine, but because it suited their purposes to have someone they could trust in a position to provide them with information.

Now I had even more freedom. So long as I had a ledger under my arm and a worried frown on my face, I could go almost anywhere I pleased inside the camp. I had more or less official access, too, to the chief registrar's books, and this added substantially to my file on the camp.

Sartorially speaking, of course, I jumped almost into the Saville Row class. Instead of my zebra trousers, I wore a pair of riding breeches, superbly tailored by a Polish prisoner. My riding boots would have done justice to a cavalry officer, and though I was not allowed to discard my striped tunic, I saw that it was neatly cut.

I was, perhaps, a little overdressed for my lowly rank, but circumstances soon remedied that. Six weeks after my appointment, Subsection A was opened as a quarantine camp for new prisoners, and I, thanks to the activities of the underground, became its first registrar.

Again, they were not acting entirely for the good of my health. Camp A and Camp D were officially watertight compartments. It was essential for the underground, however, to have someone in the new camp who could act as a go-between, and as registrar, I would have to move from one camp to the other as part of my regular duties.

I welcomed both tasks. My rank gave me privileges. My clandestine activities gave me pride. It made me feel good to think that in a few months I had graduated from being a messenger boy for Kapo Bruno to being a courier for the resistance.

The only snag, in fact, was my new block senior, a man called Albert Hämmerle, but known throughout the camp as Ivan the Terrible. He was a professional murderer who had been in concentration camps since 1933. Before that, he had been in various German prisons, and since his arrival in Auschwitz, he had built up the reputation of being the biggest killer in a camp of killers.

Nor was this hearsay. We all knew that the professional criminal kapos held contests among themselves to see who could kill the most. They notched up their victories like fighter pilots, and it was generally acknowledged that Ivan the Terrible was an ace with a record which would take some beating.

He was also a virtuoso at another little sport. He and his fellow German criminals would while away their time seeing who would be the first man to kill a prisoner with one blow of his fist. In fact, they were engaged in just such a contest when I arrived to take up my duties in Camp A.

There were three of them, *Lager Alteste* "Monkey" Tyn, chief of all block seniors, a man with the strength and physique of a gorilla; Mietek Katerzynski, a Polish block senior; and Ivan the Terrible.

I saw Monkey Tyn grab a new prisoner who was walking by and bellow, "What are you loitering about for, you bastard! I'll teach you to move fast." He grabbed him by the tunic, swung his arm back like a discus thrower, and smashed his fist into the man's face. It was a vicious blow, but slightly mistimed. The prisoner fell, unconscious but still breathing.

"Bad luck," grinned Katerzynski. "I thought you had him for a moment."

They strolled on. Katerzynski swooped on another man, abused him for some imaginary offense, then sent him crashing into the mud, where he lay, writhing.

"You're slipping, Mietek," murmured Monkey. "You need more practice."

Now it was Ivan the Terrible's turn. Without even bothering to make an excuse, he grabbed a man and felled him. He lay still, his neck broken.

They walked on, grinning. "I don't know how you do it, you old swine," said Monkey. "I think you must have an eye for the weak ones."

They went into Ivan's block, and I followed them. He turned round in his chair, looked me up and down, and said, "So you're my new registrar!"

"That's right, sir."

"D'you know what happened to the last one? D'you know how you have to write down the numbers of those who are going to die? Well, I made him write his own number down one morning!"

The three of them roared with laughter. I stood, watching them, saying nothing.

Still studying me keenly, Ivan said, "You're not afraid of me?"

He was smiling. I smiled back and said, "I don't think so."

Another gust of laughter. "Maybe I'm not so bad as they say," he said. "Sit down. Have a drink."

He clapped his hands. A prisoner hurried in. A bottle of schnapps and four glasses were produced, and I drank one of the most insincere toasts of my life.

That night, I learned why he was being so pleasant to me. While the others in the block slept five or six to a bunk, Ivan and I had our own rooms. His was splendidly decorated and painted according to his own flamboyant taste.

Just before he went to bed, he came to me and said in a surprisingly gentle voice, "Why don't you share my room until yours is decently decorated? There's plenty of space. And you'll be much more comfortable."

It was a difficult situation. As politely as possible, I said to him, "Thank you, sir, but I think it would be hardly proper for a registrar to share the block senior's room. It would be bad for discipline. After all, you're very much my senior."

He looked at me for a full minute without speaking, and then he said, "Very well. Have it your own way."

This time his voice was not gentle, and that night I put half a dozen empty tin cans just inside my door as a makeshift alarm system. On the table beside my bed, I placed the long knife which I used for cutting up the block's bread rations.

I was not being melodramatic. A man like Ivan the Terrible killed when he was crossed. I knew he would not dare to murder me during the day because he realized I had powerful friends and would not be easy to handle anyway, but at night, it was different. At night, there would be no witnesses, and in the morning, there would be plenty of excuses.

Though I knew death could come easily at any time in Auschwitz, I was determined that I was not going to die in bed at the hands of a homosexual murderer.

Nor was I exaggerating the significance of his invitation. Some time later, he was sent to the Punishment Block for having relations with a Jewish prisoner, a heinous crime in the eyes of the pure Aryan SS.

AUSCHWITZ I

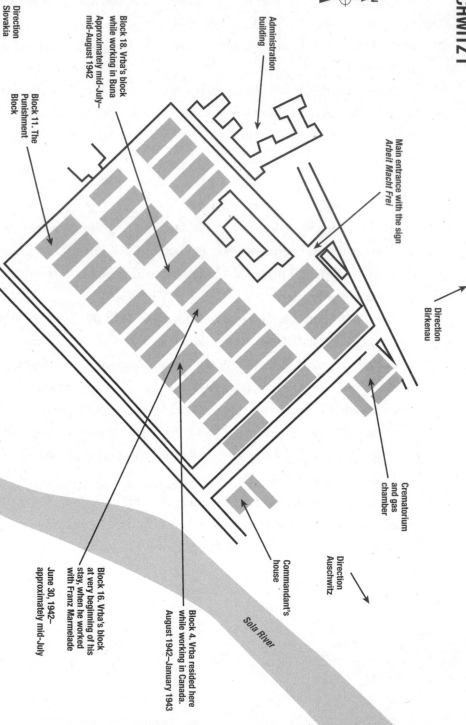

N

Main entrance with the sign
Arbeit Macht Frei

Direction
Birkenau

Administration
building

Block 18. Vrba's block
while working in Buna
Approximately mid-July–
mid-August 1942

Block 11. The
Punishment
Block

Direction
Slovakia

Crematorium
and gas
chamber

Direction
Auschwitz

Commandant's
house

Sola River

Block 16. Vrba's block
at very beginning of his
stay, when he worked
with Franz Marmelade
August 1942–January 1943

Block 4. Vrba resided here
while working in Canada.
June 30, 1942–
approximately mid-July

AUSCHWITZ ENVIRONS, SUMMER 1944

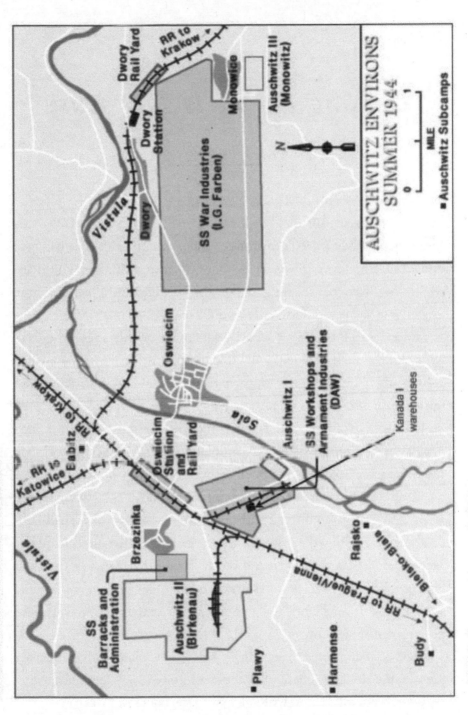

AUSCHWITZ ENVIRONS
SUMMER 1944

N

0   1
MILE

■ Auschwitz Subcamps

Dwory Rail Yard

RR to Krakow

Auschwitz III (Monowitz)

Monowice

Dwory Station

Dwory

Vistula

SS War Industries (I.G. Farben)

Oswiecim

Oswiecim Station and Rail Yard

Sola

Auschwitz I

SS Workshops and Armament Industries (DAW)

Kanada I warehouses

RR to Krakow

Babitz

RR to Katowice

Brzezinka

Rajsko

Bielsko-Biala

Vistula

SS Barracks and Administration

Auschwitz II (Birkenau)

Plawy

Harmense

RR to Prague/Vienna

Budy

— US Holocaust Memorial Museum

CHAPTER 12
"Gassing People is Not Easy"

NOBODY WHO SURVIVED CAMP A IN BIRKENAU WILL EVER forget September 7, 1943, for it was unlike any other day we had ever known. That morning, we felt wonder, elation, nostalgia, and over-whelming amazement as we gazed on a sight which most had forgotten existed and the rest doubted they would ever see again.

Into Camp B beside us, separated from us by only a few strands of wire, poured men, women, and children dressed in ordinary civilian clothes, their heads unshaven, their faces bewildered, but plump and unravaged. The grown-ups carried their luggage, the children their dolls and their teddy bears, and the men of Camp A, the zebra men who were only numbers, simply stood and stared, wondering who had tilted the world, spilling a segment of it in on top of them.

There were about five thousand of them, and as we watched them settling in, our camp buzzed with speculation. Never before had fam-ilies been kept together in Auschwitz, except in the gas chambers. Never before had they been allowed to retain their clothes and their luggage. It was a puzzle, a mystery, and, we older prisoners felt quite sure, a trick of some sort, for we soon saw that the new arrivals were getting VIP treatment.

The SS men treated them with consideration, joking with them, play-ing with the children. Then, when they had stowed away their luggage, all registrars were called in to write them into the books of Birkenau.

Here I thought I might find a clue to the mystery, but the little I learned made the situation even more bewildering. First, I noted that each of them, even the youngest children, who were about two years of age, had been tattooed with a special number that bore no relation to Auschwitz, and each had a card on which was written: "Six months quarantine with special treatment."

"Special treatment" in Auschwitz was a most sinister phrase. It meant extermination. Yet these people, who had come from Theresienstadt ghetto near Prague obviously were being kept alive for some purpose. It was a problem far beyond me, and as soon as possible, I reported everything I knew to Schmulewski, who, I had learned by this stage, was the leader of the Birkenau underground.

I found that already he was fairly well informed about these startling developments. Already, indeed, resistance cells had been formed in Camp B. A special meeting of senior members of the underground was called, however, to discuss why kid gloves were being used, why all the rules of the camp were being broken, and soon they reached what seemed to be a reasonable conclusion.

In Theresienstadt ghetto, we had learned, there were about 100,000 Jews. It was clear to us that all were scheduled for Auschwitz and ultimate death, but from what we had gathered from the new arrivals, this was not going to be a simple operation. Kid gloves, in fact, were vital, because in this particular ghetto there were International Red Cross observers.

The fiction of the resettlement areas, therefore, had to be made sound like an undeniable fact. There was no room here for doubts, for rumors, for fear because one adverse report to Geneva could wreck the whole plan. So, the first five thousand were transported in comfort, pampered on arrival, and ordered to write cheerful letters home, wish-you-were-here notes that would kill even the vaguest suspicions.

It was an old trick, of course, but this time it was played on an unprecedented scale, for this was one operation which must not fail.

Upon its success, indeed, depended the future of Himmler's extermination plans.

The SS knew, therefore, that it was pointless to order these people to write at gunpoint, for the brave and the clever could hide secret warnings between the lines. So, they decided they would give them no cause for complaint, no reason to doubt what lay ahead. They helped them settle in comfortably, even worming their way into the confidence of the children by bringing them sweets and fruit, and the parents, of course, were moved by the sight of husky soldiers cossetting their little ones, for they had yet to learn how low these killers could sink to attain their objectives.

I watched in wonder across the wire as they organized their new and temporary lives, for they believed Birkenau was merely a transit camp. I saw them set aside a barracks for the children, a nursery, no less, in the shadow of the crematorium. I saw a blond, athletic man of about thirty organizing games, then lessons, and somehow the sight of it was good for my morale, even though I had a nasty suspicion that those children were going to die.

Others, older, worldlier than I was, gazed across the wire with different thoughts in their minds. They saw attractive young girls in silk stockings and high-heeled shoes, just like the girls they had known an eon ago back home. Surreptitious flirtations began. First names were exchanged. Rendezvous were made and kept at a distance of ten yards. Suddenly, romance began to gently flourish in the heart of a private hell.

It flourished so rapidly, in fact, that the wire between the two camps soon became a serious inconvenience. The men of Auschwitz, however, were nothing if not adaptable, and soon this obstacle was overcome for the more daring. A gang who had been installing new drains parallel to the wire suddenly let their shovels slip off at a tangent, and the result was a tunnel, a tunnel of love, through which the more ardent Romeos slipped at night. They risked death, of course, but the rewards, they assured us in vivid terms afterward, were sweet indeed.

I never used that tunnel. That did not mean, of course, that I was immune to the charms of the lovely young Czech girls on the other side of the fence. Far from it. I admired them from afar, so to speak, but was much too shy to indulge in the lighthearted affairs which brightened the lives of my more experienced and more adventurous fellow prisoners.

It is true that I was nineteen and mentally somewhat older, thanks to the University of Auschwitz. When it came to girls, however, I was still a seventeen-year-old boy, still the same gauche youngster who used to boast so loudly about his conquests back home in Trnava, though in truth they had never amounted to more than a few quick, clumsy kisses after a dance.

Because of this, I suppose it was inevitable that very soon I found I was violently in love with a girl to whom I had never spoken. There in Birkenau, in the depth of death and decay and despair, I began to suffer the sweet agonies of adolescent adoration.

It happened one day when I was talking across the wire to Fredy Hirsch, the man who was in charge of the children's dormitory and was trying so hard to bring some normality into their troubled young lives. He was a German Jew who had emigrated to Czechoslovakia, a physical culture instructor by profession and a youth leader by vocation.

In fact, he was telling me about some new plan of his for the children and I was marveling at the man's enthusiasm when a girl interrupted us, and after that, I heard him only faintly, for he seemed to fade into the background.

She was about twenty-two, tall, dark, and slender, a girl with an easy grace and frank, smiling eyes.

Vaguely, I heard Fredy say, "Meet our neighbor, Alice. He's a registrar." Then he said to me: "This is Alice Munk, one of my assistants."

I mumbled some conventional phrase, some "pleased-to-meet-you" cliché and just kept on gazing into those dark-brown eyes until she lowered them in slight embarrassment and I cursed myself inwardly for being a clumsy idiot. Then she was smiling at me again and saying in a soft voice, "How long have you been here?"

It was a banal remark, of course. She spoke, in fact, as if we were dancing together for the first time in a strange ballroom and she was saying, "Do you come here often?"

Yet to me it was music, every syllable of it. I shuffled a bit and said, "About two years…"

"Two years? But you look so…strong. So different from…the others, I mean."

I smiled with the pure pleasure of it. Suddenly, I was profoundly glad that I was a registrar, that I had a well-cut pair of riding breeches and shining boots and a smartly tailored tunic, that my shorn head was covered by a neat cap. Somehow, I stammered, "Well…it's not so bad sometimes. Not when you know your way around."

So the stumbling conversation went on with its awkward pauses, its quick flood of meaningless words. Neither of us noticed Fredy Hirsch slip quietly away. Neither of us noticed anything except each other. Auschwitz with its wire and its walls and its horror seemed to fade, and a bright new sun shone on the pair of us.

After that, we met every day. Awkwardness melted away to be replaced by a gentle intimacy. We talked of each other; of her parents, wealthy industrialists in a town north of Prague; of her schooldays. She laughed when I told her about my under-the-counter Russian studies, of my arguments with my mother, and her eyes softened and saddened when she heard of my Hungarian journey, which seemed so pathetic in retrospect. We talked of the future, as if there surely was going to be one, and all the time I kept my eyes averted from the chimney stack which knew only hearts that were still.

It was, of course, self-deception, understandable escapism, for this was my first love, and my mind was trying hard to reject any thought that harm could come to Alice. It tried, but it failed, for every day I was reminded that the situation was ominous, and it was complicated further in December when yet another four thousand Czechs arrived from Theresienstadt Ghetto.

The underground, in fact, was seriously worried about the new arrivals. They were faced with a totally unprecedented situation—the children, for instance—and they worked speedily to meet it. Everyone's bread ration was reduced slightly so the very young would have more to eat. Soap and medicines were provided from heaven knows where. It was a masterpiece of rapid improvisation.

Every day, I saw Schmulewski to make my report, and every day, I thought his eyes looked harder. I had to restrain myself from asking him what was on his mind, for that would have been a breach of discipline, but as time went by, I grew more and more concerned, for I sensed that he felt they were doomed.

The first positive indication he gave me that he was pessimistic, however, was when he said one day, "I want you to find out exactly how many underground workers there are in the family camp."

"Why?" I said. "Is something wrong?"

At first, he frowned. Then he flung me a wry smile, for he knew all about Alice, and said shortly, "It doesn't look good."

That night, I talked not only to Alice, but to her friends Helena and Vera Rezek, two sisters from Prague. All three were members of the family camp underground, and I asked them to get the figures Schmulewski needed.

For a moment, they were silent. Then Helena said calmly, "What's going to happen? Is it…serious?"

I glanced quickly at Alice. She was as cool, as impassive as the other two. As steadily as possible, I said, "I don't think it could be much more serious."

Next day, Helena came to the wire and told me, "There are thirty-three members of the underground between the two groups. Any more news?"

I shook my head. Like her, I was wondering why Schmulewski wanted precise figures, and later, when I reported back to him, he must have seen the question in my eyes.

"It's not many," he said, "but it could be just enough. I can't tell you more."

As time went by, as the enigmatic deadline of March 7 drew nearer, my work as a courier became more and more pressing. Cryptic messages went to and fro between Schmulewski and the underground workers in the family camp. Every day, I analyzed them over and over again, seeking some glimmer of hope, but never with any success. From a dozen different sources, Schmulewski gleaned his scraps of information, and each one of them seemed to point in the same direction... toward the chimney. Yet all the time, I felt that he had not given up, that behind his broad, inscrutable face lay a plan which might avert disaster, which might save the Czechs, which might save Alice. What it could be, I had no idea, but I had faith in him as a man and as a leader.

It was March 4, D-Day minus three, before he revealed some of his thoughts to me, and they were not reassuring.

"This whole business stinks," he said. "In the first place, they've all been told to write home and to postdate their letters by one month. The SS say it's because they have to go to Berlin for censorship, but that's nonsense."

"But why?" I said. "Couldn't it be true?"

He shook his head. "No," he said, "I'm afraid not. The *Sonderkommando* have been ordered to stoke the furnaces for four thousand on the night of March 7. And the SS men have been talking about a special job, a difficult job."[1]

---

1   At that time, about a thousand Jews from the Czech Family Camp had died of "natural causes." --Eds.

He stared at me hard. Still, my face was blank.

"Don't you see?" he said. "It's not going to be easy, gassing those people. They're not an innocent mob off a train. They know what happens here. They could make a fight of it. Now go and tell them everything I have said."

I went back to camp, the facts Schmulewski had given me tumbling around in my mind. A fight! I thought of the children caught in the cross fire of a hundred submachine guns. I thought of the young girls who had never seen blood before. Most of all, I thought of Alice, yet slowly I realized that only by fighting had any of them a chance to survive; then it would depend on how much support they got from other prisoners. How strong was the underground? And how willing?

It was easy to say that the resistance would rise and join them, but it was demanding a tremendous sacrifice. Already, these men had survived in the face of fantastic odds. With every day, their chances of living increased. Already, indeed, some were talking of the liberation, of the Russian steamroller smashing through the Auschwitz defenses, of the SS being swept away by the swift tide of war.

Would these hardened prisoners who had seen a million die in their time risk everything for the sake of four thousand Czechs? Or would they, perhaps, be fighting for something much greater? For the demolition of Auschwitz itself, for instance? For a mass escape and flight to the forests where the Polish partisans roamed? What was in Schmulewski's mind, and what did his blunt message really mean? Silently, I cursed the discipline that forbade me to ask questions, and then I sought out Alice and Helena and Vera to report what he had said.

They listened carefully and in silence as I talked, occasionally glancing quickly at each other. Then Helena said, "Now I've news for you. I believe we're moving into your camp tomorrow. The rumor is that we're being transferred soon."

"You mean…away from Auschwitz?"

She nodded. There was excitement in her eyes, and I knew she had more faith in her own sources of information than she had in mine. For a moment, indeed, my own spirits rose, but then I realized it was merely wishful thinking.

"Maybe so, Helena," I said. "But you must tell everyone what Schmulewski said. Those are his orders."

The next day, however, the first part of her forecast came true. Suddenly, the SS moved all new prisoners out of Camp A, leaving only members of the permanent staff, like myself. As soon as it was cleared, the four thousand Czechs who had arrived in September were moved in among us.

In spite of the gloom, in spite of the rumors, in spite of Schmulewski and his grim warnings, I was thrilled. For six months, I had been in love with Alice—deeply in love. All that time, a few strands of wire had kept us apart. All that time, we had never as much as held hands, and now she was walking toward me quickly, eagerly, her brown eyes smiling and her long hair dancing in the wind.

For a moment, we stood close, and I could feel the warmth of her, smell the freshness of her. Her cheek brushed mine for an instant, and she was gone, leaving me with a message I never thought I would hear:

"See you soon, darling. In the barracks."

That night, she came to my room with Vera and Helena, and we sat for an hour or two, discussing the latest news. Alice sat beside me, her hand in mine, and the pressure of her fingers seemed to drive away my pessimism. Rumors were falling like snowflakes now, and each one of them contradicted the stem words of the underground leader.

"They say we're going north," said Helena. "To somewhere near Warsaw."

"Fredy Hirsch says they wouldn't dare kill the children," said Vera. "He says they'd be afraid the news might leak out."

"Soon, maybe, the war will be over," said Alice very softly. "And then...and then..."

I kissed her that night for the first time. It was not much of a kiss because I had not had a great deal of practice in my life, but somehow my clumsiness did not seem to matter, and that night I fell asleep, thinking, Soon, maybe, the war will be over...

These pastel-shaded thoughts were soon dispersed, however. The next morning, when I took twenty prisoners over to collect the bread ration, Schmulewski was looking grimmer than ever.

"Listen carefully," he snapped. "I haven't much time. Briefly, the situation is about as bad as it could be. You must warn them again to prepare for the worst. As soon as I hear any definite news, I'll get in touch with you. And it could come at any minute."

I hesitated. Once more, he guessed what was in my mind. Gruffly, he said, "Personally, I'm fairly sure they will die tomorrow. Is that what you wanted to know?"

I nodded. Suddenly the cheerful, hopeful rumors of the previous day seemed pale and anemic. Here was the truth from a man whose spies were everywhere, who had been face-to-face with death so often that he could smell it.

Again, I reported back. Again, that night, Helena, Vera, and Alice came to my room, but this time there was no dreaming, no wishful thinking. I made no attempt to break the news gently, to soft-pedal, for now it was too late. Now we all had to think fast.

I asked Helena, "What about the others? How do they feel about it? Do they believe Schmulewski?"

"Some do," she said with a shrug. "Some don't. But hardly any of them believe the children will die. They can't imagine people killing little children, particularly after the way the SS have been behaving."

For an hour, perhaps, we talked around the subject, tearing apart the facts, the half facts, the rumors, the whispers, and getting nowhere.

At last, Helena stood up suddenly, smiled gently at Alice and me, sitting on the bed, and said, "Well...you two probably have other things to talk about. Come on, Vera."

We were alone. For me, it was the first time I had ever been alone with a girl in my bedroom. Embarrassment clogged my mind, and though I knew what I wanted to do, a cold barrier of shyness held me back.

"I wonder what Schmulewski's going to do," I said, and my voice was stilted, unnatural. "I know he's planning something."

Alice said nothing.

"A revolt, maybe. A rising. It could mean the end of Auschwitz."

Still, she was silent.

"A lot of people would die, of course. But maybe it would be worth it. Maybe...."

"Look at me," she said softly.

Slowly, I turned and looked at her. She was curled up on the bed now, and I do not think I have ever seen anyone lovelier.

Her dark-brown hair tumbled around her shoulders. Her eyes were misty, but still smiling, and her mouth curved gently. Then she sank back and the soft line of her breasts moved delicately, subtly, beneath her pale-blue blouse.

The barriers, all barriers melted. I leaned over her, so close that the fragrance of her enveloped me, and this time there was no awkwardness.

"You smell so beautiful," I whispered stupidly, aimlessly. "Why do you smell so beautiful?"

She laughed, a rather breathless little laugh.

"Soap, darling," she murmured. "Just soap. Why do you talk so much?"

After that, I did not talk for quite a long time. Auschwitz did not matter anymore, did not exist anymore. The watch towers and the guns and the dogs; the mud; the death; the tall, evil chimney were erased, obliterated by a magic that neither of us had ever known before.

———

SOMEONE WAS SHAKING MY SHOULDER. DIMLY, I HEARD A voice saying, "Wake up, get up. Hurry!"

I fought against it. I did not want to wake up. I did not want reality anymore, but the shaking went on, and at last I sat up, sleepily. Helena was standing by the bed, her face set, her eyes clouded with anxiety.

"Schmulewski wants you," she said quickly. "He says it's urgent. The whole place is surrounded by SS men."

I blinked, and the camp, the hateful camp, swam into focus. At the end of the bed, I could see a crumpled, pale-blue blouse. Beside me, Alice was still sleeping, a wisp of a smile on her lips. She stirred, stretched luxuriously, and as she turned, her arm slid over my body.

Gently, as gently as possible, I whispered, "Wake up, darling. It's morning. I've got to go."

At once, she was awake, sitting bolt upright, and for the first time, I saw something like fear in her eyes. Then she saw Helena and pulled the blanket up round her chin.

"Hurry," Helena insisted. "For God's sake, hurry. Something terrible is happening."

She left, and I began to dress.

Alice had regained her composure now and was ready before I was. She kissed me lightly and very quietly said, "Come on, darling. You've work to do."

Together, we walked out to face the gray morning of March 7. The deadline had arrived, as deadlines always will.

Soon afterward, I marched with my twenty prisoners out of Camp A to collect the bread in Camp D and saw that Helena was right. SS men, submachine guns nestling in the crooks of their arms, were everywhere. Some I recognized. Some were strangers, but about all of them was an air of grim, silent purpose, and I knew that the commandant was preparing for anything, even a rising.

The Russians had the bread ready for me, but I stood chatting with them for a while, postponing the interview I suddenly did not want to have, avoiding the words I did not want to hear. I asked them for lemons for the children, for anything that would keep them and me occupied for just a few minutes more.

At last, however, I could fritter away no more time. I went to Schmulewski, whose eyes were heavy, like those of a man who had not slept, and he came to the point with a directness that hurt.

"The news is as follows," he snapped. "The family camp dies today."

"You mean there's going to be a selection? They're going to get rid of the old and the children and the sick?"

"No. Everyone dies. And because of that, it could be our day. This is the first time they've tried to gas a few thousand people who will know what is going to happen. This is the moment for revolt, and the SS know it."

His face was utterly expressionless, but the tension radiated from him. I knew that every fiber in him was tuned for instant action and that he was controlling himself carefully.

"Now I cannot ask our fellows to throw away their lives for a lost cause. But if the Czechs rise, if they make a worthwhile fight of it, they will not fight alone. Hundreds of us, maybe thousands, will be beside them, and with a bit of luck, we could smash this whole stinking outfit.

"Tell them that. Tell them they have nothing to lose, that they fight or die. But tell them, too, that they won't have a chance unless they have the right leader."

"Leader? Who?"

"We have selected him already, though he doesn't know it yet. But it is essential that you get it into their heads why we have chosen this man. As you know yourself, there are half a dozen different political schisms in that camp...communists, Zionists, anti-Zionists, social democrats, Czech nationalists, the lot. If we appoint a man from any of these groups, we're going to have quarrels and divisions and failure. We've got to have someone who'll be respected and obeyed by all of them without question. Someone who can tell them to fight and lead them into the fight, united."

"But who? Where the hell are you going to find a man like that?"

"As I told you, we've found him. Fredy Hirsch."

Fredy Hirsch! A German! The tall, athletic Fredy who had organized the children's dormitory. At first, I thought Schmulewski had gone mad, but slowly I realized he was absolutely right. Hirsch had won the respect of everyone. German, he certainly was. But a German Jew. He had aligned himself with the people of his adopted country, had suffered with them, and was prepared to die with them. I knew he would fight with them and for them, too.

"Now here's what you've got to do. Go back and immediately call a meeting of the underground from the first batch, the September batch who are the only ones involved so far. Tell them what I've told you. Tell them we'll fight if they fight, but that they must start it and start it well. Then call in Fredy and tell him the role he must play. Okay?"

"Okay."

"Good luck."

"Thanks."

I marched back to camp with the bread and some lemons and a couple of onions I had managed to scrounge. As soon as I got there, I passed on Schmulewski's orders to Helena, and then I went back to wait in my room, the room where a few hours earlier Alice and I had made love.

The underground workers from the family camp came in one by one and sat on the floor because there were only two chairs. I sat on the bed, and Alice was beside me, her arm around my shoulder. While they took out cigarettes or rolled them, I counted them. Just sixteen, and more girls than boys.

I tried to see them as a fighting force, as torch-bearers who would set the camp on fire and burn it to the ground; but it was not easy. They were young. They were brave. They were dedicated. But they were children, unschooled by the world, untempered by hardship or hate. I wondered just how much courage they would need to outweigh their innocence, to give them a chance in the middle of a massacre.

Bluntly, almost crudely, I told them the situation. As I spoke, I studied their faces, and when I had finished, I felt sure that their hearts were big enough for the dirty task that faced them, for they were calm and unafraid perhaps because they had yet to learn the reality of death.

Helena said, "I'll get Fredy Hirsch."

She returned with him in a few minutes, and they left us alone. I gazed across the room at this strong young German, at his open, enquiring face, and I knew here was a man who would follow his conscience, even if it meant death. Once more, I repeated Schmulewski's message.

His expression did not change. For two minutes, he sat, silent, until I said, "Fredy, you're the only man who can do it. The only man they'll follow."

He said in something like a whisper, "But what about the children?"

This was the moment I had feared. I knew how much he loved those kids, how much they loved him. He was their second father, the axis on which their young lives turned.

"Fredy," I said, "the children are going to die. That you must believe. But tens of thousands of children have died here before, and now we have a chance to put a stop to it. To smash the camp so no other kid will ever be gassed here. Think of it that way...a few hundred die today because nobody can save them. But tens of thousands of other youngsters will live."

His face was pale and tense; his hand shook as he lit a cigarette. "How can I leave them?" he said. "How can I march off to fight for my own skin and leave them to be butchered? Don't you see they trust me? They need me!"

"They're doomed, Fredy. You can't save them. Think of others. Think of all the thousands of kids all over Europe. Kids who are at home with their parents but who'll burn in Auschwitz if we don't act now."

The agony of decision was in his eyes, the agony of a man who was still civilized, who had not been long enough in Auschwitz to grow the hard skin that imprisoned emotions.

"Give me an hour," he said finally. "Give me an hour to think it over."

It was about eleven o'clock. The gassings, I reckoned, were unlikely to start before late afternoon. I said to Fredy, "Right. But remember...there's only one way you can help anybody."

Alice was waiting outside. I told her what was happening, and suddenly she said, "Are you sure? Is Schmulewski sure? Somehow it doesn't seem possible."

"I'm sure," I said. "I know the SS. For them, there is no other way."

"But the children...surely not the children."

"The children, too. But let's talk about something else."

We talked about something else. About a future that knew no barbed wire. About a world that knew no guns. About an ordinary house in an ordinary street with a grocer just around the corner. About four firm walls that held a bedroom and a kitchen and a hearth with a fire that danced and flickered in the evening. About peace which I had almost forgotten and which she could scarcely believe had ended. Splendid words. Empty words. False words, for now we were lying to each other to help each other. And lying to ourselves.

Then it was noon.

I went back into the barracks to hear the decision which might lend substance to our shadows. Fredy Hirsch was lying on the bed unconscious.

I ran to him. His heavy breath was growling in his throat. His face was blue-gray. Flecks of froth hung on his lips, and I saw all the signs of luminal poisoning.

I dashed from the barracks and searched frantically for one of the prisoner doctors. I found two of them, and they came with me at once to the man who had to live. His breathing was even heavier now, quick, urgent, desperate. Without a word, they examined him while I hung, helpless, in the background.

At last, they turned from the bed, their faces blank. The older one said to me, "I can save him."

"Thank God for that!"

"But it will take time. He won't be on his feet again for a fortnight."

"That's no bloody good!" I shouted. "He's going to die today anyway. They're all going to die. He's the only man who can save any of them! He's the only man who can make them fight!"

The two doctors looked at each other. Then the older one said quietly, "If what you say is true, let him die now. It's the best way, the kindest way, because we can do nothing."

I looked down at Fredy Hirsch, the German whose heart was too big, who could not bear to see little children suffer, and I realized that I had asked him to do too much.

Yet still there was hope. Still there was time. Schmulewski would think of something, would find a new leader, a new figurehead. Out I ran from the barracks again, and then I stopped in my tracks.

Camp A was surrounded by SS men. We were isolated.

I went to the wire that separated us from Camp B, where the second batch of Czech families still lived, and called Hugo Lenk, one of the underground leaders.

"Hirsch is dead," I told him. "For Christ's sake, get a message to Schmulewski!"

"How the hell can I?" he snapped. "The whole bloody place is sealed off."

"Try, man. Try! I can't give orders on my own. I can't tell them to fight without Hirsch. Only Schmulewski can do that."

"All right. I'll do my best. But it's going to be tough."

I knew, of course, that it was going to be tough, but now I was demanding miracles. The responsibility of the situation pressed down on my shoulders, and suddenly I felt tired, washed out, dispirited. Disconsolately, I wandered over to the barracks, where I found Alice, Helena, and Vera.

Alice's arms went round me immediately. "What's the matter?" she said. "You're ill. Darling, what's happened?"

"Hirsch is dead. There can be no rising."

"But why? We can go on without him. You give the orders, and we'll fight."

This, I had expected. They did not realize how much was at stake. They did not understand how the underground worked. They knew nothing of its iron discipline, its cold, unemotional, devastatingly logical approach to every problem.

"I can't give orders," I said wearily. "I'm only a small boy in the organization. I can't take responsibility without authority from higher up."

"But we must fight!" said Vera desperately. "We can't die like dogs. Let's set fire to the barracks…anything rather than nothing!"

Helena frowned at her, then said to me, "Have you any further orders from Schmulewski? Any orders at all?"

"I have no orders. No orders at all."

She turned again to her sister and said, "Don't be silly, Vera. We don't want to do anything which might cost the lives of other people. We must wait for instructions."

I looked at her gratefully. At least she understood.

Time went quickly after that. I probed every possible chink in the wall around the camp. I told the SS that I had to go to Camp D with some important documents. They shook their heads. I even thought of telling them I had to take poor Fredy Hirsch's body out of the camp, but I knew it was no good. I contacted Hugo Lenk in the forlorn hope that he might have managed to get a message out, but he shook his head sadly.

We were trapped. Now, I knew, it was only a matter of time, unless the miracles I demanded were delivered. Automatically, I wandered back to the barracks, to Alice and Helena and Vera.

I do not remember how long we were there or what we said to each other, but I shall never forget the sound of the lorries. They came roaring into the camp, a dozen, two dozen, forty, fifty, sixty. I never knew how many.

We moved toward the door but were too late. A swarm of kapos, strange kapos, poured into the barracks, their clubs swinging.

"Out…out…out!" they roared. *"Raus…raus…raus!"*

The clubs rose and fell. The thin wail of the women clashed with the terrified screams of the children. Alice flung herself into my arms, and as I held her close, the kapos beat and kicked and bullied their cattle out to the lorries. They swarmed all around us, ignoring us for the moment, for they saw from my clothes that I was one of them, but this, I knew, was only a temporary protection. This, I knew, was the end.

A bloodstained child fell at my feet. A mother swept up its dead body and was sent hurtling through the door by a blow on the back. Alice's face was pressed close to mine, and she was whispering into my ear.

"We'll meet again, darling. We'll meet again, and it'll be wonderful. But…if we don't…it has been wonderful."

A kapo blundered past, gave us a push, and roared, "Break it up, you two. This is no time for fucking. Get that bitch up on the lorry!"

Still we clung together, our lips pressed close, fingers biting frantically, futilely into each other's flesh.

"Come on, you bastard! Get rid of that girl or go up on the lorry with her!"

Alice heard him. Her grip relaxed. Her face was white, but there were no tears. "Go, darling," she panted. *"Go now!"*

Then she herself was gone, running for the lorry. I saw her stumble under a blow, recover, then disappear through the door.

I followed her but could not see her. Outside the barracks was ringed completely by kapos and SS men, safety catches off their submachine guns. If I stayed inside that ring, I knew that I, too, would be bundled on to the lorry, riding breeches or no riding breeches. If I ran, I would be shot immediately.

I took a cigarette from my pocket, lit it, and strolled over to a kapo I knew. I chatted to him for a moment, but he was not listening. Then, cigarette in my mouth, hands in my pockets, I walked slowly toward the green line of SS men.

"Halt!" The snout of a submachine gun jabbed my belly.

"I'm the registrar of Block Fourteen. I've been ordered to go to the block senior immediately."

"Okay. Make it snappy." He waved me through the cordon with his gun, and I walked briskly away from the barracks, away from the bedlam, away from Alice.

I stood at the door of Block Fourteen and looked back. A registrar I knew said, "You're a right bloody fool! You damn nearly ended up in the furnace!"

I did not answer him. I scarcely heard him. The lorries began to snarl again and move toward the gate like an armored division. The noise of the engines seemed to fill the camp, to drown my ears.

Then, suddenly, over this harsh, imperative note, I heard a new, sweet sound. The sound of a thousand women singing. And the song was the Czechoslovak National Anthem—"Where Is My Home...."

It faded away as the lorry disappeared. New voices took over with a new song, inspired by the same thought. This time it was the Jewish National Anthem—"Hope."

For hours, I stood outside that barracks, long after the last lorry had gone and the stench of exhaust had disappeared. I stood there, tortured, until I saw dark smoke mix with the huge yellow flame that rose from the crematorium. Then I went back to my room, back to the bed that twenty-four hours earlier had known magic.

I lay on it, but I did not sleep.

———

Filip Müller had been working all night. His face was grimy, and his eyes were tired.

With careful indifference, I said to him: "How did it go?"

"Quietly," he said. "Very quietly. They sang the Czech and Jewish national anthems all the time, and they just walked straight into the chambers."

"No resistance?"

"We were waiting for it, but it never came. Had they started a fight, we would have joined them. I suppose they were thinking of the children."

"No protests at all?"

"Nothing to speak of. Three girls made a fight of it and had to be beaten in. That was all."

Just three girls. I wondered who they might have been, but I asked Filip no more questions.[2]

---

2   Whereas the facts of the Czech Family Camp are described very precisely in the book and significantly helped historians reconstruct the course of events, the author erred by one day; the transport of the first Family Camp arrived on September 8 and was gassed on the night between March 8–9, 1944.
During the escapee's imprisonment, two additional groups of Czech prisoners arrived. The same six-month pattern of treatment was initiated, but these people were still alive when the escapees gave their report in Slovakia. In the hope that these Czechs would not be murdered, the escapees gave very precise details about the Czech Family Camp. The escapee's report reached the Czechoslovak diplomat Jaromír Kopecký in Switzerland. Almost immediately, Kopecký arranged to have excerpts relating to the Czechs broadcasted on radio. It is of interest that these Czech prisoners did not meet the same fate as their predecessors. About 3,500 healthier prisoners were selected for slave labor, out of which approximately 1,200 survived the war. --Eds.

CHAPTER 13
"Never Trust a German"

———————

APART ALTOGETHER FROM THE FACT THAT I HAD NO AU-
thority to call upon the Czechs to rise, there was another reason which
forced me to keep my silence. My own escape plans had been completed, and now it was absolutely essential that someone should get away
from Auschwitz to warn the world, for the extermination machinery
was being geared to cope with the greatest massacre it had known in
its bloodstained history.

We got our first hint of the horror to come when, in January, new
railway tracks began edging their way up the broad road that lay between Birkenau 1 and Birkenau 2. Prisoners slaved on them day and
night, under arc lights when necessary, and every morning, we could see
that they had advanced another few yards toward their objective, which,
it soon became obvious, was the gas chambers and the crematoria.

The ramp, it seemed, was to become obsolete. Here was an operation beyond the scope of lorries. Here there would be no selections, no
weeding out of the young and fit—just a direct line to death.

I discussed the situation with Filip Müller, and he was able to give
me further information. The old trenches, where the bodies were
burned before the crematoria were built, were being made ready for
action again. New trenches were being dug. The capacity even of
Auschwitz, the greatest death factory in the history of the world, was
going to be stretched to its limits.

The Nazis, we estimated, were preparing to kill at least a million people. For a while, we wondered in which country they would find so many Jews left, but gradually, as the clues filtered through to us, we realized who were destined to break all records. It was the Hungarians, whom most of us had thought were reasonably safe.

Hungary, after all, was still an independent state, and Jews had always been prominent in its hierarchy. It seemed inconceivable that a nation which had woven Jewry so intimately into its fabric could stand by, silent, while it was destroyed.

Yet suddenly it all seemed to make sense. From the German newspapers, which were forbidden to prisoners, of course, but which we old hands "organized" regularly, we learned of unrest in Hungary. Then came news that German troops had marched in to "restore order"—and then a development which seemed both fantastic and ridiculous. Sztójay had been declared prime minister. Sztójay, the little toy Nazi who had been a laughing stock in his country throughout his pathetic life!

Horthy remained head of the state, but became a puppet. Sztójay, of course, was a puppet, too, a willing lackey, but his presence in any position made it quite clear that it was the Nazis of Germany who now held absolute power.

So it was that we in Auschwitz, perhaps the most isolated spot in Europe, learned a secret that was known only to the Nazi elite in Berlin. In fact, it took some time for the truth to trickle down through the ranks, but ultimately, any doubts we may have had were removed by the SS men who worked in close contact with the *Sonderkommando* in the gas chambers and the crematoria. What confirmation we needed came from their gossip, as they joked among themselves about the Hungarian salami which soon they would be having by the ton.

I knew then that this was my moment. For almost two years, I had thought of escape, first selfishly because I wanted my freedom, then in a more objective way because I wanted to tell the world what was happening in Auschwitz—but now I had an imperative reason. It was no longer a question of reporting a crime, but of preventing one—of warning the Hungarians, of rousing them, of raising an army one-million strong, an army that would fight rather than die.

Nevertheless, I did not underestimate the difficulties ahead of me. Auschwitz was the most heavily guarded camp in Europe, a secret which the Nazis were determined would never be revealed, for once even a whisper about it escaped, the sheep would no longer walk quietly into the slaughterhouse.

Nor had I any illusions about the fate which awaited any would-be escapers who were caught. Indeed, it had been made brutally clear to me when I had been in the camp for only seven days.

We had finished our work and were marching toward our barracks for evening roll call. For some reason that we did not understand, however, the routine was changed, and we found ourselves lined up with thousands of other prisoners before the kitchen, a huge building that sported on its roof in letters ten feet tall the splendid legend: "Honesty and Cleanliness, Love of Work, and Love of Fatherland Are the Milestones to Freedom."

This noble thought, however, was wasted on us that fine summer's evening. Our eyes and our minds were distracted by the two mobile gallows which dominated the open space in front of us—and by the greatest display of SS men with submachine guns we had ever seen. There were four or five rows of them, enough to mow down most of the camp in a matter of minutes, and, while this we understood, we were puzzled by yet another row which had their weapons slung across their shoulders.

This row had large military drums, adding a hint of circus to a scene which already looked thoroughly ominous.

There were always SS officers present at roll call, but this time the parade had star status. Commandant Rudolf Hoess was there, blocky, sturdy, immaculate. So was his deputy, Camp Commander Hans Aumeier, a neat little figure of five feet two which, incidentally, gave him the double record of being the smallest and most vicious officer in Auschwitz.[1]

It was impressive and frightening. Yet we prisoners had not the faintest idea what it was all about until Oberscharführer Jakob Fries, who had the loudest voice in the camp, came forward to make a little speech. "Two Polish prisoners," he bellowed with a roar that flooded the camp, "have been caught preparing to escape. This was made quite clear by the fact that under their tunics they were found to be wearing civilian shirts.

"This is something which the camp administration will not tolerate. Any man found planning an escape will be punished by death on the gallows, as these two prisoners are about to be punished now.

"Let it be a warning to you all. The rules of the camp must be obeyed."

Josef Erdelyi beside me muttered, "He's bluffing. He's just trying to scare us. I bet they only hang them by their wrists for half an hour or so."

He had no time to say more. Another column of SS was marching up on either side of two terribly thin, barefoot prisoners who somehow were managing to hold their heads high, and as soon as they drew level with us, the two dozen drums began to roll louder and louder until they obliterated every other sound in the camp, deadening our ears, drowning our words, driving all independent thought out of our minds.

The gallows were only fifteen yards away from me. I saw the two prisoners mount the twin platforms. The hangman, a kapo, went quickly to the first one and bound his ankles and his thighs. His hands were already tied behind his back, and in a second, the noose was being adjusted expertly around his neck.

The man showed absolutely no emotion—no sign of fear or sadness or panic. Beside him, his comrade was making a speech to us all,

---

1   Both Hoess and Aumeier were hanged after the war at Auschwitz on their own gallows.

but the drums overwhelmed his words, as they were intended to do, and though he knew well we could not hear him, he kept on speaking, even when the rope was slipped around his neck.

The kapo was working fast now because he hated the job. He ran to the back of the first gallows and pulled a lever. The platform crashed open, and to our horror, the prisoner dropped no more than six inches.

There was no question of his neck snapping, of instantaneous death. He was being strangled. I could see his chest heaving faster and faster as his lungs fought frantically for air. Then his body contracted. His legs moved slowly upward until they were parallel to the ground, then just as slowly sank. Up and down...up and down they went in a rhythmical movement that made the body rotate gently before us.

Another crash above the thunder of the drums, and the second man's speech was over. Again, the reaction was the same...the quick, quick heaving of the lungs, the slow gymnastics of the legs, the twirling of the body. For three minutes, it lasted, and then it was all over. The lungs were empty. The legs were straight. Only a gentle breeze created movement now.

Suddenly, the drums stopped, leaving a vacuum of silence. Then it was filled by the drone of a thousand whispers until Jakob Fries roared, "Nobody moves! You stand there for an hour."

Commandant Hoess and Camp Commander Aumeier went home, for they had had a tiring day. The SS, drums and guns and all, marched off with fine precision. We stood there, watching the sun sink behind the kitchen, watching the slim shadows of the gallows stretching out toward us across the parade ground, watching the bodies of the men who had worn civilian shirts swaying very slightly. We were on the brink of twilight, and the words on the roof were scarcely visible anymore.

Honesty and Cleanliness, Love of Work, and Love of Fatherland are the Milestones to Freedom.

After our hour of penance for the sins of our fellows, we were allowed to move around the camp freely. I passed close to the bodies. Their tongues were stretched out grotesquely, yet in spite of that, their faces were strangely peaceful. I gazed at them for a minute and read, as I was meant to read, the notices pinned to their zebra tunics.

They were simple and effective. They read: "Because we tried to escape…"

It was primitive psychology, but I missed the point, for I was, after all, not yet eighteen and very naïve. I remember thinking, When I get out and tell people about this, they probably won't believe me!

Immediately, I began studying the layout of the camp, searching for chinks in its defenses, and what I noted I found depressing. The mother camp of Auschwitz—and a very similar system applied to Birkenau, I learned later—was divided into an outer camp in which we worked and an inner camp in which we slept.

The inner camp in Birkenau was guarded by a trench six yards wide and five yards deep. It was filled with water. Then came two barbed-wire, high-voltage fences five yards high. Arc lamps played constantly on the inner camp all night, and SS men with machine guns surveyed it from watch towers.

In the morning, these guards stood down after we had gone to work, and fresh guards manned towers on the perimeter of the outer camp, which was about four miles long. The approaches to this perimeter were absolutely barren, and no prisoner could cross them in daylight without being caught in cross fire from the towers.

If a prisoner did manage to sneak through this network, if he were reported missing from the inner camp at night, the outer towers were manned and reinforcements—three thousand men and two hundred dogs—were called in to seal off the entire area.

This massive guard stayed on duty for three days and nights while troops and dogs fine-combed the camp. If the prisoner had not been recaptured by that time, it was presumed that he had escaped beyond the camp where other SS men were searching already. The guard was dismissed then, and the matter was handed over to the authorities beyond Auschwitz.

It was clear to me that a man who could remain hidden beyond the inner perimeter for three days and three nights had a reasonable chance. It was not so clear to me, however, how this could be accomplished, and therefore, I began what was to be my first scientific study: the technique of escape. I began to study every unsuccessful escape attempt, to analyze its flaws and to correct them.

It was a slow, tedious process which led ultimately to success. Yet I do not think I would have got away completely, had it not been for one man who laid his vast experience before me and thereby saved my life a dozen times over.

He was Dmitri Volkov from Zaporozshe on the Don, one of a group of one hundred Russians whom we called our "second-hand prisoners of war." They all had been captured on the eastern front, sent to ordinary POW camps and transferred to Auschwitz for breaking the rules—trying to escape, stealing bread, or something like that. They came to Birkenau Camp A, still in their old military uniforms, and I had a good deal to do with them, principally because I was the registrar and partly because I spoke reasonable Russian.

I got to know Dmitri Volkov very well, though this took some considerable time. He was a huge man from the Cossack country with deep-set, dark eyes; dark hair; and rather prominent cheekbones—a man of obvious intelligence, yet without rank marks on his shoulders. I began practicing my Russian with him, and in return, I gave him my bread and margarine ration, which I had promised I would never eat while I could get food from other sources.

At first, he was extremely reserved. He would thank me courteously for the food and then split it meticulously into four portions for his friends who, like himself, were starving. It was only later that the SS gave them jobs in the kitchen, not because they had any concern for their empty bellies, but because they realized that in Moscow there was a record of all prisoners of war—that most of those who had come to Auschwitz had died, and that it would be wise to have a token force still alive. Dmitri and his comrades, in fact, were the SS men's insurance policy, though personally, I would not have placed too much faith in it.

These, however, were not matters which I discussed with Dmitri, who remained reticent about his background and about local camp politics. We talked, instead, about Russian literature, about Dostoyevsky or Tolstoy. Then, as we got to know each other a little better, we progressed to the great Soviet writers, Mayakovsky, Bloch, Gorky, Sholokhov, Ehrenburg, even Zoshchenko, the humorist who had earned the disapproval of his regime by being a little too funny.

It was all on a rather high plane, and therefore, I was considerably surprised one day when Dmitri said suddenly to me: "It has taken me some time to understand you. The first time you gave me bread, I was vaguely suspicious. The sixth time, I was fairly sure you were a German agent. But now I know I can trust you because no German could appreciate Russian writers the way you obviously do.

"So, let's talk openly for a change. As you've probably guessed, I'm not a private. I'm a captain, but somehow I've managed to keep this quiet ever since they captured me because, as you know, all Russian officers are shot by the Germans."

With that one sentence, of course, he was delivering his life into my hands. He was a man, however, who trusted a person completely once he had summed him up, and over the next few days, he told me about his amazing life since he had been taken prisoner.

I gathered that he had been in various concentration camps before arriving at Sachsenhausen near Berlin. It was extremely well organized and almost as difficult to break as Auschwitz. Yet Dmitri Volkov managed to get away from it.

Not only that. He traveled thousands of miles through enemy territory, right into Russia until he came to the banks of the mighty Dnieper River near Kiev, which was still occupied by the Germans.

He knew he could not cross by the bridge which was heavily patrolled. There was only one other way, and that was to swim at night for the far bank, which he could not see.

He accomplished this marathon feat, and in his moment of triumph, he made his first mistake. He was so elated to feel solid ground under his feet again that he went bounding through the bushes like a gazelle—and found himself gazing into the muzzle of a German revolver.

"It was bad luck," he said to me with a grin. "The bloody fellow wasn't even on duty. He was in those bushes with a girl and thought I was a Peeping Tom! Still, it taught me a lesson for the next time.

"And now I'm going to teach you some lessons because I know you're not the type who will go to the gas chambers. You're like me. You're going to get out or die like a soldier.

"Lesson one is this: Trust nobody. Don't tell me, for instance, when you're going to escape or how. I have my own plans, too, but I won't let you know them.

"As soon as you're reported missing, you see, they'll come to me because they've seen you giving me bread. And, maybe under torture, I'd talk. I don't think I would, but I might, because no man knows how much he can stand.

"Lesson two: Don't be afraid of the Germans. There are many of them, but each of them is small. Here in Auschwitz, they try to break your mind as well as your body. They try to convince you they're supermen, invincible. But I know they can die just as quickly as anybody else because I've killed enough of them in my day.

"Lesson three: Once you're out, don't trust your legs because a bullet can always run faster. Don't give them a chance to shoot. Be invisible. Never move by day, for that is the time to rest. And be sure you have found somewhere to sleep before it is light, somewhere you won't be seen.

"Lesson four: Carry no money. I know you can get as much as you want here from the *Sonderkommando* in the crematorium, but don't touch it. If you're starving, you'll be tempted to buy food. If you've no money, you can't. Live off the land. Steal from the fields and the lonelier farms. Keep away from people.

"Lesson five: Travel light. You'll need a knife and a razor blade. The knife for hunting or for defending yourself. The razor blade in case you're about to be captured. Don't let them take you alive.

"You'll need matches because you'll have to cook what you steal. You'll need salt because with salt and potatoes, you can keep going for months. You'll need a watch so you can time your journeys and make sure you're never caught in the open by day. You can use it as a compass, too."

He taught me how to do this. He filled in my Manual of What Every Escaper Should Know. He explained, for instance, how I could fox the tracker dogs by carrying Russian tobacco that had been soaked in petrol and dried. The smell, he said, drove them away.

"Only Russian tobacco, remember," he added. "I'm not being patriotic. I just know Machorka. It's the only stuff that works!"

He warned me, too, that while making my escape, I should never carry meat because it would attract the dogs immediately, and the last piece of advice he gave me was, perhaps, the most significant of all.

"Never forget," he said, "that the fight only begins when you're away from the camp. Never relax so long as you're in enemy territory. Never get drunk with freedom, like I did outside Kiev, for you never know who's lying in the bushes!"

It was a long briefing, spread over several days, and once it was over, we never spoke again, for Dmitri Volkov's last words to me were: "We'd better not meet again because we have been seen talking together too much already, and I intend to get out, too, remember. Good luck to you. Maybe we'll meet some other time, some other place."

Up to now, we have not met, but I hope that Dmitri survived Auschwitz. If ever he should read this book, I wish he would write to me, for I would like to thank him.

I had, of course, other tutors, but few of them survived. In fact, I learned only from the example of their death, from the fatal mistakes which they made and which I was determined I would not repeat. There was, for instance, Fero Langer, big, burly, jovial Fero with whom I had played bread skittles for salami back in Novaky at the beginning of my long journey to Auschwitz.

Inevitably, he arrived in Birkenau in dramatic fashion, because he could never do very much quietly. One day in January 1943, Schmulewski came to me and said, "Three Slovak Jews have just arrived. They're in my block now. See if you can help them."

"But how?" I said. "There hasn't been a Slovak transport. Where have they come from?"

"The Gestapo brought them in. They were caught on the Swiss border under a pile of wood on a freight train. Another few minutes, and they'd have been free."

I went to Schmulewski's block and was greeted by a roar of laughter which transported me right back to that prison cell in Novaky. Fero, looking as if he had just arrived for a holiday, flung his arms around me and bellowed, "What's all this I've been hearing about you? They tell me you're making a career for yourself here. Just look at your shoes! C'mon now, let me have them. I can't go round in these bloody wooden things!"

Fero Langer, to whose father my father owed money when he died, had not changed a bit. His humor was more boisterous than ever, and his shrewd brain was working like lightning. Although he had been in Birkenau only forty-eight hours, already he had a fair grasp of the situation.

Soon everyone knew him not as Fero Langer, but as Fero the Bull. He eased himself into the higher echelons of society, and soon, he was patronizing me, a veteran of the camp.

Once he was established, he organized his life carefully and methodically. He was never invited to join the underground, but that did not worry him, for he felt he was an underground unto himself. He made contact, for instance, with the *Sonderkommando*, and soon he had at his fingertips a fortune which would have made his wealthy parents back home in the town of Telgart in the Eastern Tatra Mountains seem poor.

In every way, he thought big and never bigger than when he began to plan an escape. Like me, he was not thinking of his own freedom. He was thinking of telling the world, but unlike me, he decided the world must be told in five languages. So, he made up his mind he would bring four others with him—a Dutchman, a Frenchman, a Pole, and a Greek.

Precisely what was in his mind, how he was going to get away with his polyglot team I did not know, for not only did we not discuss our escapes with each other, but we seldom even mentioned the word.

I sensed, however, that he felt he had made considerable progress when he came to me one day, excitement bubbling in his eyes and said very casually, "I've just met a very interesting fellow. An SS man."

"Keep your company to yourself," I said. "They only interest me when they're dead."

"Wait a minute," he said soothingly. "This lad's different. There I was, being marched out of the camp this morning, and who do you think was guarding me? An old schoolmate of mine! A lad called Dobrovolny."

"His father's Slovak—he used to work for my old man, as a matter of fact—but his mother's German. And that makes old Dobrovolny

German in the eyes of the Führer. We used to share the same desk and the same girls. We grew up together like brothers!"

"Listen, Fero," I said, "that was a long time ago. He's a bloody SS man now, and don't you forget it. Once a man puts on that green uniform, something happens to him. It turns him into a dirty swine."

"Nonsense!" said Fero. "Not old Dobrovolny. You just wait and see."

Soon I had to admit that he seemed to be right. He and his school-friend could not be seen talking together by the SS, for that would have meant death for both of them, but their old friendship seemed to be resumed, nevertheless, just where it had been interrupted years earlier in Telgart.

Fero, in fact, became more highly organized than ever. When Dobrovolny went home on leave, he carried with him a letter to old Mr. and Mrs. Langer. When he delivered it to the wealthy forest owner, he was suitably rewarded, and when he returned, he brought a reply. Fero, indeed, was not merely the one Auschwitz prisoner who got letters from home, but he actually wrote checks in the camp, or what were as good as checks. He would scribble a postscript to his letters, asking that the bearer be paid ten thousand crowns or twenty thousand crowns. To Mr. Langer, Sr., the money did not matter, so long as he heard from his son.

Inevitably, Dobrovolny became a key man in Fero's escape plan. I heard some of the details one afternoon when I went into Fred Wetzler's block for a dish of potatoes and found him talking quietly with Fred and Rosin, the only Slovak block senior in the camp. They did not invite me to join the discussion, but they did not stop talking, and I sat, listening, as I ate my dish of potatoes.

"My plan is this," said Fero softly. "Every day, a few prisoners are marched beyond the outer perimeter for work. They are guarded well, of course, and the SS man in charge has to show the boys at the gate special permits for them.

"But that's easy. Dobrovolny can lay his hands on these permit forms and sign them. I can give him enough money to buy a lorry which he'll park three or four miles from Auschwitz. Then all we have to do is walk out, pile into the lorry, and head for the Slovak border fast."

"What about the other SS men?" said Fred. "What are you going to do with them?"

"Take them with us," said Fero with a shrug. "Or deal with them on the spot. That's only a detail."

"I don't know," said Rosin slowly. "You know the old Hungarian proverb, Fero? Never trust a German!"

"Don't be silly!" said Fero. "Dobrovolny's not really a German. He's my old school pal, and he's proved it since we met here in Birkenau. And, what's more, he's going to make £100,000 out of this little trip, and that's not chickenfeed in anybody's money."

"Well," said Rosin with a sigh, "don't say I didn't warn you. But good luck all the same."

A few days later, at three o'clock one afternoon early in January 1944, the escape siren began to wail. Suddenly, the camp seemed filled with SS men and dogs. I saw some kapos running and shouting to each other: "It's Fero, the Bull!"

Silently, I wished him luck and wondered where he was. Speeding toward the Slovak border? Battling with the redundant SS men? Somehow, I felt confident he would make it, for if ever there was a man who seemed indestructible, it was Fero Langer. Indeed, as the afternoon wore on, I plotted his progress in my mind, ticking off the towns he would bypass, picturing him abandoning the lorry and disappearing into the forests of Slovakia.

Fero, however, never reached the forests. He never got very far from Auschwitz. At six o'clock that evening, they brought back his body and the bodies of his own personal International Brigade. They had been shot dead, but in no ordinary fashion. Dumdum bullets, which explode on impact like shells, had ripped their flesh to pieces.

Nor was this merely sadism. It was done with a purpose. The SS got five chairs and placed them in the middle of Camp D, where everyone would see them when they marched back from work. They strapped the bodies on the chairs and decorated them with a large notice which read: *"We're back!"*

Half Fero's face had been blown away. The others were mutilated beyond recognition.

I wondered what had happened to Dobrovolny. Perhaps, I thought, he was still being tortured, for he would suffer more than the prisoners. The next morning, however, I discovered I had been wasting my sympathy.

Walking through the camp, smiling to himself, was Fero Langer's old schoolfriend.

It was some days before we discovered exactly what had happened. It was, it seemed, a simple case of betrayal.

As soon as Fero had revealed his plan to Dobrovolny, the SS man had reported it to his superiors. The Political Department was delighted to issue the permits which would take them through the outer gates, for here was a situation out of which he could make considerable capital.

Everything, in fact, went according to plan, until they were approaching the lorry. Then the SS men flung themselves flat, and a murderous blast of fire cut the five prisoners to ribbons. At that moment, Dobrovolny had earned himself his sergeant's stripes and probably ton of money, too.

The lesson to be learned from that escape attempt was contained in the old Hungarian proverb, quoted by Rosin: "Never trust a German." Yet, for some reason I cannot understand, looking back, I only half-assimilated it. Soon afterward, indeed, I nearly fell into the same trap.

At that time, I was very friendly with a French army captain, Charles Unglick. He had been born in Czestochowa in Poland, but his Jewish parents had emigrated to France, where Charles had a French wife and two children. He had been captured at Dunkirk and earned a place in Auschwitz because of his background.

I knew him as a block senior in the Quarantine Camp where I was registrar—a great gangster, a man with a big heart, and a very powerful prisoner in the camp in or out of the underground of which, incidentally, he was not a member. Charles Unglick made a terrible enemy but a fine friend.

His physical strength was such that even the Monkey Tyn, the camp senior, was afraid of him. His contacts among the influential prisoners in general and the *Sonderkommando*, who had access to the valuables of the gas-chamber victims, in particular, were closer even than those of Fero Langer. He was a millionaire even by the standards of Birkenau, where I have seen twenty-dollar bills used as toilet paper, and he used his wealth to gain power over the SS by the simple expedient of bribery.

Two of his closest associates—I will not say friends—in the SS were Unterscharführer Buntrock and Unterscharführer Kurpanik,[2] a pair of notorious murderers. On many occasions, I saw them march drunk into the Quarantine Camp after roll call and kill for the fun of it. Their hands were never far from their revolvers, and even without provocation, they would draw them and shoot a prisoner in the face at close range.

With Charles Unglick, however, their manners were very different, as I learned one night soon after we had become friendly. We were sitting in his room, talking, when there was a timid knock on the door. A voice whispered, "Are you asleep, Charlo?"

With a grunt of irritation, he swept open the door. Outside, as diffident as two junior clerks in the presence of the boss, stood Buntrock and Kurpanik.

---

2   Both Buntrock and Kurpanik were hanged with Hoess on the Auschwitz gallows.

"Come in!" bellowed Charles. They followed him into the room, and as he flopped back into his seat, he clapped his hands. Immediately, the prisoner who was his personal servant appeared, and the master ordered a meal.

A snow-white cloth was laid on the table. Within five minutes, we were sitting down to a magnificent cold chicken supper washed down with a couple of bottles of Yugoslav Reisling. When the meal was over, Unglick marched over to his cupboard and returned with a fistful of dollars. He flung one hundred to Kurpanik and another hundred to Buntrock.

When they had gone, he spat on the floor, grinned at me, and said, "The bastards! But we've got to keep them happy. It's worth it, because you and I are going to get out of this bloody camp soon. We're going to go to Paris and live it up. I'm going to see my wife and kids again if it costs me every golden dollar in the crematorium!"

At the time, I did not take him very seriously, though I knew he had considerable influence. I grew accustomed to Buntrock and Kurpanik calling two or three times a week and collecting their dollars. In fact, when I came in one night and found Unglick talking to a strange SS man, I was quite surprised, and when I heard them talking in Yiddish, which was Unglick's mother tongue, I could scarcely believe my ears.

An SS man speaking Yiddish! It was unbelievable, but even more startling was what they were saying. They were planning an escape which to my mind seemed foolproof.

The SS man, it seemed, was a German who had been orphaned in Romania and brought up by a Jewish family. When the Germans occupied the country, he reverted to his old nationality and joined the SS, but Yiddish, which I could understand, though spoke only badly, was his mother tongue.

I listened carefully, saying nothing, as the rapid-fire conversation droned on in low tones. The SS man, I gathered, was a driver. Unglick's plan was that he should drive his lorry into the Quarantine Camp with a routine load of wood, leaving the huge toolbox at the back of the cab open. The pair of us would hop into it and he would lock it. At the gates, of course, he would be stopped by the guards, who normally searched the lorry and glanced in the toolbox, but he could easily get past them by saying he had forgotten the key, that the box had been locked when he drove in.

There was only one point I could not understand. Why was this particular SS man going to help us? I knew he must be expecting some reward, for, Yiddish or no Yiddish, he was not going to risk his neck for the memory of his dear old foster mother back in Bucharest.

That, too, Unglick explained in very precise terms. He said, "Any day now, I'm expecting to collect two pounds of gold dollars and diamonds. We'll split it three ways, and we'll be millionaires as soon as this bloody war is over!"

The SS man grinned. I grinned. Unglick grinned. Slapping his vast palm on the table, he grunted with relish: "Paris—here I come!"

When the German had gone, he said to me quietly, "This is it. We'll be out by the end of the week. I don't know exactly when we go, but our friend will tell us."

It was one of the few times I had seen him really serious, and the mood did not last long. The next minute, he was roaring, "C'mon, you bastard! How about a brandy?"

He rummaged in his cupboard, hauled out a bottle of fine French cognac, and poured it like beer. Raising his glass, he winked at me and whispered with a grin, "To the Arc de Triomphe! And the Eiffel Tower, too!"

Though he must have been tense inside, he never showed it in the days that followed. He bullied the prisoners as usual in a jovial fashion, though I never saw him hit them. He fussed about his clothes, which were the finest in the camp, and kicked up murder when one of the Polish tailors failed to deliver a new jacket. All his clothes were perfectly cut by one of Warsaw's finest tailors—his riding breeches, his jacket. His boots were made to measure from the best leather, and his shirts were silk. He was particularly proud of a magnificent white pullover which had been knitted specially for him from strands of wool teased meticulously from Dutch blankets.

In fact, he took an almost childish delight in his appearance and was constantly acquiring something new. One day that week, in fact, I was in the latrine with him and saw he had a splendid leather belt which I had not noticed before.

"Been robbing again, Charlo?" I said. "That's a new belt, isn't it?"

"Yes. A bloody fine one, too."

"How about letting your old pal have it, then? You've got dozens of them."

"You bastard!" he grinned. "Everything you see, you want! I tell you what—you can have it when I die. I'll leave it to you in my will!"

Then, without any change of mood, he whispered, "By the way, I've just learned that our car leaves in three days' time at seven o'clock after roll call. Don't be late."

The date was January 22, 1944. The next three days seemed to crawl by, but at last I found myself standing stiffly to attention during evening roll call on January 25. I could hardly believe that in a few hours I could be away, that this could be the last time I would line up before my block, or any block for that matter.

We were dismissed. It was a quarter to seven. I wandered up and down near the spot where the lorry was due to call, counting the minutes, fighting the rising excitement inside me, striving to appear relaxed and casual. I walked a hundred yards away from the spot, timing myself carefully, chatted for a while with a registrar I knew, then strolled back.

It was five to seven. I glanced toward the gate. There was no sign of the lorry. I took another short walk, afraid now to go too far from the spot.

Seven o'clock. No Unglick. No lorry. My nerves were raw, but I forced myself to walk slowly, coolly, away once more, just a few yards this time and then back. Other prisoners drifted around me, but I scarcely saw them. Already, I felt I was no longer part of them.

Five past seven. Ten past seven. Jesus, I thought, something's wrong. The SS man's squealed. Where the hell's that lorry!

"Halt!"

I jumped and whirled around. A prisoner from my block was grinning at me.

"You're as nervous as a cat," he said. "What's the matter? Thinking of running for the wire or something?"

"Sorry," I said, forcing myself to smile back. "My mind was miles away. Did you want something?"

"No. But Doctor Milar does. He asks me to present his compliments and to inform you that supper is served."

Andrej Milar was senior of my block by that time, one of the Slovak intellectuals and a man for whom I had a great respect. Normally, I would have been delighted to eat with him, but not now.

"Tell him…tell him I'm not hungry," I stammered. "I'll see him later."

"Now I've seen everything," he said in mock amazement. "An Auschwitz man who isn't hungry! I'd go if I were you. It's goulash soup."

It was seven fifteen. Either the lorry was late or it was not coming at all. I decided I would slip in to see Andrej, have a quick soup, and then return. After all, I thought, it would not take a minute, and I might never see him again.

Inside Block Seven, I found he had a bowl of goulash soup that would last for several days. He poured me out a big dish and chatted as I ate it. Somehow, I answered him, though I had no idea of what I was saying, and as soon as I had finished, I mumbled my thanks and walked out quickly.

A registrar ran up to me. "Unglick's been looking for you every-where," he said. "He seemed to want to see you badly."

My stomach turned. That bowl of soup had cost me my freedom!

"Where is he?" I snapped. "Have they brought the wood to his block yet?"

"He was over there by Block Fourteen. Yes, the wood arrived. I saw them unloading it."

I ran to Block Fourteen. The wood was there, all right, but the lorry was gone. The lorry that was to take me through the gates in its toolbox. Quickly, I went to Unglick's room and hauled up the loose plank beneath which he had hidden the gold dollars and the diamonds. Frantically, my hand probed in the dust. The bag which had weighed two pounds and held a fortune was gone!

I felt sick, weak with disappointment, disillusionment, reaction. Back I wandered to Andrej Milar, but even his company was not much com-fort because, though he was a fellow Slovak, a fellow member of the underground and my block senior, I could not tell him of the escape bid, for an unwritten law of the camp outlawed all mention of this subject.

Somehow, I managed to hide my misery, or, at least, he did not seem to notice it. Again, I carried on an aimless conversation until about eight o'clock.

Then we were interrupted. From outside came the shout: "Block Senior Fourteen!"

That was Unglick! The SS were looking for him. The call was be-ing relayed from block to block…*"Block Senior Fourteen…Block Senior Fourteen…Block Senior Fourteen!"*

I walked out quickly. Andrej Milar followed me. Down by the gate, I could see a cluster of SS men—and high-ranking ones at that. SS Sturmbahnführer Schwarzhuber, Hoess's deputy in Birkenau and Aumeier's opposite number was there, a sure sign that something im-portant was happening. I hurried down to see what it was.

Monkey Tyn was standing rigidly to attention. Schwarzhuber said with searing sarcasm: "Haven't you located Block Senior Fourteen yet, Herr Lager Eldeste?"

Red in the face, Monkey Tyn made a funnel of his hands and bellowed once more: *"Block Senior Fourteen!"*

"You bloody idiot!" sneered Schwarzhuber softly. "Here he is!"

He stood back. I saw Unglick's body on the ground behind him. The face was stained with blood, and there was a dark, red bullet hole in the breast of the white pullover. The immaculate clothes were covered in mud, for they had dragged him from wherever they had killed him.

For fully a minute, I gazed at him. Then, in a complete daze, I wandered back to my block, to Block Seven. Everybody seemed very far away, and I was acting by reflex alone. My hand took up a spoon. I began eating the goulash soup, though I did not know it. I went on eating until suddenly I realized the pot was empty. I gazed at it, puzzled, then looked up at the others.

They were standing in a half circle around me. Their faces were hostile, and I could not understand why. Somehow it did not seem important anyway until Andrej Milar broke the silence.

"That soup was for five people," he said very quietly. "I don't mind you finishing it. I just wonder how you could touch it. You've just seen your best friend lying dead. Yet all you can think of is food. I never knew quite what to make of you until now. But now I know you're just an animal!"[3]

I started to explain but stopped myself in time. I was being misjudged, but there was absolutely nothing I could do about it except walk out of the block.

---

3   Five years later, I met Doctor Andrej Milar in the University of Slovakia, where he was teaching biology. By that time, he had heard the full story of Unglick, and he said, "I'm sorry. Since I last saw you, I've learned that people under great stress may suddenly start eating. Now I understand why you ate that goulash soup!"

Charles Unglick was already on display. They had put him on a stool and propped him up with a couple of spades. I stayed beside him for about half an hour; then I went back to the block, filled a bowl of water, and took it out. I soaked my handkerchief and gently wiped the blood and the mud away from the broad, powerful face. I talked to him as I worked, and when at last I went to my room, I knew at least that his face was clean, that some of the physical ignominy of his capture had been removed.

He was still there next day. In fact, he remained propped on his stool for forty-eight hours, and in that time, I learned what had happened. The SS man had driven straight to an empty garage, had unlocked the toolbox, and had shot him dead through the heart. After that, he had simply pocketed the fortune and reported that he had foiled a prisoner who was trying to escape.

The following day, four men came from the mortuary to take him away. The hierarchy of the camp gathered round, for he had to be stripped, and it was an Auschwitz tradition that clothes should be distributed to the living in order of seniority.

Monkey Tyn was there. So was Leon Sziwy, a Polish block senior. It was Sziwy who turned to me and said, "You take what you want. He was your best friend."

I could not speak.

Sziwy said, "What do you want? The boots?"

"I want the belt," I said. "Just the belt."

"Don't be crazy. Have what you like. How about the breeches?"

"I want the belt."

"For God's sake! Why not take the zipp on his pullover. It's a bloody fine zipp."

He bent over the body, cut the zipp away, and handed it to me. I shook my head, bent over Unglick, and unstrapped the belt that he had left me in his will three days before he died. I hauled it tightly around my waist and watched while the others made their choice.

At last, Unglick's body was quite naked. Quietly, I said to the men from the mortuary, "This is Charles Unglick. He has been in the camp a very long time."

They understood. We took him to the washroom and washed his body clean. Then we wrapped him in a blanket and put another blanket over him. The four men picked up their burden gently, and we walked slowly with them as far as the gate. It opened, and we watched the men who normally dragged naked bodies through the mud carry away Charles Unglick with something very like reverence.

Today, I still wear his belt. It is the only memento I have of Auschwitz-Birkenau. It is the only memento I want to have.[1]

---

4   In 1999, the author gave the belt to the Imperial War Museum, Holocaust Exhibition Project, London, UK. When reading a French copy of this book, Charles's family recognized their father and grandfather in the book and were very grateful they could learn about his last days. They were very proud of him. The family made a trip to London to see Charles Unglick's belt. --Eds.

CHAPTER 14
Escape

THE BETRAYAL OF CHARLES UNGLICK LEFT ME WITH EMO-
tions that were thoroughly scrambled. I knew bitter sadness because I had
lost a friend; brooding anger that smoldered into hate for the man who
had killed him; primitive, selfish relief that I had been spared by accident;
and, of course, the loneliness of a disappointment I could not share.

Of these, the disappointment concerned me least of all, for I
had known it already. Earlier, I had seen my own private escape plan
shattered, and the fact that the man who destroyed it was Camp
Commandant Rudolf Hoess himself did nothing to soften the blow.

It was a simple plan, and I literally stumbled across it by accident. One night, while I was running down the ramp carrying two
large suitcases and a rucksack from a transport, I tripped on a loose
plank and fell heavily. For a moment, I lay there. Then suddenly
I realized that through a gap in the plants I could see the ground
some ten feel below me, and as I scrambled to my feet, I thought for
an instant how wonderful it would be to slip through that crack and
for just a few minutes lie hidden beneath the ramp, away from the
guns, away from the wagons, away from the work and the misery
that was all around me.

The roar of an SS man shattered that pipe dream, and on I ran, up
and down, up and down for the rest of the night until every wagon was
empty and all the loot had been collected.

Yet, as I sagged into my bunk that night, that glimpse of a haven beneath the hell on the ramp kept creeping back to me, and as I thought of it, an idea took seed and began to grow.

First, I thought of the geographical position of the ramp. It lay between the mother camp of Auschwitz and Birkenau and was outside the outer perimeters of both. A man who could evade the SS men for a reasonable length of time might have a chance of getting away.

Like any sensible hare, I began to concentrate on the hounds, to plot their movements, to examine their defenses. When the train arrived, they surrounded it completely. We began unloading at one end, and as we worked our way down, the cordon tightened around us, getting smaller and smaller all the time. There was never any hope at any stage of getting through it.

Was there, however, any hope of ducking underneath it? Under the weight of a million feet, taking their last few steps before the gas chambers, the wood of the ramp was cracking. If a prisoner could rip up a plank and slip through quickly, he would be technically free; if he worked his way back beneath the ramp toward the end of the train, which was empty now and unguarded, he would be outside the cordon and could be really free.

Food and clothes would create no difficulty, for both were there for the taking. The only immediate problem would lie at the end of the ramp, when he emerged into the open. For all I knew, the SS might have thought of this loophole and might have stationed a guard at this weak spot, but, even so, this was something which could be solved fairly simply with the aid of a sharp knife.

I began studying the weak links in the ramp, the battered, loose planks which could be pulled up for a second and then jerked back into position. I noted their positions carefully and gradually became convinced that, given luck, I had a slight chance of succeeding. I even turned down the chance of a job as registrar in Birkenau rather than be removed from my escape hatch, and I had reached the stage where I was merely waiting for a suitable moment to make my break when my whole plan was wrecked.

Suddenly Commandant Hoess decided the ramp should be reinforced with concrete. Whether he did so because he spotted this flaw in his defenses or because he feared the whole affair might collapse, thus disrupting his crematorium service, I did not know. I merely knew that while I slept one day, hundreds of prisoners got to work, and when I went down for duty that night, all cracks had disappeared. With them went my hopes.

Yet I was not too disheartened. Probably because I was young and fit, I had developed the happy philosophy of the soldier who believes the man next to him may be killed but he will remain immune.

I accepted almost as an axiom that everyone else in the camp might die, but I believed I would escape, and I cannot remember ever relinquishing that faith, not even when I saw attempt after attempt end in failure and humiliating death.

There were times, of course, when I felt frustrated. Such was the discipline in the underground that I could not attempt an escape officially without their permission. From them, indeed, I was supposed to get my passport to freedom, and these travel documents were not issued liberally.

The reason for this was basically sound. Long before I thought of the idea, the underground had been concentrating on the problem of exposing Auschwitz, revealing its secrets and warning Europe's Jews of what deportation really meant. They were utterly unselfish about it and sought merely the right plan, the right moment, and the right man. When I approached them somewhat tentatively with my own schemes, indeed, they were far from enthusiastic. In the first place, they felt I was too impetuous to succeed, that only a man of wide experience and thorough discipline could make it, and secondly, they thought I was too young to convince the world of what was going on in the camp. Who, they argued, was going to listen to a boy of eighteen or nineteen? Civilized people would find it hard enough to believe the story, they said, even if it came from a mature adult, and to a degree they were right, for when my report after my escape reached London and Washington, both Churchill and Roosevelt found it difficult to accept at first that anyone could perpetrate such atrocities on such a grand scale.

Discussing escape, indeed, with anybody was almost impossible. It was regarded as a rude word not to be mentioned in company, for the Germans were by no means fools and had their agents planted everywhere. This, of course, made the whole project even more difficult, though in this respect, I was lucky. I had one friend, Fred Wetzler from my hometown Trnava, whom I could trust implicitly.

He occupied a unique position in the camp. He was popular with everybody, with the Germans, the ordinary prisoners, and the underground, even though he was not a member of it and never knew that I was all the time we were in the camp together. Unlike most of the other prisoners, he had absolutely no interest in politics, though this by no means indicated an indifference to people. Fred's heart may have been apolitical, but it was very large.

Because of his popularity, too, his contacts were varied, invariably useful, and inspired by genuine regard rather than by bribery. Many people confided in him, not merely because they liked him but because they trusted him, and so his knowledge of the camp was deep and wide.

It was this trust which he generated that led to a strange offer from an even stranger source.

One evening, I went to his barracks in Camp D to have a meal with him and found him sharing a bowl of potatoes with an SS man called Pestek, a particularly good-looking Unterscharführer who was about twenty-six years old. As soon as I came in, Fred said to his guest, "I'd like to have a word with my friend about this. Would you excuse us for a minute?"

The German inclined his head. Fred took me to another room and said, "Listen. This fellow has an extraordinary plan which might work. He wants to help me escape by dressing me up as a senior SS officer and marching with me through the gates. After that, he says, all we've got to do is get on a train for Prague."

"Don't be a fool, Fredo," I said sharply. "Remember Fero Langer. Remember Unglick. It's a trick."

"I don't think so," said Fred. "I know this lad. We've often eaten together—got drunk together, in fact. He's different from the others, one of the few decent SS men alive."

I respected Fred's judgment of people, but the twin pictures of Fero with half his face blown away and Charles Unglick, propped up on a stool with spades, was still vivid in my mind.

"No, Fred," I said. "It's not worth the risk. Langer and Dobrovolny were like brothers, and look what happened."

For quite a while, Fred pondered the situation. Then he went back to his room and said to the SS man, "Thanks, Pestek. But I don't think it would work. And if it failed, we're both as good as dead."

The German shrugged, glanced at me, and said, "Has Fred told you about the plan?"

I nodded.

"How about you, then? I'm sure we could get away with it."

"Why are you doing it? What are you going to get out of it? Why risk your career and your neck?"

"Because I hate this whole bloody setup," he said quietly. "Because I hate seeing women and kids murdered. I want to do something, anything, to get the smell out of my mind, to make myself feel a bit cleaner."

"But how do we get past the gate? Suppose someone starts asking me questions. There are a hundred snags."

"If someone speaks to you, you just jerk your head at me. You're an Oberstumbannführer, remember. I'm your aide. You don't waste your time with little men. You don't bark yourself when you've got a dog."

"But how about the train? What happens if someone starts talking to me there? What about the ticket collectors, the military police, the frontier checks."

"You'll be asleep. An Oberstumbannführer cannot be disturbed. Your *aide* will deal with all the mundane matters."

It was a daring plan, so simple that it could succeed. I thought it over for a while in silence, searching for flaws and finding none, but the ghosts of Fero and Charlo were still too close to me.

"Thanks for the offer," I said at last. "But I don't think it's worth the risk."

A few days later, Hugo Lenk, the old Inter Brigade man who had come with the second Czech Family Camp, said to me, "You know that SS man, Pestek? He's got a plan. He wants to smuggle me out of the place in the uniform of an SS officer. It sounds crazy, I suppose, but still…"

"I know all about it," I said. "He made the same offer to Fred Wetzler and then to me. He seems all right, if you can say that about any SS man, but there's something about the whole business that stinks. If you take my advice, you'll forget the whole idea."

He took my advice, but Pestek seemed to be determined to put his plan into action. He contacted a man called Lederer, a friend of Lenk's in the Czech camp, and Lederer agreed to go with him.

I do not know precisely when they left, but I remember the alarm siren wailing. I remember thinking to myself, He'll be back soon. With his brains blown out.

Lederer, however, did not come back. He traveled to Prague with Pestek in a first-class compartment. He is alive today, living in Czechoslovakia, and he owes his life to the only honorable SS man I ever met, a man I judged by his fellows and rejected; a man who had not been brainwashed, who saw the vileness that lay beneath those smart, green uniforms and had the courage to strike against it. In fact, he struck twice, though the second time it was for more selfish, less idealistic reasons.[1]

He had fallen in love with one of the girls in the Czech camp, just as I had myself, and, encouraged by his success with Lederer, he decided to go back to Auschwitz just once more in an attempt to smuggle her out.

It was a crazy idea, doomed to failure, for by that time he was a wanted man. Love, however, seldom knows logic, and apparently, he felt sure that she, too, could become an Oberstumbannführer for a day, if only she cut her hair.

He returned to the camp, to the scene of his crime, for this one last coup. A German professional criminal recognized him, raised the alarm, and Pestek was taken to Block Eleven, the Punishment Block.

We never saw him again, though we heard about him. Some days later, a brief message reached us by bush telegraph from the *Sonderkommando*. It said: "Pestek is in the ovens…what's left of him."

I think, perhaps, I felt more disappointment over the fact that I had not trusted Pestek than I had done over the failure of my earlier plans. It did not discourage me, however. With Fred, I continued to hope, to plan, to search for the slightest gap in the defenses of Auschwitz, and sometime later, he came to me with significant news.

"Four of the boys from the mortuary—the ones who took Unglick away, as a matter of fact—are going to make a break for it," he said, "and they need our help."

I knew these prisoners well. Because their job was collecting the dead, they could move fairly freely from subsection to subsection, and this gave them an immediate advantage when it came to escaping.

---

1 Lederer's unexpected disappearance from Birkenau on the same day that the author and Wetzler selected for their escape forced them to postpone their planned escape by two days. Lederer safely reached The Protectorate of Bohemia and Moravia (the area of former Czech lands), and repeatedly tried to warn Theresienstadt Jewry and attempted to send his own report to Geneva but was ignored. He lived in Czechoslovakia in oblivion, and his death went unnoticed. --Eds.

"You know the planks they've stacked for the new camp they're building?" Fred went on. I nodded. It was to be Birkenau Three, and it was being built parallel to Birkenau Two to accommodate the flood of Hungarians.

"Well, they've bribed some kapos to pile them so there is a cavity left in the middle. A hole big enough to hold the four of them."

I saw at once what they were trying to do. The planks were in the outer camp, which at night was undefended because all prisoners were securely behind the high-voltage wires and the watch towers of the inner camp. If they could remain hidden for three days while all the guards stood to and the place was searched, they had a good chance, for at the end of three days, it would be assumed that they had got beyond the confines of Auschwitz, and the job of finding them would be handed over to the authorities there. The guard which ringed the entire camp for those three days would be withdrawn, and they would merely have to wait until night before sneaking away past the unmanned outer watch towers.

"How can we help them?" I asked. "And why have they chosen us anyway?"

"Well, one of them is Sandor Eisenbach. He seems to like the pair of us, and he trusts us."

I smiled. Sandor Eisenbach! He was a Slovak, was a good deal older than I was, and knew my parents. Ever since we had met in the camp, indeed, he had kept a fatherly eye on me.

"All they want us to do," said Fred, "is keep them posted about what's happening in the camp while they're hiding and see that they're all right."

As registrars, Fred and I had a certain freedom of movement, too, so the four prisoners were not asking much. A few days later, the sirens went, and we watched anxiously as men and dogs began sweeping the camp. Several times, they ran past the wood pile, but they never seemed to think that the men they were seeking were crouched in a little room beneath the planks.

That evening, when the search was going on at some distance, I wandered casually over to the escape chamber and, without looking at it, said softly, "Can you hear me?"

"Yes."

The voice was faint but distinct. While I pretended to study some documents I was carrying, I said, "Everything's fine. They're over by the crematoria now. They've been past here a dozen times, but they've never even looked at the wood."

"Okay. Thanks."

Frowning at my papers as if they were presenting me with a terrible problem, I strolled back toward Camp D and reported to Fred that all was well.

The following day, the search was intensified. We took turns keeping the boys briefed, and by nightfall we knew that their chances were soaring, for by that time, most of the searchers would be convinced in their hearts that their quarries had got away. The third day and night, indeed, was more or less a formality, and on the fourth morning, when I talked softly beside the planks, there was no answer.

They were free! I felt a surge of exhilaration, not merely because they had got over the first hurdle but because they had left behind a perfectly good escape launching pad which could be used again. Fred and I talked it over that night and decided we would be the next to go under the planks, though we agreed it would be wise to let a fair period of time pass before we made any detailed plans. The four ex-prisoners still had a long way to go, and I thought of Captain Dmitri Volkov's last warning: "Remember...the fight only begins when you're away from the camp."

We decided, in fact, to let a fortnight pass before we took any action. By that time, we reckoned, they would be dead, captured, or safely hidden by friends, and as the days crept by, our optimism increased.

Nevertheless, we were careful not to be overoptimistic, and unfortunately, our caution was well justified. Just one week after I had made my last call to the pile of wood, there was excitement at the gates, and I saw the four men being marched through the camp, surrounded by grinning SS men.

I felt bitter with anger and sorrow. They had failed, which was bad enough, but now it was unlikely that Fred and I would have a chance to try. I felt sure that in Block Eleven, the secret of the escape route would be squeezed out of them slowly.

Yet, as they passed me, Sandor Eisenbach caught my eye and winked.

I knew what that slight flicker of an eyelid meant. The secret had not yet been revealed, though it was obvious from the cuts and bruises on their faces that already there had been a preliminary interrogation. Now they faced the serious business which would take place in Block Eleven.

The capture of the four men from the mortuary was not the only sensation in the camp that day. A few hours later, two French Jews, a kapo and his assistant, tried to escape and were caught almost immediately. They were carrying a loaf of bread in which they had hidden diamonds worth at least a million pounds, and they, too, went to Block Eleven.

This, we felt, was going to provide Hoess with a field day. Never in the history of the camp had he had six would-be escapers on his hands. Never had he had such an opportunity to impress on the other prisoners that crimes of this nature did not pay. Nobody was surprised a few days later when two mobile gallows were wheeled out and the SS paraded with their guns and their drums.

Sturmbahnführer Schwarzhuber gave the pre-execution address. He harangued us for a few minutes about what would happen to anyone who tried to follow in the footsteps of the six miserable men who stood before us, their hands tied behind their backs. He told us the value of the diamonds which had been stolen, and then, with apparent relish, he announced: "They will die on the gallows. But first they will receive fifty lashes!"

An SS man stepped forward, cat-o'-nine-tails in his hand. One by one, the prisoners bent over the flogging block, and for half an hour not a sound was heard except the thud of the thongs on flesh.

This, however, was only the overture, for the main theme was the hanging. The drums began to roll, and the two Frenchmen mounted the steps. The prisoner executioner worked swiftly. The traps slapped open, crashing against the sides of the platform, and the dreadful contorting began.

After a few minutes, the bodies hung limply. We waited for them to be taken down to make room for the next two victims, steeling ourselves for the spectacle to which we had never grown hardened, though we had seen it many times.

Nobody around the gallows moved, however. I heard an SS man give a sharp order, and then, to my amazement, I saw the four men who had escaped from the cavity being marched off toward the Punishment Block.

They were being spared for a while, but for what? For more torture? Did this mean the SS still did not know how they had escaped and were determined to find out? That night, Fred and I examined the riddle from every angle and came to the conclusion that our hopes were slender indeed. It was only a matter of time before our friends cracked, we felt, because the human frame, the human mind, can stand only so much, and the SS were experts when it came to torture.

A few days later, however, to my astonishment, they appeared on the camp again and not on the gallows. It is true that they went straight to the vicious Punishment Block, but they were still alive. Again, Fred and I tried to find a reason for this unprecedented reprieve, and this time we were really baffled.

Nevertheless, we were not long finding an answer to the question that really mattered: had they told about the cavity in the wood? The Punishment Command was isolated from the rest of the camp, but I soon was able to find an excuse to get into it.

I passed close to Sandor Eisenbach and, without looking at him, whispered, "Do they know about it?"

With the others, he was digging a ditch with his bare hands, piling the earth into his zebra cap. Without pausing or raising his head, he grunted, "No."

"Are you sure?"

"On your father's memory, I swear it. Take it from me, you'll be leaving soon."

He picked up his cap full of frozen earth and scampered away to dump it. I went back to Fred, elated, because I knew that I could rely completely on every word Sandor had said, and mixed with my elation was a feeling of awe at the strength of the man and of his three friends.

Next day, I saw him again to thank him. He muttered, "Don't be silly. But there's one way you can repay us."

"Sure. I'll do anything I can."

"We left a little memorial in the cavity. A message, scribbled on the planks. We signed it with our numbers, and if they ever find it, we're goners."

"I'll scrub it out as soon as I get inside. But what did you say in the message?"

"Kiss our arses!"

I smothered a laugh. Then I thought of the four of them, huddled in that little hole, listening to the SS boots pounding all round them, and I wondered whether my own sense of humor would survive so well when I was there.

"What went wrong?" I whispered. "How were you captured?"

"We ran into a military patrol outside Porebka. Steer clear of that place. It's not much of a town, but it's stinking with soldiers for some reason or other and festooned with barrage balloons."

Every scrap of information was needed urgently now, for Fred and I were almost ready to go. Our clothes—expensive Dutch suits and over-coats and heavy boots—had been delivered from the Canada Command departmental store. Our Russian tobacco had been soaked in petrol and dried. Most important of all, we had organized two Poles who would replace the planks over our heads as soon as we slid into the hole.

Finally, we chose the time and the date: two o'clock on the afternoon of April 3, 1944. Keeping this rendezvous was going to be our first hurdle, because though the four of us had reasonable freedom of movement, there could be a hundred snags to prevent us from arriving at the pile of wood simultaneously.

The first day, I had no trouble leaving Camp A. I told the SS man at the gate that I had to go to the crematorium, and he just said, "Bring me back a pair of socks." The Poles, too, both of whom worked in the mortuary, managed it, but Fred was missing, and that evening I learned that he had not dared leave his camp because it would have meant passing a particularly suspicious SS man at the gate.

On the second day, I had another trouble-free trip and another request for a pair of socks. This time, however one of the Poles was missing because his kapo had some special work for him to do—and so it went on for four days. Each time I had to return, despondently, to my camp and tell the SS man at the gate that I had forgotten his socks.

I began to worry a little, in fact, in case he might become suspicious, and certainly, my forgetfulness did nothing to improve his temper. On the fifth day, he growled, "If you don't bring me back those socks this time, you needn't bother coming back at all!"

I promised him faithfully that I would not forget him and walked away from the gate, hoping that his words would come true, though not in the way he meant.

In fact, I very nearly disappeared in a way which was in neither of our minds. As I walked toward the pile of wood, two SS men grabbed me, a pair of new Unterscharführers I had never met before.

"Well!" said one of them with a sneer. "What have we got here? A civilian—or a prisoner? Have you ever seen anything like this tailor's dummy before, Fritz?"

It is true that I looked remarkably like a prosperous Dutch gentleman. This, however, would not have worried a more experienced SS man, for he would have known that, as a registrar, I had a great deal of sartorial latitude. My elaborate outfit, indeed, would have been regarded merely as an eccentricity, for most of the SS knew me and thought of me as a permanent fixture in the camp.

To these two, however, I was an oddity, and I knew that their inexperience could mean death for me, for inside my shirt, pressing against my flesh, was the watch I had stolen for the journey. If they found it, I would be sent to the Punishment Block and hanged for "attempting to escape." Already I could almost hear Sturmbannführer Schwarzhuber intoning as he stood before the gallows: "Why should a prisoner have a watch unless he was trying to get away?"

They were still joking menacingly about me, and I knew that in a minute, when they had had their fun, they would start searching me. I thought of Fred and the Poles, waiting, and silently, I cursed my luck. This was the first time in my entire Auschwitz career that I had been held up in this way!

"I wonder, Hans," said the other SS man at last, "just what the gentleman has in his fine pockets? Shall we have a look?"

He plunged a hand into my overcoat pocket and drew out a fistful of loose cigarettes. He let them dribble through his fingers into the mud and said, "Just look at that, Hans! He must be a heavy smoker!"

They emptied out a hundred cigarettes that I had stowed away quickly at the last minute, and I waited for them to start searching in earnest. I wished, indeed, that they would get on with the job, for by that stage, I was certain I was lost. Sweat began trickling down my back, but somehow, I managed to keep my face expressionless, though I was seething with frustration.

Then suddenly, almost in a daze, I realized they had not opened my overcoat. Instead, they were standing back, staring at me.

"You cheeky bastard!" said Fritz softly, drawing back his thick bamboo stick and crashing it down on my shoulder. "I'll teach you to act the gentleman around here."

The stick thumped again, and I staggered slightly.

"I'll teach you to walk around like a dressed-up monkey. I'll teach you to smuggle cigarettes that you have robbed. Take his number, Hans, because it's obviously time that Mr. Bloody Registrar here saw what the inside of Block Eleven looks like."

Over his shoulder, I saw the two Poles walking by. Their expressions did not change as they spotted me in the hands of the SS men, but their faces went pale. Suddenly, Fritz lashed me full in the face and said, "C'mon, you bastard, get going! Get out of my sight!"

My mind was wobbling all over the place with pain, with depression, with rage.

"But Block Eleven, Herr Scharführer," I stammered. "I thought you said…"

"Not now, you idiot! I've better things to do than march a louse like you around the place. I'm reporting you to the Political Department, and they can pick you up after roll call. Now get back to your section before I break your neck!"

For a split second, I stared at him, round-eyed. I was not under arrest! He was not going to search me anymore! I sped away without another word, running for my section gate, and as soon as I was out of sight, I twisted to the left and strolled casually toward my little log cabin.

I still had plenty of time to keep my appointment, but before I reached the pile of wood, there was another delay, this time one which was irritating rather than dangerous. I ran into Unterscharführer Otto

Graff, who once—it seemed years ago—had persecuted me in Canada. Now, however, he was working with the *Sonderkommando*.

Because I knew the eyes of other SS men could be watching me, I whipped off my cap and stood rigidly to attention. Otto grinned and said, "Well, you old swine, how are you?"

I cursed inwardly, for obviously he wanted to chat, and replied, "Fine, Herr Unterscharführer, and how's life with you?"

"I've been working all bloody night," he said with a grimace. "A damn sight harder than you, probably. In fact, I can hardly keep my eyes open."

"I'm sorry for you," I said with a forced grin, "but after all, there's a war on."

"Too true!" he sighed. "Here—have a Greek cigarette. They're better than nothing."

I knew then why he had been working so hard. There had been a big transport from Greece.

"No thanks," I said. "I never touch them. They're bad for my throat!"

"You fussy bastard!" he said with a laugh. "As cheeky as ever! Well…I'll be seeing you!"

He wandered off, and somehow, I felt it was almost symbolic that the handsome, brutal Otto should be the last person to whom I was to speak in the camp.[2]

I could see the wood now and the Poles on top of it, apparently working. Fred was there, too, and the three of them gaped a little when they saw me, for they felt sure I was already in the Punishment Block.

---

2   Otto Graff was the last person with whom the author spoke to in the camp, but it was not the last time they saw each other. After the war, Otto Graff—SS Unterscharführer—lived unmolested under his own name in Vienna, working as a painter of houses. In 1963, the author heard about it and started criminal proceedings against him. Graff was arrested only nine years later and charged with thirty cases of criminal acts in Auschwitz (the author was also a witness for the prosecution). Although found guilty on twenty-nine charges, he was released due to the statute of limitation. The thirtieth charge was murder; the jury was split in its decision, and in such cases in Austrian law, it is decided in favor of the defendant. --Eds.

Nobody spoke, however. The Poles moved the planks and gave us an almost imperceptible nod.

This was it. For a moment, we both hesitated, for we knew that once we were covered up, there was no going back. Then together we skipped quickly up on top of the wood and slid into the hole. The planks moved into place over our heads, blotting out the light, and there was silence.

Our eyes soon got used to the gloom, and we could see each other in the light that filtered through the cracks. We hardly dared to breathe, let alone talk. It was fifteen minutes, in fact, before we relaxed a little, and then I began examining the walls of our home carefully.

"What's the matter?" whispered Fredo so gently I could barely hear him. "What are you doing?"

"Looking for Sandor's message," I said. "We can't have dirty words written on the wall!"

I found it and scraped it off with my knife. Somehow, the task soothed my nerves, and I decided I must work instead of think. I took out my powdery Russian tobacco and began puffing it into the narrow spaces which separated some of the planks while Fredo sat, watching me in the gloom.

It took me at least an hour to impregnate our temporary prison thoroughly with dog repellant. Then I sat down; leaned against the rough, wooden wall; and concentrated on some positive thinking. I forced my mind away from all thoughts of discovery and told myself over and over again: There'll be no more roll calls. No more work. No more kowtowing to SS men. Soon you'll be free!

Free—or dead. I felt the keen blade of my knife and swore to myself that if they found me, they would never get me out of the cavity alive.

Time stood still. I glanced at the watch which had nearly cost me my life and saw it was only half past three. The alarm would not be raised until five thirty, and suddenly I realized I was longing to hear it. I felt like a boxer, sitting in his corner, waiting for the bell, or like a soldier in the trenches, waiting to go over the top.

I feared the wail of that siren. Yet I could not bear the waiting. I wanted the battle to begin.

We could not stand up and became cramped sitting. We did not dare to talk, and that made time hang even more heavily. The movements of the camp, movements we both knew by heart, drifted faintly into our hole in the wood, but somehow it all seemed far away in time, as well as in distance, for already my mind was free in advance of my body.

For the next hour, I kept glancing at my watch, holding it to my ear occasionally to see whether it had stopped. Then I disciplined myself to ignore it, grinning in the dark as I thought fatuously of my mother in her kitchen back home, shaking her finger at me and saying solemnly, "A watched pot never boils!"

In fact, it was never necessary for me to look at my watch, for the noises in the camp outside told me roughly what time it was. At last, after what seemed a week, I heard the tramp of marching feet, and at once every fiber was alert. The prisoners were coming back from work. Soon they would be lining up in their neat rows of ten for roll call. Soon we would be missed, and then there would be the siren, the baying of the dogs, the clatter of SS jackboots.

We heard the distant orders, faint, disembodied, like lonely barking at night. We saw in our minds the entire scene which would never be part of our lives again. The rigid rows of the living. The silent piles of the dead. The kapos and block leaders, snapping at their charges, fussing, panicking. The SS, aloof, superior, totting up their units.

I thought of my own block leader, Doctor Andrej Milar, and wondered how he would react. Since I had shocked him by eating the goulash soup the night Charles Unglick died, our friendship had cooled a little, but I knew that he would wish me luck, that he would want me to get away. I thought of Monkey Tyn, scampering to the SS to report that his registrar, who everyone thought was built into the bricks of Auschwitz, was missing. I thought of what lay ahead, and suddenly, I realized that if everything went well, I would be free on April 10.

I permitted myself the luxury of a glance at my watch. It was five twenty-five. Five minutes from siren time. Already, they must have missed us. Already, they must be debating what to do, whether we had been delayed somehow or whether we had escaped, whether they should raise the alarm and risk ridicule if we turned up, or whether they should wait and risk the rage of Hoess and Schwarzhuber if it turned out we had gone.

Five thirty. And silence. Fredo and I stared at each other, and though we did not speak, we shared the same thoughts. Five forty-five, and still not a sound. I felt a tremor of panic, for this was ominous. It could mean big trouble—the end, in fact.

Someone, for instance, could have squealed. In a few minutes, perhaps, we would hear the planks being dragged back and see the muzzles of submachine guns. Instinctively, my grip tightened on my knife, and I strained my ears for some sound, any sound that might give me a hint of what was going on.

Six o'clock. The silence was torturing our nerves now. I whispered to Fred, "They're toying with us, playing with us. They must know where we are."

He said nothing, but I knew he agreed with me. Someone walked by. We both froze and held our breath. The footsteps faded in the distance. We heard voices, German voices, but they were too far away for us to understand what was being said. The walls of our wooden home seemed to grow smaller, pressing in on us, crushing our minds, our morale, wrapping us up in a neat little box that would be handed over with mock ceremony to some sneering Oberscharführer. I heard the drums. I saw the notices: "Because they tried to escape…" My mind squirmed at the humiliation of it, recoiling from the jeers and the laughter and the smug triumph that would greet our capture.

Then the siren split my thoughts asunder, scattering them, pulverizing them, whisking away fear, sweeping the cavity clean of depression, thrusting a challenge into my heart and into my mind.

The wail rose triumphantly to its thin apex, clung there for a few minutes, then died sadly. I could see Fred's eyes gleaming, and I could hear chaos being born, maturing, pounding all around us. A hundred, two hundred, five hundred feet beat a tattoo. A thousand voices shouted, and two thousand answered them. Orders ricocheted from barracks to barracks, and the dogs gave anxious, plaintive tongue.

The search was on. The long, meticulous, painstaking search that would continue for three days until every inch of Birkenau had been examined, every known hiding place upended. We felt something very near to exhilaration as we heard it drawing near and visualized the scene we knew so well.

The voices were close now. I heard Unterscharführer Buntrock rasp, "Look behind those planks! You're supposed to be searching this place, not taking the air. For Chrissake, use your heads as well as your eyes!"

Boots scrabbled up over the planks above us, sending a little shower of grit down on top of us. The pounding raised the dust and we covered our noses in case we sneezed. More boots and the heavy breathing of men. Then the dogs, snuffling, panting, their nails scraping the wood as they slithered and tumbled from plank to plank. My knife was out, and I could see Fred poised, his teeth clenched in a smile of tense anticipation.

Then the cacophony faded. Distance mellowed the grating discord, and silence filled our hideout, a silence that carried with it a strange sense of security. We had won the first round. Our nerves had been hacked against the wooden walls, and they had not failed us.

The viciousness seeped out of Fred's grin. He winked at me and said, "The stupid bastards!"

Soon, of course, they were back, sweeping ground already swept, scraping in corners, probing a little more desperately now. Again, we heard the boots; again, the dogs and the exasperated curses of frustrated men.

So it went on all through the night, the noises rising and falling, fading, returning, reverberating around us. We had bread and margarine, but we could not bring ourselves to eat; wine, but we could not drink. Even when the searchers moved away, we dozed, but we did not rest, for our minds chased the fantasies of dreams, then were jerked back to the reality of our twilight by noises we had never noticed before.

We could hear the sentries on the outer ring being checked, passwords being exchanged. Then the lorries began roaring by, forty, fifty, sixty of them on their way to the gas chambers with their victims, for outside our wooden walls, it was business as usual in Birkenau. We thought of them, filing quietly into the "showers," and after an hour or two, we heard the harsh clanking of the iron grills as they rattled into the ovens with load after load of dead flesh, twisted, and sent it cascading into the flames.

It was a monotonous sound, a sinister sound, yet it was a challenge to us, for we knew that only by escaping successfully could we do anything to silence it.

The second day was a crucial period. The camp authorities knew that time was against them now and were whipping their men on mercilessly. They swirled around us and over us. The voices were harsh and strained, the intervals of silence shorter, and as the tension increased outside, it filtered through to us in a gross, distorted fashion because we could not see what was happening. Our nerves were frayed and hypersensitive, and our stomachs were knotted with strain. Again, we could neither eat nor drink, though we had had neither food nor liquid for over twenty-four hours.

Night brought no relief. The stumbling, hurrying men kept rumbling overhead, and it was only with the dawn that the pressure seemed to ease.

"Just a day and a half more," said Fred. "And it shouldn't be too bad. By now, they must be sure we're miles away."

In a way, he was right, for this third day was more relaxed, the quietest we had known, in fact. In another way, however, he was very wrong.

At about two o'clock that afternoon, we heard two German prisoners talking outside. One said, "They can't have got away. They must be in the camp still."

For a while, they swapped wild theories about where we might be hiding. Then the second prisoner said, "Otto...how about that pile of wood? Do you think they might be hiding under there somehow? Maybe they built themselves a little alcove or something."

"The dogs have been over it a dozen times," said Otto. "They'd have smelled them...unless, of course, they've some way of killing the scent."

There was a long silence. Fred and I crouched motionless and heard Otto say slowly, "It's a long shot...but it's worth trying. C'mon!"

We heard them climbing onto the pile of wood, and we drew our knives. They heaved one plank aside, then a second, a third, a fourth. Only about six inches of wood separated us from the enemy now, and we stood poised to lunge, not daring to breathe. I braced my back against one wooden wall, crouching because there was not room to stand.

Suddenly there was uproar on the other side of the camp. We could hear excited shouts and the quick patter of scurrying feet. The two Germans above us were silent now and motionless. Then Otto said, "They've got them! C'mon...hurry!"

They slithered off the planks and dashed off to answer a false alarm that had saved our skins.

"One thing about Auschwitz," muttered Fred bitterly. "You meet a nice class of person. The dirty swine!"

On the night of April 9, we had a shock of a different nature. At about eight o'clock, we suddenly heard the distant rumble of heavy aircraft, something which we had never known in all the time we had been in Auschwitz. They came closer and closer; then bombs began to crunch not far away.

Our pulses quickened. Were they going to bomb the camp? Was the secret out? Were high explosives going to rip away the high-tension wires and the watch towers and the guards with their dogs? Was this the end of Auschwitz?[3]

The explosions were nearer now, heavier. Then suddenly, almost beside us, it seemed, there was a new sound—the harsh, urgent crash of anti-aircraft fire from guns on the camp itself. The planks trembled with every salvo. Grit tumbled around us, and as the flashes lit up the cavity, I said to Fred, "What about it? Will we make a break? They won't see us in all this chaos."

Fred, however, was less impetuous. He said, "No. We'll sit tight. Those boys out there are soldiers, remember. Bombs or no bombs, the fellows ringing the camp and manning the watch towers will stick to their job, and that's catching us!"

He was right, of course, but at least that air raid served one purpose. The thunder of guns and bombs gave us cover to talk in tones that were almost normal. In fact, we were sorry when the planes droned away and we could again hear the clank of the grills.

---

3   Auschwitz was not bombed that day. The author in a letter to the scholar David S. Wyman, dated December 8, 1976, clarified: "What I heard was a bombing somewhere in the vicinity. Also, I was very close at that time to anti-aircraft artillery located directly in the perimeter of the camp, and from my position, the tremors caused by artillery fires could well be mistaken for bombs." Franklin D. Roosevelt Presidential Library, Vrba's Collection, box 7. --Eds.

The last twenty-four hours passed quietly enough. The search went on, but there was little heart left in it. The hours creaked by, and our tension rose as we waited for the signal which for us meant action, for the dismissal of the outer cordon.

We knew just how it would happen. An SS man would take the order to the nearest watch tower. It would be shouted from tower to tower, circling the camp, an admission of temporary defeat. The towers would empty. The guards would march back to the camp. The coast would be comparatively clear.

Then we heard it, the first sing-song shout: *"Postenkette abziehen!"*

"Cordon down!" The shout seemed to echo as it was taken up from tower to tower. It grew fainter and fainter until we could hear it no more, but soon we picked it up again as it completed its circle of the camp. It grew louder and louder as it came nearer, and then at last it stopped.

It was six thirty on April 10, 1944. We heard the tramp of marching feet, then nothing more except the drone of mild activity in Birkenau. Officially, we were out!

Yet still we did not move, for isolation had magnified our suspicions and our fears. I said to Fred, "We'd better wait a while. It could be a trick. They could be foxing, just waiting for us to show ourselves."

So, we waited. Seven o'clock came…eight…nine. Without a word, we stood up simultaneously and began pressing cautiously against the wooden planks that formed our roof.

Then a moment of panic. They would not move!

Grunting, straining, sweating, we used every ounce of our combined strength. Gradually, almost painfully, the planks rose an inch and now we could grip their rough edges. We heaved them sideways, and suddenly we could see stars above us in the black, winter, moonless sky.

"Thanks be to God those bloody Germans nearly found us!" whispered Fred. "If they hadn't moved those other planks, we'd have been trapped!"

We scrambled out into the cold air and replaced the planks carefully in case someone else might be able to use the escape chamber later, and for a moment we sat on the pile of wood, motionless, invisible, gazing at the inner camp, which we were determined never to see again.

For the first time, I was seeing Auschwitz from the outside, viewing it as its victims viewed it. The brilliant lights painted a soft yellow patch in the darkness, giving the whole place a mysterious aura that was almost beautiful. We, however, knew that it was a terrible beauty, that in those barracks, people were dying, people were starving, people were intriguing, and murder lurked around every corner.

We turned our backs to it, slid to the ground, flung ourselves flat, and began to crawl slowly on our bellies, foot by careful foot, away from the toothless watch towers and toward the small forest of birch trees that hid the old-fashioned pits of fire and gave Birkenau its name. We reached it, rose, and ran, stooping, through it until we came to open ground again and began to crawl once more.

As I wriggled forward, I remembered Dmitri Volkov. The battle was just beginning.

I remembered something else he'd said, too. Beware of mines.

This was a chance we just had to take, for it was dark, and if we did not keep going, the dawn would catch us in the open. We moved on, and then, when we least expected it, we came to an entirely unexpected obstacle.

At first, I thought it was a river. It was about eight yards wide, a whitish ribbon stretching as far as I could see on either side. I knelt to examine it, put down my hand and found sand...yard after yard of smooth white sand which presumably surrounded the entire Auschwitz-Birkenau camp. It was worse than water, for once we trod on it, our footsteps would be arrows for the patrols to follow as soon as it was light. As I gazed at it, in fact, I realized it could be even more menacing than it seemed. It could easily conceal the mines of which Dmitri Volkov had spoken.

Nevertheless, that was another risk we had to take. Together, we plunged across the miniature desert and found ourselves on open moor land, thick with bracken. Here and there were sign posts which I thought might be warnings about mines, but it was too dark to read them and too risky to strike a match. So, we just kept walking steadily until at last we could see the outline of another forest ahead of us just as the sky began to lighten. We quickened our pace instinctively because we had no cover, though I paused for a moment close to one of the signposts to see what it said.

I read: "Attention! This is Auschwitz Concentration Camp. Anyone found on these moors will be shot without warning!"

We were still within the confines of the camp, and the forest seemed just as far away. By the time it was quite light, in fact, we were still exposed. The moor had ended, giving way to a field of young corn. We paused to get our bearings, glanced around quickly, and flung ourselves to the ground.

Five hundred yards away, we could see a band of women prisoners, heavily escorted by SS men!

For a moment, we lay there, panting. Then, cautiously, we raised our heads. The column was on its way to work somewhere, and obviously, they had not seen us.

Nevertheless, we did not dare to stand up. Instead, we wriggled along on our bellies, making use of every hollow, every dip, every ditch we could find. To hurry would have been madness, and it was another two hours before we reached the safety of the trees.

We rested briefly, then pushed on through the thick firs. The green umbrella soothed our taut nerves—until suddenly we heard voices: the voices of dozens of children.

We plunged behind some bushes, peered cautiously through the heavy branches, and saw a huge party of Hitler Youth making their way through the forest, rucksacks on their backs. To our horror, they sat down beneath the trees less than thirty yards away and began to eat sandwiches. We were trapped, not by the SS this time, but by their children!

We must have lain behind that bush for an hour, but then our luck changed dramatically. Heavy drops of rain began to fall. The Hitler Youth glanced up and went on eating, but the shower became a downpour, and at last they rose and scampered off, squealing at one another.

We resumed our march. The ground was soggy beneath our feet, but our boots were strong. The rain beat down through the trees onto our bare heads, but it could not penetrate our fine Dutch overcoats. We felt almost happy as we ploughed on, and not even the sight of an SS patrol with another band of women prisoners could depress us. We simply hid in a ditch until they had passed out of sight.

At last, I said to Fred, "It's time we slept. Let's find somewhere to hide, somewhere that not even the SS would bring women."

For half an hour, we searched until we found a large clump of bushes. We wormed our way into the center and lay down in the bracken, confident we could not be seen.

A watery April sun filtered through the branches. The more enthusiastic birds twittered over our heads, and Fred lectured me amiably on the finer points of chess until we fell asleep. He was an expert. The champion of Auschwitz, in fact, and I am glad to say that he retired, unbeaten.

AUSCHWITZ II (Birkenau)

With Wetzler and Vrba's working places in Birkenau and their hiding place used for the escape

yards
0   200   400

0   200   400
metres

woods

pits for
burning
bodies

woods

B III

"Mexico"
camp extension under construction

"Mexico" - approximate
location of Vrba and
Wetzler's hiding place

S.S. guard
dog kennels

S.S. barracks

Gas Chamber and
Crematorium V

Gas Chamber and
Crematorium IV

← road to Gas Chambers IV and V

Camp
Commandant

"Canada"

B IIf   B IIe   B IId   B IIc   B IIb   B IIa

Gypsy   men's   men's   family
camp   camp   camp   camp

quarantine
camp

Gravel Pit -
approximate position
of Mordowicz and
Rosin's bunker

"Sauna"
bathhouse

perimeter fence

road to Gas
Chambers IV
and V

Vrba's office in
Quarantine Camp
June 1943 –
April 1944

to Auschwitz

birch   wood

Gas Chamber and
Crematorium III

Main Gate

rail spur built
spring 1944

Gas Chamber and
Crematorium II

women's camp   women's camp

New ramp built in
early 1944 for
anticipated arrival
of Hungarian Jews

Mortuary -
Wetzler's
office

B Ib   perimeter fence   B Ia

Potato
Store

B Ib - men's
section until
June 1943

B IId - main camp for men
Wetzler was Schreiber in
Block 24.

In mid-January 1943, the Canada workforce
was moved from Auschwitz I to Birkenau;
Vrba resided in this Block until June 1943.

© Sir Martin Gilbert 2009

Reproduced by permission from *Routledge Atlas of the Holocaust*, Fourth Edition,
Taylor & Francis Books UK, *http://www.martingilbert.com*

Specific notes regarding Vrba and Wetzler added by Nikola Zimring, Rudolf Vrba Archives, LLC 2018.

CHAPTER 15
Hiding Out

———

THE SLOVAK BORDER IS ABOUT EIGHTY MILES FROM Auschwitz as the crow flies. Unfortunately, Fred and I were only Jews, which meant we had to walk, and the road which lay ahead ran through dangerous country.

All Germans, military and civilian alike, had orders to shoot obvious strangers on sight. The Poles had been told clearly that they and their families would be shot if they helped escaping prisoners, and many, indeed, paid this penalty. So, even if we made no mistakes, those eighty miles prickled with hazards, and we were far from infallible.

In fact, the night after Fred had lulled me to sleep with his talk of knights and bishops and castles, we excelled ourselves. It was pitch dark, and we wandered right into the outer confines of a concentration camp!

We saw the empty watch towers, the shadowy outlines of huts, and all the paraphernalia of work, and though we tried desperately to find our way out of this threatening, frightening maze, our steps kept leading us back to the type of surroundings which we knew only too well and from which we had risked our lives to escape.

Our knowledge of camp routine, far from helping us, merely put an extra strain on our nerves. We knew the watch towers would be manned as soon as it was light and that we would be caught on flat, open ground. Yet, because we did not know the plan of the camp, we might as well have been innocents straight from home.

So, we simply had to blunder on in the hope that we would find some sign that would lead us to safety, and just as the sky was turning from black to dark gray, I spotted what looked like a wood, which I knew must be outside the camp boundaries. We reached it safely, came across a clump of large bushes, disappeared into the interior, and covered ourselves with leafy branches which we broke from the trees.

After that, we relaxed a little, feeling if not secure, at least more comfortable than we had been in the shadow of the watch towers, but as the sun eased itself into the sky, it chased away any confidence we might have had.

We were not in a wood. We were in a public park, and as the morning grew older, we saw it was a very special park, indeed, one used by SS men with their girlfriends, wives, or children. From our pathetic little bower, we watched them strolling around in their green uniforms, relaxing, resting from their labors among the wicked enemies of the Reich.

Some had dogs which snuffled and bounded everywhere, and these worried us so much that we overlooked even more dangerous animals—the children. They bounced, laughing and squealing, past our hideout, and we ignored them, until we saw to our horror that a little boy and a little girl were bearing straight down upon us. Fifteen paces behind them strolled an Oberscharführer in uniform, pistol at his belt, plump, blond wife on his arm.

We held our breath. The children danced to and fro, like fireflies, approaching our bushes, veering away, returning, playing violent discords on our nerves, but at last the awful inevitable happened, and we found ourselves gazing into two pairs of round, unblinking, blue, Aryan eyes. We saw two mouths form incredulous circles, and then came the cries.

"Papa...Papa...come here...there are men in the bushes...funny men."

Fred and I had our knives out now. We saw Papa's head jerk up and a frown sweep away his indulgent smile. He strode over toward the bushes and gazed down upon us for fully ten seconds. We gazed back, ready to lunge. Then we saw the amazement fade from his eyes and in its place came an expression of cold understanding. Quickly, he gathered his chicks under his wing and swept them away from the scene.

We watched them disappear. The Oberscharführer was talking earnestly to his wife, and she was looking suitably shocked. After all, things had come to a pretty pass when a respectable German hausfrau could not take her children for a walk in a public park without finding men lying together in the bushes!

This slight upon our morals, however, saved our lives. We remained in the bushes, undisturbed, for the rest of the day, and as soon as it was dark again, we continued our journey, traveling slowly, carefully, for Volkov had warned me that haste inevitably led to death.

Though Volkov's advice was useful constantly, he had never managed to teach me how to see in the dark, and in spite of the fact that we were learning rapidly from experience, we got lost again on the fifth day of our journey.

We were heading for the Bezkyd Mountains, a group adjoining the Tatras and spanning the frontier. When we saw the lights of what we felt must be the town of Bielsko in the distance, we knew we were going in the right direction. We were correct, but unfortunately, when the lights went out, we lost our bearings, and instead of skirting the town, we ambled right into the center of the place.

One moment, it seemed, we were in the heart of the country, moving smoothly; the next, we were threading our way through streets with tall buildings frowning down upon us. We tried to retrace our steps, to abandon unwelcome civilization, but those buildings kept following us, and we both knew we could run into a patrol of armed militia men at any moment.

Still, we managed to keep cool and, as dawn was breaking, disentangled ourselves from Bielsko. That did not mean, however, that we transferred ourselves immediately to the safety of the fields, but rather that we moved from major to comparatively minor danger, from Bielsko to the village of Pisarovice. By that time, it was quite light, and we knew we could travel no farther.

Here, indeed, was a considerable crisis. It would be madness to try and get out of the village without being seen. That meant we would have to seek help. For the first time since our escape, we would have to speak to people and, even more frightening, to trust them.

We might knock on a German door. Even if we struck lucky, however, and found a Polish house, which was, of course, more likely, we could not blame the occupier if he turned us away. After all, by harboring us, two total strangers, he was risking not only his own life, but those of his wife and his children.

Nevertheless, it had to be done. We chose a house more or less at random. As we made our way round to the yard at the back, chickens darted around our feet, and somewhere, a goose honked indignantly. An old woman dressed in the voluminous black frock and white head scarf of a Polish peasant came to the door, and we could see the worried face of a girl of about eighteen behind her.

In our best Polish, we greeted her in traditional fashion: "Praise be to the name of Christ."

"May His name be praised forever, amen," she intoned. "Please come in, gentlemen."

We went into a large kitchen with a stone floor and felt reasonably confident. The old lady was not stupid. She knew that our fine clothes were stolen, that we were on the run, for otherwise we would not be calling at her humble home.

Yet the calm dignity of her eyes, the proud tilt of her head convinced us that she would not betray us to the Germans, and this she tried to convey to us immediately, if indirectly.

"I'm afraid my Russian is not very good," she said, "but you speak Polish well. Now you must be hungry."

She turned to the girl, who had yet to speak, but whose wide eyes had never left us, and said, "Maria, get some breakfast for our guests."

Obviously, she thought we must be Soviet soldiers who had escaped from some POW camp, and though she must have been afraid, she certainly did not panic. Indeed, as we sat down gratefully to a meal of coffee and potatoes which Maria set before us, she lectured us calmly on local conditions.

"The mountains are quite far from here," she said. "To reach them, you must cross open country which is watched constantly by the Germans because there are partisans in the area. If you attempt to cross those open spaces by day, you will be caught; you must stay here until it is dark. If my sons were here, they might be able to give you more help, but one is dead and the other is in some concentration camp, and so you will have to rely on my poor advice."

We thanked her sincerely and then leaped to our feet as the door opened. The old lady smiled and said, "Don't worry. It is an old friend of mine."

An elderly man, smoking an even more elderly pipe, pottered into the big kitchen and bade us good morning as if strangers wearing obviously foreign clothes were seen every day in the village.

"You've come at the right time, boys," he said. "There's a pile of wood in the back that needs to be chopped. Perhaps you could help us out."

We agreed immediately, took off our heavy coats, and got down to work. At about one o'clock, the girl came to us timidly and summoned us in to a meal of potato soup and potatoes. After that, we finished chopping the wood and then we went into the house and promptly fell asleep.

It was three o'clock in the morning when I felt someone shaking my shoulder. I was on my feet immediately, but saw in the gloom that it was the old lady.

"I'm sorry if I gave you a fright," she said with a smile, "but it's time for you to go. Wake up your friend and have some coffee."

I woke Fred, and we drove the sleep out of our systems by swallowing down two or three cups of hot, ersatz coffee from a jug which the old lady had brought us. She watched us, her sad smile reflecting concern for us rather than for herself. Then, quickly, she pressed four marks, about a pound, into my hand and said, "Take this. You have worked hard all day."

For two reasons, I did not want to take her money. In the first place, I felt we owed her much more than she did us. Secondly, I was thinking of Volkov's cardinal rule—take no money or you'll be tempted to spend it—and was determined not to break it.

"Thank you," I said gently, "but we don't want money. We don't need it. You've been kind enough already, and we were only too glad to help in any way we could."

"Please take it," she pleaded. "Just for luck."

Reluctantly, I shoved it in my pocket. For her, it was a lot of money—more, I knew, than she could afford. I felt, however, that perhaps she was thinking of her two sons, one who was dead and the other who was in some camp—perhaps, indeed, Auschwitz. We thanked her again, set off in the darkness, and within three hours reached the mountains which were flecked with snow.

Our progress was slower now. In another two days, however, ten days after we had left our wooden hideout, we reached the halfway mark on our journey. It was encouraging, though the landmark by which we were able to pinpoint our position made us feel uneasy. It was the town of Porebka, where Sandor Eisenbach and his three friends had been captured. We saw it nestling in a valley below us with fat, gray barrage balloons lowering sullenly in the sky above it, and Sandor's ominous words came back to us.

"Steer clear of Porebka....It's stinking with soldiers."

We decided to take his advice, though those marks were burning in my pocket now, begging to be spent, and as we lay down to rest on a hillside, we felt both proud and smug that we had resisted temptation.

We did not realize, however, that the stink was not confined to the town of Porebka. It spread up the mountainside. As we lay back with our eyes closed, a rifle cracked and a bullet sang over our heads.

In a flash, we were on our feet. Seventy yards away on another hill was a German patrol with dogs. We ran, scrambling, stumbling up our hill through the snow. If we could reach the top and disappear into the valley on the other side, we had a chance, but we had to cover that ground under fire, and the Germans were blazing away accurately.

Fred was ahead of me. He reached the safety of a huge rock and flung himself behind it. I drove myself after him, tripped, and fell flat. The rock was only a few yards away, but it might as well have been a million miles, for the bullets were buzzing like bees around me now, chipping the shale and the boulders. I pressed my face into the ground and lay quite still.

I was not playing possum. For a moment, I was simply too scared to move, and that twinge of fear, of panic saved my life. In the crisp, clean air of the mountainside, I heard the order, loud and clear: "We've got him! Cease fire!"

They began slithering down the hillside. I leaped up, flung off my overcoat, and hurled myself toward the safety of the rock. Another shout, and the firing began again, but by that time, I was hidden.

"C'mon!" snapped Fred. "Head for the trees!"

Halfway up the hill that lay ahead was a small wood, but at the bottom of the valley was a wide, fast-moving stream. We careened toward it, urged on by the baying of the dogs, plunged into the icy water, and struggled toward the bank. The cold bit into our marrow. The flow snatched at our heavy clothes. Twice I fell and submerged, but at last we made it, hauled ourselves up the bank, and lumbered on, gasping for breath, through snow that sometimes reached our waists.

We reached the friendly shelter of the trees before the Germans had breasted the hill, and now the advantage was with us. The stream would puzzle the dogs, and the delay would give us time to lose ourselves. On we went, zigzagging through the tall firs until we could hear no more baying, and then we fell, exhausted, into a ditch that was rich with bracken and bushes.

For an hour, we lay there, our ears straining for the slightest sound, but all we heard was the rustle of melting snow as it tumbled through the trees and the intimate whispering of the wood's secret life.

After that scare, we pressed on fast, sure that soon we would be out of Poland. We kept to the most desolate tracks, for the thought of a last-ditch capture was unbearable and people were dangerous—sometimes deliberately, sometimes by accident—but dangerous nevertheless. Yet people, unfortunately, have a habit of appearing in the most unlikely places, and a day later, as we worked our way through a field, we stumbled across an old Polish peasant woman.

For quite a while, we stood in silence, gazing at one another, trying to assess the situation. The old woman showed no fear, but she knew we meant trouble, that we were on the run. If she helped us, the Germans might kill her. If she did not help us, we might kill her. It was as simple as that.

At last I said, "We're heading for the Slovak border. Can you show us the way? We've escaped from a concentration camp, from Auschwitz."

It was pointless trying to deceive her, and suddenly I realized that, for the first time, I was talking about Auschwitz to someone outside the camp. It meant nothing to her, of course, but I felt that if I died that moment, at least I had told one person.

"You'll have to wait here," she said slowly, never taking her eyes off our faces. "Tonight, I'll send a man who will help you. And I'll send you some food right away."

I realized then that we were starving. Food had been scarce on the mountain, but tension had blunted our appetites after our encounter with the German patrol. We had drunk from streams and hardly eaten a bite for several days.

We thanked her, but we did not trust her. As she walked away, we studied our position and saw that she would have to cross a bridge about a thousand yards away. About two hundred yards away in the opposite direction was a forest. If she tipped off the Germans, we would see them crossing the bridge and would have plenty of time to reach shelter before they even saw us.

Two hours later, we saw someone approaching the bridge—not a soldier, but a small boy of about twelve. He skipped up the hill to us and with a shy smile handed us a big parcel. We opened it, found it contained a kilo of cooked potatoes and some meat, and gobbled it greedily. The boy's grin broadened as he watched us, and he said when we had finished, "My grandmother will be back when it is dark."

The food appeased our hunger but did little to lull our suspicions. If she returned when it was dark, we would not be able to see who was with her when she crossed the bridge. For a while, we debated whether we should press on, but in the end, we decided we would be able to gauge from the sound of the footsteps how many were with her and whether we should bolt for the trees.

For hours, we waited. I shivered without my overcoat as the sky darkened and the chill of evening seeped into my bones. I soon forgot the cold, however, when, peering through the deepening dusk, I saw the old woman returning with a man who wore the rough clothes of a peasant.

Still we did not relax, for this, too, could be a trick. We waited without speaking until they were quite close to us, and then we saw a pistol in man's hand.

Instinctively, we closed our hands on the knives in our pockets. The situation was dangerous, but by no means hopeless, for if he were taking us back to the Gestapo, we still had a long road to travel, and both of us were desperate. We knew we could kill him before he fired in the dark, and we were prepared to do so.

The old woman, however, behaved just as she had that morning, calmly and without fear. She gave us another big parcel and said, "Here's some more food. You look as if you need it."

The man with the gun never spoke, and our eyes never left him as we crammed the food into our mouths. Because we were still famished, we finished it in a few minutes, and then, to our amazement, he roared with laughter.

Shoving the gun into his pocket, he said, "You're from a concentration camp, all right. Only really hungry men could eat like that. But at first I thought you might be Gestapo agents."

"Gestapo agents?"

"Yes. Sometimes they try to trick us. They know we help the partisans, and so they dangle decoy ducks in front of us, hoping we'll show our hands. But it's easy enough to tell the real from the sham.

"Now you'd better come with me. You can stay the night in my place, and tomorrow night, I'll see you safely across the border."

We rose to our feet, grinning like children. The border…people who spoke Slovak…friends…safety…home. It seemed too good to be true.

As we moved off, however, I wondered if I would make it. My feet, which had been giving me trouble for a long time, were now so swollen that I could not walk properly; I could only hobble.

He took us to his home, a small, neat cottage in the valley. There, I flopped in a chair and tried to ease off my boots. They would not budge. I tugged at them, wincing with agony, while Fred and our host watched me anxiously.

"There's only one thing for it," said Fred. "You'll have to cut them off. You'll get nowhere if you wear them."

He was right. Once inside Slovakia, I felt confident I could lay my hands on a pair of boots or shoes, and I was determined to cross that border, even if it meant walking on my hands.

From an inside pocket, I took my razor blade, the suicide blade that Volkov had told me I must carry. Carefully, I cut through the fine Dutch leather, and my feet expanded with relief as the boots fell away.

"You can't travel in your socks," grunted the Pole. "Here…take my carpet slippers. They're all I can spare."

That night, we knew the luxury of sleeping in a bed. All the next day, we stayed in the cottage while our friend went off to work. When he returned, we had supper, and then he said, "It's time to go. But first let me tell you what you're facing. This border is patrolled fairly well. The guards, however, stick to a routine, the idiots, and that means I can gauge fairly accurately where they are at any given time. So long as you do exactly what I say, I'll get you across."

Ten minutes later, we left. The old man moved surprisingly swiftly and silently for his age, and I had quite a job keeping up with him in my carpet slippers. At last, however, he stopped and consulted a heavy gunmetal watch.

"A German patrol passes here every ten minutes," he said casually, as if he were announcing the time of the next train. "We'll have to let the next one go by."

We hid in the bushes. Soon, we heard the crunch of marching feet, and as we peered cautiously through the branches, the soldiers passed so close to us that we could have touched their green uniforms.

The journey lasted longer than we had anticipated—two days, in fact. At last, however, we came to a clearing, and our guide stopped.

"See that forest over there?" he said. "That's Slovakia. At this point, the German patrols pass every three hours. So you'd better wait until the next bunch appears before you move on."

We gazed at the forest fifty yards away, dampening down the urge to dash for it right away. Then we turned to the tough old Pole and thanked him.

"I'm glad I could help," he said with a grin. Then he glanced at my feet and added, "I hope the slippers hold out!"

He disappeared without another word. We hid in the trees on the edge of the clearing until the patrol came and went, and then we dashed for Slovakia. For the first time since we had climbed from the pile of wood, we felt really free, even though the country was still ruled by Monsignor Tiso with his Hlinka Guards and was well populated with Quislings.

Freedom, however, was not enough. It was not the primary reason for our escape. We still had to contact the *Judenrat*[1] with whose help the Germans were able to arrange the deportations. We had to tell them that resettlement areas really meant gas chambers, and we knew that making this vital contact was not going to be easy.

It meant walking into a town without papers, exposing ourselves to spot checks by the Hlinka Guards or the Germans, asking our way, seeking the addresses of the Jews, revealing ourselves, in fact, as strangers from God knew where.

It would have been safer, indeed, to stay in the forests, to join the partisans, to fight with them, but that was a luxury which would have to wait until we had finished the job we had set out to do.

After marching through the forest for about two hours, we came to open country. A peasant working in a field straightened himself and stared at us as we approached. Now I was on more familiar ground, for

---

1   *Judenrat* (German for Jewish Council) was a widely used administrative Jewish agency imposed by the Nazis during World War II that was forced to implement Nazi policies. --Eds.

I knew my own people, and as I studied him carefully, I had a feeling that I could trust him.

Bluntly, for deception would have been pointless, I said, "Where are we?"

"Near the village of Skalite. Not far from the town of Cadca."

I knew both places. I took another good look at the man in the field. He was tall and hardy with dark-brown eyes and an inscrutable face. My instincts still insisted he was reliable, though my suspicious mind, tempered by Auschwitz, warned me to be careful. Fred, I knew, was thinking much as I was, and after a while, we both came to the conclusion that now we had to trust him anyway. Obviously, he was no fool. He knew we were strangers, and he knew we wanted to reach the nearest town or village. Even if we left him, he could still betray us and have us picked up within the hour.

"We need help," I said. "We must get to Cadca."

He looked us up and down and grinned. Then he said, "You'd better come to my place first because you're not going to get far in those clothes. By the way, my name is Canecky."

We looked at each other and saw how right he was. We no longer looked like two impeccably dressed Dutch businessmen, which would have been bad enough. We looked like two Dutch businessmen who had been rolled in the mud and torn through a very large bramble bush. Without another word, we followed him to his cottage.

There he fed us, and while we ate, he searched his own sparse wardrobe and came back with some peasants' clothes which would give us a veneer of respectability in that farming community. We changed quickly and then sat down to give him a brief outline of our story.

"We must contact the Jewish leaders in Cadca," I said finally. "And we must contact them fast."

Speed, in fact, was now vital. A wall calendar that advertised seeds told me the date was April 21. I knew it could not be long before the Hungarian transport began rolling on its dismal journey to Auschwitz.

"Well, one thing is sure," said our host who, we gathered, was a small farmer. "You've got to get farther from the border. But you've got to have a good excuse for traveling, too, once you reach a town.

"Now, in three days' time, I'm bringing some pigs into the market at Cadca. You help me along with them, and nobody will ask any questions. But in the meantime, you'll have to stay here and I'll have to carry on with my work because if I'm not seen out and about, someone'll get suspicious."

Fred and I glanced quickly at each other. The farmer understood and said with a grin, "Don't worry, gentlemen. I'm not going to give you away. You have my word for that...my Slovak word! And once we get to Cadca, I can put you in touch with a Jewish doctor I know, a Doctor Pollack."

So, for three days, we stayed in the cottage while Mr. Canecky went about his business. Early on the fourth day, we set off for the town, driving ten pigs in front of us, and as we mingled in the market, I felt a light-headed happiness sweep over me.

All around me, I heard the music of the Slovak language. The bargaining mingled with a brisk, swift banter that needed no translation in my mind. Beside me, a woman offered a keen price for her hens, put her hands on her hips, and asked her customer sadly, "What are you? A Jew...or a human?"

I laughed. I was back where I belonged.

We sold our pigs for a good price, and Mr. Canecky was in high good humor. We were glad for him, but as we wandered away from the market, we realized his pleasure was quite unselfish.

"We don't have to worry anymore, gentlemen," he said. "I've money now, and it's all yours if you need it. So, let's go and find Doctor Pollack."

When we reached the doctor's surgery, indeed, the farmer tried to press some of the money onto us, but we refused. Already, he had risked his life for us, yet when we tried to thank him, he just laughed and said, "I wish you'd take some crowns. Poverty's no disgrace I know, but it can be uncomfortable!"

Then, still laughing, he wandered away.

We turned toward the large building where the doctor had his surgery—and stopped. At the main door stood two soldiers of the Slovak Quisling Army. Slowly, we approached it, and suddenly, we realized we were about to enter Army Headquarters, where, apparently, the doctor had a room!

"To hell with it," Fred muttered. "Can't we be sick, just like anybody else?"

Why not? The sentry did not even glance at us as we walked past him, and a few minutes later, we were sitting in an antiseptic little room, telling our story to Doctor Pollack.[2] He listened carefully, occasionally interrupting with a quiet question. Then he said, "Tonight, you sleep at my place. Tomorrow, I'll take you to the leaders of the Jewish community in Zilina. They'll know what's best to do."

———

THE FOLLOWING DAY, APRIL 25, FRED AND I WERE SIPPING sherry at the Zilina headquarters of the Jewish Council and telling our story to Doctor Oscar Neumann, spokesman for all Slovakia's Jews,

---

2 The author had actually met Dr. Pollack previously, in Novaky, where they had both been awaiting the deportation. Because a disproportionate number of physicians in Slovakia were Jews, and their deportation would have led to the collapse of the health care system, the physicians and their immediate families were usually granted a working exemption from deportation. For this reason, Dr. Pollack was removed from the "resettlement list" at the last moment. The familiarity with each other helped them establish trust. --Eds.

Oscar Krasnyanski,[3] Erwin Steiner, and a man called Hexner. We were still talking when they led us into a dining room where we sat down at a table covered with a gleaming white cloth and gleaming cutlery. We continued while we waded through the finest meal either of us had had in our lives, and we still had merely scratched the surface of Auschwitz when the liqueurs and cigars were produced.

I looked around the table at the faces of our hospitable hosts, and suddenly, I had a horrible feeling that they did not believe a word we were saying.

Why should they, after all? How could they? Human minds had yet to be trained to absorb the thought of mass murder on an Auschwitz scale.

After the meal, however, they began probing. They took us to another room and produced some large books. These, they told us, were records which showed exactly when and from where every deported Jew had left Slovakia.

"When, for instance, did you leave?" they asked me.

"June 14, 1942."

The pages flipped. The heads nodded. Another voice said, "Where did you leave from?"

"Novaky."

More nods. Then: "Can you name any of the people on the transport with you?"

I reeled off about thirty names of those I remembered from my own wagon. A finger traced slowly down a page of the big ledger. I saw the faces before me change slowly, suspicion fading from the eyes, and in its place was absolute horror. They realized, I think, at that moment that the heavy covers of their books held nothing but obituaries, that their original purpose would never be served, that after the war, they

---

3   Oskar Krasnyanski—whose name is spelled in slightly different ways in various documents, e.g., Krasnanski, Krasnansky, Krasnyansky or Krasznyansky—immigrated to Israel after the war and changed his name to Karmiel. --Eds.

would not be able to bring their deported people back to Slovakia as they had planned. The myth of the resettlement areas was melting in their minds, and the shock was terrible.

Yet, understandably, they were still dubious. They did not want to believe us, and for that, I do not blame them. To their credit, however, they did not dismiss us as lunatics or troublemakers. They took us each into a different room and asked us to make separate statements.

For hours, I dictated my testimony. I gave them detailed statistics of the deaths. I described every step of the awful confidence trick by which 1,760,000 in my time in the camp alone had been lured to the gas chambers.[4] I explained the machinery of the extermination factory and its commercial side, the vast profits that were reaped from the robbery of gold, jewelry, money, clothes, artificial limbs, spectacles, prams, and human hair. I told them how even the ashes were used as fertilizer.

I gave them, in fact, the whole ghastly picture, the information I had been gathering so carefully for so long, and when I had finished, I repeated the very first words I had spoken to them.

"One million Hungarians are going to die," I said. "Auschwitz is ready for them. But if you tell them now, they will rebel. They will never go to the ovens. Your turn is coming. But now it is the Hungarians' hour. You must tell them immediately."

"Don't worry," they said soothingly. "We are in daily contact with the Hungarian Jewish leaders. Your report will be in their hands first thing tomorrow."

I sagged back in my chair, and I felt weak—not because of my journey from Auschwitz and the strain of it; not because I had been talking

---

4   The exact number of Auschwitz victims is impossible to establish. The estimates differ considerably. Franciszek Piper, the leading expert on Auschwitz, maintains the dead toll was 1,095,000 lives. The author and Wetzler estimated that up until the time of their escape, at least 1,765,000 were murdered; the author thought that the final number of victims was 2,500,000; the commander of Auschwitz, Rudolf Hoess, calculated the victims to be approximately 3,000,000. --Eds.

for hours, stripping my mind and my heart; but because relief suddenly struck me with all the force of a physical blow.

"You're tired," they said. "You and Mr. Wetzler must stay here. We will get you some decent clothes and will organize your papers so you can move about without fear of arrest. And you need not worry about money."

I slept quietly that night on a soft, soft bed. I had done what I had set out to do. My mind was free, for I was quite confident that Auschwitz would never know another transport. The truth about its diabolical purpose would be transmitted swiftly, not only to Hungary, but to every Jewish community left in German-occupied Europe.

The next morning, an elderly maid brought me my breakfast in bed. Then she disappeared and came back quickly with a complete new outfit for me, an expensive suit, socks, shirt, underwear, tie, and a silk handkerchief. There was only one item missing.

"What about shoes?" I said with a smile. "I can't go out in my socks!"

"They haven't been able to get them yet," she said with a sad smile. "They told me to tell you you'd have them tomorrow."

I got up; had a long, leisurely bath; shaved; dressed in my finery; and went downstairs in my stockinged feet, for all my old clothes had been removed. Dr. Neumann and Oscar Krasnyanski were waiting for me, and again I raised the question of footwear.

"Don't worry," they said. "You'll get your shoes soon. And you can't go out anyway until we fix you up with papers. In the meantime, just try to relax."

"Have you sent my report?" I asked. "Have the Hungarians got it yet?"

"Yes, it is in their hands. At this very minute, it is being examined by Dr. Kastner, the most important man in the whole Hungarian committee."

I tried to relax. The food was splendid, and soon, I told myself, I would be able to wander round Zilina, looking at the shops, sitting in cafés, maybe meeting some girls with Fred. I had done my part, and I felt I could leave the rest to Dr. Kasztner.

Every day, I asked casually for news from Hungary, expecting all the time to hear of a revolt. My hosts, however, said quietly, "Dr. Kasztner is looking after everything. He knows how to handle the situation. We can rely on him to take the right action at the right time. He's a man of vast experience."

I was happy to hear these reassuring words until one morning my sad, elderly maid came into my room with my breakfast. She was crying quite openly, and immediately, I asked her what was the matter.

"They're deporting the Hungarians," she sobbed. "Thousands of them. They're passing through Zilina in cattle trucks!"[5]

---

5   Two transports of Hungarian Jews passed through Zilina on April 28, 1944. --Eds.

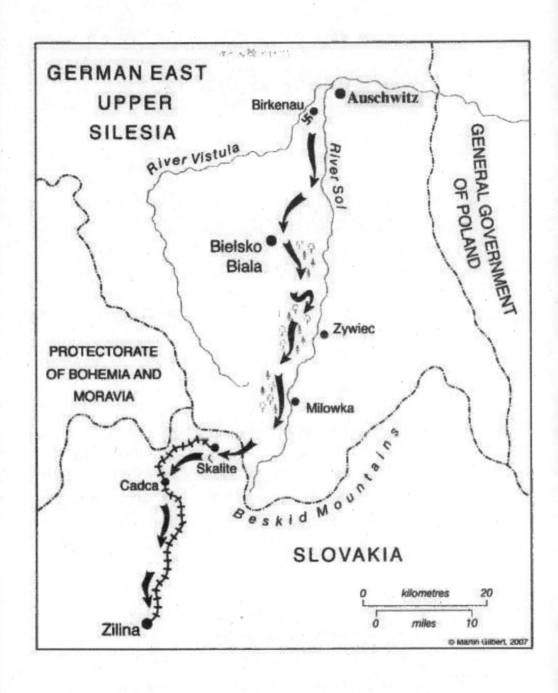

GERMAN EAST
UPPER
SILESIA

Birkenau ● **Auschwitz**

River Vistula

River Sol

Bielsko
Biala

Zywiec

PROTECTORATE
OF BOHEMIA AND
MORAVIA

Milowka

Skalite

Cadca

B e s k i d M o u n t a i n s

SLOVAKIA

Zilina

| 0 | kilometres | 20 |
| 0 | miles | 10 |

© Martin Gilbert, 2007

CHAPTER 16
We Get the Word Out

"THEY ARE DEPORTING HUNGARIANS. THOUSANDS OF THEM. They're passing through Zilina in cattle trucks."

A simple statement from a simple woman. An obituary notice, a ghastly piece of crime reportage, an indictment, a defeat, all wrapped up in less than a score of words. They swirled around my head as I walked downstairs, plaguing me, mocking me, stirring the bile of cold anger inside me, an anger made all the sharper by frustration.

There was no sign of Neumann, of Krasnyanski, of Steiner. Only Hexner,[1] a very minor official, was there, and he explained to me, "They've all gone to Bratislava."

"Don't they know what's happening? The trains are rolling. The Hungarians are on their way to Auschwitz. What are they doing? What's Kasztner doing? What in Christ's name is happening?"

His face puckered with bewilderment. These were questions far beyond him, and even the thought of the answers worried him.

"They're doing what they can. Last night, they sent sandwiches down to the transports and milk for the children…"

"Sandwiches and milk! Holy God, are they mad? Don't they know those poor bloody people are frying in the ovens now? Didn't they tell them what was happening? Didn't they warn them?"

---

[1] Hexner had faith in his leaders, but no knowledge of their innermost policies or actions. He died in Auschwitz with his family.

He heaved a sigh that came from his heart. Like a weary, word-worn parrot, he said, "You must keep calm. They know what they're doing. Dr. Kasztner is a very influential man, a man of great experience, a…a powerful man. He knows best."

I was not listening. I was pacing the floor, sick, trembling, talking to myself rather than to Hexner, spewing out my thoughts perhaps because I wanted to convince myself that I was not going mad.

"Why did I escape? What was the point? Don't they realize how many people are going to die, that those Auschwitz butchers have been preparing for this for months? Those crematoria are going to be working twenty-four hours a day until they've swallowed up a million people. Didn't they understand me? Didn't they believe me?"

"You must keep calm. They know best. They're clever men, cleverer than you or I."

I sat down in a chair and lit a cigarette. Consciously, I fought to get a grip on myself. I tried not to panic. Could Hexner be right? Was I just a blundering idiot who understood only the crudities of Auschwitz, an inexperienced boy who could not understand the subtleties of my elders? Were they playing a deep, skillful game that was beyond me? Were they sacrificing a few to save many? Did they honestly know best? Now it was my turn to sigh, for the answers were beyond me. I merely knew that the triumph of my escape had suddenly seemed to turn sour.

"Listen, sir," said Hexner, and there was a pleading note in his voice. "They left a message for you, an important message. Maybe it will convince you that they know what's going on, that they are not fools."

He paused and took a deep breath. Somehow, it gave me the impression that he was trying to convince himself rather than me. Then he said, "They learned last night that the Gestapo have given an order that you and Wetzler must be captured at all costs. So, they've arranged for the pair of you to go with false papers[2] to Liptovsky Svaty Mikulas in the Tatras, where the organization will look after you. They've even arranged for you to get five hundred crowns[3] each a week. You won't want for anything, and you'll be safe."

Another pause. Then: "We all know you've had a terrible experience. We know the sacrifices you've made and the risks you've taken to bring us this dreadful news, and we're proud of you. But for your own sake, you must go away today. Stay there until you hear from us, and try to enjoy yourself. You've earned a rest."

That day, Fred and I, papers in our pockets to show we were well-to-do students, went to Liptovsky Svaty Mikulas, for there was nothing else we could do. We were not even cogs in the machine anymore because we had done our work. Our youth and our strength had been useful. Without them, the message would never have been delivered, but the tasks which lay ahead were for skilled men only, not for apprentices.

We were, in fact, apprentices at the art of living because for so long we had thought only of survival. We did not fit smoothly and suavely into the world at first, not even into the little world of the train that brought us to our new home. We grew tense at the sight of soldiers. We jumped when the ticket collector came to us, and when a Hlinka Guard checked our papers in the street, we were poised to kill him.

That was the only creed we knew. Kill or be killed. Run or be caught. Trust nobody. Never relax. Live a little longer, but never just live.

Gradually, however, our nerves grew calmer as we got used to life again. After a while, we could wander into a café and have a beer

2   The author, who was born as Walter Rosenberg, chose the name Rudolf Vrba. He liked the Czech sound of it. Perhaps, because the name meant a new beginning for him, the chance of a new life, he accepted it as his own and legalized it as soon as he could in liberated Czechoslovakia in 1945. –Eds.
It is of interest that at the time, he was unaware that there was already another Rudolf Vrba (1860–1939), a Czech Catholic priest, journalist, and writer "exemplary" anti-Semite who self-published most of his anti-Semitic leaflets and books.
Alfred Wetzler's false identity was Josef Lánik, which he used after the war as his literacy pseudonym. --Eds.
3   Approximately $140 in 2017. --Eds.

without flicking glances over our shoulders or seeing an enemy in every face. We learned to raise our arm and say "Heil Hitler" to all the right people, and we learned to laugh at ourselves afterward. Ultimately, in fact, we felt that we had become integrated.

This I realized the first time I went to have my hair cut. It had grown for the first time in two years while I was living in the Jewish organization's headquarters at Zilina, and now I was going to a barber who, unlike his Auschwitz counterparts, would not dream of cutting a customer's throat just for the hell of it. For me, it was going to be quite an experience.

I arrived at the door simultaneously with an impeccably uniformed Unterscharführer. Immediately, he jumped back, clicked his heels, and said with a smile, "After you, sir."

This time, I did not go tense. I smiled back and said equally politely, "No...please...after you."

"Sir...I insist."

With a slight bow, I went in first. We sat in adjacent chairs, and the SS man offered me a cigarette. I took one, and he followed up quickly with a light, and as the barbers worked on the pair of us, he tried to make light conversation in halting Slovak. I answered him politely, also in Slovak, and wondered what he would do if he knew I had come from Auschwitz. I wondered, too, how he would behave after one week in the camp.

That, of course, was the trouble. We thought we were being integrated, but always there was a barrier. Always there was something to remind us of the immediate past. We found ourselves relating everything to Auschwitz, judging everything by Auschwitz standards which nobody else knew or understood. Always, just as we thought we were human beings again, a jagged edge came out of the past and scratched us.

One day, for instance, we were wandering down the main street when a column of Slovak soldiers went by. Suddenly, one of them shouted: "Fredo!"

He detached himself from his comrades and came over to us, a lad of about twenty-three. Immediately, he grabbed Fred's hand, pumped it up and down, and said, "You old devil, where have you been hiding. It must be six months at least since I saw you!"

Fred's eyes widened in mock amazement. "Hell, no!" he said. "It can't be as long as that! Doesn't time fly?"

"I'm stationed here now. I'll see you downtown tonight maybe."

Then he was gone, scampering down the street after his column. Fred shook his head slowly, smiled, and said, "We used to play football together. Six months? My God, if he only knew it was a lifetime since we last met."

So it was. To others, those two years seemed no more than six months. To us, they were a century. Somehow, it did not seem quite right that the world should have ambled along while Auschwitz was in action, that people should have laughed and joked and drank and made love while millions died and we fought for our lives.

We were not wallowing in the past. In fact, we were trying desperately hard to break with it. We went out and got drunk together. We flitted from girl to girl, living it up, for we had plenty of crowns in our pockets. With a determination that was almost grim, we set out to enjoy ourselves, to obey the instructions given to us at Jewish headquarters in Zilina, and we almost succeeded.

The shadow of death, however, kept drifting over our minds. We tried to lose ourselves and our thoughts, wandering by Slovak streams, but always they reflected faces we would never see again. We went back to places where we had played before the war, trying to recapture an almost forgotten gaiety, but the stones of the streets we knew were flecked with the blood of the people we had known.

Inevitably, perhaps, there were times when we wondered whether we would ever be happy again or whether Auschwitz, scene of so much death, was immortal and would live in our minds until we, too, died, and then live on to haunt those who understood. These were somber moments in which we feared that never again, perhaps, would we be able to live normal lives. Yet, looking back, I think we were right and others were ignorant of the truth. This was no time for pleasure, and soon it palled on us.

After six weeks in Liptovsky Svaty Mikulas, in fact, I began to get bored and restless. I decided to take a chance, to get out of it for a while, to go to Trnava and see my mother. Returning to my hometown, of course, was a calculated risk, but I felt it was well worth taking.

As soon as I got off the train, I went straight to the house of a friend. He gazed at me as if I were a ghost and then said slowly, "So your mother isn't mad after all!"

"What do you mean—mad?"

"She's been telling everyone you'll be back this summer, that you're not the sort of boy who will sit around in one place for longer than two years. We all thought she was going round the bend because nobody ever comes back."

I grinned. Obviously, my mother had not changed.

"Slip around to her," I said. "Tell her I'm here. You needn't break it to her gently because obviously she's expecting me."

About half an hour later, she came into the room, looking a little older, a little more settled, but otherwise much the same as I had left her. She nodded to me, looked around the room with a frown, and said to my friend, "When is my son coming?"

She had not recognized me! Suddenly, I realized that I was the one who had changed. I had gone away a seventeen-year-old boy, and though only two years had passed, I had returned very much older. I had seen 1,760,000 people die, and that had left a mark on my face.

"There he is," said my friend. "Do you think he's grown?"

For a moment, she stood motionless. Then she embraced me swiftly, thoroughly, and stepped back to have a good look at me, as if I had just come in off the streets late for supper with dirty knees.

"You're a dreadful boy," she said at last. "You know, you never wrote to me once. You never even sent me your address."

"I'm sorry, Momma," I said. "It was a bit difficult. You see, we were…very busy all the time."

"Never mind. I knew you'd be back this summer. You never were a one who would stick in a place for long. As a matter of fact, I've made some of your favorite jam. I didn't bother last year because I knew you wouldn't be here."

She flicked a tear from her cheek and rattled on. Where was I living? Had I a job? Did anyone air my sheets? Who did my laundry? Where did I get my suit?

At last, I managed to get a word in edgeways. I said, "Please, Momma, sit down for a moment. I've a good deal to tell you."

She sat down. As briefly as possible, I told her where I had been, cutting out as many of the grim details as I could. When I had finished, she was silent for quite a while, and then she said, "Well…I suppose it was difficult for you to write. And now you can't come home. Never mind. Wait here, and I'll fetch the jam."

She bustled out, and I knew she understood. Indeed, I was proud of the way in which she controlled her emotions, for I was quite sure she had not been fooled for a moment by my expurgated version of life in Auschwitz. She filled in the gaps, and she kept quiet about them, for she sensed that was the way I wanted it.

That night, I returned to Liptovsky Svaty Mikulas, carrying my jam with me. I was not looking forward particularly to jumping back abroad the lazy roundabout again because roundabouts never get anywhere, and I was tired of an aimless existence. The following day, however, I had a visitor who provided me with just the target I was seeking.

It was Oscar Krasnyanski from Zilina. He seemed ill at ease and worried, and at last, after some meaningless small talk, he said, "I'm a little anxious about the way matters are working out. I'd like you to know that I sent a copy of your report to the Papal Nuncio in Slovakia."

"What do you mean?" I asked. "Is there some trouble? What's the Papal Nuncio got to do with it?"

He shrugged and said, "Never mind about that for the moment. The point is that he wants to see you. In fact, I've arranged for you to meet him at a monastery near Svaty Jur, and I don't need to tell you that it would be better if the meeting were kept a secret."

Svaty Jur is near Bratislava. I traveled there a few days later and was ushered by a monk into a large, plainly furnished room where the Nuncio was waiting for me.

He was a tall, elegant man of about forty, and as he rose to greet me, I saw that he had a copy of my report in his hand. After a few preliminary courtesies, he got down to business and for six hours cross-examined me with all the skill of an experienced lawyer. He went through the report line by line, page by page, returning time after time to various points until he was satisfied that I was neither lying nor exaggerating, and by the time we had finished dissecting the horrors about which I had written, he was weeping.

"I shall carry your report to the International Red Cross in Geneva," he said at last. "They will take action and see that it reaches the proper hands."[4]

4   *The Report* was sent to Msgr. Angelo Burzio, who was not Papal Nuncio, but was in fact charge d'affaires in Slovakia (the lower rank of an apostolic delegation), since there was no nunciature in Slovakia at that time. But Krasnyanski—by mistake—referred to him as Nuncio, and this is why the author referred to him as Nuncio as well. The author actually met with Msgr. Mario Martilloti, who came to Bratislava on an errand from Switzerland, and who was a member of the Vatican nuncio office.
The author visited Svätý Jur with Czeslaw Mordowicz, the Birkenau prisoner who escaped six weeks after Vrba and was able to reach Slovakia. The author left him out from the book, which caused friction between them. Here is the author's explanation why he excluded Mordowicz: "I did not mention Mordowicz at all because at the time of its writing (1963), I lived in England, having left Communist Czechoslovakia in 1958. Mordowicz at that time still lived in Bratislava under the neo-Stalinist regime of Antonín Novotný. To publicly describe in England a close connection between myself and Mordowicz might have caused him problems, including accusations of having been 'a Vatican spy,' or 'closely connected with the exiled heretic R. Vrba.'" --Eds.

At the time, I did not realize the significance of this meeting. I did not know that the mission which I had undertaken when first I had begun to compile statistics in Auschwitz had yet to be completed.

I did not know that Dr. Kasztner had not warned the Hungarian Jews that they were going to die, that he was conducting mysterious negotiations with Adolf Eichmann in Budapest.

I did not know that the Hungarian transports were going day and night to Auschwitz, that the SS were breaking all records by murdering 12,000 Hungarians every twenty-four hours.

I did not know that already 200,000 of these I had tried to save, those whom I thought, indeed, I had saved, were already dead.

I did not know that others were about to act while the Jewish leaders in Budapest talked with the man whose job it was to exterminate one million of their people; that, to quote the British historian Gerald Reitlinger, the bombardment of Admiral Horthy's conscience was about to begin.

The Papal Nuncio took my report to Geneva. From there, it went to Pope Pius XII, to Prime Minister Winston Churchill, and to President Roosevelt.[5]

On June 25, 1944, exactly two calendar months after I had dictated my report in Zilina, Monsignor Angelo Rotta, Papal Nuncio in Hungary, handed a letter from Pope Pius XII to Admiral Horthy, the regent.

It was evasively worded, but nevertheless, it was undoubtedly a protest against the deportation of Hungarian Jews. The fact that it came from a Pontiff who hitherto had refrained from censuring directly Hitler's murder of the Jews made it particularly significant. Certainly, it must have appeared so to Horthy, since was a Roman Catholic

The Pope's letter was followed the following day by a note from Mr. Cordell Hull, the US Secretary of State, who threatened reprisals

---

5   The version of The Report that reached President Roosevelt is permanently archived at the Franklin D. Roosevelt Presidential Library. As a matter of interest, Rudolf Vrba's personal papers are also archived there. --Eds.

against those responsible for the deportations. The King of Sweden offered to help the Hungarian Jews to emigrate.

The Regent did not answer, but the chips, nevertheless, were down. On July 7, Mr. Anthony Eden, Britain's Foreign Secretary, announced in the House of Commons that "700,000 to 1,000,000 Hungarian Jews" were in process of extermination, information, I understand, which he gathered from my report.

By that time, too, the Swiss government had raised its censorship of the subject in its newspapers, and the world knew at last about Auschwitz. My escape, in fact, had not been in vain.

Horthy stopped the deportations, and of the 1,000,000 earmarked for the gas chambers, "only" 400,000 died. Had the warning which I gave on April 25 been passed on by Kasztner to his people immediately, of course, the death toll, I feel sure, would have been substantially smaller.

When I spoke with the Papal Nuncio at Svaty Jur, of course, I had no idea of the international repercussions which would result from our meeting.

Indeed, I returned to Liptovsky Svaty Mikulas merely intrigued by this strange rendezvous in a quiet monastery. I did not quite see the point of it, for I was confident that already the Jewish leaders in Budapest had warned their people and killed forever Eichmann's operation. Krasnyanski, however, seemed still perturbed, and he told me soon after I arrived: "You're to meet Rabbi Weissmandel in Bratislava."

I had heard strange, romantic stories about Rabbi Michael Dov Weissmandel;[6] how, single-handed and under the noses of the Nazis,

---

6   In August 1944, some months after I met him, Rabbi Michael Dov Weissmandel was captured by the SS and put on a train for Auschwitz. In a piece of stale bread, he concealed a coil of emery thread which could cut through steel. That night, he cut a hole in the sealed car and leaped to freedom in the darkness. Later, he resumed his clandestine rescue work. After the war, he went to New York, where he founded a rabbinical school. He continued to live an utterly austere life, rejecting all the offers of financial help pressed upon him by rich American Jews, and died there in 1957.
[The author visited Weissmandel with Mordowicz as well, and for the reasons explained in detail previously omitted his presence from the book. See also note 4. --Eds.]

he had saved hundreds of Jews from deportation; how he lived a life of utter austerity, teaching in his secret rabbinical school; how he was not merely a profoundly religious man, a mystic, perhaps, who inspired his pupils, but a rare symbol of resistance.

I had yet to learn that three weeks after I wrote my report, he smuggled his own accurate account of Auschwitz in general and the plans for Hungary's Jews in particular to the Jewish leaders in Turkey, Switzerland, and Palestine. In it, he begged for action. He pleaded with them to publicize this mass murder throughout the world, to let the Allies know so Auschwitz and the railway lines leading to it could be bombed, particularly those leading from Eastern Hungary and persistently the bridges in the neighborhood of Karpato-Rus.

It was a cry almost of despair in which he said, "Drop all other business to get this done. Remember that one day of your idleness kills 12.000 souls.

"You, our brothers, sons of Israel, are you insane? Don't you know the Hell around us? For whom are you saving your money?

"How is it that all our pleadings affect you less than the whimperings of a beggar standing in your doorway?

"Murderers! Madmen! Who is it that gives charity? You who toss a few pennies from your safe homes? Or we who give our blood in the depths of Hell?

"There is only one thing that may be said in your exoneration— that you do not know the truth.

"This is possible.

"The villain does his job so shrewdly that only a few guess at the truth.

"We have told you the truth several times. Is it possible that you believe our murderers more than you believe us?

"May God open your eyes and give you heart to rescue in these last hours the remainder…"

Rabbi Michael Dov Weissmandel got no answer to that letter.

They took me to his secret school in one of the oldest parts of the city. I passed down a corridor that ran between a line of rooms in which zealous young men were studying the Talmud, and then I found myself facing a tall, dark man with exceptionally vivid eyes. He was only about forty, but his heavy black beard made him look older. I felt at once that I was in the presence of a very remarkable personality, in spite of his shabby clothes; his collarless, buttonless shirt; his mud-stained trousers; and his battered shoes. One, I noticed, was tied with string. The other was not tied at all.

He greeted me in Slovak, which amazed his students because normally he spoke only Hebrew and insisted on an interpreter translating into Hebrew anything said to him in any other language. Then, dismissing the students in his room with a gesture, he said, "So you have escaped from Auschwitz. Therefore, I must address you as the Ambassador of 1,760,000 people."

I understood what he meant. He had quoted the number who died in Auschwitz while I was there, and I knew then that he had read my report.

For a considerable time, we discussed it. I learned to my horror that he shared Krasnyanski's unspoken fears, that he believed the transports were still leaving Budapest every day, for he did not seem surprised when I told him of the two which, to my knowledge, had left while I was still in Zilina.

"Can't something more be done?" I asked. "Can't they be warned? Can't they be told they must fight because they have nothing to lose?"

He sighed, and then he said, "I will do everything in my power. If I had two guns, I would shoot with both hands."

Was this the answer I had been waiting to hear? I thought of his quiet words all the way back to Liptovsky Svaty Mikulas; and, by the time I arrived in the station, I was convinced that this man of wisdom and of courage had told me what I had to do. There would be no more roundabouts.

I went to members of the underground with whom I had made pre-liminary contacts already and said as casually as possible, "My friends, I need a pistol. Someday, a bright SS man is going to see through my false papers, and when that happens, I don't want the argument to be one-sided."

To my amazement and fury, they said sternly, "We don't issue pis-tols to lads like you."

Then they grinned and added, "We issue submachine guns!"

Three months later, I went to Western Slovakia, to a village near Nove Mesto, where Laco Fischer had his home, and reported to Sergeant Milan Uher, who was on the way already to becoming a legend. After the war, indeed, as Captain Uher, he was posthumously awarded the title of Hero of the Insurrection.[7]

They accepted me readily, gave me about twenty-four hours of rapid training, and told me, "Tomorrow night, we've a bit of a fight on our hands. There are about seven hundred SS men holed up in the schoolhouse at Stara Tura. They have to be wiped out, not just because they are SS men, though that's a good enough reason, but because they have been drafted into the area to wipe us out."

"How many of us will attack?"

"About a hundred and twenty. With submachine guns and grenades."

The following night, we filtered into Stara Tura, blending into the buildings, heading for the schoolhouse. Silently, foot by foot, we edged toward it. Then Sergeant Uher shouted, and we hurled ourselves at its walls and its windows.

A flash of fire came from a doorway. A dozen flashes answered it. Two men beside me fell, but I scarcely noticed them. I was running

---

7   The described events were part of the Slovak National Uprising that broke out at the end of August 1944. For his actions in the uprising, Vrba was decorated with the Czechoslovak Medal for Bravery, the order of Slovak National Insurrection and Medal of Meritorious Fighter. There is a commemorative plaque in Lubina, North-West Slovakia, recognizing the author's and Wetzler's (Wetzler joined the uprising later on) bravery during the uprising. --Eds.

now, and tears of happiness were coursing down my cheeks. I was running forward, not backward.

We reached the wall of the schoolhouse and hurled our grenades through the windows. We heard them roar, and then we heard the screams of pain, of fear, of death. We burst through the door into a fiery chaos and sprayed the room with bullets.

Then we withdrew from Stara Tura, our mission accomplished, and I was laughing with the elation of it. I knew that the answer given to me by Rabbi Michael Dov Weissmandel was the only answer.

Other words drifted back to me. The words of Captain Dmitri Volkov, who had told me, "Don't be afraid of the Germans. There are many of them, but each of them is small. Here in Auschwitz, they try to break your mind as well as your body. They try to convince you that they're supermen, invincible. But I know they can die just as quickly as anybody else because I've killed enough of them in my day."

He was right, too. SS men died and screamed just as their victims in Auschwitz, old men, women, and children, had died and screamed. They were not invincible.

I thought of the mystical rabbi and the Soviet soldier. It seemed strange, somehow, that their views should be so close, their answers so similar.

Or was it so strange? Suddenly, I realized I had known this answer for a long time, ever since my childhood, in fact, when I was being taught to understand the Scriptures.

I remembered reading: "It is evil to assent actively or passively to evil as its instrument, as its observer or as its victim…"

At that moment outside Stara Tura, those words made splendid, brilliant sense. They still do.

EDITOR'S NOTE

WHAT FOLLOWS IS AN ASSORTMENT OF DOCUMENTS AND articles closely related to the story of Rudolf Vrba's escape.

We will start with an epilogue, the author's reflection of the events that followed his escape, especially the controversial acts of the Hungarian Jewish leadership.

The second document is a replica of the exact copy of the Vrba-Wetzler Report, which reached the USA for first time in mid-October 1944. This includes the Mordowicz-Rosin Report. We have explained a few ambiguities in footnotes.

The third document is an article by Nikola Zimring describing the escape of Vrba's friends Mordowicz and Rosin from Auschwitz-Birkenau and their mutual effort to spread *The Report*.

We will conclude this section with Vrba's article, which explains in more detail the circumstances and consequences of his escape. We hope this will be useful for those readers who still have questions after reading Vrba's memoir.

Epilogue

IN THIS BOOK, I HAVE PREFERRED FACT TO OPINION. THE mind of the world, however, is not yet shockproof, and 2,500,000 cannot die without creating at least a ripple of controversy, for that would be the ultimate in cynicism.

Inevitably, a major subject of debate is how it was all possible. Why did hundreds of thousands walk without resistance to the gas chambers? One answer has been given by Judge Benjamin Halevi of the Jerusalem District Court.

In May 1953, just nine years and two weeks after my report on Auschwitz reached Jewish leaders in Budapest, he entered his tiny courtroom to hear the case of the State of Israel versus Malchiel Gruenwald.

Malchiel Gruenwald was seventy-two years of age, an unknown writer who distributed his smudged, badly mimeographed pamphlets around the coffee bars of Jerusalem. Now he was accused of criminal libel against Dr. Rudolf Kasztner, once head of the Jewish Agency Rescue Committee in Hungary and at the time of the trial editor of Israel's most popular Hungarian-language newspaper and spokesman of the Ministry of Trade and Industry.

In one of his broadsheets, it was alleged, he had branded Kasztner as a Nazi collaborator.

In June 1955, after a trial which rocked Israel, Judge Benjamin Halevi found old Malchiel Gruenwald not guilty. Delivering his verdict, he said, "The masses of Jews from Hungary's ghettos obediently boarded the deportation trains without knowing their fate. They were full of confidence in the false information that they were being transferred to Kenyermeze.

"The Nazis could not have misled the masses of Jews so conclusively had they not spread their false information through Jewish channels. The Jews of the ghettos would not have trusted the Nazi or Hungarian rulers, but they had trust in their Jewish leaders. Eichmann and others used this known fact as part of their calculated plan to mislead the Jews. They were able to deport the Jews to their extermination by the help of Jewish leaders."

In January 1958, the Supreme Court of Israel, on a split decision of three judges to two, reversed the district court's decision on the point of collaboration. It did not question, however, the basic fact that Kasztner bought 1,684 Hungarian Jews of his choice, including members of his own family, from Eichmann at a time when 400,000 others were on their way to the ovens of Auschwitz at the rate of 12,000 a day, and 600,000 were awaiting their turn.

Kasztner paid for those 1,684 lives with his silence. During the trial, he admitted that Eichmann had told him he did not want another Warsaw. He did not want a repetition of that twenty-seven-day battle during which 33,000 men, women, and children held at bay thousands of Wehrmacht and SS troops, armed with tanks and cannon.

He admitted that he had been warned that all his negotiations with Eichmann were only for the purpose of keeping the Jews from the knowledge of their extermination and added, "I also felt the same thing in my heart."

He admitted that toward the end of April 1944, he had received information from Auschwitz[1] that they were preparing to receive the

---

1   The information to which he referred was contained in *The Report* which I dictated to the Jewish leaders at Žilina and sent to Budapest. As soon as he received it, Kasztner went at once to Eichmann and told him he knew his secret. At that moment, Eichmann knew he would have to bargain with this man, for under his command he had only 150 SS men to supervise the deportations. He did not dare risk a revolt.

Hungarian Jews and, in reply to Judge Halevi, said that from the middle of May 1944, he knew Jews were being deported from Hungary at the rate of 12,000 a day.

Why did Dr. Kasztner betray his people when he could have saved many of them by warning them, by giving them a chance to fight, a chance to stage the second "Warsaw" which Eichmann feared? According to Judge Benjamin Halevi, he "sold his soul to the German Satan."

Could there have been any other reason? Supreme Court Judge Shlomo Chesin said in his verdict that Kasztner concealed the bitter truth because "he did not think it would be useful and because he thought that any deeds resulting from information given them would damage more than help."

I bow, naturally, to the learned judge's intimate knowledge of Kasztner's thoughts, even though they reflect sadly upon the fighting spirit of the Hungarians. After all, the Hungarians had thirty times the numerical strength of their Polish brothers and sisters. They faced German and Quisling Hungarian forces which, combined, were only a pittance compared with the Wehrmacht and SS units that were halted in their tracks for nearly a month in Warsaw.

Could it be, therefore, that the defeatist mood of Dr. Kasztner was reinforced by the memory of words used by Dr. Chaim Weizmann, first President of Israel, when he addressed a Zionist convention in London in 1937?

He said, "I told the British Royal Commission that the hopes of Europe's six million Jews were centered on emigration. I was asked: 'Can you bring six million Jews to Palestine?' I replied: 'No.' The old ones will pass. They will bear their fate or they will not. They are dust, economic and moral dust in a cruel world...only a branch will survive....They had to accept it....If they feel and suffer they will find the way—*beachareth hajamin*[2]—in the fullness of time...I pray that we may preserve our national unity, for it is all we have."

---

2   "When the Messiah comes, all the dead will be revived."

"Only a branch will survive…" Did Kasztner, like Hitler, believe in a master race, a Jewish nation created of Top People for Top People by Top People? Was that the way in which he interpreted Dr. Chaim Weizmann's somber oration, and was he right in so doing? If so, who was going to select the branch? Who was going to say which grains would form the heap of moral and economic dust destined to await the coming of the Messiah?

Throughout Europe, it is true, there were Jews who had their champions. The communists, the socialists, and the true nationalists had the underground. The wealthy had their money. The Zionists had their Kasztners.

What of the rest? What of the mass of simple people who were not communists, socialists, millionaires, or Zionists—people like my brother Sammy who was murdered in Majdanek, like my mother whom I managed to save only because I had escaped to Slovakia with the secrets of Auschwitz and was a valuable property in Zionistic eyes?

They, presumably, formed the dust which was to be swept into the ovens by the Nazis who used Jewish leaders as their brooms, and the diligent manner in which these jackbooted dustmen worked is not only a matter of interest to historians, but a warning to future generations.

There is no doubt that the Nazis operated a system of mass extermination which was suitable not only for Jews, but for any other ethnical, political, social, national, or religious group. Documents which were captured after the defeat of Nazi Germany make it clear that they were intending to apply these methods to the Czechs, Poles, or anyone else who might oppose them or who might be useful to them dead.

It was a diabolically clever system of corruption and murder, for even today, in spite of technical advances, it would be difficult to exterminate 6,000,000 people spread all over Europe. The Nazis managed it twenty years ago because they made full use of political intrigue, nepotism, and bribery, not merely in connection with their "Final Solution," but in the extermination of about 14,000,000 non-Jews throughout Europe.

The creation of Quislings, voluntary or otherwise, was, in fact, an important feature of Nazi policy. Kasztner knew from my report in April 1944 precisely what was planned for 1,000,000 of his Jewish fellow-countrymen. He kept silent, and as a result, 400,000 of them went innocently and passively to their deaths in the gas chambers.

This policy of creating Quislings was practiced with spectacular success in every country occupied by the Nazis. It was particularly tragic where Jews were concerned only because it led to the destruction of nearly four-fifths of Europe's Jewish population.

Argument, however, will not bring 20,000,000 people back to life; nor will it revive Dr. Kasztner, who was murdered outside his home, 6 Emmanuel Street, Tel Aviv, in March 1957. It can answer, however, a question that is more immediate, sway a debate concerning those who still live.

Nineteen years after the Soviet Army liberated Auschwitz, the Federal Republic of Western Germany is putting on trial some of the men who operated its efficient machinery. I remember many of them—ex-Oberscharführer Josef Klehr, for instance, who injected phenol into the hearts of those unfit to work, and ex-Oberscharführer Wilhelm Boger, who was a virtuoso on a particularly vicious torture known as the Spanish Swing. I remember others who are not in the dock—ex-Oberscharführer Jakob Fries, for example, who, for me, will always be Mr. Auschwitz, but that is beside the point, though naturally I regret that he is not sharing the dock with his former comrades.

The importance of ranging these men before the bar of German justice, however belatedly, is that it will present the Auschwitz story in its proper perspective. It will correct, for instance, a popular belief that Hitler created his mass murder machine merely to satisfy his hunger for dead Jews.

Undoubtedly, his obsessional anti-Semitism produced the seeds from which the extermination camps in general and Auschwitz in particular grew; but the Nazi system, which abhorred waste, soon turned this obsession to profit. Killings were carried out with an efficiency which few time-and-motion experts would fault, and they paid rich dividends.

There was sadism, too, of course, but it was merely an ancillary product of a vast business enterprise which did much to bolster up German's economy and the morale of her soldiers and civilians.

In three years, for instance, six tons of gold were sent from this one camp to the Berlin State Bank. Part of this bullion was used to manipulate the foreign exchange through Swiss banks so the Allied economy would suffer, and the gold which was taken from the mouths of the victims as well as their pockets was reinforced with currency not only from occupied Europe, but from all parts of the world. A fortune in black-market dollars, pounds, and Swiss francs found its way to Auschwitz.

Gold and money, however, were only part of the loot. Clothes were carefully segregated, according to size, quality, and so on, and distributed throughout the Reich, which was becoming more and more threadbare as the war went on.

Fur coats were remodeled and sent to troops on the Eastern front. In the last six weeks alone of the camp's life of three years 222,259 men's shirts and 192,652 women's blouses were sent to Germany to bring some comfort into the lives of the war-torn civilian population.

All this had a sound psychological as well as material value. Hans might be sweating it out on the Russian front, cursing the war, worrying about his wife, Erika, in her blitzed Hamburg garret and about his baby who needed clothes.

Then he would get a letter from Erika telling him that the Führer had provided a complete outfit for their little son, and out Hans would go again to fight to the death for the compassionate Saint who had found time amid all his worries to remember Erika. If he fought hard enough, his Iron Cross might be augmented by a gold watch from the Auschwitz departmental store.

Artificial teeth and limbs, spectacles, prams...they all flowed back to Germany. Nothing was wasted, not even the victims' hair or the bones and ashes, which became fine fertilizer.

Here, indeed, was a multipronged secret weapon. The German General Staff used mass murder and robbery as freely as it used guns, tanks, and bombs, though this its ex-generals have been denying with monotonous regularity for many years. General Warlimont, once deputy to General Jodl, for instance, has stated categorically that the German Army took no part in any atrocities which is akin to a defendant in court saying that he took no part in the murder of a night watchman during a robbery, though he knew very well that murder was an essential part of the plot.

Yet the main charge at Frankfurt is mass murder, and the main problem facing the court is how it will punish the guilty. Judge Benjamin Halevi, I imagine, could advise its members well, but he is unlikely to be consulted.

Certainly, it is to be hoped that they will be treated less leniently than have other war criminals with which German courts have dealt in recent years. In Karlsruhe, for instance, the leader of an extermination squad which murdered more than 1,000 Jewish men, women, and children, was sentenced to twelve years' imprisonment. At Giessen, three men, found guilty of complicity in the murder of one hundred and sixty two people, were given sentences ranging from two years and nine months to three years and three months. At Munich, a man who took part in the murder of 15,000 got away with ten years, and at Ansbach, another man who was found guilty of the murder of nine Poles was sentenced to fifteen months imprisonment, from which eleven months of preventive arrest were deducted.

It may well be, of course, that the passage of time has blurred the edges of memory, that the stench of blood has gone and the stain has faded. At Frankfurt, however, I believe the judges must be more realistic when it comes to the point of punishing the guilty. They might bear in mind, for instance, a letter written by Britain's Prime Minister to his foreign secretary on July 11, 1944, after he had received my Auschwitz report.

Winston Churchill wrote: "There is no doubt that this persecution of the Jews in Hungary and their expulsion from enemy territory is probably the biggest and most horrible crime ever committed in the whole history of the world and it has been done by scientific machinery by nominally civilized men in the name of a great State and one of the leading races in Europe.

"It is quite clear that all concerned in this crime who may fall into our hands, including the people who only obeyed orders by carrying out the butcheries, should be put to death, if their association with the murderers has been proved.

"I cannot therefore feel that this is the kind of ordinary case which is put through the protecting powers as, for instance, the lack of feeding or sanitary conditions in some particular prisoners' camps.

"There should, therefore, in my opinion, be no negotiations of any kind on this subject. Declarations should be made in public so that everyone connected with it will be hunted down and put to death."

Since then, of course, nearly half a century has passed and there has been a development which will make it difficult for the Frankfurt judges to take heed of Sir Winston's advice, even though they may agree with it in their hearts.

One of the first acts of the West German Federal Government on its foundation was to abolish the death penalty. Many people applauded this piece of progressive legislation, forgetting as, perhaps, did the government itself, that some crimes are so gargantuan that they are beyond the scope of ordinary laws for run-of-the-mill murderers.

I believe, however, that what Winston Churchill wrote then remains true today. I believe the guilty men of Auschwitz must be put to death. I believe the Federal Republic of Western Germany must accept the precedent created by the Israeli Government which faced just such a dilemma in 1961.

When the State of Israel was founded, there was no place in its laws for the death penalty. Its people had seen too many gallows, not only in Palestine itself, but throughout Europe.

Then it was faced with Adolf Eichmann, and for this man, it introduced the death penalty.

I shall be accused, I know, of bitterness for advocating such a course. It will be said by those who were spared the sight of the crematoria chimneys that I am poisoned by a corrupting desire for revenge at a time when I am in a position to display charity and tolerance.

It is true, certainly, that I cannot forget Auschwitz and that I cannot forgive the men who made it the mightiest murder apparatus ever. Yet these are not the reasons for which I demand their death.

I cannot forget Auschwitz. But neither can I forget the country which produced Beethoven, Mozart, and Mendelssohn; Kant and Hegel, Goethe and Thomas Mann, Einstein and Heisenberg, even if I find it hard sometimes to believe that one nation could achieve the twin peaks of barbarity and humanity.

It is for the sake of this other Germany that I call for the execution of the guilty. Nothing less will convince the world that the people of music, of poetry, of philosophy, of science, even of genius, have triumphed and that the dark elements which swamped them have been obliterated forever. It is not merely a question of punishing criminals, for what punishment could fit the crime, but of purging a nation's conscience in public.

Nor is that, vital though it may be, the most important consideration. Auschwitz is not only a lesson for the world, but a warning, too, which men of every race must scrutinize carefully before they condemn lightly. The Nazis, it is true, created this monstrous machine, but in so doing, they demonstrated with Teutonic thoroughness the depths to which man can sink.

Let us make quite sure that their methods will never be aped, that never again will human beings of any nationality degrade their fellows on such a scale.

THE VRBA-WETZLER REPORT

Including the Mordowicz-Rozin Report

**LEGATION OF THE
UNITED STATES OF AMERICA**

Bern, October 12, 1944.

~~Confidential~~

Franklin D. Roosevelt Library
DECLASSIFIED by State
Dept. per telephone to Director,
FDRL, 2-7-64.

Mr. John Pehle,
    Director, War Refugee Board,
      Washington.

Sir:

    Subject: Transmitting two reports on the German
              concentration and extermination camps for
              Jews and political prisoners of AUSCHWITZ
              (Oswieçim) and BIRKENAU (Rajsko) in Upper
              Silesia previously referred to in the
              Legation's 4291 and 4295 of July 6, 1944.

    I have the honor to send to the War Refugee Board, enclosed herewith, three copies each of two reports dealing with the German SS-controlled concentration and extermination camps for Jews and political prisoners from various occupied countries in Europe located at Auschwitz (Germanization of the Polish name of Oswieçim) and Birkenau (the name of the Polish village was Rajsko) in Upper Silesia. The enclosed reports constitute, in English translation, the full texts, a condensation of which was cabled to the War Refugee Board in the Legation's telegrams Nos. 4291 and 4295 of July 6, 1944.

    These reports reached Switzerland during June 1944 from Bratislava, having been forwarded through Czech underground channels. They were delivered to Dr. Jean Kopecky, Representative of the Czechoslovak Government in Geneva, although that written by the two young Slovak Jews was addressed to Mr. Nathan Schwalb, Representative in Switzerland of the Hechalutz Organization (the left labor wing of the Zionists).

    While it is of course impossible to directly vouch for their complete authenticity, I have every reason to believe that they are, unfortunately, a true picture of the frightful happenings in these camps.

                                       In

Image courtesy of the FDR Presidential Library.

-2-

In the case of the first report by the two young Slovak Jews I had occasion to speak here in Bern with a member of the Bratislava Papal Nunciature who had personally interviewed these two young men and declared the impression they created in telling their story to be thoroughly convincing. I further understand that responsible members of the Bratislava Jewish community closely cross-examined the authors of this report so that the material finally incorporated into it includes only that about which there was no uncertainty or equivocation in their minds or in the minds of their examiners.

The report of the Polish Major (No. 2) was composed quite independently of the story of the two young Jews and was communicated to the Czech Resistance Movement in Slovakia, which in turn forwarded it to Dr. Kopecky. Dr. Kopecky vouches for the reliability of the man who composed it and for its authenticity. It arrived originally in Polish from which a German translation was first made. I in turn carefully corrected the translation from German into English enclosed herewith.

The figures concerning the size of the Jewish convoys arriving and the numbers of men and women admitted to the two camps cannot be taken as mathematically exact; and, in fact, are declared by the authors to be no more than reliable approximations. A precise statistical record of the numbers of persons murdered at Asuchwitz and Birkenau, however, would not detract in any appreciable degree from the value of these reports as testimony to the enormity of the crime perpetrated here.

The indications given concerning the periods of arrival and countries of origin of Jewish convoys check very closely with information possessed by various reliable Jewish and non-Jewish organizations in Switzerland regarding the departure of such deportees from various European countries. I myself, for example, was in southern France during the deportation of large convoys of foreign Jews from such internment camps as Rivesaltes, Gurs, Les Milles and Récébédou, in August and September of 1942, and have considerable first-hand information with respect to their composition, number and dates of departure.

The episode of the postcards written by members of the first Theresienstadt convoy, which had to be dated March 23 and 25, 1943, recounted in the report of the two young Jews, is, to cite another small example, fully confirmed by the fact that a number of these cards were received here in Switzerland.

Numerous

In paragraph 2. The Polish Major's Report is not published in this book. Interested readers can find the entire report at FDR Presidential Library, Hyde Park, New York (FDRPL), General Correspondence, Box 7. http://www.fdrlibrary.marist.edu/_resources/images/wrb/wrb0139.pdf

331

-3-

Numerous other similar examples could be given if one were to go into this question at length.

Although, in the main, I personally feel that the handling of such material as the enclosed reports cannot be considered as a positive contribution to real relief or rescue activities, it does constitute a tragic side of the whole problem, an awareness of which plays a necessary role in developing and implementing programs destined to bring whatever aid possible to these people. I therefore submit them to the War Refugee Board for its own and for the information of whatever other agencies the Board deems advisable.

Respectfully yours,

Roswell D. McClelland,
Special Assistant to
the American Minister.

Enclosure:

Two reports.

RDM/mjb
In triplicate to War Refugee Board.

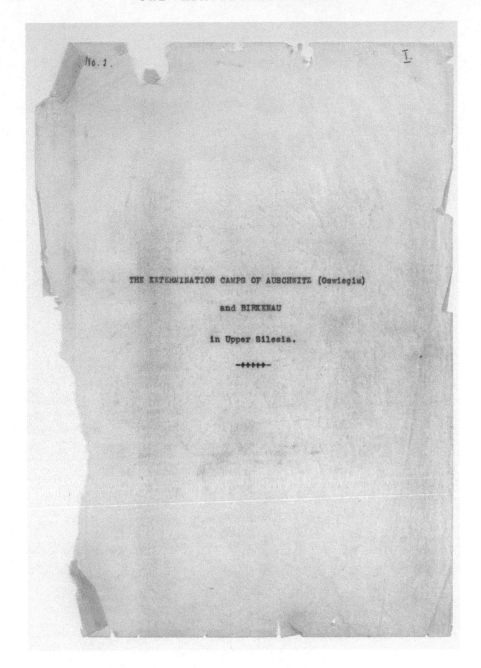

No. 1.   I.

THE EXTERMINATION CAMPS OF AUSCHWITZ (Oswiegim)

and BIRKENAU

in Upper Silesia.

-+++++-

FORWARD.

—┼┼┼┼┼—

Two young Slovak Jews – whose names will not be disclosed for the time being in the interest of their own safety – have been fortunate enough to escape after spending two years in the concentration camps of BIRKENAU, AUSCHWITZ and LUBLIN-MAJDANEK, where they had been deported in 1942 from SLOVAKIA.

One of them was sent on April 13, 1942 from the assembly camp of SERED directly to AUSCHWITZ and then to BIRKENAU, while the other was sent from the camp of NOVAKY to LUBLIN on June 14, 1942 and after a short stay there, transferred to AUSCHWITZ and, later, BIRKENAU.

The following report does not contain everything these two men experienced during their captivity, but only what the one or both together underwent, heard or experienced at first hand. No individual impressions or judgments are recorded and nothing passed on from hear-say.

The report starts with the story of the young Jew who was removed from SERED. The account of his experiences in BIRKENAU begins at the time the second Jew arrived there and is therefore based on the statements of both. Then follows the individual narrative of the second Jew who was sent from NOVAKY to LUBLIN and from there to AUSCHWITZ.

The declarations tally with all the trustworthy yet fragmentary reports hitherto received and the dates given with regard to transports to various camps agree with the official records. These statements can therefore be considered as entirely credible.

———

This forward was written by Oskar Krasnyanski, a member of Slovakian Jewish underground movement, who recorded the statement from Vrba and Wetzler as mentioned in Chapters 15 and 16 of the book.

On the 13th April 1942 our group, consisting of 1,000 men, was loaded into railroad cars at the assembly camp of SERED. The doors were shut so that nothing would reveal the direction of the journey and when they were open after a long while we realized that we had crossed the Slovak frontier and were in ZWARDON. The train had until then been guarded by Hlinka men but was now taken over by SS. guards. After a few of the cars had been uncoupled from our convoy we continued on our way arriving at night at AUSCHWITZ, where we stopped on a side-track. The reason the other cars were left behind was apparently the lack of room at AUSCHWITZ. They joined us, however, a few days later. Upon arrival we were placed in rows of five and counted. There were 643 of us. After a walk of about 20 minutes with our heavy packs (we had left Slovakia well equipped) we reached the concentration camp of AUSCHWITZ.

We were at once led into a huge barrack where on the one side we had to deposit all our luggage and on the other side completely undress, leaving our clothes and valuables behind. Naked, we then proceeded to an adjoining barrack where our heads and bodies were shaved and desinfected with lysol. At the exit every man was given a number which began with 28,600 in consecutive order. With this number in hand we were then herded to a third barrack were so-called registration took place. This consisted of tattooing the numbers we had received in the second barrack on the left side of our chest. The extreme brutality with which this was effected made many of us faint. The particulars of our identity were also recorded. Then we were led in groups of a hundred into a cellar, and later to a barrack where we were issued striped prisoners clothes and wooden clogs. This lasted until 10 a.m. In the afternoon our prisoner's outfit was taken away from us again and replaced by the ragged and dirty remains of Russian uniforms. Thus equipped we were marched off to BIRKENAU.

AUSCHWITZ is a concentration camp for political prisoners under so-called "protective custody". At the time of my arrival, that is in April of 1942, there were about 15,000 prisoners in the camp, the majority of whom were Poles, Germans and civilian Russians under protective custody. A small number of prisoners came under the categories of criminals and "work-shirkers".

AUSCHWITZ camp headquarters controls at the same time the work-camp of BIRKENAU as well as the farm labor camp of HARMENSE. All the prisoners arrive first at AUSCHWITZ where they are provided with a prisoner's immatriculation number and then are either kept there, sent to BIRKENAU or, in very small numbers, to HARMENSE. The prisoners receive consecutive numbers upon arrival. Every number is only used once so that the last number always corresponds to

- 3 -

the number of prisoners actually in the camp. At the time of our escape, that is to say at the beginning of April 1944, the number had risen up to 180,000. At the outset the numbers were tattooed on the left breast, but later, due to their becoming blurred, on the left forearm.

All prisoners, irrespective of category or nationality, are treated the same. However, to facilitate identification, they are distinguished by various coloured triangles sewed on the clothing on the left breast under the immatriculation number. The first letter indicates the nationality of the prisoner. This letter (for instance "P" for Poles) appears in the middle of the triangle. The coloured triangles have the following meaning :

red triangle		political prisoners under protective custody.
green	"	professional criminals.
black	"	"dodgers" (labor slackers), "anti-socials" (mostly Russians).
pink	"	homosexuals.
violet	"	Members of the religious sect of "Bibelforscher".

The Jewish prisoners differ from the Aryan prisoners in that their triangle (which in the majority of cases is red) is turned into a David's star by adding yellow points.

Within the enclosure of the camp of AUSCHWITZ there are several factories : a war production plant, Deutscher Aufrüstungswerk (DAW), a factory belonging to the KRUPP works and one to the SIEMENS concern. Outside the boundary of the camp is a tremendous plant covering several square kilometers named "BUNA". The prisoners work in all the aforementioned factories.

The prisoners' actual living quarters, if such a term may at all be used, inside the camp proper cover an area of approximately 500 by 300 meters surrounded by a double row of concrete posts about 3 meters high which are connected (both inside and outside) to one another by a dense netting of high-tension wires fixed into the posts by isulators. Between these two rows of posts, at interwals of 150 meters, there are 5 meters high watch-towers, equipped with machine-guns and searchlights. In front of the inner high-tension circle there is further an ordinary wire fence. Merely touching this fence is answered by a stream of bullets from the watch-towers. This system is called "the small or inner chain of sentry posts". The camp itself is composed of three rows of houses. Between the first and second row is the camp street and between the second and third there used to be a wall. The Jewish girls deported from Slovakia in March and April 1942, over 7,000 of them, lived in the houses separated by this wall up to the middle

On line 24 "Aryan" is an incorrect translation, more precise term is Gentile.

- 3 -

of August 1942. After these girls had been removed to
BIRKENAU the wall between the second and third row of
houses was removed. The camp entry road cuts across the
row of houses while over the entrance gate, which is of
course always heavily guarded, stands the ironic in-
scription : "Work brings freedom".

At a radius of some 2,000 meters the whole camp is
encircled by a second line called "The big or outer chain
of sentry posts" also with watch-towers every 150 meters.
Between the inner and outer chain of sentry posts are the
factories and other workshops. The towers of the inner
chain are only manned at night when the high-tension
current is switched into the double row of wires. During
day-time the garrison of the inner chain of sentry posts
is withdrawn, and the men take up duty in the outer chain.
Escape through these sentry posts – and many attempts have
been made – is practically impossible. Getting through
the inner circle of posts at night is completely impossible,
and the towers of the outer chain are so close to one another (one every 150 meters, i.e. giving each tower a
sector with a 75 meters radius to watch), that approaching
unnoticed is out of the question. The guards shoot without warning. The garrison of the outer chain is withdrawn
at twilight, but only after it has been ascertained that
all the prisoners are within the inner circle. If the roll-
call reveals that a prisoner is missing, sirens immediately sound the alarm.

ROUGH GROUND PLAN OF AUSCHWITZ

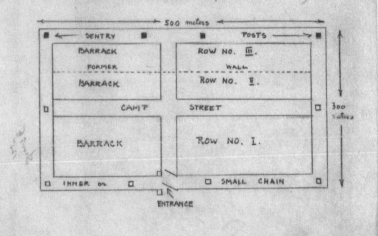

337

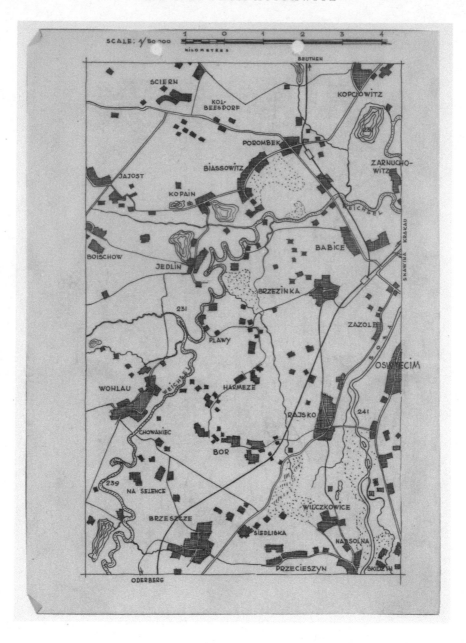

The men in the outer chain remain in their towers on the look-out, the inner chain is maned, and a systematic search is begun by hundreds of SS guards and bloodhounds. The siren brings the whole surrounding countryside to a state of alarm so that if by miracle the escapee has been successful in getting through the outer chain he is nearly certain to be caught by one of the numerous German police and SS. patrols. The escapee is furthermore handicapped by his clean-shaven head, his striped prisoner's outfit or red patches sewn on his clothing, and the passiveness of the thoroughly intimidated inhabitants. The mere fact of neglecting to give information on the whereabouts of a prisoner, not to speak of extending help, is punished by death. Provided that the prisoner has not been caught sooner, the garrison of the outer chain of sentry posts remains on the watch for three days and nights after which delay it is presumed that the escapee has succeeded in breaking through the double circle. The following night the outer guard is withdrawn. If the escapee is caught alive he is hanged in the presence of the whole camp but if he is found dead, his body - wherever it may have been located - is brought back to camp (it is easy to identify the corpse by means of the tattooed number) and seated at the entrance gate, a small notice clasped in his hands, reading : "Here I am". During our two years imprisonment many attempts to escape were made by prisoners but, with the exception of two or three, all were brought back dead or alive. It is not known whether the 2 or 3 escapees who were not caught actually managed to get away. It can however be asserted that among the Jews who were deported from SLOVAKIA to AUSCHWITZ or BIRKENAU, we are the only two who were lucky enough to save ourselves.

As stated previously, we were transferred from AUSCHWITZ to BIRKENAU on the day of our arrival.

Actually there is no such district as BIRKENAU. Even the word BIRKENAU is new in that it has been "adopted" from the nearby birch forest (BREZINSKY). The district now called BIRKENAU was and is still called "RAJSKA" by the local population. The existing camp center of BIRKENAU lies 4 kilometers distant from AUSCHWITZ. The outer control zones of both BIRKENAU and AUSCHWITZ meet and are merely separated by a railway track. We never found anything out about NEW-BERUN, probably about 30 to 40 kilometers away which, oddly enough, we had to indicate as postal district for BIRKENAU.

At the time of our arrival in BIRKENAU we found there only one huge kitchen for 15,000 people and three stone buildings, two of which were completed and one under construction. The buildings were surrounded by an ordinary barbed wire fence. The prisoners were housed in these buildings and in others later constructed. All are built according to a standard model. Each house is about 30 meters long and 8 to 10 meters wide. Whereas the height

of the walls hardly exceeds 3 meters the roof is dis-
proportionately high — about 5 meters —, so that the
house gives the impression of a stable surmounted by a
large hay-loft. There is no inner ceiling, so that
the room reaches a height of 7 meters in the center; in
other words the pointed roofing rests directly on the
four walls. The room is divided in two by a partition
running its whole length down the middle and fitted with
an opening to enable communication between the two parts
thus separated. Along both side-walls as well as along
the middle partition, two parallel floors, some 80 centimeters apart, have been built which are in turn divided
into small cells by vertical partitions. Thus there are
3 floors : the ground floor and the two built in the
side-walls. Normally 3 people live in each cubicle. As
can be judged from the dimensions indicated, these cubic-
les are too narrow for a man to lie stretched out and not
high enough for him to sit upright. There is no question
of having enough space to stand upright. In this way
some 4 to 500 people are accommodated in one house or
"Block", as they are also called.

The present camp of BIRKENAU covers an area of some
1800 by 500 meters which is surrounded — similar to AUS-
CHWITZ — by a so-called small or inner chain of sentry
posts. Work is now proceeding on a still larger compound
which is to be added later on to the already existing
camp. The purpose if this extensive planning is not known
to us.

Within a radius of 3 kilometers as with AUSCHWITZ,
BIRKENAU, is also surrounded by an outer chain of sentry
posts with the same type of watch system as at AUSCHWITZ.

The buildings we found on our arrival had been erected by 12,000 Russian prisoners of war brought there in
December 1941. In severe winter weather they had to work
under inhuman conditions as a result of which most of them,
with the exception of a small number employed in the kitchen, died of exposure. They were numbered from 1 to
12,000 in a series which had no connection with the ordinary
camp numbering system previously described. Whenever fresh
convoys of Russian prisoners arrived, they were not issued
the current AUSCHWITZ prisoner numbers, but received those
of deceased Russians in the 1 to 12,000 series. It is therefore difficult to estimate how many prisoners of this category passed through the camp. Apparently Russians were
transferred to AUSCHWITZ or BIRKENAU on disciplinary grounds
from regular prisoner of war camps. We found what remained
of the Russians in a terrible state of destitution and ne-
glect living in the unfinished building without the slightest protection against cold or rain. They died "en masse".
Hundreds and thousands of their bodies were buried super-
ficially, spreading a stench of pestilence. Later we had
to exhume and burn the corpses.

- 6 -

A week before our arrival in AUSCHWITZ, the first group of Jews reached the camp :(the women were dealt with separately and received numbers parallel to those of the men; the Slovak women received serial numbers from 1 to 8,000) 1,320 naturalized French Jews from Paris. They were numbered from 27,500 onwards. It is clear, therefore, that between this French group and our convoy, no other men arrived in AUSCHWITZ, since we have already pointed out that our numbers started with 28,600. We found the 700 French Jews who were still alive in terrible condition, the missing 600 having died within a week after their arrival.

The following categories were housed in the three completed buildings :

I.   The so-called "prominencia" : professional criminals and older Polish political prisoners who were in charge of the administration of the camp.

II.   The remainded of the French Jews, namely some 700.

III.   The 643 original Slovak Jews to whom were added a few days later those who had been left at ZWARDON.

IV.   Those Russians who were still alive and housed in the unfinished building as well as in the open air and whose numbers diminished so rapidly that as a group they are scarcely worth mentioning.

Together with the remaining Russian prisoners the Slovak Jews worked at the construction of buildings, whereas the French Jews had to do spade work. After 3 days, I was ordered, together with 200 other Slovak Jews, to work in the German armament factories at AUSCHWITZ but we continued to be housed in BIRKENAU. We left early in the morning returning at night and worked in the carpentry shop as well as on road construction. Our food consisted of 1 litre of turnip-soup at midday and 300 grams of bad bread in the evening. Working conditions were inconceivably hard, so that the majority of us, weakened by starvation and the inedible food, could not stand it. The mortality was so high that every day our group of 200 had 30 to 35 dead. Many were simply beaten to death by the overseers - the "Capos" - during work, without the slightest provocation. The gaps in our ranks caused by these deaths were replaced daily by prisoners from BIRKENAU. Our return at night was extremely painful and dangerous, as we had to drag along over a distance of 5 kilometers our tools, fire wood, heavy caldrons and the bodies of those who had died or had been killed during the working day. With these heavy loads we were forced to maintain a brisk pace and anyone incurring the displeasure of one of the "Capos" was cruelly knocked down, if not beaten to death. Until the arrival of the second group of Slovak men some 14 days later, our original number had dwindled to 150. At night we were counted, the bodies of the dead were piled up on flat, narrow-gauge cars

In the middle part of the last paragraph, left hand margin "Capos" is another possible spelling of Kapo.

341

or in a truck and brought to the birch forest (BREZINSKY)
where they were burnt in a trench several meters deep and
about 15 meters long. Every day on our way to work we
met a working party of 300 Jewish girls from Slovakia who
were employed on ground work in the vicinity. They were
dressed in old Russian uniform rags and wore wooden clogs.
Their heads were shaven and unfortunately we could not
speak to them.

Until the middle of May 1942, a total of 4 convoys
of male Jews from Slovakia, arrived at BIRKENAU and all
received similar treatment to ours.

From the 1st and 2nd transports 120 men were chosen
(including myself) and placed at the disposal of the administration of the camp of AUSCHWITZ which was in need
of doctors, dentists, intellectuals and clerks. This
group consisted of 90 Slovak and 30 French Jews. As I
had in the meantime managed to work my way up to a good
position in BIRKENAU — being in command of a group of 50
men, which had brought me considerable advantage — I at
first felt reluctant to leave for AUSCHWITZ. However, I
was finally persuaded to go and left. After 8 days, 18
doctors and attendants as well as three further persons
were selected from this group of 120 intellectuals. The
doctors were used in the "sick building" or "hospital"
at AUSCHWITZ, while we three were sent back to BIRKENAU.
My 2 comrades, Ladislav Braun from Trnava and Gross from
Vrbové (?), both of whom have since died, were sent to
the Slovak block while I was ordered to the French section where we were employed at collecting "personal data"
and at "nursing the sick". The remaining 99 persons were
sent to work in the gravel pit where they all died within
a short time.

Shortly thereafter a so-called "sick-building"
(Krankenbau) was set up. It was destined to become the
much dreaded "Block 7" where at first I was chief attend-
ant and later administrator. The chief of this "infirmary" was a Pole named Viktor Mordarki, prisoner No. 3550.
Actually this building was nothing else than an assembly
centre for death candidates. All prisoners incapable of
working were sent there. There was no question of any
medical attention or care. We had some 150 dead daily and
their bodies were sent for cremation to AUSCHWITZ.

At the same time the so-called "selections" were introduced. Twice weekly, Mondays and Thursdays, the camp
doctor indicated the number of prisoners who were to be
gassed and then burned. These "selectees" were loaded
into trucks and brought to the Birch Forest. Those still
alive upon arrival were gassed in a big barrack erected
near the trench used for burning the bodies. The weekly
"draft" in dead from "Block 7" was about 2,000, of whom
1,300 died of natural "death" and about 800 through "selection". For those who had not been "selected" a death

342

certificate was issued and sent to the central administration at ORANIENBURG, whereas for the "selectees" a
special register was kept with the indication "S.B."
("Sonderbehandelt" - special treatment). Until January
15, 1943, up to which time I was administrator of "Block
7" and therefore in a position to directly observe happenings, some 50,000 prisoners died of "natural death" or by
"selection".

As previously described, the prisoners were numbered
consecutively so that we are able to reconstruct fairly
clearly their order of succession and the fate which befell each separate convoy on arrival.

The first male Jewish transport reaching AUSCHWITZ
for BIRKENAU, was composed, as mentioned, of 1,330 naturalized French Jews bearing approximately the following numbers :

27,400 - 28,600	
28,600 - 29,600	In April 1942, the first convoy of Slovak Jews (our convoy).
29,600 - 29,700	100 men (Aryans) from various concentra-tion camps.
29,700 - 32,700	3 complete convoys of Slovak Jews.
32,700 - 33,100	400 professional criminals (Aryans) from Warsaw prisons.
33,100 - 35,000	1900 Jews from Cracow.
35,000 - 36,000	1000 Poles (Aryans) - political prisoners.
36,000 - 37,300	In May 1942 - 1300 Slovak Jews from LUBLIN-MAJDANEK.
37,300 - 37,900	600 Poles (Aryans) from RADOM, amongst them a few Jews.
37,900 - 38,000	100 Poles from the concentration camp of DACHAU.
38,000 - 38,400	400 French naturalized Jews who arrived with their families.

This whole convoy consisted of about 1,600 individuals
of whom approximately 200 girls and 400 men were admitted
to the camp, while the remaining 1,000 persons (women, old
people, children as well as men) were sent without further
procedure from the railroad siding directly to the Birch
forest, and there gassed and burnt. From this moment on
all Jewish convoys were dealt with in the same manner.
Approximately 10 % of the men and 5 % of the women were
allotted to the camps and the remaining members were immediately gassed. This process of extermination had already
been applied earlier to the Polish Jews. During long months,
without interruption, trucks brought thousands of Jews from
the various "ghettos" direct to the pit in the "Birkenwald".

38,400 - 39,300	800 naturalized French Jews, the remain-der of the convoy was - as previously described - gassed.

39,200 - 40,000   800 Poles (Aryans), political prisoners.

40,000 - 40,150   150 Slovak Jews with their families.
   Outside of a group of 50 girls sent to the women's
camp, all other members were gassed in the Birch forest.
Among the 150 men who came to camp there was a certain
Zucker (Christian name unknown) and Sonnenschein, Viliam,
both from Eastern Slovakia.

40,150 - 43,800   approx. 4,000 French naturalized Jews,
almost all intellectuals. 1,000 women were directed to
the women's camp, while the balance of about 3,000 persons
were gassed in the usual manner.

43,800 - 44,200   400 Slovak Jews from LUBLIN, including
Matej Klein and No. 43820, Meiloch Laufer from Eastern
Slovakia. This convoy arrived on June 30, 1942.

44,200 - 45,000   200 Slovak Jews. The convoy consisted of
1,000 persons. A number of women were sent to the women's
camp, the rest gassed in the Birch wood. Among the prisoners sent to camp were : Jozef Zelmanovic, Snina - Adolf
Kahan, Bratislava - Walter Reichmann, Sucany - Esther Kahan,
Bratislava. I had the opportunity to speak to the latter
on April 30, 1944. She is the "Block eldest" in the women's
camp.

45,000 - 47,000   2,000 Frenchmen (Aryans), communists and
other political prisoners, among whom were the brother of
Thorez and the young brother of Léon Blum. The latter was
atrociously tortured, then gassed and burned.

47,000 - 47,500   500 Jews from Holland, in the majority
                  German emigrants. The rest of the convoy,
                  about 2,500 persons, gassed.

47,500 - 47,800   About 300 so-called Russians under pro-
                  tective custody.

48,300 - 48,620   320 Jews from Slovakia. About 70 girls
were transferred to the women's camp, the remainder, some
650 people, gassed in the Birch wood. This convoy included
about 80 people who had been handed over by the Hungarian
police to the camp of SERED. Others from this convoy were :
Dr. Zoltan Mandel (since deceased) - Holz (Christian name
unknown), butcher from PIESTANY, later sent to WARSAW -
Miklos Engel, Zilina - Chaim Katz, Snina, now employed in
the "mortuary" (his wife and 6 children were gassed).

49,000 - 64,800   15,000 naturalized French, Belgian and Dutch
Jews. This figure certainly represents less than 10 % of
the total convoy. This was between July 1st and September
15, 1942. Large family convoys arrived from various European
countries and were at once directed to the Birch wood. The
special squad ("Sonderkommando") employed for gassing and
burning worked in day and night shifts. Hundreds of thousands of Jews were gassed during this period.

*On line 21 "April 30, 1944" must be a typographical error, since the author
escaped Auschwitz-Birkenau on April 7, 1944.*

64,800 - 65,000   200 Slovak Jews. Out of this transport about 100 women were admitted to the camp, the rest of them gassed and burnt. Among the newly arrived were : Ludwig Katz, Zilina - Avri Burger, Bratislava - Poprad (wife dead) - Mikulas Steiner, Povazska Bystrica - Juraj Fried, Trencin - Buchwald - Josef Rosenwasser, Eastern Slovakia - Julius Neuman, Bardejov - Sandor Wertheimer, Vrbove - Misi Wertheimer, Vrbove - Bela Blau, Zilina.

65,000 - 68,000   Naturalized French, Belgian and Dutch Jews. Not more than 1,000 women were selected and sent to the camp. The others, at the lowest estimate 30,000, were gassed.

71,000 - 80,000   Naturalized French, Belgian and Dutch Jews. The prisoners brought to the camp, hardly represent 10 % of the total transport. A conservative estimate would be that approx. 65 to 70,000 persons were gassed.

On December 17, 1942, the 200 young Slovak Jews, the so-called "special squad" employed in gassing and burning the condemned, were in turn executed at BIRKENAU. They were executed for having planned to mutiny and escape. A Jew betrayed their preparations. This frightful job had to be taken over by a group of 200 Polish Jews who had just arrived at camp from MAKOW. Among those executed were : Alexander Weiss, Fero Wagner, Oskar Scheiner, Dezider Wetzler, Aladar Spitzer, and Vojtech Weiss, all from Trnava.

The change thus effected in the "special squad" deprived us of a valuable contact which soon had a detrimental effect on our "private supplies". In spite of having all their luggage confiscated at AUSCHWITZ, these "death convoys" brought with them considerable sums in foreign currency, especially paper and gold dollars, large quantities of gold jewelry and valuable stones as well as foodstuffs. Although all valuables naturally had to be surrendered it was unavoidable that articles found in searching the clothing of the deceased (especially gold dollars) disappeared into the pockets of our boys. In this way they brought considerable means into the camp, not to speak of foodstuffs. Officially nothing could be bought with this money in the camp but one could do considerable "trading" with S.S. guards or other civilian workmen employed as specialists on various jobs in the camp who had the opportunity to bring with them food and cigarettes. The prices were naturally in relation to the abnormal circumstances. For a few 100 cigarettes one had to produce a 20 dollar gold coin. Bartering also flourished. The increase in price had no effect on us as we had money enough. Through the "special squad" we were also able to exchange our rags for the better clothing of the gassed. The coat I am still wearing to-day belonged to a Dutch Jew and on the lining one can still see the label of an Amsterdam tailor.

The men belonging to the "special squad" lived separately. On account of the dreadful smell spread by them people had but little contact with them. Besides they were always filthy, destitute, half wild and extraordinarily brutal and ruthless. It was not uncommon to see one of them kill another. This was considered by the others a sensation, a change. One simply recorded that number so-and-so had died.

Once I was an eye-witness when a young Polish Jew named Jossel demonstrated "scientific" murder on a Jew in the presence of an SS. guard. He used no weapon, merely his bare hands, to kill his victim.

No. 80,000 marks the beginning of the systematic extermination of the Polish ghettos.

80,000 - 85,000 approx. 5,000 Jews from various ghettos in MLJAWA - MAKOW - ZICHENOW - LOMZA - GRODNO - BIALOSTOK.

For fully 30 days truck-convoys arrived without interruption. Only 5,000 persons were sent to the concentration camp, all the others were gassed at once. The "special squad" worked in two shifts, 24 hours daily and was scarcely able to cope with the gassing and burning. Without exaggerating it may be said that out of these convoys some 80 to 90,000 received "special treatment". These transports also brought in a considerable amount of money, valuables and precious stones.

85,000 - 92,000   6,000 Jews from GRODNO, BIALOSTOK and CRACOW as well as 1,000 Aryan Poles. The majority of the Jewish convoys were directly gassed and daily about 4,000 Jews were driven into the gas chambers.

During mid-January 1943 3 convoys of 2,000 persons each from THERESIENSTADT arrived. They bore the designations "CU" "CR" and "R". (The meaning of these signs is unknown to us). These markings were also stamped on their luggage. Out of these 6,000 persons only 600 men and 300 women were admitted to the camp. The remainder was gassed.

99,000 - 100,000   End of January 1943 large convoys of French and Dutch Jews arrived : only a small proportion of them reached the camp.

100,000 - 102,000   In February 1943, 2,000 Aryan Poles, mostly intellectuals.

102,000 - 103,000   700 Czech Aryans. Later, those still alive were sent to BUCHENWALD.

103,000 - 108,000   3,000 French and Dutch Jews and 2,000 Poles (Aryans).

During the month of February 1943, 2 contingents
arrived daily. They included Polish, French and
Dutch Jews who, in the main, were sent to the gas
chambers. The number gassed during this month can
well be estimated at 90,000.

At the end of February 1943 a new modern crematorium
and gassing plant was inaugurated at BIRKENAU. The gassing and burning of the bodies in the Birch forest was
discontinued, the whole job being taken over by the four
specially built crematoria. The large ditch was filled
in, the ground levelled and the ashes used as before for
fertilizer at the farm labour camp of HERMENSE, so that
to-day it is almost impossible to find traces of the
dreadful mass murder which took place here.

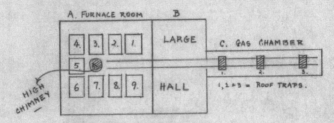

ROUGH GROUND PLAN OF

CREMATORIA: TYPES I & II IN BIRKENAU

At present there are four crematoria in operation at
BIRKENAU, two large ones, I and II, and two smaller ones,
III and IV. Those of type I and II consist of 3 parts,
i.e. : a) the furnace room; b) the large hall; and c) the
gas chamber. A huge chimney rises from the furnace room
around which are grouped nine furnaces, each having four
openings. Each opening can take three normal corpses at
once and after an hour and a half the bodies are completely burnt. This corresponds to a daily capacity of about
2,000 bodies. Next to this is a large "reception hall"
which is arranged so as to give the impression of the anti-
chamber of a bathing establishment. It holds 2,000 people
and apparently there is a similar waiting room on the
floor below. From there a door and a few steps lead down
into the very long and narrow gas chamber. The walls of
this chamber are also camouflaged with simulated entries
to shower rooms in order to mislead the victims. The roof
is fitted with 3 traps which can be hermetically closed
from the outside. A track leads from the gas chamber towards the furnace room. The gassing takes place as follows:
the unfortunate victims are brought into hall (b) where
they are told to undress. To complete the fiction that
they are going to bathe, each person receives a towel and a
small piece of soap issued by two men clad in white coats.

Then they are crowded into the gas chamber (c) in such numbers that there is of course only standing room. To compress this crowd into the narrow space shots are often fired to induce those already at the far end to huddle still closer together. When everybody is inside the heavy doors are closed. Then there is a short pause, presumably to allow the room temperature to rise to a certain level, after which SS. men with gas masks climb on the roof, open the traps and shake down a preparation in powder form out of tin cans labelled "CYKLON" "For use against vermin" which are manufactured by a Hamburg concern. It is presumed that this is a "CYANIDE" mixture of some sort which turns into gas at a certain temprature. After 3 minutes everyone in the chamber is dead. No one is known to have survived this ordeal, although it was not uncommon to discover signs of life after the primitive measures employed in the Birch wood. The chamber is then opened, aired and the "special squad" carts the bodies on flat trucks to the furnace rooms where the burning takes place. Crematoria III and IV work on nearly the same principle but their capacity is only half as large. Thus the total capacity of the four cremating and gassing plants at BIRKENAU amounts to about 6,000 daily.

On principle only Jews are gassed; Aryans very seldom, as they are usually given "special treatment" by shooting. Before the crematoria were put into service, the shooting took place in the Birch wood and the bodies were burnt in the long trench; later, however, executions took place in the large hall of one of the crematoria which has been provided with a special installation for this purpose.

Prominent guests from Berlin were present at the inauguration of the first crematorium in March 1943. The "program" consisted of the gassing and burning of 8,000 Cracow Jews. The guests, both officers and civilians, were extremely satisfied with the results and the special peep-hole fitted into the door of the gas chamber was in constant use. They were lavish in their praise of this newly erected installation.

* *

109,000 - 119,000 At the beginning of March 1943, 45,000 Jews arrived from Saloniki. 10,000 of them came to the camp including a small percentage of the women; some 30,000 however went straight to the cremating establishment. Of the 10,000 nearly all died a short time later from a contageous illness resembling malaria. They also died of typhus due to the general conditions prevailing in the camp.

Malaria among the Jews and typhus took such toll among the prisoners in general that the "selections" were

On line 10, "CYKLON" is another possible spelling of Zycklon.

temporarily suspended. The contaminated Greek Jews were
ordered to present themselves and in spite of our repeated
warnings many of them did. They were all killed by intra-
cardial Phenol injections administered by a lance-corporal
of the medical corps assisted by imprisoned Czech doctors.
The latter : Dr. Honsa Cespira, of Prague (previously in
BUCHENWALD) and Dr. Zdenik STICH, also from Prague via
BUCHENWALD, did their utmost to alleviate the sufferings
of these victims.

Out of the 10,000 Greek Jews, some 1,000 men remained
alive and were later sent, together with 500 other Jews,
to do fortification work in Warsaw. A few weeks later
several hundred came back in a pitiful state and were
immediately gassed. The remainder presumably died in Warsaw. 400 Greek Jews suffering from malaria were sent for
"further treatment" to LUBLIN after the Phenol injections
had been stopped and it appears that they actually arrived.
Their fate is not known to us, but it can be taken for
granted that out of the original number of 10,000 Jews not
one eventually remained in the camp.

Simultaneously with the stopping of the "selections"
the murdering of prisoners was forbidden. Prominent murderers
such as :
the Reich German professional criminals Alexander Neumann,
Zimmer, Albert Haemmerle, Rudi Osteringer, Rudi Bechert, and
the political prisoners Alfred Kien and Alois Stahler, were
punished for repeated murder and had to make written declaration that they had killed so and so many prisoners.

At the beginning of 1943 the political section of AUSCH-
WITZ received 500,000 discharge certificates and we thought
with ill-concealed joy, that at least a few of us would be
liberated. But the forms were simply filled out with the
names of those gassed and filed away in the archives.

119,000 - 130,000   1,000 Poles (Aryans) from the PAWIAK
                     penitentiary in Warsaw.

130,000 - 123,000   3,000 Greek Jews part of whom were sent
                     to replace their comrades in Warsaw.
                     The remainder quickly died off.

123,000 - 124,000   1,000 Poles (Aryans) from RADOM and
                     TARNOW.

124,000 - 126,000   2,000 from mixed Aryan convoys.

In the meantime ceaseless convoys of Polish and a few
French and Belgian Jews arrived and without exception were
dispatched to the gas chambers. Among them was a transport
of 1,000 Polish Jews from MAJDANEK which included three
Slovaks, one of whom was a certain Spira from Stropkow or
Vranov.

The flow of convoys abruptly ceased at the end of July 1943 and there was a short breathing space. The crematoria were thouroughly cleaned, the installations repaired and prepared for further use. On August 3rd, the killing machine again went into operation. The first convoys consisted of Jews from BENZBURG and SOSNOWITZ and others followed during the whole month of August.

132,000 - 136,000   only 4,000 men and a very small number of women were brought to the camp. Over 35,000 were gassed. Of the aforementioned 4,000 men, many died as a result of bad treatment, hunger or illness; some were even murdered. The main responsibility for these tragedies lies with the criminal TYN (a Reich German) from the concentration camp of SACHSENHAUSEN and the Polish political prisoner No. 8516, Mieczislav KATERZINSKI, from Warsaw.

The "selections" were introduced again and this time to a murderous extent, especially in the women's camp. The camp doctor, an SS. "Hauptsturmführer" and the son or nephew of the police president of Berlin (we forget his name) outdid all the others in brutality. The selection system has been continued ever since, until our escape.

137,000 - 138,000   At the end of August 1,000 Poles came from the PAWIAK prison and 80 Jews from Greece.

138,000 - 141,000   3,000 men from various Aryan transports.

142,000 - 145,000   At the beginning of September 1943, 3,000 Jews arrived from Polish working camps and Russian prisoners of war.

148,000 - 152,000   During the week following September 7, 1943, family transports of Jews arrived from THERESIENSTADT. They enjoyed quite an exceptional status which was incomprehensible to us. The families were not separated and not a single one of them received the customary and "normal" gas treatment. Their heads were not even shaven, they were able to keep their luggage and were lodged in a separate section of the camp, men, women and children together. The men were not forced to work and a school was even set up for the children under the direction of Fredy HIRSCH (Makabi, Prague). They were allowed to correspond freely. The worst they had to undergo was mistreatment at the hands of their camp eldest, a certain professional criminal by the name of Arno BÖHM, prisoner No. 8. Our astonishment increased when we learned of the official indication given to this special transport :

"SB" - transport of Czech Jews with 6 months quarantine -

We very well knew what "SB" meant ("Sonderbehandlung") but could not understand the long period of 6 months quarantine and the generally clement treatment this group received. The longest quarantine period we had witnessed

so far was only three weeks. Towards the end of the six
months' period, however, we became convinced that the
fate of these Jews would be the same as that of most of
the others — the gas chamber. We tried to get in touch
with the leader of this group and explain their lot and
what they had to expect. Some of them declared (especially Fredy HIRSCH who seemed to enjoy the full confidence
of his companions) that if our fears took shape they would
organise resistance. The members of the "special squad"
also swore that they would join the movement. Thus, some
of them hoped to instigate a general revolt in the camp.
On March 6, 1944 we heard that the crematoria were being
prepared to receive the Czech Jews. I hastened to inform
Fredy HIRSCH and begged him to take immediate action as
they had nothing to loose. He replied that he recognized
his duty. Before night-fall I again crept over to the
Czech camp where I learned that Fredy HIRSCH was dying;
he had poisoned himself with luminal. The next day, March
7, 1944, he was taken, unconscious, along with his 3,791
comrades who had arrived at BIRKENAU on September 7, 1943,
on trucks, to the crematoria and gassed. The young people
went to their death singing, but to our great disapoint-
ment nobody revolted. The men of the "special squad",
ready to join, waited in vain. Some 500 elderly people
had died during quarantine. Of all these Jews only 11
twins were left alive. They are being subjected to various
medical tests at AUSCHWITZ, and when we left BIRKENAU,
they were still alive. Among the gassed was Rozsi FÜRST,
from SERED. A week before the gassing, that is to say on
March 1st., 1944, everyone in the Czech group in the camp
had been asked to inform his relatives about his well
being. The letters had to be dated March 23 to 25, 1944
and they were requested to ask for food parcels.

153,000 - 154,000   1,000 Polish aryans from the PAVIAK
                     penitentiary.

155,000 - 159,000   During October and November 1943, 4,000
    persons from various prisons and smaller transports of
    Jews from BENZBURG and vicinity who had been driven out
    of their hiding places; also a group of Russians under
    protective custody from the MINSK and VITEBSK regions.
    Some more Russian prisoners of war arrived and as stated
    they as usual received numbers between 1 and 12,000.

160,000 - 165,000   In December 1943, 5,000 men originating
    from Dutch, French, Belgian transports and, for the
    first time, Italian Jews from FIUME, TRIESTE and ROME.
    Of these at least 30,000 were immediately gassed. The
    mortality among these Jews was very high and in addi-
    tion the "selection" system was still decimating all
    ranks. The bestiality of the whole procedure reached
    its culminating point between January 10th and 24th,
    1944 when even young and healthy persons irrespective
    of profession or working classification — with the ex-
    ception of doctors — were ruthlessly "selected".

Every single prisoner was called up, a strict control was established to see that all were present and the "selection" proceeded under the supervision of the same camp doctor (son or nephew of the Police President of Berlin) and of the Commandant of BIRKENAU, SS "Untersturmführer" SCHWARZHUBER. The "infirmary" had in the meantime been transferred from "Block 7" to a separate section of the camp where conditions had become quite bearable. Its inmates, nevertheless, were gassed to the last man. Apart from this group, this general action cost some 2,500 men and over 6,000 women their lives.

165,000 - 168,000   On December 30, 1943 a further group of 3,000 Jews arrived from THERESIENSTADT. The convoy was listed under the same category as the one which had reached the camp on September 7, i.e. "SB" - transport, Czech Jews with 6 months quarantine". On their arrival, men, women and children all joined the September group. They enjoyed the same privileges as their predecessors. 24 hours before the gassing of the first group took place, the latest arrivals were separated from the rest and placed in another part of the camp where they still are at present. Since they know what their fate is to be, they are already planning organised resistance, under the leadership of Ruzenka LAUFSCHNER and Hugo LANGSFELD, both from Prague. They are gradually collecting benzine and other combustible goods and intend to set the blocks of their section on fire when the crucial moment comes. Their quarantine ends on June 20, 1944.

168,000 - 170,000   1,000 people in small groups, Jews, Poles and Russians under protective custody.

170,000 - 171,000   1,000 Poles and Russians and a number of Yougoslaves.

171,000 - 174,000   At the end of February and beginning of March, 3,000 Jews from Holland, Belgium and for the first time long established French Jews (not naturalized) from VICHY, in France. The greater part of this transport was gassed immediately upon arrival.

Small groups of BENZBURGER and SOSNOWITZER Jews who had been dragged from hiding arrived in the middle of March. One of them told me that many Polish Jews were crossing over to Slovakia and from there to Hungary and that the Slovak Jews helped them on their way through.

After the gassing of the THERESIENSTADT transport there were no further arrivals until March 15, 1944. The effective strength of the camp rapidly diminished and men of later incoming transports, especially Dutch Jews, were directed to the camp. When we left on April 7, 1944 we heard that large convoys of Greek Jews were expected.

• • •

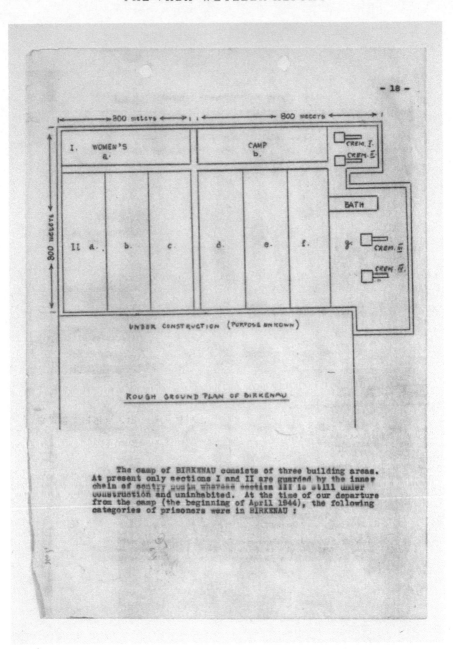

- 18 -

ROUGH GROUND PLAN OF BIRKENAU

The camp of BIRKENAU consists of three building areas. At present only sections I and II are guarded by the inner chain of sentry posts whereas section III is still under construction and uninhabited. At the time of our departure from the camp (the beginning of April 1944), the following categories of prisoners were in BIRKENAU :

- 19 -

<u>Section I.</u> (Women's concentration camp).

	Slov. Jews.	Other Jews.	Aryans.	Remarks.
I a and I b	app. 300	app. 7,000	app. 6,000	In addition to the 300 Slovak Jewish girls, app. 100 are employed in the administration building of AUSCHWITZ.

Section II.

	Slov. Jews.	Other Jews.	Aryans.	Remarks.
IIa Quarantine camp.	2	" 300	" 800	One of the 2 Slovak Jews is Dr. Andreas MULLER from Podolinec, (block eldest).
IIb Jews from THERESIENSTADT.	-	" 3,500	-	With a 6 months quarantine.
IIc At present uninhabited.	-	-	-	
IId "Stammlager"	58	" 4,000	" 6,000	
IIe Gipsy camp.	-	-	" 4,500	This is the remainder of some 16,000 gipsies. They are not used for work and die off rapidly.
IIf Infirmary.	6	" 1,000	" 500	The 6 Slovak Jews are all employees of the building, namely

No. 36832	Walter SPITZER, block eldest from NEMSOVA, came to LUBLIN from BIRKENAU.
" 29867	Jozef NEUMANN ("overseer of the "corpse crew") from SNINA.
" 44989	Josef ZELMANOVIC. "staff" from SNINA.
-	Cham KATZ. "staff" from SNINA.
" 30049	Ludwig SOLMANN, "clerk" from KESMAREK.
" 32407	Ludwig EISENSTADTER, tattooist from KREMPACHY.

The internal administration of the camp of BIRKENAU is run by specially selected prisoners. The "blocks" are not inhabited according to nationalities but rather according to

On line 2 "Slov." is an abbreviation for Slovakian

354

working categories. Each block is supervised by a staff
of 5, i.e.

> a block eldest,
> a block recorder,
> a male nurse, and
> two attendants.

The block eldest.

He wears an arm band with the number of his block, and
is responsible for order there. He has power over life
and death. Until February 1944, nearly 50 % of the block
eldests were Jews but this was stopped by order of BERLIN.
They all had to resign with the exception of three Slovak
Jews who in spite of this order were able to keep their
posts. They are :

> Arnost ROSIN (Hacek), ZILINA - Block eldest of Block
> 34, head of the clearing squad and arti-
> san from BENZBURG.

> Dr. Andreas MULLER, PODOLINEC - Block eldest of Block
> 15, the quarantine camp.

> Walter SPITZER, NEMSOVA - Block eldest in Block 14,
> the "Infirmary".

The Block-recorder.

He is the block eldest's right hand, does all the
clerical work keeping the index cards and records. His
work is of great responsibility and he has to keep his led-
gers with painful exactitude as the index cards only indicate the number and not the name of the prisoners; and
errors are fatal. For instance, if the recorder has noted
down a death by mistake - and this often occurs with the
unusually high mortality - the discrepancy is simply straightened out by killing the bearer of the corresponding number.
Corrections are not admitted. The block recorder occupies
a key post which is often misused.

Nursing and "room" duties.

They consist in keeping the inside of the barracks clean
and carrying out small manual jobs in and around the block.
Of course there is no question of really taking care of the
sick.

The camp eldest supervises the whole camp; he is also
a prisoner. This post is at present held by :

Franz DANISCH, Number 11,182, a political prisoner, from
KONIGSHUTTE, Upper Silesia. He is undisputed master of the
whole camp and has power to nominate or dismiss block-eldests
and block-recorders, hand out jobs, etc.. He is impartial,
cannot be bribed and is correct towards the Jews.

Further we have a "chief recorder" whose position is undoubtedly one of the most powerful in the camp. He is in direct contact with camp head-quarters, receiving their orders and reporting on all matters. All camp-recorders are directly subordinated to him and have to submit all their reports to him. The chief recorder of BIRKENAU is :

Kasimir GORK, Number 31,029, a Pole from WARSAW, a former bank clerk. Although an antisemite, he has never directly harmed the Jews.

The supreme control over the blocks lies in the hands of 6 to 8 "Block leaders", all SS men. Every night they hold roll-call, the result of which is communicated to :

The Camp Leader, "Untersturmführer" SCHWARZHUBER, from the Tyrol. This individual is an alcoholic and a sadist. Over him is the camp commander who also controls AUSCHWITZ where there is a second subordinate camp leader. The camp commander's name is :

HOESS.

The Chief of a work squad or group is called the "Capo".

During work the "Capo" has full authority over his group of prisoners and not infrequently one of these "Capos" kills a man working under him. In larger squads there may be several "Capos" who are then under the orders of a "Capo in chief". At first there were many Jewish "Capos" but an order from BERLIN prohibited their being employed. One Jew, however, has been able to keep his post; he is :

ROTH, from MICHALOVCE, a fitter by profession.

Supreme control over work is carried out by German specialists.

II.

MAJDANEK.

On June 14, 1942, we left NOVAKY, passed through ZILINA and arrived at ZWARDON toward 5 o'clock in the evening. We were assembled, counted and SS. men took over our convoy. One of these guards voiced his surprise at the fact we had made the journey without water by shouting : "Those Slovak barbarians, give them no water !". The journey continued and we reached LUBLIN two days later. Here the following order was issued : "Those fit for work aged between 15 and 50 are to leave the cars. Children and old people remain". We struggled out of the freight car and discovered that the station was surrounded by Lithuanians in SS. uniforms all armed with automatic pistols. The cars containing the children and old people were immediately closed and the train moved on. We do not know where they went and what happened to them.

On line 18 "HOESS" is another possible spelling of Höss.

356

The SS. troop leader in command informed us that we had a long way ahead of us but that whoever wanted to take his luggage with him could do so. Those who preferred to put it on a truck would certainly receive it later. So some of us dragged along our luggage whereas others loaded it on the truck.

Behind the town stood a clothing factory called the "Bekleidungswerke". In the courtyard, waiting for their noon meal some 1,000 prisoners in dirty striped clothing, obviously Jews, were lined up and the sight of them was none too encouraging. Arriving on a small hill we suddenly sighted the vast barrack camp of MAJDANEK surrounded by a 3 meter high barbed-wire fence. No sooner had we gone through the entrance gate than I met Maco WINKLER from TRNAVA who warned me that all our personal belongings would be taken away. Around us stood Slovak Jews in a wretched condition, their heads shaven, in dirty prison clothes and wooden clogs or simply bare-footed, many of them having swollen feet. They begged us for food and we gave them what we could spare, knowing very well that everything would be confiscated anyway. We were then conducted to the stock room where we had to leave everything we possessed. At double time we were herded into another barrack where we had to undress, were shaved and given a shower. After this we were issued a convict outfit, wooden clogs and a cap.

I was assigned to "working section No. 3" as the whole camp was divided into 3 such sections separated by wire fences. Section No. 3 was occupied by a number of Slovak and Czech Jews. For two full days we were taught how to remove and put on our caps when we met a German. Then, in the pouring rain, we practiced roll-calling for hours.

The barrack accommodations were quite original to say the least. Three long tables (nearly as long as the barrack itself) had been placed one on top of the other. These comprised our "bunks" (4 floors of them, that is ground floor plus the three tables). A small passage was kept open along the walls.

Our food consisted of a fairly thick "soup" early in the morning which had to be eaten with the hands. We got the same soup again at lunch. The evening meal consisted of a brew called "tea", 300 grams of bad bread and some 20 to 30 grams of marmalade or artificial fat of the worst quality.

Great importance was attributed during the first few days to the learning of the "camp song". For hours we stood singing :

> From the whole of Europe came
> We Jews to Lublin
> Much work has to be done
> And this is the beginning.
>
> To manage this duty
> Forget all about the past
> For in fulfillment of duty
> There is community.

- 23 -

Therefore on to work with vigour
Let everyone play his part
Together we want to work
At the same pace and rhythm.

Not all will understand
Why we stand here in rows
Those must we soon force
To understand its meaning.

Modern times must teach us
Teach us all along
That it is to work
And only to work we belong.

Therefore on to work with vigour
Let everyone play his part
Together we want to work
At the same pace and rhythm.

(This is a literal translation of
the song).

Working section No. I was occupied by Slovak Jews
"   "   " II "   "   " Slovak and Czech Jews
"   "   " III "   "   " Partisans
"   " IV & V was being built by the Jews of Sectors
I & II.

The Partisans in section III were locked up in their
barracks without having to work and their food was thrown
at them as if they had been dogs. They died in great numbers in their overcrowded barracks and were shot at the
slightest excuse by the guards who did not dare venture too
near them.

The "Capos" were Reich Germans and Czechs; whereas the
Germans were brutal, the Czechs helped wherever they could.
The camp eldest was a gipsy from HOLIC by the name of
GALBAVY. His adjutant, a Jew from SERED called MITTLER,
certainly owed his post to his brutal actions. He took full
advantage of the power conferred upon him to torment the
Jews who, as it was, already had their full share of hard-
ships. The evening roll-call brought us more brutal treatment from the SS. men and for hours we had to stand in the
open after a hard day's work and sing "the camp song". A
Jewish orchestra leader was forced to conduct from the roof
of one of the barracks. This was the occasion of much
hilarity among the SS. men.

During these "concert parties" the SS. guards were very
generous with blows and physical punishment. A tragic end
befell Rabbi ECKSTEIN from SERED who was suffering from
dysentry and once came a few minutes too late for the roll-
call. The group leader had him seized and dipped head first
into one of the latrines, then poured cold water over him,
drew his revolver and shot him.

The crematorium was located between working sections
I and II and all the bodies were burned there. With an
effective strength of 6 to 8,000 men per working section,
the mortality was about 30 a day. This figure later increased five and sixfold. In other instances 10 to 20
inmates were removed from the sick room, brought to the
crematorium and burned after having been put to death in
a manner which I have not been able to find out. This
crematorium was electrically heated and the attendants
were Russians.

Illnesses increased as a result of the bad food and
intolerable living conditions. Serious stomach troubles
and a seemingly incurable foot disease spread throughout
the camp. The feet of the victims swelled up to the point
where they could not walk. More and more of the sick were
now being taken to the crematorium and when on June 26,
1942 the number thus treated rose to 70, I decided to take
an opportunity which was offered to me and applied for a
transfer to AUSCHWITZ.

On June 27, 1943 I discarded my prisoner's outfit and
travelled to AUSCHWITZ in civilian clothes.

After a journey of 48 hours during which we were co-
uped up in freight cars without food or water, we arrived
at AUSCHWITZ half dead. At the entrance gate the huge
poster "Work brings freedom" greeted us. As the courtyard
was clean and well kept and the brick buildings made a good
impression after the dirty and primitive barracks of
LUBLIN, we thought that the change was for the best. We
were taken to a cellar and received tea and bread. Next
day, however, our civilian clothes were taken away, our
heads were shaved, and our number was tattooed on our forearm in the usual way. Finally we were issued a set of
prisoner's clothes similar to those we had worn in LUBLIN
and were enrolled as "political prisoners" in the concentration camp of AUSCHWITZ.

We were billeted in "Block 17" and slept on the floor.
In a adjoining row of buildings, separated from ours by a
high wall, the Jewish girls from Slovakia, who had been
brought there in March and April of 1942, were quartered.
We worked in the huge "BUNA" plant to which we were herded
every morning about 3 a.m. At midday our food consisted
of potato or turnip soup and in the evening we received
some bread. During work we were terribly mistreated. As
our working place was situated outside the large chain of
sentry posts it was divided into small sectors of 10 X 10
meters, each guarded by an S.S. man. Whoever stepped outside these squares during working hours was immediately
shot without warning for having "attempted to escape".
Often it happened that out of pure spite an SS. man would
order a prisoner to fetch some given object outside his
square. If he followed the order he was shot for having
left his assigned place. The work was extremely hard and
there were no rest periods. The way to and from work had
to be covered at a brisk military trot; anyone falling out

of line was shot. On my arrival about 3,000 people, of
whom 2,000 were Slovak Jews, were working on this em-
placement. Very few could bear the strain and although
escape seemed hopeless, attempts were made every day.
The result was several hangings a week.

After a number of weeks of painful work at the "BUNA"
plant a terrible typhus epidemic broke out. The weaker
prisoners died in hundreds. A immediate quarantine was
ordered and work at the "BUNA" stopped. Those still alive
were sent, at the end of July 1942, to the gravel pit but
there work was even still more strenuous. We were in such
a state of weakness that, even in trying to do our best, we
could not satisfy the overseers. Most of us got swollen
feet. Due to our inability to perform the heavy work
demanded of us our squad was accused of being lazy and
disorderly. Soon after a medical commission inspected all
of us; they carried out their job very thoroughly. Anyone
with swollen feet or particularly weak was separated from
the rest. Although I was in great pain, I controlled myself and stood erection front of the commission who passed
me as physically fit. Out of 300 persons examined, 200
were found to be unfit and immediately sent to BIRKENAU and
gassed. I was then detailed for work at the DAW (Deutsche
Aufrüstungswerke) were we had to paint skis. The prescribed
minimum to be painted each day was 120. Anyone unable to
paint this many was thoroughly flogged in the evening. It
meant working very hard to avoid this punishment. Another
group was employed at making cases for hand-grenades. At
one time 15,000 had been completed but it was found that
they were a few centimeters too small. As punishment
several Jews (one of whom was a certain ERDELYI who is said
to have relatives in BANOVCE) were shot for sabotage.

Somewhere around the middle of August 1942 all the
Jewish girls from Slovakia who lived next to our quarters,
on the other side of the wall, were transferred to BIRKENAU.
I had the opportunity to talk to them and was able to see
how weak and half-starved all of them were. They were
dressed in old Russian uniform rags and wore wooden clogs.
Their heads were shaven clean. The same day we again had
to undergo a strict examination and those suspected of having
typhus were removed to the Birch wood. The remainder was
shaved afresh, bathed, issued with a new set of clothes and
finally billeted in the barracks the girls had just left.
By chance I learned that there was an opening in the "clearance squad" and I handed in my application. I was detailed
to this task.

This squad consisted of about a hundred Jewish prisoners. We were sent to a far corner of the camp, away from
all our comrades. Here we found huge sheds full of knap-
sacks, suitcases and other luggage. We had to open each
piece of baggage and sort the contents into large cases
specially prepared for each category of goods, i.e. combs,
mirrors, sugar, canned food, chocolate, medecines, etc. The
cases were then stored away. Underwear, shirts and clothes
of all kinds went to a special barrack, where they were
sorted out and packed by Jewish girls. Old and worn clothes

were addressed to the "TEXTILE FACTORY" at MEMEL whereas the usable garments were dispatched to a collecting
center in BERLIN. Gold, money, bank notes and precious
stones had to be handed over to the political section.
Many of these objects were however stolen by the S.S.
guards or by prisoners. The head of this department was
Albert DAVIDOVIC from SPISSKA NOVA VES. He still holds
this post and has become quite an expert in the matter.
A brutal and vile individual who often struck the women
is commander of this squad. He is SS. "Scharführer"
WYKLEFF.

Every day the girls who came to their work from
BIRKENAU described to us the terrible conditions prevailing there. They were beaten and brutalized and their
mortality was much higher than among the men. Twice a
week "selections" took place and every day new girls replaced those who had disappeared.

During a night shift I was able to witness for the
first time how incoming convoys were handled. The transport I saw contained Polish Jews. They had received no
water for days and when the doors of the freight cars were
opened we were ordered to chase them out with loud shouts.
They were utterly exhausted and about a hundred of them
had died during the journey. The living were lined up in
rows of five. Our job was to remove the dead, dying and
the luggage from the cars. The dead; and this included anyone unable to stand on his feet, were piled in a heap.
Luggage and parcels were collected and stacked up. Then
the railroad cars had to be thoroughly cleaned so that no
trace of their frightful load was left behind. A commission
from the political department proceeded with the selection
of approximately 10 % of the men and 5 % of the women and
had them transferred to the camps. The remainder were
loaded on trucks, sent to BIRKENAU and gassed while the dead
and dying were taken directly to the furnaces. It often
happened that small children were thrown alive into the
trucks along with the dead. Parcels and luggage were taken
to the warehouses and sorted out in the previously described
manner.

Between July and September 1942 a typhus epidemic had
raged in AUSCHWITZ, especially in the women's camp of BIR-
KENAU. None of the sick received medical attention and in
the first stages of the epidemic a great many were killed
by phenol injections, and later on others were gassed whole-
sale. Some 15 to 20,000, mostly Jews, died during these
two months. The girl's camp suffered the most as it was not
fitted with sanitary installations and the poor wretches
were covered with lice. Every week large "selections" took
place and the girls had to present themselves naked to the
"selection committee" regardless of weather conditions. They
waited in deadly fear whether they would be chosen or given
another week's grace. Suicides were frequent and were mostly committed by throwing oneself against the high-tension
wires of the inner fence. This went on until they had
dwindled to 5 % of their original number. Now there are only

On line 11 "WYKLEFF" is also possibly spelled as Wyklef.

400 of these girls left and most of them have been able to secure some sort of clerical post in the women's camp. One of them, KATJA by christian name (family name unknown), from POVAZSKA BYSTRICA, (where she has relatives by the name of LANGBELDER) has risen to the important post of chief recorder. About 100 girls hold jobs at the staff building in AUSCHWITZ where they do all the clerical work connected with the administration of the two camps. Thanks to their knowledge of languages they are also used as interpreters. Others are employed in the main kitchen and laundry. Of late these girls have been able to dress themselves quite well as they have had opportunities to complete their wardrobes which, in some cases, even include silk stockings. Generally speaking they are reasonably well off and are even allowed to let their hair grow. Of course this can nor be said of the other Jewish inmates of the women's camp. It just so happens that these Slovak Jewish girls have been in the camp the longest of all. But if to-day they enjoy certain privileges they have previously undergone frightful sufferings.

I was not to hold this comparatively good job with the "clearance squad" for long. Shortly afterwards I was transferred to BIRKENAU on disciplinary grounds and remained there over a year and a half. On April 7, 1944 I managed to escape with my companion.

———

Careful estimate of the number of Jews gassed
in BIRKENAU between April 1942 and April 1944 (according
to countries of origin).

Poland (transported by truck) ....approximately	"	300,000
" " " train	"	600,000
Holland	"	100,000
Greece	"	45,000
France	"	150,000
Belgium	"	50,000
Germany	"	80,000
Yougoslavia, Italy and Norway	"	50,000
Lithuania	"	50,000
Bohemia, Moravia and Austria	"	30,000
Slovakia	"	30,000
Various camps for foreign Jews in Poland	"	300,000
	approximately	1,765,000

III.

On August 6, 1944, a report was received in Switzerland covering the happenings in Birkenau during the period
between April 7 and May 27. This second report was drawn-
up by two other young Jews who succeeded in escaping from
this camp and reaching Slovakia. Their declarations
complete the first report, particularly as regards the
arrival of the Hungarian Jews in Birkenau, as well as
adding certain new details not contained in the previous
accounts. It has not been possible, however, to check the
origin of this "second report" as closely as it was the
first.

          o
        o   o

After the flight of the two Slovak Jews from Birkenau
on April 7, 1944 great excitement reigned in the camp. The
"Political Division" of the Gestapo instituted a thorough-
going investigation, and the friends and superiors of the
two escapees were closely questioned, although in vain.
Since the two had held posts as "Block Recorders" all Jews
exercising such functions, by way of punishment and also as

Bottom 1/3 of page at "III." This III. designates the beginning of the Mordowicz Rosin Report.

a precautionary measure, were removed and, as the Gestapo (justifiably) suspected that they had succeeded in escaping through building No. 3, the outer chain of sentry posts was considerably shortened so that now it cuts through the middle of Building No. 3.

· · ·

At the beginning of the month of April, a transport of Greek Jews arrived, of whom about 200 were admitted to the camp. The remainder of circa 1,500 were immediately gassed.

Between the 10th and 15th of April some 5,000 "Aryans" arrived in Birkenau, mainly Poles, some 2,000 to 3,000 women among them being from the abandoned camp of Lublin-Majdanek. They were given numbers running from approximately :

176,000 to 181,000   Among the women were about 300 Jewish girls from Poland. The greater part of the new arrivals were ill, weak and very run down. According to their information the healthy ones had been sent from Lublin to German concentration camps. Concerning the fate of the Jews held in the camp of Lublin-Majdanek, we learned from them, especially from the Jewish girls, that on November 3, 1943 all Jews in this camp, that is some 11,000 men and 6,000 women were killed.

We recalled that about this time the SS. in Birkenau had reported that Lublin had been attacked by partisans and in order to fight against the latter a number of the SS. personnel from Birkenau had been temporarily transferred to Lublin. It was now clear to us for what purpose our SS. had gone to Lublin.

Apparently the Jews had been compelled to dig a long, deep grave in Field V of the camp of Majdanek and on November 3, they were brought out in groups of 2 to 300, shot and thrown into the grave. Within 24 hours everything was over. During the execution loud music was played to drown out the shots.

Three hundred girls who were active in Lublin on the "clearing-up Commando" and as Recorders were left alive. Three days after their arrival in Birkenau they were all gassed and burned on special order of Berlin. Through an error on the part of the "Recorder" two of the girls were not sent to the gas chamber. This was discovered, however, the next day, and the girls were immediately shot and the Recorder replaced.

The fate of the Lublin Jews caused great depression among the Jews in the camp of Birkenau who became afraid that one day the whole of Birkenau would suddenly be

On line 5 there was an error in translation, the authors meant section no.3 not "Building 3". Section 3 was referred in the camp as "Mexiko".

"liquidated" in the same way.

Approximately No. 182,000   Toward the end of April more
                            Greek Jews were brought to
Birkenau. Some 200 were admitted to the camp and about
3,000 exterminated.

183,000 to 185,000   At the beginning of May 1944
                            smaller transports of Dutch,
French, Belgian and Greek Jews arrived, as well as Polish
"Aryans". Most of them were put to work in the BUNA plant.

On May 10, 1944, the first transport of Hungarian Jews
arrived in Birkenau. They were principally from the
prisons of Budapest, including those who had been arrested
in the streets and railroad stations of the city. Among
the women with whom we spoke were :

                Ruth Lorant from Zilina,
                Mici Lorant   "   "   (her sister),
                Ruth Quasztler from Bratislava,
                Irene Roth from Michalovce and later from Krialy-
                                                        helmec,
                Frau Dr. Barna Fuchs from Michalovce.

The transport was received in Auschwitz and Birkenau
according to the well-known procedure (heads shaved, numbers
tattooed, etc..) The men were given numbers beginning with
186,000 and the women were placed in the women's camp. About
600 men, of whom some 150 were between the ages of 45 and
60, were brought to Birkenau where they were divided up among
various work detachments. The remainder stayed in Auschwitz
where they worked in the BUNA plant.

The members of the transport were all left alive, and
none of them, as had been customary, were sent directly to
the crematoria. In the postcards which they were allowed to
write, they had to give "Waldsee" as return address.

On May 15, mass transports from Hungary began to arrive
in Birkenau. 14 to 15,000 Jews arrived daily. The spur
railroad track which ran into the camp to the crematoria was
completed in great haste, the crews working night and day,
so that the transports could be brought directly to the
crematoria. Only about 10 % of these transports were admitted to the camp; the balance was immediately gassed and
burned. Never had so many Jews been gassed since the establishment of Birkenau. The "Special Commando" had to be
increased to 600 men, and after 2 or 3 days to 800 (people
being recruited from among the Hungarian Jews who had arrived
first). The size of the "Clearing Commando" was stepped up
from 150 to 700 men. Three crematoria worked day and night
(the 4th was being repaired at that time), and since the
capacity of the crematoria was not enough, great pits 30
meters long and 15 wide were once more dug in the "Birkenwald" (as in the time before the crematoria) where corpses
were burned day and night. Thus the "exterminating capacity"
became almost unlimited.

- 31

The Hungarian Jews who were left alive (about 10 %) were not included in the normal camp "enrollment". Although they were shaved and shorn, and received convicts clothing, they were not tattooed. They were housed in a separate section of the camp, section "C", and were later transferred to various concentration camps in the German Reich : Buchenwald, Mauthausen, Grossrosen, Gusen, Flossenburg, Sachsenhausen, etc. The women were temporarily quartered in the "gypsy camp" in separate Blocks and then also transferred elsewhere. Jewish girls from Slovakia were "Block Eldest" there.

The first Hungarian transports came from : Munkacs, Nagyszöllös, Nyiregyhaza, Ungvar, Huszt, Kassau, Beregszasz, Marmarossziget, Nagyberezna. Among those remaining alive were :

    Robert and Ervin Waizen (brothers) from Kassau,
    Stark from Kassau,
    Ehrenreich from Ubla (included in the transport from
                                Nagyberezna),
    Katz, Chaim from Snina,   "   "   "

The last two have already been transferred. The parents of the Waizen brothers were gassed.

The transports of Hungarian Jews were under the particular control of the former Camp Commander "Hauptsturmbannführer Höss, who travelled continually between Auschwitz and Budapest. The Commandant of Birkenau at this time was Höss' former adjutant, "Hauptsturmführer" Kramer.

187,000 to 189,000   1800 French "Aryans", almost exclusively intellectuals and prominent persons, including a small number of Polish "émigrés". Among the French were high officers, members of leading French financial circles, well-known journalists and politicians, and even, it was said, former ministers. On their arrival some of them rebelled but were put down in an exceedingly brutal fashion by the SS, some of them being shot on the spot. The French were very courageous and self-possessed. They were strictly isolated in Birkenau and no one was allowed to have any contact with them. After two weeks, on orders from Berlin, they were sent to Mauthausen (near Linz, in Austria.)

Since the middle of May the newly arrived Jews no longer received consecutive numbers as formerly. A new numbering system was inaugurated beginning with No. 1 preceeded by the tattooed letter "A". We do not know the reason for this measure. At the time of our flight on May 27, 1944 about 4,000 Jews had received these new numbers. The 4,000 were composed of 1,000 Dutch, French and Italian Jews and 3,000 Jews from Theresienstadt who reached Birkenau on May 23, 1944. These were treated exactly as the previous 2 transports from Theresienstadt. They were quartered (unshorn) with the members of the previous convoy from Theresienstadt (who have been in Birkenau since Dec. 20, 1943 and whose "quarantine" is due to be up on June 20, 1944) in Section II/b.

According to the statement of a Jew from the "Special Commando", "Reichsführer" Himmler was said to have visited Birkenau on the 15th or 16th of May. On one of these days I myself saw 3 automobiles and 5 men in civilian clothing drive toward the crematoria. The Jew who made this statement declared that he, as well as others, recognized Himmler, who had visited crematorium No. 1 and after a stay of about half an hour had again driven off with those accompanying him. On the day after there was an account in the Silesian newspapers of Himmler's visit to Cracow, so that this report could be true.

One other happening should not be forgotten which was told to us by the men of the "Special Commando". In the late summer of 1943 a commission of 4 Dutch Jews - distinguished looking men - came to Auschwitz. Their visit had already apparently been announced to the camp Commander, for the Dutch Jews in Auschwitz received better clothes, as well as regular eating equipment (plates, spoons, etc.) and better food. The commission of 4 were very politely received and were shown over the camp buildings and particularly those portions which were clean and made a good impression. Dutch Jews from the camp were brought to them who reported that only a portion of the Dutch Jews were in this camp, the others being in other similar camps. In this manner the 4 men were satisfied and signed a statement according to which the commission had found everything in good order in Auschwitz. After the signing the 4 Dutch Jews expressed a desire to see the camp of Birkenau and particularly the crematoria about which they had heard some stories. The camp authorities declared themselves quite willing to show them both Birkenau and the crematoria, the latter being used, they said, to cremate those who died in the camp. The commission was then taken to Birkenau, accompanied by the camp leader, Aumayer, and immediately to crematoria No. 1. Here they were shot from behind. A telegram was supposedly sent to Holland reporting that after leaving Auschwitz the four men had been victims of an unfortunate automobile accident.

There is a biological laboratory in Auschwitz where SS., civilian and internee doctors are occupied. The women and girls on whom experiments are performed are housed in Block 10. For a long time the "block eldest" there was Magda Hellinger from Michalovce and a girl named Rossi (family name unknown) from Humenné. Experiments were carried out only on Jewish girls and women, although to date no Slovakian girls have been used. Experiments were also performed on men but the latter were not housed separately. A great many died as a result of these experiments. Often gypsies were used. Block 10 where the "subjects" of the experiments are housed is completely isolated, and even the window openings are walled up. No one whatsoever had admission to it.

The Commandants of Auschwitz and Birkenau have been to date the following : Aumayer, Schwarzhuber, Weiss, Hartenstein, Höss, and Kramer.

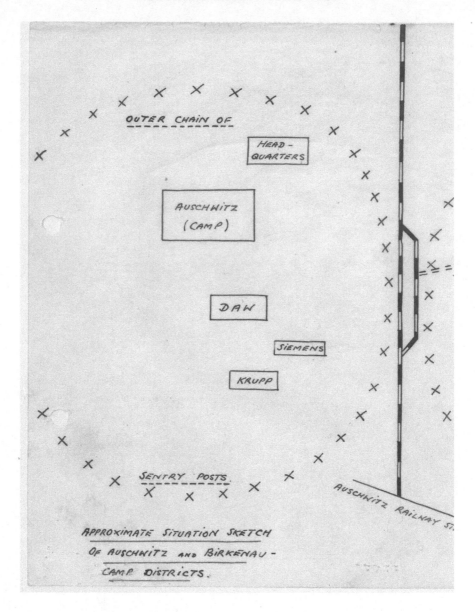

The upper part of the map which usually is North is in fact facing South. Vrba explained his error in a letter dated August 12, 1980, to Martin Gilbert: "This is the result of a peculiarity of the way my mind works, and until this day whenever I draw a location of a particular place, the north will be on the bottom of the map.

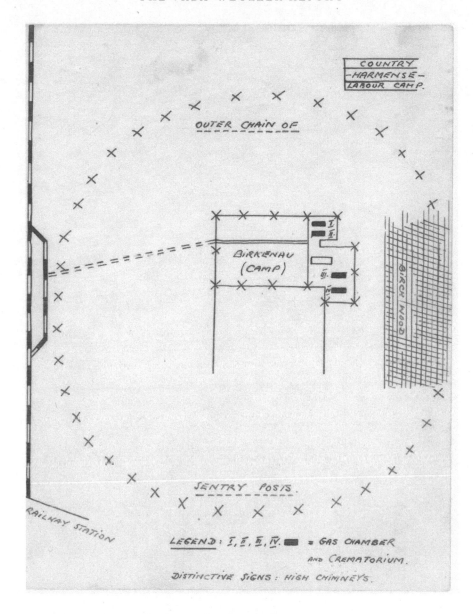

This error is not inborn but originates from an error of a teacher of mine in my school who explained to me (at my age of ten) that our school is 200 yards south of Danube In fact, it was two hundred yards north of Danube and since then north in my maps appears on the bottom I hardly ever doubted the wisdom of my teachers." FDRPL, Vrba's Collection, Box 2.

A TALE OF DARKNESS:

Story of the Mordowicz-Rosin Report
by Nikola Zimring

THE AUSCHWITZ PROTOCOLS, OR AUSCHWITZ REPORT, IS A COL-
lection of three reports by five contributors, all escapees from Auschwitz:[1]

1. Jerzy Tabeau, a non-Jew, was imprisoned in Auschwitz I and escaped on November 19, 1943. His portion of *The Report* is also known as the "Polish Major's Report."

2. Rudolf Vrba and Alfred Wetzler escaped from Auschwitz-Birkenau on April 7, 1944. They wrote the most comprehensive portion, which is sometimes referred to as the Auschwitz Protocols on its own.

3. Czesław Mordowicz and Arnošt Rosin escaped also from Auschwitz-Birkenau on May 27, 1944, six weeks after the Vrba-Wetzler escape. When Mordowicz and Rosin reached Slovakia, they contacted the same people as Vrba and Wetzler. Their seven-page report detailed events that took place in Auschwitz-Birkenau after Vrba and Wetzler's escape. It was attached to the Vrba-Wetzler Report and never stood by itself.[2]

The four Auschwitz-Birkenau escapees reunited in Slovakia and continued their efforts to warn the prospective victims about the real meaning of the "resettlement" that was being forced on Jews.

---

1   Auschwitz consisted of a complex of over forty camps spread over an area of forty square kilometers. The three major units were Auschwitz I, a concentration camp; Auschwitz II (Birkenau), the killing center; and Auschwitz III (Buna-Monowitz), the slave labor complex.
2   The full version of the Auschwitz Protocols can be found at the Franklin D. Roosevelt Library (FDRPL), General Correspondence, Box 7.

Since Mordowicz and Rosin's lives were so intensely intertwined with Vrba and Wetzler, this book is a good place to tell their stories. Who were they, how did they find themselves in Auschwitz-Birkenau, and how did they escape from there? What were the circumstances of their escape and their contribution to the Auschwitz Report, and what were their connections to Vrba and Wetzler?

CZESŁAW MORDOWICZ

CZESŁAW MORDOWICZ WAS BORN IN MŁAWA, POLAND, IN 1919, just a few kilometers from the German border. When the Nazi offensive against Poland started on September 1, 1939, the first skirmishes took place in the Mława area. To avoid danger, Mordowicz's family first escaped to Warsaw, but Warsaw was under attack with heavy bombing. Therefore they decided to return back home. Mordowicz however remained with friends in Płonsk, (the birthplace of the Israeli founding father and the first prime minister, David Ben Gurion), where his family had made a stop on their way home. His parents and sister continued to Mława.[3]

After a short fight, Poland succumbed to German and Soviet aggression and the area in which Mordowicz resided was incorporated into the German Reich. In the summer of 1941, the Germans attacked the Soviet Union and captured the remainder of Poland. Numbering 3.3 million, and comprising 10 % of the population of Poland, the Polish Jewish community was the largest in all of Europe. Under the German regime, the Jews were systematically stripped of their civil rights and property ownership, then imprisoned in ghettoes and shipped to their

---

3   Interview with Czeslaw Mordowicz on October 24, 1995, and October 30, 1996, United States Holocaust Memorial Museum, pp.1–6. http://collections. ushmm.org/oh_findingaids/RG50.030.0354_trs_pl.pdf (downloaded: January 15, 2016). (Cited hereafter as Mordowicz's interview.)

deaths at various extermination camps: Chełmno, Sobibor, Bełżec, Treblinka, Majdanek, Auschwitz. It is estimated that three million Polish Jews—90% of the pre-war community in Poland—perished in the Holocaust.[4]

Mordowicz was also subjected to the escalating anti-Jewish policies. He was ghettoized in Płonsk ghetto. Despite the horrendous circumstances, he found a wife and fortuitous employment with a German who "took over" a Jewish furniture factory. Since the new owner did not know how to run the business, Mordowicz quickly became the chief manager and proved indispensable to the enterprise. Partly for this reason, when the Płonsk Ghetto was liquidated in the fall of 1942, Mordowicz was offered the opportunity to go into hiding with the family of his employer. He declined, refusing to abandon his wife and mother-in-law. All three were transported to Auschwitz.

Upon arrival, Mordowicz was separated from his wife and mother-in-law, whom he never saw again. Within days of his arrival in Auschwitz, Mordowicz had an emotional reunion with his father from whom he learned that his mother and sister were dead, murdered in the gas chambers. To make matters even worse, Mordowicz never saw his father again, as his father died shortly after their meeting. Only the vision of possible escape gave him hope and chased away suicidal thoughts.

Still, there was a little bit of luck on Mordowicz's side as he was able to obtain a "job" as a *Schreiber*—the administrative "right hand" of a blockleader (kapo). This luck meant he could avoid hard labor, had sufficient food, was sheltered from bad weather, and, to a certain extent, was protected by his kapo. This tipped the chances for survival slightly in Mordowicz's favor.[5]

---

4   Jan T. Gross, *Fear, Anti-Semitism in Poland after Auschwitz: An Essay in Historical Interpretation* (New York: Random house, 2006), p.4.
5   Mordowicz's interview, pp. 7-24.

ARNOŠT (ERNST) ROSIN

FAR LESS IS KNOWN ABOUT ARNOŠT ROSIN'S PRE-AUS-chwitz whereabouts. He was born in 1913 in Snina, then part of the Austro-Hungarian Empire and later part of the newly founded Czechoslovakia. On March 14, 1939, the Slovaks broke their union with the Czechs and declared themselves an independent state.[6] Almost immediately, the Slovaks adopted a number of anti-Semitic laws—the first one as early as one month after the establishment of independent Slovakia—in part to satisfy their own anti-Semitism and in part to appease the Germans. In 1942, Slovakian anti-Jewish policies peaked, and the regime started to "resettle" the impoverished Jews— impoverished due to the laws that gradually stripped them of their civil rights, property and means to make money. From 89,000 Slovak Jews, between March and October 1942, the Slovak government de-ported 58,000 Jewish men, women and children—only a handful ever returned.[7] Rosin (as well as Vrba and Wetzler) was among the deport-ees. While visiting his parents in April 1942, he was arrested by Hlinka Guards,[8] paramilitary forces, modeled after the SS, and deported to Auschwitz-Birkenau.[9]

6   The same day, German soldiers marched on what was left from Czechoslovakia and, on March 15, established the Protectorate of Bohemia and Moravia on the pretense of ensuring peace in the unstable area.

7   It is not clear whether the proposition to "resettle" the Jews originated in Berlin or in Bratislava, but this "solution" was welcomed by the Slovakian officials with relief and even excitement. The Slovak government paid Germany 500 Reichsmarks as a "resettle-ment fee" for each deported Jew with the promise they could keep the Jewish property and that the Jews would not return. It is also very important to note that Slovakia was the only unoccupied country in Europe that executed the deportations of its Jews with its own administration and forces, without any pressure on the part of German authorities. Hans Safrian, *Eichmann's Men* (Cambridge University Press, 2009), pp. 142-145.

8   The Hlinka Guards were created by Andrej Hlinka (1864-1938), a Catholic priest and politician and founder of the anti-Semitic Slovak People's Party. Today, he is openly celebrated as one of the founding fathers of Slovakia, and virtually every Slovakian city has either a street or square named after him, including Sered and Nováky, where the labor and transit camps for Jews were located.

9   Arnošt Rosin's interview with Erich Kulka conducted in 1965, Yad Vashem Archives, P.25/21, pp.1-2. (Cited hereafter as Rosin's interview.)

A few days after his arrival to Auschwitz-Birkenau, Rosin was selected for *Sonderkommando*, the "special work unit" whose task it was to dispose of the bodies of the murdered victims as well as prisoners who died in the camp from "natural causes." The gas chambers and crematoria had not yet been built. Arriving prisoners were murdered in improvised gas chambers at two original Polish farm houses (residue of the farm that had existed there before). These people were buried and/or burnt in the outside trenches. Rosin was among the prisoners who dug those trenches, and was initially under the impression that this work assignment was for defensive purposes. When he learned what it was he was actually doing, Rosin was absolutely horrified and desperately wanted to get out of there. About three weeks later, Rosin received a loaf of bread from his friend who worked in the "farm house" and had taken it from a murdered new arrival. Inside the loaf of bread, Rosin found a long gold chain, which the owner had hoped to hide from the greedy hands of the Nazis. With the chain, Rosin bribed his block *Schreiber*, Leo Polák, to be transferred to another position.[10] According to historian Erich Kulka, Rosin was the only survivor of this specific *Sonderkommando*, which consisted of three hundred Slovakian Jews deported to Auschwitz-Birkenau in April 1942.[11]

Later Rosin became the Blockleader at the Block 24, where he met and became close friends with Alfred Wetzler (who was a *Schreiber* at the same block) and Rudolf Vrba. Although Rosin knew about Vrba and Wetzler's plan to escape, the details were kept secret from him to protect him from revealing anything under a possible Nazi torture.

10   Rosin's interview, p.4-5.
11   Erich Kulka, "Attempts by Jewish Escapees to Stop Mass Extermination," in *Jewish Social Studies 47*, 3/4 (1985), p.304.
In Auschwitz, or for that matter in any Death Camp, the members of *Sonderkommando* were always executed after a certain period of time, since they were inconvenient witnesses of the mass crimes. According to Rosin, "his" group tried to organize a collective escape but were discovered and executed.
Other notable survivor of another *Sondekommando* was Slovakian Jew Filip Müller, who was friends with Rosin, Vrba, and Wetzler, and who recorded a very intense account of the events he witnessed firsthand in the book *Eyewitness Auschwitz: Three Years in the Gas Chambers* (Chicago: I. R. Dee, 1999). Müller is described extensively in the present book in chapters 7,11,12 and 13.

Rosin even helped them in various ways in maneuvers connected with the preparations for their escape.[12] As a precaution, in order to protect Rosin, Wetzler had himself transferred to another block two months prior to the escape. Nevertheless, Rosin was accused of conspiracy, interrogated, and beaten. By pretending to be very angry at Vrba and Wetzler for not taking him with them, he managed to convince the Nazis he knew nothing about the escape.[13]

As punishment for Vrba and Wetzler's escape on April 7, 1944, all Jews were suspended from any position that held even the slightest power. Mordowicz and Rosin found themselves working in a hard labor unit in a gravel pit.[14] Security measures were intensified: the prisoners were counted every two hours, and the number of the guards was increased.[15]

THE HUNGARIAN JEWS

FROM THE START BIRKENAU FUNCTIONED AS A DEATH CAMP. Jews from all over Nazi dominated Europe arrived in mass transports, about 10–15% of them were selected for slave labor and about 85–90% were immediately sent to their deaths in the gas chambers. At first, farm cottages were converted into gas chambers and the bodies were disposed in pits outside. Next, four "modern" gas chambers and crematoria were built and designed specifically for mass killing with a maximum capacity of 6,000 murders per day. In January 1944, work was started to extend the railway line so that it ended directly at the entrance of the crematoria.[16] In May of 1944, the number of incoming transports and victims increased dramatically.

---

12   Vrba's letter to Martin Gilbert, July 30, 1980, FDRPL, Vrba's Collection, Box 3.
13   Rosin's interview, p.8.
14   Mordowicz Rosin Report
15   Mordowicz's interview, p.28; Rosin's interview, p.13.
16   Initially, the newly arrived victims intended for immediate death had to either walk three kilometers or be transported by trucks, which demanded logistical planning and resources—one truck could take a maximum of one hundred souls.

After the German occupation of Hungary in March 19, 1944, Adolf Eichmann together with his top experts on the Final Solution, Dieter Wisliceny, Hermann Krumay, and Otto Hunsche orchestrated their evil "masterpiece".[17] The last large Jewish community in Europe was disappearing to Auschwitz-Birkenau at the overwhelming speed of 12,000 people a day, all but a few murdered in cold blood on the spot in gas chambers.[18] The bodies were burned day and night, and the *Sonderkommando* could not keep up with the greatly increased "work load." The newly arrived people were forced to wait patiently in line for their deaths. The crematoria were working at full capacity, but it was not enough, so additional trenches had to be dug to burn bodies. The fire in the trenches hissed and covered the area with black smoke; flames licked the crematoria chimneys that cracked from the heat; all of Birkenau was filled with heartbreaking shouts, weeping, curses, and commands. Even the experienced *Sonderkommando* prisoners, used to bearing Auschwitz-Birkenau's cynical and industrial murder daily were now sick to their stomachs. Birkenau had become hell. It was an

---

17   Hunsche and Krumay were tried for their crimes in 1969 (!), in Frankfurt, and Rudolf Vrba was a witness for the prosecution. About the trial he wrote to his friend: "For me this trial was quite ridiculous. I was brought in as a witness to the Landgericht in Frankfurt and the presiding judge *Oberlandesgerichtsrat* Schmied interrupted me several times (when I was on the witness stand) on account of my improper use of German grammar, apparently that was to him more important than what I tried to convey to the Court. So finally I got fed up and I told the judge that if my German is not understandable on account of my wrong use of the German version of the conjunctivum cum accusativo, he can get me a Slovak-German translator and we can start from there. After that the judge cooled down a bit." Krumay received five years, and Hunsche was acquitted. Letter to Benno Müller-Hill, June 25, 1997, FDRPL, Vrba's Collection, box 4.

18   Hungary then had a Jewish population of 725,007, as well as approximately 100,000 converts and Christians who were identified as Jews under the racial laws then in effect. Despite the numerous Anti-Jewish laws as well as the deaths of approximately 60,000 Jews caused by Hungarians between 1941 and March of 1944, Hungarian Jews still felt relatively secure and "survived the first four-and-one-half years of the Second World War almost oblivious to what was happening to the other Jewish communities in Nazi-dominated Europe.

Randolph L. Braham, "Rescue Operations in Hungary: Myths and Realities", *Yad Vashem Studies 32* (2004), pp. 21-57.

image of the end of the world, and everybody, including Mordowicz and Rosin, wished to escape.[19]

THE ESCAPE

MORDOWICZ PLANNED THE ESCAPE WITH THE SUPPORT OF Kapo Adam Lužnicky, a Polish criminal prisoner. Together with Polish prisoners, Mordowicz prepared a tiny bunker in the gravel pit, approximately four hundred meters from the train ramp where the victims arrived. It was in the "outside perimeter" of the camp, where the prisoners worked during the day. In the evening, the prisoners were confined to the "inner perimeter" of the camp, the sleeping quarters, and only the inner camp was guarded. Whenever a prisoner was reported missing, the procedure was to search the camp and its immediate surroundings meticulously for three days, after which time it was assumed that the prisoner had escaped or was dead and the search was halted. If the escapees could hide for those critical three days in the "outer perimeter" of the camp, they would have a reasonable chance of slipping out during the night unobserved, after the search was called off. It was the same principle that was used by Vrba and Wetzler for their escape; their hiding place was also in the "outer perimeter," the building site known as "Mexico."[20]

Mordowicz initially wanted to take his friend Borenstein from Płonsk, but Borenstein was unfortunately selected for the new *Sonderkommando* shortly before the escape was to take place. From the *Sonderkommando* there was no way back. Mordowicz had to improvise and chose to take Rosin, mainly for his physical capability even though he barely knew him.[21]

---

19   Rosin's interview, p.11.; Mordowicz-Rosin Report; Lanik, Jozef, *Oswiecim, hrobka styroch milionov ludi (Auschwitz, tomb of four million people)* (Košice: Wiko, 1946)., pp.63-65. (Note: Jozef Lanik was the literary pseudonym of Alfred Wetzler.)
20   Vrba discussed extensively the Auschwitz-Birkenau security system as well as his escape in the present book in Chapters 13 and 14.
21   Czeslaw (Bezalel) Mordowicz, "I Have Come Out Alive Twice from Auschwitz." *Yalkut Moreshet*, Tel Aviv, (November 1968) (in Hebrew), p.10.

As soon as they entered the small poorly constructed bunker at noon on Saturday, May 27, 1944, gravel poured in. Then by accident they spilled their supply of water, and the pipe that was supposed to supply fresh air proved insufficient. Soon both Mordowicz and Rosin were suffocating. As they were unable to loosen the opening of the bunker, they feared they were buried alive. Finally, by Sunday night they succeeded in opening the lid and freeing themselves from the bunker, whereupon they immediately fainted. Even though they only stayed hidden for a day and a half, they could not face the prospect of going back to the bunker.

That night, two trainloads of Hungarian people arrived, and the kapos and the SS were busy with organizing the murder of all these victims. This "chaos" in Birkenau had taken their toll on the kapos and the SS as well—their alertness was weakened. The service dogs, which would under regular circumstances be used to look for the missing prisoners, were "assisting" at the railway ramp. Mordowicz and Rosin decided to take the risk and proceeded with their escape immediately. The commotion surrounding the transports helped them disappear unobserved from the camp into the darkness. [22]

The plan was to go north to Cracow and then Warsaw. They hoped either to join the Red Army or possibly to reach Gdansk and maybe even cross the Baltic Sea to neutral Sweden. They were forced to change their plans, however, after being warned by a Polish peasant woman, whom they met on the way, that Germans were picking up young men to dig trenches on the Eastern Front. [23]

Years later, in an interview with Erich Kulka, Rosin made the chilling confession that they actually considered returning to Auschwitz! The initial euphoria experienced by Rosin and Mordowicz upon their escape and regained freedom was quickly replaced by abject fear of the

22   Rosin's interview, p.12–14, Lanik, p.66.
23   Rosin's interview, p.14. Martin Gilbert, *Auschwitz and the Allies* (New York: Henry Holt and Company, 1982), p.215. (Based on interview with Mordowicz on December 22, 1980.)

outside world, which had ceased to be familiar and seemed intractable. People appeared to them unfriendly at best, and they were in constant fear of denunciation. As experienced prisoners in Auschwitz, at least they knew how to avoid dangerous situations and how to "postpone death," and in a way they felt safer there.[24]

Mordowicz and Rosin decided to go south to Rosin's native Slovakia. They took the bold step of boarding a train in the direction of Nový Targ. They traveled on the roof and to their horror passed a road sign indicating the distance (twelve kilometers) to Auschwitz! They jumped off the train before it arrived at the station in Nový Targ and on foot finally reached Slovakia, in an area close to Spišská Stará Ves. It was June 6, 1944, an easy day to remember since it was the day of the Allied invasion at Normandy.[25]

As soon as he reached his homeland, all the fear left Rosin. He felt relieved and safe, totally disregarding the fact that Slovakia was actually a Nazi satellite, and abandoned all security precautions. Even Mordowicz (after initial reservations) was affected by this carelessness of Rosin and came to share it. Rosin went to buy beer and cigarettes at a small kiosk, where he was refused service. They learned about D-Day from a peasant and from that the defeat of Nazis seemed to them within reach, so they decided to celebrate in the nearest tavern, where they were all arrested. It turned out that the kiosk owner alerted police about two suspicious individuals. Their fear of denunciation actually materialized as soon as they put their guards down.[26]

Fortunately, at the court building at Spišská Stará Ves, Rosin caught sight of an old acquaintance from Snina, Juhas Aladar, with whom he was able to exchange a few words. Aladar swiftly contacted representatives of the remainder of the Slovakian Jewish community, who organized help for both prisoners. The Jewish Community representatives—Mangel and

---

24   Rosin's interview, p.16.
25   Rosin's interview, p.16–18; Mordowicz's interview, p.40
26   Mordowicz's interview, p. 44; Rosin's interview, pp. 17–18.

Moskovič—provided Rosin and Mordowicz with dollar bills, and managed to have them charged as smugglers, thereby successfully avoiding exposure of their real "crime." Since their violation was now a financial matter, requiring a different court, they were taken by train to the district city Liptovský Svätý Mikuláš. To Mordowicz and Rosin's profound surprise, Vrba greeted them on the platform when the train arrived at the station. They hugged each other—it was the most genuine hug of Rosin's life. Vrba and Wetzler also visited the two in prison.[27] Mordowicz and Rosin were sentenced to eight days, and the Jewish community paid the 5000-crown fine on their behalf. Mangel and Moskovič also contacted the members of the Slovakian Jewish underground movement "Working Group,"[28] and Oskar Krasnyanski immediately arrived from Bratislava.[29]

ASSEMBLING THE REPORT

WHEN RELEASED FROM PRISON, MORDOWICZ AND ROSIN provided detailed information about the crimes being committed in Auschwitz-Birkenau. Krasnyanski immediately recognized the credibility of the prisoners and the importance and gravity of their testimony because, by strange coincidence, six weeks earlier he had interviewed two other escapees from Auschwitz-Birkenau, Rudolf Vrba and Alfred

---

27   Rosin's interview, p.21.
28   The "Working Group" came into existence spontaneously in 1942 as a counterpart of the *Judenrat* (Jewish Council appointed by the regime), when the deportation of Slovakian Jews to the "East" was in full swing. Their goal was to pursue any idea that might lead to even the remotest chance of stopping the deportations. The most notable members were Gisi Fleischmann, Rabbi Dov Michael Weissmandel, Oskar Krasnyanski, and Oskar Neumann. By the time Mordowicz and Rosin came in contact with the "Working Group," its members were already seasoned activists with well-established domestic as well as international contacts in Hungary, Switzerland, and Turkey.
29   Erich Kulka, "Five Escapes from Auschwitz," in *They Fought Back* (ed. Yuri Suhl) (New York: Schocken books, 1975), p.209. (Oskar Krasnyanski—whose name is spelled in slightly different ways in various documents, e.g., Krasnanski, Krasnansky, Krasnyansky or Krasznyansky—immigrated to Israel after the war and changed his name to Karmiel.)

Wetzler, who also provided detailed information about the killing center and warned about the imminent danger to the Hungarian Jewish Community. Mordowicz and Rosin corroborated Vrba and Wetzler's account fully and added details of their observation of the events at the camp subsequent to Vrba and Wetzler's escape, mainly the slaughter of the Hungarian Jews. Between May 15 and their escape on May 27, 1944, Rosin and Mordowicz estimated that over 100,000 Hungarian Jews were transported to Birkenau, where most of them were immediately murdered in the gas chambers.[30] Swiftly, the Slovakian Jewish leaders drafted a seven-page report focusing on the events that took place after Vrba and Wetzler's escape, attached it to Vrba and Wetzler's Report, and distributed it to their contacts. The report is today known as the Mordowicz-Rosin Report, or Second Auschwitz Protocol, and it is part of the so-called Auschwitz Protocols—it never stands by itself. For security reasons, the names and tattoo numbers of the escapees were omitted from the report. As was the case with Vrba and Wetzler, the "Working Group" provided Mordowicz and Rosin with fake papers and a monthly salary.[31]

THE EFFORTS OF THE ESCAPEES

THE SLOVAKIAN JEWISH LEADERS WHO RECORDED THE TESTImony provided by Vrba and Wetzler reassured them that the report would immediately get into the right hands, to Hungarian Jewish leaders, and in particular to Rudolf Kasztner,[32] who had experience

30   Mordowicz Rosin Report.
31   Rosin's new name was Štefan Roháč, Mordowicz's was Petr Podulka, Kulka, "Five Escapees," p.210.
32   Rudolf Kasztner was a highly controversial figure. On one hand, he was a bold member of the Hungarian Jewish Underground Movement *Va'adat Ezra ve'Hatsala*, which helped to smuggle Jews from Slovakia and Poland to then safer Hungary; on the other hand, he withheld information regarding the true purpose of Auschwitz-Birkenau, probably in order to protect his own rescue plans, which involved negotiations with Adolf Eichmann. After the war, he moved to Israel, where he was assassinated in 1957 after an Israeli court convicted him of having collaborated with the Nazis. In 1958, the Supreme Court of Israel overturned the verdict.

and who would act effectively on the information. Vrba and Wetzler felt betrayed by the Slovakian Jewish leaders, when they learned that Hungarian Jews were arriving at Auschwitz at a horrific rate totally unaware of what awaited them. All four ex-prisoners decided to rely on themselves, moved to Bratislava, and distributed the report without the collaboration of the "Working Group."

Historically the Slovakian and Hungarian Jewish communities were closely intertwined and often members of the same families. In order to expose their report to the Jewish population still alive in Hungary, the escapees secured the help of some of the Slovak Jews who were illegally visiting their families in Hungary.[33] Gerta Sidonová (later Vrbová), Vrba's childhood friend and future first wife, copied the report with a typewriter at her office after working hours.[34]

In the meantime, Krasnyanski was contacted by the nunciature, which had previously received a copy of the Vrba Wetzler Report. The Spanish clergyman Msgr. Mario Martiotti, came to Bratislava on a Vatican errand and asked to speak to the people who "gave the report."[35] A secret meeting was set up on June 20, 1944 at a monastery in Svätý Jur, approximately forty kilometers from Bratislava. Too many people visiting the monastery could attract unwanted attention, so it was decided that only Mordowicz, as a witness of the Hungarian massacre, and Vrba, who was briefly imprisoned in Majdanek, Krasnyanski and "Kalb," a translator would attend.[36] The meeting lasted several hours. Martiotti naturally wanted to be reassured of the authenticity of the escapees' report; he even took pictures of their

33   Vrba's letter to Robert A. Graham, July 2, 1976, FRDPL, Vrba's Collection, Box 1.
34   Between 1942 and 1944, Gerta Vrbová was in hiding in Hungary. With the arrival of the Germans, it was safer to return to Slovakia, so she obtained fake identification papers and an office job and reunited with her childhood sweetheart Rudolf Vrba. Gerta Vrbová, *Trust and Deceit: A Tale of Survival in Slovakia and Hungary, 1939-1945* (Mitchell Vallentine & Company, 2006).
35   Oscar Karmiel's (formerly Krasniansky) Deposition under Oath, 1961, FDRPL, Vrba's Collection, Box 16.
36   Vrba's letter to Robert A. Graham, July 2, 1976, FRDPL, Vrba's Collection, Box 1.

tattoos. Martiotti was well connected, politically, and just before their meeting he had lunch with Josef Tiso, president of the Slovak state as well as a Catholic clergyman.[37] Martiotti was supposed to travel to Switzerland the next day. Krasnyanski and the escapees begged him to deliver their report to the Pope and to the free world, in order, finally, to expose the German crimes and warn the potential victims. Martiotti promised to do so.[38] It is unclear how fully this interview was relayed to the Vatican and even less clear whether it encouraged Pope Pius XII to issue an open telegram to Miklós Horthy, the Hungarian leader, five days later on June 25, 1944.[39] The telegram may have been prompted instead by the sudden intense press and radio campaign that occurred at the same time.

THE MEDIA CAMPAIGN

IN JUNE 1944, THE REPORT REACHED TWO FEARLESS, BRIGHT and bold personalities in Switzerland who instantly recognized the magnitude of its message and arranged to have it published immediately. Dr. Jaromír Kopecký, a representative of the Czechoslovak exile government in Switzerland, received the Vrba-Wetzler Report together with the Polish Major Report (probably) on June 10, 1944. He did not receive the Mordowicz-Rosin Report, or even portions of it; however, the cover letter to the report contained the

---

37   After the war Tiso, a Catholic priest, was tried as a war criminal, condemned to death, and hanged. Today he is celebrated by some as a victim of the struggle for political power between the Czechs and Slovaks and perceived as one of the founding fathers of the Slovak Nation. See for example Gila Fatran, "Holocaust and Collaboration in Slovakia in the Postwar Discourse," in *Collaboration with the Nazis: Public Discourse after the Holocaust* (ed. Roni Stauber) (Routledge, 2010), pp.186–211, pp.197–206.

38   Oscar Karmiel's (formally Krasniansky) Deposition under Oath, 1961, FDRPL, Vrba's Collection, Box 16.

39   Randolph L. Braham, *The Politics of Genocide: The Holocaust in Hungary* (New York: Holt, Rinehart and Wiston, 1981), p.714.

information that 12,000 Hungarian Jews were being deported daily to Auschwitz.[40] Kopecký had the shortened version of the report broadcasted by British radio.[41]

The second of these men was George Mantello, a Jewish diplomat of Romanian origin. Mantello was a wealthy businessman who served as a representative for El Salvador in Switzerland. A very shortened version of the report reached him on June 21, 1944. According to David Kranzler, this five-page summary of the first Auschwitz report already included the shortened testimony of Mordowicz and Rosin on the "continuing mass murder of Hungarian Jews."[42] Mantello forwarded the information to the British journalist Walter Garrett, who represented the British News Service in Switzerland. On June 24, Garrett sent four lengthy telegrams to his central office in London containing many dramatic details. Based on these telegrams, over the course of the following 18 days, 383 articles were published in the Swiss press appealing to the international community's conscience.[43] Garrett concluded his telegrams with the following, possibly referring to Martiolli's activity: "ABSOLUTE EXACTNESS ABOVE REPORT UNQUESTIONABLE AND DIPLOMAT CATHOLIC FUNCTIONARIES WELL KNOWN VATICAN DESIRE WIDEST DIFFUSION WORLDWIDE."[44]

---

40   Richard Lichtheim, *Aktenvermerk Betreffend Birkenau und Auschwitz (File reference Concerning Birkenau and Auschwitz)*, June 23, 1944, enclosed in correspondence between John S. Conway and Miroslav Kárný, FDRPL, Vrba's Collection, Box 1.
41   Gilbert, pp.232–234.
42   David Kranzler, *Man Who Stopped the Trains to Auschwitz: George Mantello, El Salvador, and Switzerland's Finest Hour* (New York: Syracuse University Press, 2000), pp.87–89.
43   Werner Rings, *Advokaten des Feindes. Das Abenteuer der politischen Neutralität* (Advocates of the enemy. The Adventure of Political Neutrality) (Vienna: Econ, 1966), pp.144–146, Gilbert, pp.248–9.
44   The full text of the telegrams can be found in Jenó Levai, *Zsidósors Európáhan* (Budapest, 1948), pp.68–72.

THE INTERNATIONAL OUTCRY

THE ADVANCE OF THE SOVIET ARMY ON THE EASTERN Front and the Normandy landings, as well as the obviousness of the impending defeat of Germany created a favorable ground for spreading and publishing the report, since the world was surely now more prepared to pay attention and show empathy toward the Jewish tragedy. The press campaign caused an international outcry. President Franklin D. Roosevelt of USA as well as Pope Pius XII and King Gustav of Sweden sent strong warnings to Hungarian leader Miklós Horthy to stop the outgoing transports of Hungarian Jews to Auschwitz-Birkenau. Horthy submitted on July 7, 1944, via an order that became effective by July 9. Other decisive factors for Horthy's decision might have included the bombarding of Budapest by the Allies and news of a coup d'etat planned against him with the close collaboration of Germans within Hungarian security. Two hundred thousand Jews in Budapest were thus saved from the Auschwitz-Birkenau gas chambers (although not from murderous rage of the Hungarian Arrow Cross Party). Sadly, 437,000 Hungarian Jews were deported to Auschwitz between May 15 and July 9 of 1944.[45]

EPILOGUE

AT THE END OF AUGUST 1944, THE SLOVAKIAN NATIONAL Uprising broke out. It had massive participation, with up to 60,000 soldiers and 18,000 partisans, a disproportionate number of which were Jews. Vrba joined immediately; Wetzler followed shortly after. The insurgents were supposed to open the Dukla pass and other Carpathian passes in order to assist the Red Army's advance. Germans helped Tiso's men to crush the rebellion and then renewed the deportations

---

45   Braham, *The Politics*, p.1144.

of Slovakian Jews to Auschwitz-Birkenau, with brutal determination.[46] By great misfortune, Mordowicz was arrested again together with Wetzler's sister-in-law and sent to Auschwitz for the second time. Out of fear that he would be recognized by Auschwitz personnel and the prisoners who had helped him escape might be afraid he would reveal their involvement, Mordowicz attempted to chew off his tattooed number. He was recognized upon arrival at the camp, but friends helped to conceal his real identity—his tattooed number was altered into another tattoo (of either a fish, leaf or flower)—and arrangements were made to have Mordowicz placed in a transport for forced labor in Friedland labor camp. There he remained until early May 1945, when the Friedland camp was liberated by the Red Army. Mordowicz returned to Bratislava. He knew his family was dead, so he had no intention to return home to Poland; instead, he longed to be reunited with his friends from Auschwitz. [47] They all attended Vrba's wedding to Gerta Sidonová in Bratislava in 1947; then their paths separated as they tried to rebuild their lives and put behind them the terrible past.[48]

---

46   Safrian, p.207.
47   Mordowicz's interview, pp.66–78.
48   Gerta Vrbová, *Betrayed Generation, Shattered hopes and disillusion in post war Czechoslovakia* (Great Britain: Zuza Books, 2010), pp.69–78.

THE PREPARATIONS FOR THE HOLOCAUST IN HUNGARY:

An Eyewitness Account
by Rudolf Vrba[1]

CONTENTS

Introduction..389
Streamlined Methods of Mass Murder and Robbery
    in Auschwitz (June 1942–April 1944)................................393
The Significance of Changes in Auschwitz-Birkenau in 1944.........404
Escape from Auschwitz..410
Contacting Jewish Representatives after Escaping from Auschwitz.....417
Meeting Representatives of the Vatican and of Orthodox Jewry.....428
Controversial Aspects Relevant to the Holocaust in Hungary.........432
Figures...444

INTRODUCTION

UNTIL MARCH 18, 1944 HUNGARY WAS AN "INDEPENDENT" ally of Nazi Germany, whereas after that date an influx of German troops as well as a number of imprecisely defined "legislatic" changes marked the "occupation" of Hungary. The Regent Admiral Miklós

---

1   This article was originally published in *The Nazis' last victims: The Holocaust in Hungary* (ed. Randolph L. Braham and Scott Miller) (Detroit: Wayne State University Press, 1998). Reprinted with Randolph L. Braham's permission. –Eds.

Horthy remained in power, but the German presence became more and more intrusive. Significantly, Horthy's police and gendarmerie apparatus continued to function throughout this period. Beginning on April 5, Jews were compelled to wear the Yellow Star. Shortly thereafter, within four to six weeks, massive deportations of Jews began, clearly with Horthy's approval. On July 7, after various appeals and threats of reprisals had been issued by neutral and allied powers, Horthy ordered these deportations to cease. But by that time, 437,000 Jews had been deported to Auschwitz. About 400,000 were murdered on arrival. The rest were sent to slave labor. Less than five percent of these deportees ever returned.[2]

Historians are often puzzled by the remarkable swiftness of this whole operation. Between March 18 and July 7 less than four months elapsed. However, it is not often appreciated that preparations for the murder of these Hungarian Jews had begun in Auschwitz much earlier. I myself learned about these preparations as early as January 15, 1944, in Auschwitz, where I had been a prisoner since June 1942. The previous procedures employed by the Nazis, which had been used for the mass murder of Jews arriving from all the Nazi-occupied countries throughout Europe from September 1942 to March 1944, were now to be changed. Specifically, a new railway ramp, giving direct access to the gas chambers and crematoria, was to be constructed in Auschwitz-Birkenau, allowing for the much more rapid and effective mass murder of the hundreds of thousands of victims scheduled to be transported from Hungary—the last and largest surviving Jewish community in Europe.

Secrecy was essential for the success of this mass murder program.[3] I escaped from Auschwitz, together with my fellow prisoner Alfred Wetzler, on April 7, 1944, with the intention of alerting the Jewish Council in Hungary about the impending and imminent danger facing

2   Randolph L. Braham, *The Politics of Genocide: The Holocaust in Hungary* (New York: Columbia University Press, 1981), p. 1144.
3   Rudolf Vrba, "Footnote to the Auschwitz Report," *Jewish Currents*, vol. 20, no. 3 (1966), p. 27.

the Jews in Hungary. Here, I shall describe the principal relevant events before, during, and after our escape to Slovakia. In brief, within 14 days after escaping from Auschwitz we were able to make contact with the Jewish Council in Slovakia, and they gave us the facilities to write down our experiences in a document known as the Vrba-Wetzler Report,[4] sometimes also referred to as the Vrba-Wetzler statement[5] or anonymously as "Auschwitz Notebook"[6] or "Auschwitz Protocols."[7] At the same time we reported on the preparations being made in Auschwitz for the impending "reception" of the Hungarian Jews. This report was in the hands of the Jewish council in Hungary before the end of April 1944.

Post factum, we can say that none of the 437,000 Hungarian Jews deported between May 15 and July 9, 1944, to Auschwitz was ever given this information. There can be no doubt that the failure of the Jewish official representatives in Hungary to inform the Hungarian Jewish population about the death-mills in Auschwitz contributed to Adolf Eichmann's stunning success in organizing so rapidly the deportation of the majority

4   John S. Conway, "Frühe Augenzeugenberichte aus Auschwitz," *Vierteljahrshefte für Zeitgeschichte*, vol. 27, 1979, pp. 260–84; -, "The First Report About Auschwitz," *Simon Wiesenthal Center Annual*, vol. 1 (1984), pp. 133–51; -, "Der Holocaust in Ungarn," *Vierteljahrshefte für Zeitgeschichte*, vol. 32, no. 2 (1984), pp. 179–212; -, "The Holocaust in Hungary" in *The Tragedy of Hungarian Jewry*, ed. Randolph L. Braham (New York: Institute for Holocaust Studies of The City University of New York, 1986), pp. 1–48; Martin Gilbert, *Auschwitz and the Allies* (New York: Holt, Rinehart & Winston, 1981), p. 367; Frank Baron and Sándor Szenes, *Von Ungarn nach Auschwitz. Die verschwiegene Warnung* (Munster: Westphalisches Dampfboot, 1994), p. 13.
5   David S. Wyman, *The Abandonment of the Jews. America and the Holocaust* (New York: Pantheon Books, 1984), p. 289.
6   Jenö Lévai, *Zsidósors Európában (Jewish Fate in Europe)* (Budapest: Magyar Téka, 1948), p. 49, Sándor Szenes, *Befejezetlen múlt (Unfinished Past)* (Budapest: The Author, 1994), p. 335.
7   Braham, *The Politics*, p. 708; The Vrba-Wetzler Report ("Auschwitz Protocols") may be found at the Yad Vashem Institute Archives in Jerusalem under no. M-20/149. At the Nuremberg trials it was submitted in evidence under NG-2061, but neither I nor Wetzler were called to testify. *The Report* was mentioned anonymously, as a testimony of "two young Slovak Jews." For references to other versions of *The Report*, see Braham, *The Politics*, p.728, John S. Conway, "Auschwitz Bericht von April 1944," *Zeitgeschichte*, vol. 8 (1981), pp. 413–42. For French version, see Rudolf Vrba with Alan Bestic, *Je me suis évadé d'Auschwitz* (Paris: Edition Ramsay, 1988), pp. 361–98.

of the Hungarian Jews. It is my contention that this tragedy could have been greatly impeded if our warnings had been effectively and swiftly communicated to the intended victims. Of course, the full and enthusiastic cooperation of Horthy's gendarmerie was another crucial factor. The result was that the annihilation of this community proceeded more swiftly than any other in the whole tragic history of the Holocaust.

Lately, some historians have tried to argue that I and Wetzler were not acting on our own initiative, but were only "messengers" of some mythical organization also operating in Auschwitz. Others indicate that we were able to describe only those events which took place in Auschwitz during the period of our incarceration (i.e., from April 1942 for one of us, or June 1942 for the other, to April 7, 1944). They claim that we were not aware of the impending fate facing the Hungarian Jews,[8] and hence were not in position to alert anyone in Hungary of what was about to happen. But quite apart from the fact that the information contained in the Vrba-Wetzler Report was detailed and graphic enough to alert any potential victim of the dreadful danger, there is evidence that leading Jews in both Slovakia and Hungary immediately recognized the importance of our eyewitness account and the reliability of our prediction that the Hungary was imminent. As evidence I quote here the letter sent by Rabbi Michael Beer Weissmandel (signed M.B.) and Gisi Fleischmann (signed G. Fl.), a leading Zionist in Slovakia and a relative of Rabbi Weissmandel's, both of whom were active members of the Jewish Council of Slovakia. This letter,[9] which

8   Miroslav Kárný, "Historie osvětimské zprávy Wetzlera a Vrby" (History of the Auschwitz Report by Wetzler and Vrba) in *Tragédia slovenských židov* (The Tragedy of Slovak Jews), (ed. Dezider Tóth) (Banská Bystrica: Datel, 1992), p. 175. See also his "The Vrba and Wetzler Report" in *Anatomy of the Auschwitz Death Camp*, (eds. Yisrael Gutman and MichaelBerenbaum) (Bloomington: Indiana University Press, 1994), pp. 553–68.
9   See below. I am grateful to David S. Wyman for a copy of this letter. The letter is in German marked Hechaluz Geneva Office, Abschrift and Uebersetzung der beigelegten Hebr. Kopic. Box 60, War Refugee Board (WRB), Franklin D. Roosevelt Presidential Library (FDRPL), General correspondence of Roswell McClelland. F. Misc. Docs. Re: "Extmn. Camps for Jews in Poland." The Hebrew original of this letter is mentioned in Braham's *The Politics of Genocide*, p. 938, footnote 40.

was dispatched from Bratislava in Slovakia to *Hechalutz* in Switzerland on May 22, demonstrates that the Jewish Councils in both Slovakia and Hungary were well informed, on the basis of the report submitted by Wetzler and myself, as early as the end of April 1944 about the preparations made in Auschwitz expressly and specifically for the impending mass murder of the Hungarian Jews. Hence the urgency of their appeals to their contacts in Switzerland for help. Even though no immediate response was forthcoming from the recipients, the subsequent publication of the contents of the Vrba-Wetzler Report in the West resulted in pressure upon Horthy's government in Hungary,[10] and the massive deportation of Hungarian Jews was stopped early in July 1944. Thereafter the death toll among Jews in Hungary declined in absolute numbers, although the Horthy regime was soon replaced by the more radically pro-Nazi government of Ferenc Szálasi and his Arrow Cross organization.[11]

STREAMLINED METHODS OF MASS MURDER AND ROBBERY IN AUSCHWITZ (JUNE 1942–APRIL 1944)

ON JANUARY 15, 1944 (I.E., ABOUT TWO MONTHS BEFORE the formal occupation of Hungary) at about 10:00 a.m., I heard for the first time about the impending mass murder of about a million Hungarian Jews who were then still living in Hungary in relative freedom. This news was communicated to me in Birkenau at the southern end of Section BIIa, also known as the Quarantine Camp. The bearer of the news was a German kapo (a prisoner who was a trustee of sorts and had been assigned to administrative or specialized duties), a

10   Gerald Reitlinger, *The Final Solution: The Attempt to Exterminate the Jews of Europe, 1939–45* (London: Valentine, Mitchell, 1968), p. 469.
11   Braham, *The Politics*, p. 1144; J. S. Conway. "Der Holocaust in Ungarn," p. 208; - , "The Holocaust in Hungary," p. 36.

Berliner identified by a political prisoner's Red Triangle whose first name was Yup (Joseph), who at that moment was standing on the other side of the southern end of the electric fence surrounding Section BIIa of the camp (see Fig. 1). Specifically, he was standing on the road between Sections BI (women's camp) and Section BII (men's camp), about 30 meters west of the main entrance into Camp Birkenau on the road leading directly into Crematorium II and Crematorium III, both situated about one kilometer west of this point, within the internal perimeter (*Kleine Postenkette*) of Birkenau. I had known Kapo Yup for well over a year, but had not seen him for at least a year before the meeting I am describing took place. Various circumstances were favorable in connection with our acquaintance and our January meeting; furthermore, it was a lucky break that he managed to pass on this communication which, under the circumstances, was highly confidential. This German political prisoner risked his life by giving me this information. In fact, a certain mutual trust had become well established a long time before our accidental meeting in mid-January 1944.

At the time of this event I had been a prisoner in Auschwitz (under my former name Walter Rosenberg, prisoner number 44070) for more than a year and a half, and on the basis of my previous experience in this place I had good reasons to believe that the information communicated to me by Kapo Yup was reliable. In order to explain the background of my past experiences in Auschwitz and why I believed this information to be true, I shall have to start this story from June 30, 1942 when I was transferred to Auschwitz from the concentration camp Majdanek near Lublin.

While a prisoner in Auschwitz I, less than two months after my arrival there, in August 1942, I was included in a special working group of prisoners which was called *Aufräumungskommando*. This name, which translated into English means a "clean-up working group" or "putting-in-order working group," was a Nazi euphe-mism. The actual assignment of this group (comprising two hun-dred to eight hundred prisoners at various periods) was to eliminate the traces of the routinely organized murder and robbery of trans-ports of Jews brought by the German administration to Auschwitz under the pretext of "resettlement." These transports arrived at a ramp specially built for this purpose. The first such ramp (the so-called "old ramp" to differentiate it from the "new" one built in 1944) was a wooden platform I estimated to be about three hundred to five hundred meters long. Along this ramp the arriving deportees were unloaded from the freight cars, made to leave their luggage on the ramp, and hurried down a wooden staircase stretching along the whole ramp and then to the eastern dead end of a special road that reached another dead end about two kilometers to the west, at the gates of the gas chambers in Birkenau. The ramp was situated between camps Auschwitz I and Auschwitz II (i.e., Birkenau), on a piece of ground which belonged to neither camp and was the-oretically "civilian territory." This oddity was due to the fact that the main railway line connecting Vienna to Cracow passed between Auschwitz I and Auschwitz II; from this railway line a short side-line branched off, and it was this side-line along which the ramp had been built (see Fig. 2).

The prisoners belonging to the *Aufräumungskommando* (also called the "Canada" commando in the prisoners slang)[12] were housed in Block (i.e., barrack) Four in Auschwitz I. However, on January 15, 1943, these prisoners were transferred to Birkenau and housed in Block Sixteen (Birkenau, Section Ib) where we stayed until June 8, 1943. The

---

12   In the storage areas of the *Aufräfumungskommando* there were clothing, shoes, blankets, food and kitchen utensils, medicine, jewels, gold and hard currency all brought by the arriving deportees, i.e., their last possessions. These storage areas appeared to represent a "plentiful paradise" in the eyes of the Polish prisoners, and because by tradition in the eyes of Polish peasants the image of a "plentiful paradise" was the country of Canada, the storage areas of the *Aufräumungskommando* were named "Canada" in the camp slang.

general procedures on the old ramp and in the *Aufräumungskommando* remained unchanged during this time, except that the prisoners of the *Aufräumungskommando* were marched there from Birkenau rather than from Auschwitz I.

I had first become acquainted with Kapo Yup While I was still imprisoned in Auschwitz I, before I was moved to Birkenau, in 1942. He was a former German trade unionist (not a Jew) who had been arrested in the thirties for failure to comply with the Hitlerian "new order." He spent a number of years in various concentration camps until finally he was transferred as a German kapo to Auschwitz I. He was known to me as "red" kapo (wearing the Red Triangle denoting a political prisoner). Although outwardly he complied with the concentration camp system (and what else could he do?!), inside he remained an anti-Nazi. Among the non-Jewish German prisoners in Auschwitz there were a very few of this kind. I got to know him through common friends (other "red" prisoners in Auschwitz), and he was aware that I had had some involvement with "leftist" anti-Nazi activities before I was brought to Auschwitz, which resulted in a certain amount of mutual trust between us. After I was transferred to Birkenau, I did not see him again for at least a year, when he suddenly and unexpectedly appeared in Birkenau at the place I described above. As I will describe below in more detail, the reasons for his being in Birkenau in January 1944 were connected with the building of a new ramp for unloading the arriving deportees.

The work of the group of prisoners to which I had been assigned in the *Aufräumungskommando* had the following routine. Whenever the arrival of a transport was announced (by telephone from one of the railway stations situated near to Auschwitz), an SS man on a motorcycle arrived at the barrack where the prisoners belonging to the *Aufräumungskommando* spent the nights. A group of these prisoners (one hundred to two hundred men depending on the size of the expected transport) was then marched out from the heavily guarded camp to the ramp (as previously mentioned, this is the ramp I often refer to for clarity as the "old ramp" even though at this time it was really still the only ramp in operation) while surrounded by a group of about a dozen heavily armed SS men. When we arrived at the ramp, a group of about fifty SS men with firearms at the ready would surround the ramp. Numerous lampposts along the ramp were lit so that the light was as bright as in daytime, no matter whether it was summer or winter, rain, snow, or fog. After a group of SS officers accompanied by NCO's (all carrying bamboo walking canes, not truncheons) arrived, the train (usually consisting of twenty to forty but occasionally fifty to sixty freight cars) was pulled into the illuminated area by a steam locomotive and positioned along the now surrounded and brightly illuminated ramp. (As mentioned earlier, the ramp was situated between the outer chains of guards of Auschwitz I and Auschwitz II respectively.)

The freight cars were unlocked by the SS and opened in rapid succession all along the length of the train. More or less the same sight was unveiled to us each time, although these transports arrived from various countries in Europe, i.e., from France, Belgium, Holland, Bohemia (Theresienstadt), Slovakia, Poland, Ukraine (mainly from Grodno and Byalistok), and Greece. During the time I worked in the *Aufräumungskommando* (August 1942 to June 1943), I estimate that I saw well over one hundred (but less than three hundred) such transports arrive on the ramp. As I never made any written notes on these events during my incarceration in Auschwitz, I cannot give a closer estimate about the exact number of arriving transports during that time, although I tried to keep (and kept) a reasonably good mental record of the total number of people who arrived in this way.[13]

The floors of the freight cars were covered with luggage on which cowered the mass of the deportees, usually eighty per freight car, sometimes a hundred or in certain cases even more. In such extreme cases of overcrowding, the number of dead on arrival could be several dozen people, since the transports traveled in these locked and heavily guarded freight cars for two to ten days. As a rule, the deportees carried along enough food in their luggage, but they were not given enough drinking water during the journey and usually arrived in a hardly imaginable stage of hygienic, physical, and mental deterioration and were tormented by thirst. Thus, they were generally willing to obey any order when promised water, a promise hardly ever kept. Most of them (80 to 90 percent) were killed soon after their arrival in the nearby gas chambers, and died thirsty. They were first ordered

---

13   According to the Vrba-Wetzler Report, a careful estimate of the total number of people murdered in Auschwitz by gassing was 1,765,000 at the date of our escape. It was relatively very well established that after April 7, 1944 (i.e., after the Vrba-Wetzler Report was released), there were further 400,000 victims from Hungary alone; moreover, transports of Jews from the Theresienstadt and Lodz Ghettos, Greece, Berlin, Paris, Trieste, Belgium, Northern Italy, Slovakia, Poland, Holland, Vienna, Kovno, and other places arrived in Auschwitz after April 7, 1944, which would bring the number of victims close to 2.5 million in total. On the other hand, Yehuda Bauer in the *Jerusalem Post* of September 22, 1989, claims that the figure for Jews murdered by gassing [in Auschwitz, R.V.] is 1,323,000, (which is about a half of the Vrba-Wetzler estimate). He writes: "The basis for these figures is the clandestine registration carried out by a group of very courageous men and women who worked as clerks in the camp administration and had a fairly clear picture of what was going on." Bauer does not state who these very courageous men and women were, what sorts of documents they saw and why their "new" figures were published only in 1989. See also Henryk Swiebocki, "Raporty Uciekinierów z KL Auschwitz" (Reports of Escapees from the Auschwitz Concentration Camp), *Zeszyty Oswiecimskie. Numer Specjalny IV* (Oswiecim: Wydawnictwo Panstwowego Muzeum w Oswiecimiu, 1991), pp. 77–129 and pp. 207–8. In the "Report of a Polish Major" (Dr. Jerzy Tabeau) who escaped from Auschwitz in November 1943, an estimate of 1.5 million victims was given, which is in good agreement with the Vrba-Wetzler estimate (1.75 million) made in April 1944. The estimates made by former SS officers in Auschwitz about the number of victims murdered there are of great interest in this connection. Hermann Langbein collected numerous statements made independently of one another, and these all point to a number of two to three million. See his *Menschen in Auschwitz* (Vienna: Europa Verlag, 1972), p. 79. This is in good agreement with the estimate in the Vrba-Wetzler Report.

by the SS noncommissioned officers, swinging their walking canes, to leave the freight cars and descend the staircase of the ramp onto the wide dead-ended road built along the ramp, while leaving their luggage in the freight cars. "*Raus, raus, alles liegen lassen, raus*" was most often the order barked at the arrivals by the SS men, who usually added more emphasis by an indiscriminate use of the walking canes which they wielded as truncheons. The deportees were marshaled into a column that had to pass by an SS doctor who performed the "selection," dividing the arriving deportees into those destined for the gas chambers and the "others," i.e., those found suitable for slave labor which were immediately marched off from the ramp either into Auschwitz I or Auschwitz II (Birkenau) for registration as prisoners. No additional registration was made of the larger group of deportees, who were immediately transported on trucks (not marched) to the gas chambers.

A fleet of heavy trucks—not too many, perhaps half a dozen—used for this purpose were parked on the dead-end road. Those identified as "unfit for work" (all women with children, all children, all the old and infirm) were immediately ordered to ascend a wooden portable staircase and were loaded onto the platforms of one of these trucks. Any given truck started on its way to the nearby gas chamber in Birkenau as soon as exactly one hundred persons had been loaded. In the meantime, the prisoners working in the *Aufräumungskommando* would have sprung into feverish activity, frequently prodded on by a hail of well-directed blows with walking canes by the SS supervisors. Their first task was to empty the freight cars of their contents. The dead and the dying were dragged *im Laufschritt* (a Nazi euphemism for frantic running under a hail of blows by walking canes) to one of the waiting trucks, which departed as soon as one hundred dead or dying deportees had been loaded and went directly to the crematoria. The trucks then returned to the dead-end road near the ramp ready to be reloaded, either with a further batch of people destined for the gas chambers, or with the luggage of the victims.

Collection of this luggage was also a task of members of the *Aufräumungskommando*. The trucks loaded with luggage went in the opposite direction, into a separate storage area (called "Canada" in the camp's slang) situated in Auschwitz I, very near the facilities of DAW (*Deutsche Ausrüstungswerke*, see Fig. 2). Altogether, then, the trucks followed a pendulum-style trajectory from the dead-end road: when carrying victims, they moved westward about two kilometers to the crematoria in Auschwitz II, and when carrying the luggage of the newly arrived deportees they moved eastward about two kilometers to the "Canada" storage areas in Auschwitz I. When all the freight cars were empty, the workers of the *Aufräumungskommando* meticulously cleaned the cars of all traces of the former human cargo (blood, excrement, rubbish, etc.). After a strict inspection confirmed the cleanliness of the cars and the train departed, the last traces had to be eliminated from the ramp and carted away; a dozen SS guards would then march the *Aufräumungskommando* back into their barracks. No more than two to three hours elapsed from the arrival of each transport to the removal of its last traces from the ramp. By the time we prisoners belonging to the *Aufräumungskommando* left the scene, 80 to 90 percent of the arrivals were dead in the gas chambers and were already being "processed" in the crematoria, their luggage was already stored in the "Canada" storage areas in Auschwitz I, and the ramp was again immaculately clean and ready to receive the next transport. Thus, outwardly visible signs of this well-organized robbery and mass murder disappeared within two to three hours after a train arrived at the ramp. When we prisoners were not working on the ramp we worked in the "Canada" storage areas where, under close supervision of the SS, we broke the locks or ripped the luggage of all the new arrivals regardless of their further fate and sorted the contents. We burned all papers, books, documents, and photo albums. Hundreds of thousands of first- to third-quality men's suits and women's clothes, blankets, underwear, furs, kitchenware, baby carriages, eyeglasses, medicaments, shoes, etc., were carefully sorted, packed according to quality, and dispatched to Germany from the "Canada" storage areas in more or less irregular transports, as the goods accumulated. Fourth-quality clothing not deemed worth disinfecting was dispatched to a paper factory in Memel. Almost every day we would fill an entire separate suitcase with hard currency (dollars, pound sterling, Swiss francs) as well as diamonds, gold, and jewelry that had been found more or less well hidden in the luggage or its contents, e.g., inside a can of shoeshine cream or toothpaste, in the heel of a shoe, sewn into a seam or disguised pocket in clothing. These valuables were carried away daily by the SS, presumably for the *Reichsbank*. Sometimes the collection suitcase was so full with jewelry and banknotes that the SS men "in service" (usually SS-Unterscharführer Otto Graf from Vienna or SS-Unterscharführer Hans Kühnemann from Duisburg, North Rhine-Westphalia)[14] had to use their boots to press down the contents so that the suitcase could be closed. Prisoners attempting to hide any valuables or declared guilty of not finding them ("dereliction of work duties") were usually disciplined on the spot by clubbing or by a pistol shot, sometimes both.

---

14   SS-Unterscharführer Otto Graf lived unmolested under his name in Vienna after the war. I heard about this in 1963 when I lived in London, and I started criminal proceedings against him. He was finally arrested in Vienna in 1972 and at the *Landsgericht* Vienna was accused of thirty cases of criminal acts in Auschwitz. I acted as one of numerous witnesses for the prosecution. The jury found him guilty in twenty-nine cases, but because of the statute of limitation valid at that time, Otto Graf was released and lives at present (1994) in Vienna in retirement.
SS-Unterscharführer Hans Kühnemann returned after the war to his native Essen in Nordrhein-Westphalia and became a singer in the local opera. I learned about this only in 1989, and I started criminal proceedings against him (for robbery, multiple murders, and active participation in mass murder) in October 1989 at the public prosecutor's office (*Oberstaatsanwalt*) in Frankfurt/Main. Kühnemann was arrested in April 1990 but released on bail after one year. He was then tried at the *Landsgericht* Duisburg (Nordrhein-Westphalen) during 1991–1993. I acted as one of many witnesses for the prosecution. The trial of Kühnemann was stopped by the Supreme Court in Germany in 1993 because of his heart ailment. He lives at present (1994) in Essen as a retired opera singer.

While I was a member of the *Aufräumungskommando* (from August 1942 to June 1943), I of course had firsthand experience on the number of "resettled" Jews arriving in Auschwitz from Europe. I stopped being a member of the *Aufräumungskommando* on June 8, 1943, when certain major administrative changes took place in Birkenau. During this reorganization, I became a *Blockschreiber* in Block Fifteen of the Quarantine Camp (BIIa). *Blockschreiber* as a word is typical Nazi concentration camp slang and means "barracks pen pusher," although the translators of the Vrba-Wetzler Report[15] in Washington sometimes translated it as "Registrar" for lack of a better English equivalent. This new assignment again gave me an excellent observation post for obtaining firsthand information on the number and origin of virtually all arriving transports, as I will explain in more detail below.

Until June 8, 1943, all prisoners in Auschwitz II (Birkenau) occupied Section I, which was divided into Section BIa, a women's camp, and Section BIb, the men's camp. Meanwhile, during 1942–43 a new section, BII, was under construction. It was divided into six subsections, BIIa through BIIf (the capital B denotes *Bauabschnitt*, i.e., section). On June 8, 1943, all the (male) prisoners in BIb were transferred into BIId, and both BIa and BIb became female camps. BIIa became a "Quarantine Camp" for new arrivals, i.e., for those men from each transport who were chosen for slave-labor and given a prisoner number, while the rest of their transport was murdered in the nearby gas chambers. Sections BIIb, BIIc, and BIIe remained empty for some time after the major reorganization on June 8, 1943, and Section BIIf became a *Krankenbau* (sick bay) where sick prisoners were deposited either to recover (primitive medical treatment was sometimes available) or to die on their own or to be sent in due course to the crematorium to be gassed and cremated.

Although I was no longer a member of the *Aufräumungskommando* after June 8, 1943, from my new placement in BIIa (see Fig. 1), I again

15   See notes 7 and 13.

was able to observe the influx of new victims into Auschwitz very well, for the following reason. From the old ramp there were only two possible roads to the gas chambers: (a) As described above, trucks carrying new arrivals passed under the main gate to Birkenau and continued between Section I and Section II to crematoria II and III with their adjacent gas chambers; (b) Other trucks did not enter the main gate but instead made a ninety-degree turn to the right, continued eight hundred meters northward along BIIa until they reached the northern end, then made a ninety-degree turn to the west (left) and continued along the northern edge of BIIa through BIIf for about one kilometer into the complex of crematoria IV and V with the adjacent gas chambers (see Fig. 1). In both cases, the trucks passed about fifty meters or less from Block Fifteen of Quarantine Camp BIIa, where I was *Blockschreiber*. As I was well aware from my previous experience on the ramp that each truck carried exactly one hundred people, counting the number of trucks passing by gave me a good estimate of the size of each transport. Moreover, those men of each transport who were not gassed on arrival were (after a shower, disinfection, and change into prisoner's garb) first brought into BIIa, where they were registered. During the process of registration, I as a *Blockschreiber* of course had the opportunity to talk to them and to find out from which country and locality their transport had come. These new prisoners also usually knew how many persons had been included in their particular transport. This gave me a means of double-checking the estimates based on counting the number of trucks carrying the new arrivals into the crematoria. (I could easily count these trucks at night as well as in the daytime since the whole barrack shook when one passed by.) From the spring of 1942 to January 15, 1944, according to my calculations, more than 1.5 million Jews had been murdered in Auschwitz.[16] All these masses of people had arrived on the old ramp, and their robbery and murder had been carried out smoothly and without a hitch when viewed from the point

16   Ibid.

of view of the SS. I was convinced that if at this point the SS wanted to introduce major changes in the well-established and smoothly running procedure, there would have to be a very good reason.

THE SIGNIFICANCE OF CHANGES IN AUSCHWITZ-BIRKENAU IN 1944

ON JANUARY 15, 1944, AT ABOUT 10:00 A.M., I SAW FROM my barrack in BIIa that a group of unusual-looking prisoners were being marched through the arched gate of Birkenau into the space between Sections BIa and BIIa (see Fig. 1). These prisoners were relatively well dressed, and therefore it was obvious to me that they were neither Jews nor from Birkenau. (In some cases, groups of "old" Polish prisoners in Auschwitz I were better dressed.) When I approached the electric fence that separated them from me, I could hear them speak Polish among themselves and I could see they were putting up tripods with theodolites, carrying around calibrated rods, and recording measurements like land surveyors before a new building project is started. I soon became aware that the kapo who was at the head of this group of prisoners was Kapo Yup, whom I had met while a prisoner in Auschwitz I. The kapo recognized me, approached the electric fence, and (in a conversation across the barbed wire of the fence) first expressed great surprise to see me, then expressed his pleasure at seeing that I was still alive and "looking well," and then wondered whether I could provide ("organize," in camp slang) some cigarettes, as indeed I could. Thereafter, I asked him what he and "his men" were doing here, and he told me (emphasizing that it was a secret) that they were building a new railway line leading straight to the crematoria. I expressed surprise and I mentioned that not so long the existing ("old") ramp had been repaired. Kapo Yup then told me that he overheard from the SS that about a million Hungarian Jews would be arriving soon and that the system on the old ramp would not be able to handle such masses of people quickly enough. I immediately believed this piece of information. From my past experience, I knew that the annihilation of such an enormous number of victims within a very short time would necessitate some changes of the well-established procedures on the ramp. We knew in Birkenau that Hungary was the only possible and indeed last major community of Jews in Europe, whose rapid annihilation would indeed require modification of the routine procedures used in Auschwitz at that time. Principally, the relatively minor change of extending the railway connection about two kilometers—from the "old" ramp directly to the crematoria—would eliminate the need to transport a million victims from the ramp to the crematoria on many thousands of separate truck rides accompanied by armed guards on motorcycles.

In my mind, I immediately accepted as a fact that the Germans were then preparing the mass murder of Hungarian Jews and that Yup was giving me perfectly truthful and reliable information. Many historians still do not appear to appreciate that the Germans had planned the mass murder of Hungarian Jews well in advance of the so-called "occupation" of Hungary on March 19, 1944. As we know now, Eichmann and his henchmen arrived in Budapest immediately thereafter, with detailed plans on whom to contact among the Jewish dignitaries and notables in Hungary.[17] They expected to use the files and connections of these Jews and their organizations as well as those of the Hungarian authorities for a rapid administrative ghettoization of the Jewish masses, followed by their rapid deportation to the mass murder machinery in Auschwitz. Obviously, they planned the "occupation" of Hungary well in advance and the role of Auschwitz was an important part of this planning.

---

17   Fülöp Freudiger, "Five Months," in *The Tragedy of Hungarian Jewry* (ed. Randolph L. Braham) (New York: Institute for Holocaust Studies of The City University of New York, 1986), p. 237.

After my meeting with Kapo Yup on January 15, 1944, I was daily reminded of the fate impending for the Hungarian Jews, as Yup's working group was soon followed by hundreds of other prisoners, now mainly locals from Birkenau, who were put to work on the new ramp. It was soon clear, even to an untrained eye, that a railway section was being built that would extend directly to the crematoria.

The news about the fate awaiting the Hungarian Jews also reached me by other channels. In Quarantine Camp BIIa there was an active group of mostly criminal kapos (German prisoners identified by Green Triangles, denoting *Berufsverbrecher*, "professional criminals") organized by a *Lagerälteste* (camp elder, the highest prisoner rank in a camp section) named Tyn, a German professional criminal with a Black Triangle (denoting an "anti-social element"). This Tyn and his cronies in the camp kept close contact with the two SS Unterscharführers named Buntrock and Kurpanik[18] who represented the SS in the Quarantine Camp. Both Buntrock and Kurpanik were alcoholics; the money for their expensive habits was provided by Tyn and his cronies, who terrorized the newly arrived prisoners (the *Zugang*) to extort gold and money that some of them had managed to retain secretly on their bodies. These SS NCOs were talkative when inebriated—which was often the case—and I soon learned by this confidential grapevine that "Hungarian salami" was coming soon. It was a fact of Auschwitz that transports from various countries were characterized by certain country-specific long-lasting edible provisions in the deportees' luggage that reflected what kind of food was still available in various countries in war-torn German-occupied Europe. This food was taken from the new arrivals along with all the rest of the luggage, as described earlier, and from the "Canada" storage areas the perishable as well as canned foods found their way to the dining rooms of the SS officers and SS NCOs. Some of the food

---

18 Both SS Unterscharführers Buntrock and Kurpanik were tried in Cracow after the war for war crimes and hanged.

was also, at great risk, smuggled by prisoners into the camp. When a series of transports of Jews from the Netherlands arrived, cheeses enriched the wartime rations. It was sardines when series of transports of French Jews arrived, it was halva and olives when transports of Jews from Greece reached the camp, and now the SS were talking of "Hungarian salami," a well-known Hungarian provision suitable for taking along on a long journey.

Secrecy as to the true purpose of Auschwitz and of the industry of death practiced there for almost two years was of course very important for the continuing "business" of Auschwitz but, remarkably, within the confines of Auschwitz-Birkenau itself secrecy was not strictly guarded. The SS assumed that in spite of an active "grapevine communication" inside the camp, which they could not stop, no information would leak out of the camp. Obviously, this assumption was quite justified, inasmuch as until my and Wetzler's escape from Auschwitz-Birkenau in April 1944 the real purpose of Auschwitz-Birkenau, the capital of the mass murder and robbery machinery organized by the Nazis, remained a secret to the outside world. This incredible preservation of the secrecy of Auschwitz to the outside world has been well documented after the war by various historians.[19] Inside of Auschwitz, virtually all prisoners knew that most newly arrived Jews would be killed in the gas chambers. However, throughout my stay in Auschwitz from June 1942 until April 1944, during which time hundreds of transports of Jews arrived from all over Europe, I never met a single prisoner who had known anything about the gas chambers of Auschwitz before he arrived. The puzzling ignorance about their true destination by all the new arrivals over such a long period was astonishing not only for me but for all other prisoners living in Auschwitz at that time,

19   Gilbert, pp. 339–41; Walter Laqueur, *The Terrible Secret; Suppression of the Truth About Hitler's "Final Solution"* (Boston: Little, Brown, 1980), p. 145; Wyman, p. 288. See also note 20.

and has remained well established in the subsequent writings of many survivors of Auschwitz.[20]

The preservation of the secrecy of the Auschwitz death factory was the cornerstone of the success of the mass murder and robbery routinely practiced in Auschwitz virtually daily over a period of two years. The alleged passivity of hundreds of thousands of Jewish mothers and fathers who brought their children to their sordid execution in the gas chambers in Auschwitz was not the result of "Jewish inferiority," as the Nazis claimed. Neither was it their "inability to comprehend the truth," as the Israeli historian Yehuda Bauer suggests.[21] Nevertheless, I learned from the Jewish prisoners who were not murdered on arrival that before they left home they had been gravely worried about their sinister, unknown destination. Until the Nazi rule was established in their hometowns, they had spent their lives in a normal civilized society. After the Nazi or pro-Nazi administrations were set up, they were subjected to a total deprivation of civil liberties and systematically terrorized by Nazi and pro-Nazi gangs in all German-occupied or

20   Langbein collected testimonies of numerous survivors of various nationalities who arrived in Auschwitz at various dates in the period 1942–1944. They all testify not to have heard about Auschwitz and its meaning until they arrived there. See his *Menschen in Auschwitz*, pp. 140–42; A. Fiderkiewicz, formerly a Polish prisoner in Auschwitz-Birkenau, describes in his memoirs the numerous talks he had with newly arrived Jewish prisoners from Hungary in May–June 1944: He was still astonished by the fact that even at that time the new prisoners from Hungary had not the slightest suspicion that their children and parents would be murdered on arrival in the resettlement area. See his *Brzezinka, Birkenau* (Warsaw: Czytelnik, 1962), p. 246. See also Judith Magyar Isaacson, *Seed of Sarah. Memoirs of a Survivor* (Chicago: University of Illinois Press, 1991), pp. 58–82.
In this connection, a particularly informative statement was made by Elie Wiesel: "We were taken just two weeks before D-Day and we did not know that Auschwitz existed. How is it possible? Everyone knew, except the victims. Nobody cared enough to tell us: Don't go." Recorded by William Nicholls, *Christian Antisemitism. A History of Hate* (Northvale, NJ: Aronson, 1993), p. 353.
21   Yehuda Bauer, *A History of the Holocaust* (New York: Franklin Watts, 1982), p. 314. Bauer claims that "knowing the facts is not always the same as accepting the facts. To survive, many had to deny what they knew. The later claim that had someone—their leadership, Kasztner or anyone else—only told them, they would have behaved differently, cannot be taken at face value." This implies that the "leadership" and Kasztner had the ability to know and accept facts, but those who were deported to Auschwitz did not. See also note 57.

semi-occupied countries. The fascist and pro-Nazi regimes in Europe protected murderous gangs such as the Hlinka Guards in Slovakia or the Ustashas in Croatia. Similar paramilitary anti-Semitic terrorist organizations were active throughout the whole of German-occupied Europe, where with the help of the ruling authorities—sometimes disguised in priestly habits like Josef Tiso in Slovakia, or veiled in nationalistic fervor like Henri Philippe Petain in France, or Ante Pavelic in Croatia—they created a pogrom-type atmosphere. The Jews were inclined to hope that by obedience they might escape the increasing violence in their hometowns. They even optimistically believed that they would be safer if moved to less dangerous "resettlement areas" or hoped that their children at least would have a chance to survive the war in some sort of Jewish reservation in the East. Against this background the Jews were hoodwinked into going willy-nilly into the deportation trains. When they arrived in Auschwitz and realized that they had been swindled, they were already inside the confines of the mass murder camps (sometimes also called "extermination camps" in line with the Nazi imagery likening Jews to insects), in most cases at the very gates of the gas chambers and crematoria. Their only choice at that point was between being wounded and tortured to death or dying less elaborately. Often they were killed before they had time to contemplate the alternatives, because speed was the vital part of the mass-murder technique practiced by the Nazis in Auschwitz and other death camps.

I believed that if I escaped the confines of Auschwitz and managed to get back into the world outside and spread the news about the fate awaiting potential candidates for "resettlement," I could make some significant difference by breaking the cornerstone of the streamlined mass murder in Auschwitz, i.e., its secrecy. I had no doubts whatever as to my abilities to communicate the realities of Auschwitz to the outside world, since I was relatively very well acquainted with the machinery of

Auschwitz including its detailed geography and operational principles as well as with what went on there during my imprisonment. Because in Auschwitz we prisoners were frequently subjected to meticulous inspection of our assigned work and habitation spaces as well as to bodily searches, I avoided making any notes whatever and relied exclusively on my reasonably reliable memory—the slightest evidence or suspicion that I was keeping track of events for possible communication to anyone outside the camp would have immediately condemned me to a difficult way of dying.

ESCAPE FROM AUSCHWITZ

I FIRST PLANNED TO ESCAPE ON JANUARY 26, 1944, together with Charles Unglick, a Jewish prisoner from Poland, born in Czestochova in 1911, who had lived in France before his arrest and been a prisoner in Auschwitz since June 1942. But on January 26, due to a technical hitch, I could not get to the place where we were supposed to meet on time. Faced with the dilemma of going alone or waiting for another opportunity, he chose to try it alone and was killed the same day.[22]

The next plan to escape was worked out with another Jewish prisoner from Slovakia, Alfred Wetzler, born in 1918 in Trnava. Wetzler had been in Birkenau since April 1942 (his prisoner number was 29162). He worked as a *Schreiber der Leichenkammer* (pen-pusher in the morgue) in Birkenau BIb and later, after the reorganization of the camp in June 1943, as *Blockschreiber* in Block Nine in BIId, which became the main male camp at that time. I knew Wetzler from Trnava, where I had lived (although I was born in Topolčany), before my deportation from Slovakia in 1942. Well over six hundred Jewish men

---

22   Rudolf Vrba and Alan Bestic, *I Cannot Forgive* (New York: Grove Press, 1964), pp. 209–15. See also note 24.

from Trnava were deported to Auschwitz from Slovakia in 1942 (including Wetzler's father and two brothers). Of all these people, only Alfred Wetzler and I were still alive in the spring of 1944. With all our friends and acquaintances from Trnava murdered outright or slowly succumbed to the camp conditions (mainly in 1942), we became close friends and trusted each other. This mutual trust was the fundamental link in the chain of many small step-by-step operations needed to prepare the escape. I want to stress that there was no resistance "group" or "organization" of any sort which decided that we two should escape[23] or where we should go or what we should do when and if we survived the massive hunt which was routinely organized after every escape attempt. Our escape was planned for Monday, April 3, 1944, but due to unforeseen technical hitches we had to delay it until April 7. The alarm was sounded in Auschwitz-Birkenau on Friday, April 7, at 6:00 p.m. We managed to stay hidden between the "small" and "large" (i.e., inner and outer) chains of guards in the confines of Birkenau until Monday, April 10, at 9:00 p.m. when, after three days and nights (the standard time period), the hunt for us was called off as unsuccessful. Then we started our trek southward to Slovakia.

I am often asked how we escaped from Auschwitz and how we knew the way to Slovakia. I shall not now describe the technical details of our escape, as I did this previously in a book that was published in numerous editions in several languages.[24] Moreover, it is not really relevant to the main subject of the present article, except for the fact I stressed above, that no "resistance organization" and no person whatever knew in which direction we were going to move in case our escape from the

23   I left Czechoslovakia in 1958. After my departure, various clumsy efforts were made to present my and Wetzler's escape as a result of an activity of a mythical resistance organization. See, for example, the account by Adolf Burger, *Ďáblova Dílna* (The Devil's Workshop) (Prague: Československá Redakce MON, 1988). Evidence to the contrary of such claims was presented by Langbein, pp. 78, 301. See also notes 26, 29, and 46.
24   Rudolf Vrba and Alan Bestic, *I Cannot Forgive* (London: Sidgwick and Jackson, 1963). The book has appeared in many editions in English, French, Dutch, German, Czech and Hebrew languages, some under slightly different titles.

camp itself proved successful. Neither in Germany nor in Poland (territories through which we inevitably had to move), neither in Slovakia nor in Hungary (territories toward which we were moving) was there a living person who knew anything in advance about our escape. At the moment of our escape, all connections with all friends and social contacts we had in Auschwitz were severed, and there was absolutely no one waiting for us outside of the death camp where we had spent the past two years: de facto, we had been written off by the world from the moment we were loaded into a deportation train in the spring of 1942. Thus, we had to step into a complete "social vacuum" outside of Auschwitz—we did not even know who, if anyone, was still alive of our family members. The only administrative evidence of our existence was an international warrant about us distributed telegraphically to all stations of the Gestapo, Kripo (criminal police), SD (*Sicherheitsdienst*, Security Service), and Grepo (*Grenzpolizei*, border police). (A photocopy of this warrant was published more than three decades after the end of the war.[25])

Inside of Auschwitz-Birkenau there existed a complex network of informers among the prisoners. It had been built up by the SS camp police (called *Politische Abteilung*, Political Department) whose objective was mainly to prevent a revolt in the camp or escape from it. The danger of being denounced to this body was an ever-present reality. Therefore, I never spoke with anyone about my plans regarding the route we would take after our escape, not even with Wetzler. Wetzler and I, though, had agreed in advance to go south, i.e., to our native country Slovakia, the only place in the world where our accents would not betray us immediately as "suspicious foreigners" and where we had some sort of connections before our deportation. There we intended to look for contacts that would enable us to make public what had been happening before our eyes in Auschwitz over the previous two

25   Gilbert, pp. 192–93. See also Swiebocki, p. 26 for a good copy of another warrant.

years and what was being prepared there in the near future for the Hungarian Jews.

To be curious in Auschwitz-Birkenau about the geography of the place might have attracted the ears of ubiquitous informers who would consider it an indication of preparing an escape, and hence invite the attention of the "Political Department" and its torture chambers. However, I had gained some insight into my exact geographical location during my first six months in Auschwitz. Since I had worked in the *Aufräumungskommando* from August 1942 to June 1943, I had quite a good idea about the relative position of Auschwitz I to Auschwitz II (Birkenau) because the railroad ramp was between these two camps and I was marched to this ramp either from Auschwitz I during the second half of 1942 or from Birkenau during the first half of 1943 (see Fig. 2). The church spire of the town Auschwitz could be seen from the "Canada" storage areas (located next to DAW, Fig. 2) on clear days at a distance of less than five kilometers away, and I knew from having been marched around Auschwitz I for odd jobs on one or two occasions that the Auschwitz I camp was separated from the town of Auschwitz by a minor river called the Sola.

While I was working in the "Canada" storage areas, the luggage of the victims there frequently contained books and notebooks of children, as their parents obviously had been inveigled to believe that the children would go to school in the new "resettlement areas." One of our tasks was to burn any papers found in the luggage. On one occasion I saw a children's atlas among the papers to be burned. At an opportune moment I took the risk of opening the book and tearing out a map of Silesia, an area which I knew from my school years to be situated around the triangle where the prewar borders of Germany, Poland, and Czechoslovakia met. I took the map under my shirt to the latrine, where I was able to study it for a few minutes before disposing of it. I learned that the town Auschwitz on the Sola river is about fifty kilometers north of the borders of northern Slovakia, that the river Sola originates directly on the borders of Slovakia, and that between the town Auschwitz and the Slovak border this river flows in an almost straight line from south to north, through the communities of Sol (on the Slovak border), Rajcza, Milowka, Saybusch (Zywiec), Kety, Auschwitz (see Fig. 3). So, it was clear to me that if I escaped from Auschwitz all I would have to do, in terms of orientation, was to follow the river Sola against its flow to reach the border of Slovakia by the shortest possible route, passing by the above-named settlements.

As mentioned above, I escaped with Alfred Wetzler on Friday, April 7, 1944; as part of our plan, we first remained hidden in Birkenau about three hundred meters east from Crematorium V in the unfinished section BIII, and we only left Birkenau after the intensive manhunt for us was called off on Monday evening, April 10. For the first week after that, we moved only at night, in a southerly direction (toward the mountains) through the rather flat terrain around Auschwitz, which was studded with several minor Auschwitz-satellite camps for slave labor. We tried to avoid contact with the civilian population since this part of Silesia—formerly Polish but now annexed by Germany—was heavily "repopulated" by German "colonists," while a good part of the former Polish inhabitants had been driven out from their homes by the Germans. We started out from Birkenau with about three to four kilograms of bread, which we carefully rationed during the night marches, and we drank water from the streams we crossed. During the night marches, we frequently lost orientation; indeed, we soon found out that we had wandered much too far to the west from my planned route when we hit the town of Bielsko-Biala on Thursday, April 13. When at the light of dawn we were still lost in the maze of Bielsko-Biala and there was no way out but to look for a temporary hideout lest we be spotted by the vigilant German security apparatus, we knocked at the doors of a rundown Polish peasant house in the suburb of Pisarowice.

The owner of the house was an old Polish peasant woman who lived there with her daughter. After a traditional Polish greeting ("Praised be the name of Jesus Christ"), both were willing to harbor us two strangers for one day and to give us bread, potato soup, and imitation coffee. As both Wetzler and myself were fluent in Polish, we gained a general outline of the situation in which we had landed. The villages around—so we learned—had been "Germanized," and the German civilians went to work in the fields armed and instructed to shoot unidentifiable strangers on sight. The Polish households were farther away from the river and the communication lines. However, any help to strangers was punished by executions, often of whole families. Many people in Polish households had already been executed for giving food or shelter to Polish- or Russian-speaking German *agents provocateurs* who paraded as fugitives.

We left these helpful Polish women in Pisarowice during the next night, and at dawn we reached the mountainous region at the end of the main valley through which the Sola flows. We moved southward along the western banks of the river on the forest-covered slopes of the valley. The isolated Polish households closed their doors and windows when we approached, and the people did not answer when we spoke to them; however, frequently a Polish peasant girl would run across our path and drop a half loaf of bread as if she had lost it while running.

Our presence in the region must have come to the notice of the German authorities. On Sunday, April 16, when we emerged from the forest and were resting on a clearing close to Porebka, a fanned-cut group of about a dozen German field gendarmes with dogs on leashes approached us concentrically and opened fire without warning as soon as we tried to move. Fortunately, we managed to reach the nearby forest through a hail of fire without being hit, although we had to abandon all of our provisions and overcoats and continue without them through forests still partially covered in snow.

Three days later, on Wednesday, April 19, we stumbled on a Polish woman attending her goats close to the forest on the hills above Milowka. She realized that we were fugitives from the Germans and offered us food and rest in her goat-hut. She also connected us with a helpful Pole who, on the night of April 20–21, hiked with us by a relatively short and safe route to the vicinity of the Slovak border and gave us some information about the frequency and usual path of German border patrols. In accordance with the habits of those times, no names or addresses were exchanged so that in case we were captured by the Germans we could not divulge under torture who had helped us. On Friday morning, April 21, we crossed the Slovak border and soon stumbled onto a Slovak peasant alone with his horse, ploughing his field in the vicinity of the Slovak-German (formerly Slovak-Polish) border. The peasant (Andrej Čánecký from the nearby Slovak village of Skalite) at that point knew nothing about us except what he had himself seen from distance, that we had crossed the border without passports.[26] He was not sure whether we were smugglers or another kind of clandestine traveler—I myself was relatively very well dressed in a Dutch tweed jacket, a white woolen sweater, woolen riding breeches, and excellent high boots (all "organized," i.e., stolen, from the "Canada" storage areas in Auschwitz). Alas, my elegance was somewhat tainted by a fortnight of life in fields and forests: I carried my boots over my shoulder as I had had to cut them off my feet with a razor due to gross swelling caused by marching and deficient diet since I had eaten little else but bread during the previous fortnight.

Čánecký offered us a chance to wash up and rest in his house, and gave us dinner. During the meal, he gave me a geographical picture of the local surroundings (nearest town Čadca, names of villages). He also mentioned the names of Jewish doctors in the villages as well as the

26 During the 1990s, some attempts were made to depict our contact with Čánecký as having been arranged by an underground organization. For references to this "linkage theory," see H. Swiebocki *Zeszyty Oswieczinskie*, p. 27, and Peter Gosztonyi's article in *Ménora*, Toronto, May 27, 1994. See also notes 23, 29, and 46.

name of a Dr. Pollack who practiced medicine in Čadca. This attracted my attention, as I had met this same Dr. Pollack just before I was deported from Slovakia in June 1942 in a transport of Slovak Jews destined for "resettlement" and in due course dispatched across the border from the camp in Nováky on June 14, 1942. At that time, Dr. Pollack had also been scheduled to be "resettled" with the same transport; I made his acquaintance in the camp in Nováky. However, due to an "exception," he had been removed from the list of Jews to be deported and returned to a medical practice in Slovakia. The "exceptions" for physicians were granted for the following reasons: A high percentage of medical practitioners in Slovakia were Jews, and when Tiso's pro-Nazi regime in Slovakia started to "resettle" the Jewish doctors in the spring of 1942, many protests were raised when the villagers suddenly found themselves lacking even basic medical assistance. Consequently, the Tiso regime, trying hard to curry favor with the peasantry, gave a reprieve to Jewish medical doctors who were not yet deported and released them to practice medicine in the smaller settlements, providing basic services to the peasantry and making it possible for the few "Aryan" doctors left in the villages to also move to the more prestigious towns and major hospitals.

CONTACTING JEWISH REPRESENTATIVES AFTER ESCAPING FROM AUSCHWITZ

WHEN I LEARNED THAT DR. POLLACK, WITH WHOM I ONCE shared a stage of the Jewish fate in Slovakia, was now stationed in the nearest small town, Čadca, I immediately decided to use him as our first contact with the surviving Jewish community. My companion, Alfred Wetzler, agreed. Čánecký then explained to us that a night march to Čadca might be unsafe and might take two to three nights, but that he thought he had a better idea. He said he intended to go to the market in Čadca by train on the next Monday to sell his hogs, and offered to harbor us during the weekend, disguise us in peasant clothing, and take us along: while helping with the transport and sale of his hogs, we were unlikely to attract the attention of the police, gendarmerie, and informers. We accepted Čánecký's magnanimous offer and stayed in his house until Monday morning, then traveled with him and his hogs the thirty kilometers to Čadca by train. On Monday afternoon, I presented myself as a patient in Dr. Pollack's surgery. This doctor's office in Čadca was situated in the army barracks. When Dr. Pollack saw me in the privacy of his doctor's office, with a shaven head (no hair was allowed in Auschwitz) and dressed as a peasant, he at first did not recognize me. But when I told him who I was and where we had met, and that I had come back to Slovakia from whence I was deported in 1942, he finally remembered me. His astonishment was not surprising, inasmuch as Wetzler and I represented the first case in the tragic history of Slovak Jews of a return after the deportations of Jews from Slovakia were temporarily stopped in October 1942. Between March and October 1942, about 60,000 Jews had been deported from Slovakia (about 30,000 to Auschwitz, the rest to Majdanek, Treblinka, Bełżec, and Sobibor) out of the total Jewish population of about 85,000 in the territory of the Slovak State at that time. When I escaped from Auschwitz, only sixty-seven of the Slovak Jewish men were still alive in Auschwitz and about four hundred young women. The rest of the "resettled" Slovak Jews died in the camp (or were murdered on arrival) in 1942.

When Dr. Pollack was given a reprieve from deportation in the spring of 1942, it covered his wife and children along with him but not his parents, brothers, and sisters and their families. He asked me whether I knew anything about the fate of his deported relatives, and I had to tell him that they were dead. He had heard nothing from his relatives since 1942 and knew nothing about the further fate of the deportees except that their silence and traceless disappearance were foreboding. He then asked me what he could do for me. I wanted to know whether there remained any representatives of any Jewish organizations in Slovakia. He assured me that he could discreetly arrange for an immediate contact with the Jewish Council in Bratislava (*Ustredna Zidov*; UZ), representing the 25,000 Slovak Jews who had not been deported in 1942 and were still living in Slovakia.

Wetzler and I spent the night in Čadca in the household of Mrs. Beck (a relative of the well-known rabbi Leo Baeck),[27] who at that time still lived in Čadca under the aegis of the Jewish Council. The next morning—still in our peasant outfits—we traveled by train to the nearby major Slovak town of Žilina and were met in the park in front of the railway station by Erwin Steiner, a representative of the Jewish Council. He took us to the Jewish Old People's Home, which had been converted into offices of the Jewish Council after the old people were "resettled" in 1942. There we were joined by his wife, Ibolya Steiner (who acted as a typist), and Oskar Krasnyanski, also an important representative of the Jewish Council. The chairman of the Jewish Council, Oscar Neumann, arrived the next day. My identity as well that of Alfred Wetzler could be established immediately as the Jewish Council had lists of deportees of each transport that had left Slovakia as well as a personal file that included a photograph of each deportee. (In fact, the files of the Jewish Council had been used in the organization of the transports .[28])

After relatively brief preliminary discussions, when the impending mortal danger to the largest—almost intact—surviving Jewish community in Hungary was clearly outlined, we agreed to dictate the

27   Rabbi Leo Baeck as a member of the Theresienstadt *Judenrat* participated in the conspiracy to withhold the truth about Auschwitz from "common" Jews, when he decided not to tell ghetto inhabitants that the transport to Poland meant death. See Bauer, *A History of the Holocaust*, p. 220, and Braham, *The Politics*, p. 722.

28   Ivan Kamenec, *Po stopách tragédie (Tracing the Tragedy)* (Bratislava: Archa, 1991), p. 169: "In preparation of the deportation also the Jewish Council (Ústredna Židov) involuntarily participated. Its department for special tasks was preparing special evidence and various lists, which served as basic materials for preparing the personal lists of the deportation transports." See also note 46.

substantial facts we knew about Auschwitz to Krasnyanski, who was a good shorthand stenographer; he then dictated from his notes, in our absence, to the typist, Ibolya Steiner. Krasnyanski wanted separate statements so that what I said should not influence Wetzler's statements and vice versa. He therefore first locked himself into an office with me. I started with a drawing (by hand, and giving estimated distances from memory) of the inner layout of Auschwitz I Camp, the layout of Auschwitz II Camp, and the position of the old ramp in relation to the two camps (see Fig. 2). I then proceeded to explain the internal organization and working of the Auschwitz camp complex, describing both the facilities constructed for the massive slave labor contingent serving the giants of the German industry (Krupp, Siemens, IG Farben, D.A.W.) and the mass murder machinery of gas chambers and crematoria. Because of my wide firsthand experience on the ramp and from Quarantine Camp BIIa, I was able to reconstruct with a considerable degree of exactness the history of all arriving transports. I particularly emphasized the fate of the so-called Czech Family Camp, which at the time of my escape was located in BIIb. In this camp about 4,000 Czech Jewish men had been "put on ice" (temporarily held prisoner) with their families, including children, for exactly six months starting September 8, 1943 and then killed on March 8, 1944, only one month before my escape. Another family transport of Czech Jews from Theresiendstadt had been "put on ice" in BIIb around December 20, 1943, scheduled to be murdered six months later (in June 1944).

The expression transport "put on ice" meant, in practical administrative terms at that time, that the transport was given the administrative denotation "*Sonderbehandlung mit 6 Monaten Quarantäne*" (Special Treatment with 6 Months Quarantine—"special treatment" was the code phrase for murder in the gas chambers). Since the two Czech family transports were held in Birkenau Section BIIb, and as I was a *Blockschreiber* in the neighboring Section BIIa, I could easily make contact with these people by talking to them across the electrified barbed-wire fence which divided the two sections (see Fig. 1). They were all Czechoslovakians with whom I shared a common language and in part a common background, so it was natural that I formed personal ties with several of them over the last six months of their life. The fate of these Jews was even closer to my heart (because they were less anonymous) than the fate of the other victims arriving from various places in Europe that had no personal associations for me who were murdered on arrival. For these reasons, these Czech family transports have a relatively more prominent role in the Vrba-Wetzler Report than the actual number of these Czech "Family Camp" victims of Auschwitz (less than 9,000) would de facto merit in comparison to the total of 1.75 million people I estimate had been murdered in Auschwitz while I was there.

In summary, the statistics in the Vrba-Wetzler Report are based mainly on the fact that until June 8, 1943, I was in the *Aufräumungskommando*, which "worked" on the old ramp. Thus, I was present at the arrival of each transport during this time and I was in a good position to prepare the statistics by memorization and using a simple mnemotechnical method. As I stated earlier, neither I nor Wetzler carried any papers when we escaped from Birkenau, nor was there any preliminary consultation with any mythical "committee" before our escape. For the rest of my time (after I was "discharged" from the *Aufräumungskommando*) in Auschwitz II I was a *Blockschreiber* in Quarantine Camp BIIa, so that I was able to continue to keep up my statistics by direct observation of transports passing in front of my eyes as well as by speaking to the new arrivals who were stationed in the Quarantine Camp at the start of their imprisonment in Auschwitz. Normally, only those who survived the "Quarantine" stage were distributed into the various slots in the slave labor force. These *Zugang* people (new arrivals) as a rule of course knew where their transports came from and how many persons they had comprised at their point of departure, i.e., before the "selection" for the gas chambers. From my work assignment in BIIa, I could also see the arrivals who were not selected for slave labor, on their way to the gas chambers (see Fig. 1), even when I was no longer working on the ramp after June 8, 1943.

My companion in the escape, Alfred Wetzler, was probably just as well informed as I was about the events and history of Auschwitz, and he could and did corroborate my data by his independent statement to Krasnyanski, although I obviously do not know exactly what he dictated to Krasnyanski in my absence. The latter then used the protocols of both our statements and in great haste combined these editorially into one typewritten report. In a preface to the final text of the report, Krasnyanski stated that the document contained the statement of two Jews who escaped from Auschwitz (starting with the statement of the first Jew). From the time the second Jew arrived there, the Report is based on the statement of both (Wetzler arrived in Auschwitz in April 1942 and I in June 1942). It would of course be difficult to disentangle which part of the report stems from me and which from Wetzler, and it is right to consider it the result of the efforts of both of us, an effort we both made to the best of our knowledge and abilities.[29] We also added a special appendix to the report in which my experiences from a short imprisonment (twelve days) in the concentration camp of Majdanek were recorded. (I had been

---

29   During the sixties, in Czechoslovakia as well as in Israel, various innuendos were aimed systematically to indicate that I and Wetzler were only "messengers carrying mail for a major organization" (sometimes "international-proletarian," sometimes "Jewish Zionist") which provided us with information about Auschwitz and prepared our escape. See in this connection: Kárný, "Historie osvětimské zprávy Wetzlera a Vrby," pp. 167–68, and p. 180; Kamenec, pp. 250–51. In Israel especially, there have been several attempts not to identify me and Wetzler as the authors of the Report by simply referring to "two young people who succeeded in escaping from Auschwitz." See, for example, the statement by Oskar Isaiah Karmiel (formerly Krasnyanski) of February 15, 1961 ("A Declaration Under Oath"), made in preparation for the Eichmann trial, and Livia Rothkirchen, "The Final Solution in Its Last Stages" in *The Catastrophe of European Jewry* (eds. Israel Gutman and Livia Rothkirchen) (Jerusalem: Yad Vashem, 1976), p. 326. In connection with this phenomenon see also Braham, *The Politics*, p. 711, and note 46.

transferred to Auschwitz from Majdanek, rather than coming directly to Auschwitz from my native country of Slovakia.) All discussions with the representatives of the Jewish Council in Žilina were conducted in Slovak. The report was originally prepared in a Slovak version, to my knowledge immediately translated into German and Hungarian, and later also translated into English and French.[30] The further fate of this report need not to be discussed here in detail, as this was done before in various extensive studies.[31] Here I would only add that all work on the Vrba-Wetzler Report was finished and the final version was typed by Thursday, April 27, 1944. Although in this Report what was said by myself and what was the contribution of my companion Wetzler was clearly mixed up, I approved of the Report as it stood, because the most relevant factor was the need for an urgent warning to the Hungarian Jews about their imminent mortal danger. To make further corrections or retype the Report in order to eliminate minor errors or to increase the accuracy of unimportant details at that point would have meant a loss of time at a crucial moment. Indeed, at least one transport of Jews from Hungary passed through Žilina as early as April 28, and the mass deportation of Hungarian Jews to Auschwitz began about two weeks after our Report was approved, signed, and released by Wetzler and myself.

On Friday, April 28, 1944, a secret conference was convoked by the Slovak Jewish Council in the Jewish Old People's home in Žilina. Perhaps a dozen people were present, including the chairman of the Slovak Jewish Council, Oscar Neumann, and some representatives of Hungarian Jewry. Wetzler and I were asked to answer their questions and to give some further explanations. In accordance with the informal rules of illegal work under Nazi occupation, no names were exchanged at this meeting. One

30   Only in the sixties did I learn that at least one translation into English of the Vrba-Wetzler Report from a Hungarian copy was made by Blanche Lucas, who after the war became a member of Goddard & Son, the London law firm. During the war she was the secretary of Walter Garrett, the British Correspondent in Zurich, who first brought the Report to the knowledge of the British Government. Werner Rings, *Advokaten des Feindes* (Vienna: Econ Verlag, 1966), p. 144.

31   Braham, *The Politics*, pp. 691-731. See also note 4.

of the gentlemen present was a lawyer who had great difficulty believing that people were de facto executed in the heart of "civilized Germany" without the benefit of a legal defense before execution. All were impressed with my tweed jacket with its fashionable Amsterdam tailor's address on the inside, a real rarity in wartime Slovakia.

By then, May 1 was imminent and the Slovak Jewish Council was anxious that we leave the premises of the Jewish Council in Žilina before that date, since on this day (a traditional trade union holiday) the state police took special precautions against anti-Nazi demonstrations. By tradition, they were likely to check any existing Jewish premises, on the assumption that all Jews are traditional "Judeo-Bolshevik agitators." Wetzler and I moved to a small town near the High Tatras (Liptovský Svätý Mikuláš; Liptószentmiklós in Hungarian). However, after our escape from Auschwitz, in view of the fugitive warrants we presumed had been issued, we of course used different names—I picked the name Rudolf Vrba (a not uncommon name in Czechoslovakia). I subsequently retained this name as my "nom de guerre" and had the change of name legalized as soon as a normal legal system was reestablished in Czechoslovakia after the defeat of the Nazis. Meanwhile, in April 1944 in Žilina, the Slovak Jewish Council provided me with a set of fake documents of excellent quality which showed that I, Rudolf Vrba, was certified as a "pure Aryan" for three generations back; with these papers, I was able to move around Slovakia without the danger of being picked up by one of the frequent police raids on the streets, in restaurants, trains, and railway stations. We were reassured by Krasnyanski that our Report was now "in the right hands" both in Budapest (the name of the "Zionist leader in Hungary" Rudolf Kasztner was mentioned in this connection with particular reverence) and Bratislava, and that we had nothing more to worry in this matter. So, my task, dictated exclusively by my conscience (not by a mythical committee in Auschwitz or elsewhere), to warn the Hungarian Jews about the exact nature of their imminent mortal danger, was finished.

Wetzler and I spent the next six weeks in Liptovský Svätý Mikuláš. I traveled frequently to Bratislava, where I had a friend, Josef Weiss,[32] a Jew from Trnava whom I knew well from before my deportation. Weiss had successfully avoided deportation in 1942, and in 1944 was working in Bratislava in the Office for Prevention of Venereal Diseases. This agency kept very confidential personal data on carriers of venereal diseases, and its offices were well protected (even from the police); it was therefore very suitable for clandestinely making copies of our Report. Weiss distributed these copies to several young Jewish men who then tried to distribute them secretly in Hungary.[33] One of these copies of the Report found its way to Switzerland and Bern (via Moshe Kraus, director of the Palestine Office in Budapest) and was smuggled to George Mandel-Mantello, a Hungarian Jew living in Switzerland, who made successful efforts to have the Report published there.[34] The publication of the Report in Switzerland then led to a wide newspaper campaign[35] and to an international chain reaction which has been described elsewhere[36] that finally induced Horthy, the Regent of Hungary, to stop the deportations on July 7, 1944.

---

32   Josef Weiss survived the war and emigrated to Israel, where he became a bus driver for the Egged Company. I met him again in 1959 during my stay in Israel.

33   In the spring of 1944, there was a considerable increase of illegal traffic across the Slovak-Hungarian border because many surviving Slovak Jews traveled illegally to Hungary, seeking to rescue some members of their families who had previously fled to Hungary to escape the Slovakian deportations of 1942. Now all were threatened by the start of the Nazi measures in Hungary. But this was also an opportunity to carry *The Report* across the border from Bratislava to Budapest or elsewhere in Hungary.

34   See Conway, "Frühe Augenzeugen-Berichte aus Auschwitz," p. 278; —, "The First Report About Auschwitz," p. 144.

35   Jenö Levai, *Zsidósors Európaban*, pp. 327–29. Levai lists more than two hundred major articles published in the Swiss Press in the summer 1944. See also Rings, p. 146. Rings noted 383 articles and various abstracts.

36   Reitlinger, p. 466. ". . . On April 7 the two Slovak authors of the War Refugees Board Report made their sensational escape from Birkenau to Bratislava. Yet news of the annihilation of Hungarian Jewry was slow in reaching the Western newspaper public. It was not until the beginning of July, when they had almost ceased, that the allied and neutral press reported the massive gassings. Had this happened sooner, 200,000 Jews or more might not have left Hungary." See also pp. 467–71.

Wetzler and I rested in Mikuláš for six weeks. During May 1944, we heard only scanty rumors about the deportation of Jews from Hungary. As I learned after the war, the Slovak Jewish Council knew well about the massive deportations from Hungary;[37] nevertheless, no information on this matter was passed on from the council to either Wetzler or me about these events. All we knew was the rudimentary information on the deportation of the Hungarian Jews published in the pro-Nazi press of Tiso's Slovak State. Then, on June 6, 1944 (D-day in Normandy), two more prisoners from Auschwitz arrived in Slovakia, and they brought us news from Auschwitz.

The two new escapees from Birkenau (Auschwitz II) were also Jewish prisoners: Arnost Rosin, born in 1912 in Snina, Slovakia (prisoner number 29858), and Czeslaw Mordowicz, from Mlava in Poland, born in 1921 (prisoner number 84216). Both had been in Auschwitz since 1942, i.e., had been "old prisoners" like Wetzler and I, and they had escaped together on May 27, 1944. After a difficult trip, they crossed the Slovak border on June 6, 1944, east of the High Tatra Mountains, about two hundred kilometers to the east of where Wetzler and I had crossed it. Over a public radio loudspeaker in the first Slovak village (Nedeca) they passed through, they heard about the Allied landing in Normandy and somewhat naively imagined the war was over. They went to the nearest bar and tried to pay for their consumption with dollars they had brought along from Auschwitz. They promptly were arrested but instead of being treated as Jews, they were accused of the much smaller crime of violating the currency laws. After a week in prison and payment of a stiff fine, they were released. The fine was paid by the Jewish Council of Slovakia, whose connections as well as the rapidly changing political situation in Slovakia (this was only three months before the Slovak National Uprising against the Nazis, and

---

37   The letter sent by Rabbi Weissmandel on May 22, 1944 (see note 9) from Bratislava contains extensive information on the progress of the deportation of Jews in Hungary from the very start.

the Soviet Army was already close to the Slovak borders) also played a significant role in the release of Rosin and Mordowicz.

Wetzler and I knew Rosin and Mordowicz personally from Birkenau, where all four of us were "old prisoners" who had survived in Auschwitz for more than a year. Those survivors were few and were frequently connected by bonds of mutual aid where any was possible; there was a sort of "old hands' Mafia" in all German concentration camps, in which survival time in the camp was a measure of distinction. In Auschwitz, more than a year of survival meant considerable seniority. Thus, Wetzler and I did not need to be introduced to the two new escapees. From Rosin and Mordowicz, we learned that in the short time between May 15 and their escape on May 27, 1944, over 100,000 Hungarian Jews had arrived in Birkenau, and most of them had promptly been murdered.

The Mordowicz-Rosin Report, an addition to the Vrba-Wetzler Report in which the ongoing slaughter of Hungarian Jews in Auschwitz was described, was recorded by Krasnyanski. It reported that the victims arriving in Auschwitz from Hungary had no knowledge whatever about what "resettlement" really meant, just like the almost two million other victims who were killed before Wetzler and I escaped from Auschwitz and prepared our Report. I only learned after the war that more than 400,000 Hungarian Jews were brought to Auschwitz after our escape and died a terrible death there up to mid-July 1944 without ever having been warned by the Hungarian Jewish Council about the true nature of "resettlement." They had entered the deportation trains hoping to land in some sort of Jewish "reservation" or ghetto where they would have a respite from the incredibly brutal terror inflicted upon them by the Hungarian Gendarmerie of Horthy's regime. They had been induced by this terror to "voluntarily" enter the deportation trains to avoid reprisals against their infirm family members. But after a horrifying journey, most of those deportees found themselves in the hands of cruel and merciless

German executioners in the German death factory in Birkenau. A lucky ten percent of them were found suitable for slave labor and later "distributed" into various slave labor camps all over Germany. Some of these survived their captivity in German hands.

MEETING REPRESENTATIVES OF THE VATICAN AND OF ORTHODOX JEWRY

IN CONNECTION WITH OUR REPORT, WETZLER AND I WERE involved in two events during June 1944 at the request of the Jewish Council of Slovakia. I was asked to speak personally to a representative of the Vatican on June 20, 1944, and a few days later to visit Rabbi Michael Beer Weissmandel, who at that time was considered the leading Jewish religious authority in Slovakia and Eastern Europe. At the request of the Slovak Jewish Council, on both visits I was not accompanied by Wetzler but by Mordowicz,[38] so that both pairs of escapees would be represented.

On June 20, 1944, Krasnyanski and a translator met with me and Mordowicz in the monastery in Svätý Jur,[39] about forty kilometers from Bratislava, where we were received by an elegant priest whom I thought at the time to be the Apostolic Delegate, Msgr. Burzio, but who was in fact a Vatican diplomat, Msgr. Mario Martilotti, a member of the Vatican's nunciature in Switzerland.[40] Martilotti—who told us he was to travel to Switzerland the next day—was well acquainted with our Report, as he had already read a German translation. He himself understood my German very well but spoke it with some difficulty—his French was

---

38   In *I Cannot Forgive* I did not mention Mordowicz at all because at the time of its writing (1963) I lived in England, having left communist Czechoslovakia in 1958. Mordowicz at that time still lived in Bratislava under the neo-Stalinist regime of Antonín Novotný. To publicly describe in England a close connection between myself and Mordowicz might have caused him problems, including accusations of having been a "Vatican spy" or "closely connected with the exiled heretic R. Vrba."

39   Vrba and Bestic, *I Cannot Forgive*, p. 256.

40   John S. Conway, "The First Report About Auschwitz," p. 143.

much more fluent. He obviously wished to be reassured about the authenticity of the escapees. Our discussions lasted several hours, but as far as we know today, this meeting did not have any far-reaching consequences other than to provide reliable information for the private ears of the Vatican. The publication of the Vrba-Wetzler Report in the West in late June 1944 was not accomplished with the help of the Vatican, as was sometimes believed, but through other channels.

The visit with Rabbi Weissmandel in Bratislava took place after our visit in Svätý Jur. This must have been toward the end of June 1944 and was even more puzzling to us than the other meeting. The real intent of this belated invitation (late June 1944) was not obvious: Wetzler and I had already been in Slovakia for two months by the time Rabbi Weissmandel invited me to come for coffee and a chat. Even after I accepted the invitation (I was invited along with Mordowicz), I remained puzzled. Perhaps this invitation was only a piece of rabbinical self-justification, so we couldn't say that we did not get a hearing. We were received by the rabbi in his study at the Yeshiva in Bratislava. Neither Krasnyanski nor a translator were present. During our relatively brief meeting (about one hour), I noticed that the rabbi clearly was very well acquainted with all the details of our Report. On the other hand, he did not mention to us that he had received previous independent information about the mass murder of Jews going on in Treblinka, Sobibor, and Belżec as well as some information about Auschwitz, the so-called Polish Major's Report[41]—I learned all this only after the war from reading a letter he wrote on May 22, 1944.[42] Rabbi Weissmandel also did not tell us that he had direct and indirect connections with the SS, particularly through Dieter Wisliceny, the German Berater (government advisor) in Slovakia, a close collaborator of Eichmann's who had helped

---

41   The account by the "Polish Major" was written after November 1943 when the Polish prisoner Jerzy Tabeau (known in Auschwitz as Jerzy Wesolowski) escaped from Auschwitz. A full text of his account was recently published in Swiebocki's *Zeszyty Oswiecimskie*, pp. 77–129.

42   See note 9.

to mastermind the deportation of 60,000 Slovak Jews from Slovakia to Auschwitz, Treblinka, Majdanek, Sobibor, and Belżec in 1942 and the deportation of Greek Jews to Auschwitz in 1943. And he told us nothing about his truly harebrained "Europa Plan" under which he and the Jewish Council in Slovakia undertook to pay two million dollars—money which he did not have and could not pay—if the Germans agreed to refrain from deporting European Jews to Poland. (Since the Jews of most of Europe had already been deported, the two million dollars would be buying, almost exclusively, a promise to stop the deportation of Hungarian Jews).[43] From the perspective of the daily realities of Auschwitz, to me this "Europa Plan" is at best nothing but a product of a tortured and incapacitated human mind. Alternatively, it may have served the rabbi and the Jewish Council as an alibi or pretext for unsavory "negotiations" with the SS, as will be discussed further below.

During the meeting, the rabbi was very polite and treated us, to use his words, as the emissaries of almost two million Jews who (by that time) had perished in Auschwitz. I want to add here a few personal recollections as background to my meeting. The Yeshiva of Rabbi S. D. Ungar and later of his son-in-law, Rabbi M. B. Weissmandel, was originally located in Nitra, where I spent some years during my childhood (1930–1933). We lived on the same street as the rabbis, my maternal grandfather (Bernat Grünfeld, from Nitra, later murdered in Majdanek) was a member of their congregation, and there was direct personal contact between my family and this congregation. I vividly remember Rabbi Ungar, who once when I was eight years old took me on a particular occasion (it was meant to be a great distinction for a child) into his conference room, where I was allowed to sit with grown-ups and was served tea and cake. Since

43   Gila Fatran, "The Working Group," in *Holocaust and Genocide Studies*, vol. 8, 1994, pp. 164–201. The same view has been adopted by some historians, including Yehuda Bauer, who have praised Weissmandel and others for their readiness to negotiate with the Germans. See, for example Yehuda Bauer, *The Jewish Emergence from Powerlessness* (Toronto: University of Toronto Press, 1979), p. 24. See also Asher Cohen, *La Shoah. L'anéantissement des juifs d'Europe, 1933–1945* (Paris: Editions de Cerf, 1990), pp. 107–8.

this cake treatment, my relation to this Jewish group had always been cordial. After the majority of the Jews of Nitra (including my grandparents) were "resettled" in 1942, the Yeshiva of Rabbi Weissmandel and its students were allowed to stay in Nitra. The rabbi and to some extent his pupils were protected from deportation in 1942 because Slovakia under President Tiso was a "Catholic State," and therefore religious schools (even a Jewish one) were to be left unmolested. However, the Yeshiva was vandalized by local fascist hooligans, and apparently for this reason was transferred to Bratislava—where "it could be better protected"—sometime in 1943. When I returned from Auschwitz in the spring of 1944, I was surprised to see that the Yeshiva of Rabbi Weissmandel was almost in the center of Bratislava, obviously under at least temporary protection of both the pro-Nazi Slovak and the German authorities who were in power in Bratislava at that time. The visibility of Yeshiva life in the center of Bratislava, less than 150 miles south of Auschwitz, was in my eyes a typical piece of Goebbels-inspired activity and brazen Nazi humor. There— before the eyes of the world—the pupils of Rabbi Weissmandel could study the rules of Jewish ethics while their own sisters and mothers were being murdered and burned in Birkenau. At that time, only two months and 150 miles away from an Auschwitz working at highest capacity, this Yeshiva in the center of Bratislava struck me as merely a circus with Rabbi Weissmandel as its main, albeit tragicomic, clown.

After the visit with Rabbi Weissmandel, I had little further contact with the Slovak Jewish Council except that they supported me financially. I got two hundred Slovak crowns per week, at that time an average worker's salary and sufficient to sustain me comfortably in an illegal life in Bratislava. On August 29, 1944, the Slovak Army revolted against the Nazis and the reestablishment of Czechoslovakia was proclaimed. My connections with the Slovak Jewish Council stopped at that point, as I immediately volunteered to enlist in the Army. Because of the rapid military advance of the Germans into Slovakia and the retreat of the regular

Slovak Army, I was directed into the Partisan Unit of Captain Milan Uher ("Hero of the Slovak National Uprising in Memoriam"). In early September 1944, in Uher's home village of Lubina in Western Slovakia, I received my Czechoslovak uniform and my gun and ammunition, and continued my war against the Nazis by conventional means until my official discharge from the Army at the end of the war in May 1945. I left for Prague in the same year to study chemistry and biochemistry, as I had intended to do even before I was sent to Auschwitz. With a distinguished military record gained during the Slovak National Uprising (I was decorated several times) and my newly legalized Czechoslovak name, the doors of all schools were open for me in Prague. There, I finished my university studies and postgraduate training and started my career in science (biochemistry and neurochemistry). I voluntarily left Czechoslovakia in 1958 and continued my teaching and research activities in Israel (Ministry of Agriculture), the UK (Medical Research Council), the USA (Harvard Medical School), and Canada (Medical Research Council of Canada and the University of British Columbia).

CONTROVERSIAL ASPECTS RELEVANT TO THE HOLOCAUST IN HUNGARY

AT THE TIME OF WRITING THIS ARTICLE, MORE THAN FIFTY years have elapsed since the events described, and much has been written about them. There are some controversies with respect to the contents of the Vrba-Wetzler Report as well as its handling after it was written. Some salient points need further clarification. The Czech historian M. Kárný wrote[44] in 1992 that neither I nor Wetzler had known anything about the preparations made in Auschwitz for the mass murder of Hungarian Jews: "In the whole Report of Wetzler and Vrba there is no mention whatever

---

44   Miroslav Kárný. "Historie osvětimské zprávy Wetzlera a Vrby," pp. 174–75. Also see note 8.

about what supposedly was a public secret in Auschwitz—namely that it was the turn of the Hungarian Jews and that preparations were already being made in Auschwitz for their murder. If such a public secret had existed in the camp, certainly the escaped prisoners from Auschwitz would have considered it necessary to place special emphasis on these preparations in their Report." Kárný further claims to have found evidence for my and Wetzler's ignorance about these preparations by quoting verbatim the end of the chronological part of the Vrba-Wetzler Report, which stated: "Small groups of Jews from Benzburg and Sosnovitz, who had been dragged from hiding, arrived in the middle of March. One of them told me that many Polish Jews were crossing over to Slovakia and from there to Hungary and that the Slovak Jews helped them on their way through Slovakia. After the gassing of the Theresienstadt transport there were no further arrivals until March 15, 1944. The effective strength of the camp rapidly diminished and 'selected' men of transports arriving later, especially Dutch Jews, were directed to the camp. When we left on April 7, 1944, we heard that large convoys of Greek Jews were expected."

M. Kárný further develops his ideas by saying: "If Wetzler and Vrba considered it necessary to record rumors about the expected transports of Greek Jews, why would they have not put on record that transports of hundreds of thousands Hungarian Jews were expected, if their expected arrival was indeed a public secret in Auschwitz? If they recorded the help of Slovak Jews to the Polish Jews escaping to Hungary, why would they not warn these Polish escapees of the danger threatening them immediately, particularly in Hungary?"

And, he claims, "[Wetzler and Vrba]...did not know that the Final Solution in Hungary was imminent." In other words, Kárný implies that preparations for the Holocaust of Hungarian Jews were not passed along because they were not revealed by us at the time.

To my present knowledge, a copy of the Slovak original text of the Vrba-Wetzler Report has not been preserved, so that I cannot state categorically whether the warning about the imminent Holocaust in Hungary was or was not recorded in the original Slovak version of the Report. However, I clearly remember that, during the checking of the final version of the Report, I had a discussion with Krasnyanski on this very point, I insisted the warning should be included, whereas Krasnyanski was of the opinion that only murders which had already taken place in Auschwitz should be recorded so that the final report would be a record of facts only that would not be weakened by "forecasts" and "prophecies." I do not remember whose opinion prevailed. But I do recall very well that Krasnyanski reassured me that the Jewish as well as other authorities would be immediately acquainted with all of the details I and Wetzler had provided about the preparations made in Auschwitz for the mass murder of the Hungarian Jews.

Indeed, there is incontrovertible evidence showing that these preparations in Auschwitz, as described by Wetzler and myself, were made known to the leading Jewish authorities in Slovakia, and subsequently to their partners in Hungary. Furthermore, this information was later passed on to the above-mentioned Jewish contacts in Western countries, specifically in Switzerland shortly thereafter. The above-mentioned letter by Rabbi Weissmandel and Gisi Fleischmann, dated May 22, 1944,[45] was written one month after Wetzler and I arrived in Slovakia from Auschwitz but well before the escape from Auschwitz and arrival in Slovakia of Mordowicz and Rosin (June 6, 1944), i.e., could not have been based on their later information. This letter (five ledger-size pages, single-space typed) was sent by a reliable courier to Switzerland, with the original addressed to the general office of Hechalutz in Bern.

This letter starts with twelve paragraphs, labeled (a) through (m), giving detailed information about the practices at Auschwitz. Paragraph (1) states: "(1) In December and January [1944] a special railway line [in Birkenau; R.V.] has already been built leading into station, in order

45   See note 9.

to prepare the new work of annihilation of Hungarian Jews [italics add-ed—R.V.]. That was said by knowledgeable people there in that were in that hell; there they discuss it without scruples, without suspecting that someone outside will learn about it since they assume, in general, that no one in the country knows anything whatever about the work in this hell."

In paragraph (m), Rabbi Weissmandel stated: "This is their system in Auschwitz, where since yesterday they are deporting [from Hungary] 12,000 Jewish souls daily; men, women, old people, children, sick per-sons and healthy people, and there every day they are asphyxiated and burned and converted into fertilizer for the fields."

In other parts of this letter the rabbi and Gisi Fleischmann describe the inhuman methods of transporting the deportees to Auschwitz and their immediate fate afterward as follows: "(e) These transports arrive in Auschwitz after two to three days of travel without air, without food and without water, body pressed upon body. In this manner a consid-erable number of persons already die during the journey; the survivors go naked into special compartments of large halls, believing that they are going to have a bath. There they 2,000 souls per section—will be gassed by cyanide."

In paragraphs (f) and (g), they state "According to an authentic message from a few witnesses, there were in Auschwitz at the end of February [1944] four such annihilation halls and according to rumors these facilities are being expanded.... The bodies and burned in ovens specially built for this purpose...."

Not surprisingly, Rabbi Weissmandel's letter did not name his sources of this crucial information, but he says on page 3 of his letter that "two Jews recently escaped from Auschwitz" are the source. We can therefore be certain that his dispatch was based on the fact that he had studied our Report at some time between April 28 and May 22. The presumption must be that this was the case, for no other eyewit-nesses escaped from Auschwitz during this period, and no alternative source has ever been suggested. And, as noted above, when I met the rabbi toward the end of June 1944, he was well acquainted with the details of our report. In view of the facts evidenced by the May 22 letter, there can be little doubt that the rabbi based his appeal to Switzerland on the information about Auschwitz provided by Wetzler and me. No other explanation is credible.

It follows that those historians are mistaken who have recently sought to show that Wetzler and I knew nothing before our escape about the preparations being made in Auschwitz for the mass murder of the Hungarian Jews. We in fact did know about these preparations and we explained it clearly; the post-war testimony of the chairman of the Jewish Council in Slovakia, Oskar Neumann, provides an eloquent confirmation of this.[46]

It is of interest to note that the rabbi was well informed about many details of the deportations of Jews then in progress in Hungary, although he lived in Bratislava, Slovakia. He says in his letter that the deportation of Hungarian Jews began east of the river Tisa (Theiss), that 12,000 are being deported daily, that each freight car contains sixty or more people, that each train contains forty-five freight cars, etc. This demonstrates that the Jewish leadership in Bratislava and Budapest was in regular contact and that channels for rapid exchange of information from distant parts of Hungary were available to the Jewish Council in Bratislava, and from provincial Czechoslovakia to

---

46   In this connection, the testimony of Oskar Neumann is of great importance, because Neumann was the Chairman of the Jewish Council in Slovakia and it was under his aegis, and with the technical assistance of Krasnyanski and Mrs. Steiner, that the Vrba-Wetzler Report was prepared. In his postwar memoirs, Neumann describes my and Wetzler's escape from Auschwitz without identifying us by name, claiming, among other things, that it was his organization that helped us cross the Slovak border. However, he also stated: "These chaps did also report that recently an enormous construction activity had been initiated in the camp and very recently the SS often spoke about looking forward to the arrival of Hungarian salami." See his *Im Schatten des Todes* (Tel Aviv: Olamenu, 1956), pp. 178–81. See also notes 23 and 29.

that of Budapest, before and during the deportations of Hungarian Jews in spring 1944, even though Jews were forbidden to travel.

The Catholic and Protestant churches also had no difficulty, relatively speaking, in obtaining the same information about the progress of deportation of Jews from Hungary; there is plenty of evidence showing that they were all perfectly aware of these events in detail, as a very recent monograph again describes.[47] The inevitable conclusion is that in May 1944 at the latest, the representatives of all major denominations (Jewish, Catholic, and Protestant) knew that the deported Hungarian Jews were being taken for slaughter, and that for some reason all religious representatives chose not to warn the masses about the scheduled fate of the deportees. The Jewish authorities, for their part, duly informed their contacts in Switzerland about the preparations made in Auschwitz for the Holocaust of Hungarian Jews and about the progress of the deportations, but this vital information was withheld from those who were actually being deported.

The interpretation of all these events is of course a painful affair, and my interpretation—as could be gathered from what I have said above—is very different from the interpretation given by Yehuda Bauer, Asher Cohen, and other mainly Israel-based Holocaust scholars who extol the "meritorious work" of Weissmandel, Dr. Kastzner, and other "negotiators." I am forced to regard these interpretations as the product of scholars who would like to improve not only the Jewish future but also the Jewish past. Perhaps part of this problem lies elsewhere: it may be that many of those who did not have direct experience with the Nazis at that time are unable to comprehend the truly pernicious nature of Nazism and the absolute futility of any negotiations unless the negotiator could prove that the group he represented was physically as strong or stronger than the Nazis. For those of us who saw the Nazis in action in Auschwitz, this basic precondition is easier to understand. If the Nazis entered into any "negotiations" with Jews

47   See for example Frank Baron and Sandor Szenes, *Von Ungarn nach Auschwitz*.

in Bratislava or Budapest, to me it merely means that they had their own deceitful plans as to how to use the Jewish Councils for their own objectives, which were very simple: to rob the Jews swiftly of their personal property, to prepare lists of those to be deported on the basis of names and addresses supplied by the Jewish Councils, to make those on the lists enter the deportation trains without causing difficulties, and to kill the deportees economically and efficiently in Auschwitz, all the while preserving the secret of their murderous empire. The fact that the Nazis in Budapest also took personal bribes from a Jewish notable, Fülöp von Freudiger,[48] and from other prominent Jews in Budapest and elsewhere means very little as far as their dedication to the general objectives of the Final Solution was concerned. For instance, it is well known that in Auschwitz, all SS without exception were dedicated not only to killing Jews but also to pilfering, from camp commander Rudolf Ferdinand Hoess to the lowliest SS man serving in the camp. Indeed, this was an unofficial part of their reward for their murderous activity. To the SS robbing, pilfering, and cheating Jews—or for that matter any other non-Germans in a weak and vulnerable position—was as natural as murdering them. Blackmailing the Jewish "negotiators" and taking large sums as bribes did not really oblige the Nazis to anything and was part of their cynical game. In this connection, I would like to point out a few relevant facts recorded by other participants in the drama of the extremely swift mass murder of Hungarian Jews.

Rabbi Weissmandel's close contact in Hungary and his confidant was an important member of the Jewish Council of Hungary, Fülöp von Freudiger, who was also the son-in-law of the late Chief Rabbi of Bratislava (Akiba Schreiber) and had studied at a Yeshiva in Slovakia.[49] In a subsequent report, Freudiger noted that on March 19, 1944, the very day the German troops crossed the western border of Hungary, Eichmann's *Sondereinsatzkommando* contacted the Jewish

---

48   Freudiger, p. 266.
49   Ibid., p. 238.

Council and various influential Jewish notables. These officers of Eichmann's staff were SS-Obersturmbannführer Hermann Krumey, SS-Hauptsturmführer Otto Hunsche, SS-Standartenführer Kurt Becher, and the above-mentioned Dieter Wisliceny. Wisliceny even brought with him a letter written in Hebrew by Rabbi Weissmandel to Freudiger, stating that "they could trust Wisliceny."[50] Freudiger also states that he quite regularly received mail from Bratislava (mainly from Rabbi Weissmandel) via a courier of the Hungarian Legation who traveled from Bratislava with the evening express train[51] (the distance is only about one hundred miles). Freudiger also stated that during the second week of May 1944 Weissmandel had informed him that, according to information obtained from the Slovak Ministry of Transportation, permission had already been granted to transport 310,000 Hungarian Jews through Slovakia on their way to Auschwitz. Of course, by that time, more than three weeks after Wetzler and I released our Report in Slovakia, Rabbi Weissmandel must have known not only what Auschwitz meant but also about the special preparations made there for the reception and mass murder of the *Zugang* from Hungary. Freudiger confirms that the copy of the Report he received from Rabbi Weissmandel contained information not only about the history of events in Auschwitz, but also about the special preparations made for the mass murder of Hungarian Jews.[52] Freudiger also claims that subsequently members of the Jewish Council spread the information contained in the Report to Members of Parliament, Bishops and even Horthy.[53] However, it is a fact that between May 15 and July 9, 1944, those earmarked for deportation, i.e., those who most needed the information contained in the Vrba-Wetzler Report, were kept in the dark about their destination.

---

50   Ibid., pp. 239, 245.
51   Ibid., p. 262.
52   Ibid.
53   Ibid., p. 263.

On the other hand, the negotiations of the Jewish Council members (particularly of the Zionist faction led by Kasztner) did obtain a limited success. In August 1944, a transport of about 1,800 Jewish people from Hungary was sent by Eichmann not to Auschwitz but to Switzerland, albeit by a long route. Obviously, those traveling in this transport were not the poverty-stricken Jews of Hungary. Freudiger records[54] that, as a partial payment for this transport, the Economic Department of the SS under SS-Obersturmbannführer Kurt Becher received cash, foreign currency, 18 kilograms of gold, and 180 carats of diamonds plus 1,000 or 2,000 US dollars per person, an incredible cash fortune for an average person in Hungary in 1944 when the black-market value of a dollar was astronomical. Whether the preservation of secrecy about the death-mills in Auschwitz was self-imposed by the Jewish Councils or was also part of the payment for the release of a small number of privileged Jews cannot be documented, for obvious reasons, but it is surely not far-fetched to suggest that it was well worth Eichmann's while to grant the release of those 2,000 relatively rich and well-connected Jews to Switzerland as a reward for keeping what was happening at Auschwitz a secret to the remainder of their fellow Jews. It is clear that these prominent Jews themselves had already become acquainted with the information contained in our Report. Andreas Biss, a close collaborator of Kasztner and von Freudiger, describes a remarkable episode on this journey when the train on its way westward was switched toward Auspitz (not Auschwitz). A terrible panic occurred, because the passengers did not understand the difference between the two.[55] Thus, while there were 437,000 Jews in Hungary who were not given any information about the nature of Auschwitz or about the preparations made there for their murder, a tiny minority of 1,800 Jews who traveled to Switzerland knew very well what the implications of the name Auschwitz meant. The simultaneous existence in one small country of these two contrasting groups is amazing but well documented.

---

54   Ibid., p. 269.
55   Andreas Biss, *A Million Jews to Save* (London: New English Library, 1973), p. 81.

Further evidence of the collaboration between the Nazis and certain favored groups of Jews can be seen from the fact when the deportation of Hungarian Jews was stopped by Horthy in July 1944, and the Jewish Council became useless for the Germans, Wisliceny advised Freudiger to flee to Romania, which he did.[56] Yehuda Bauer writes that shortly before the Russians liberated Bratislava from the Nazis (April 4, 1945), through Becher's efforts a group of sixty-nine people, most of them from Bratislava, left the city on March 31, 1945 and reached Vienna on April 3 and then traveled to Switzerland. Among them was Rabbi Weissmandel.[57] The Becher referred to is the same SS-Colonel Kurt Becher mentioned above. *Res ipsa loquitur.*

It appears that during these critical times, the Jewish masses in Slovakia and Hungary generally placed their trust either in the "Zionist leadership" (e.g., Kasztner, Biss) or in Orthodox and Rabbinical Jewish leaders (e.g., Rabbi Weissmandel, von Freudiger). The Nazis were aware of this and therefore chose exactly these circles for "negotiations." That the negotiators and their families were in fact pathetic, albeit voluntary, hostages in the hands of Nazi power was an important part of these "deals." From the testimony of survivors such as Elie Wiesel, it seems clear that the Jewish masses assumed that if something truly horrible was in store for them, these respectable leaders would know about it and would share their knowledge. But as detailed above, these leaders did in fact learn what Auschwitz meant but did not share this new knowledge with the Jews earmarked for deportation. The puzzlingly passive trip of enormous masses of Hungarian Jews into the sordid gas chambers of Birkenau was in fact the result of a successful confidence trick by the Nazis that resulted in a death toll three to four times larger than that recorded after the atomic bombing of Hiroshima. This was an incredible and unprecedented organizational

---

56   Freudiger, pp. 277–78.
57   Yehuda Bauer, *American Jewry and the Holocaust* (Detroit: Wayne State University Press, 1981), p. 449.

success, even for Auschwitz. It is my contention that a small group of informed people, by their silence, deprived others of the possibility or privilege of making their own decisions in the face of mortal danger.

One must, of course, also not forget that although 400,000 Jews from Hungary were murdered and burned, their property was not burned. I am not speaking about the gold crowns extracted from their mouths before they were cremated in Birkenau or about the luggage that was stolen from them and ended up in the "Canada" storage areas. The majority of the Hungarian Jews belonged to the middle-class, and they left behind their homes, their gardens, their fields, their stocks and shares, their bank accounts, their "shops on Main Street," their furniture, their cars, their bicycles, their kitchen utensils, their radios, their fur coats, and many other things that were scarce and valuable in the bombed-out territories of Germany and occupied Europe. This partially explains why Horthy and his clique (with the help of his bloodthirsty gendarmerie) were so keen to be rid of the unfortunate Jews. It was Horthy and his gendarmerie who were still in power during the deportations of Jews from Hungary to Auschwitz; confiscated Jewish property was redistributed among Hungarians who demonstrated their loyalty to Horthy, and was used to reinforce the shaky loyalty of Horthy's followers at a time when the war was obviously going badly. If we assume that the average per-person value of all the property of the deported Hungarian Jews, from their houses and bank accounts to their last luggage and the gold crowns in their mouths, was only $100, then 400,000 victims represent a profit of $40,000,000 in valuable goods available for immediate redistribution, a tremendous windfall in a war-torn country. In fact, of course, the property was worth many times more than the $100 estimate, and the distribution of Jewish goods and wealth had more political appeal than a distribution of dubious wartime paper money. These are the reasons why I believe Rabbi Weissmandel's idea to stop the deportation of Hungarian Jews with his Europa Plan and a $2,000,000 bribe to the Nazis was harebrained. No doubt the Nazis were amused by these unrealistic, ridiculous, and truly childish ideas, but these "negotiations" were useful to them as long as the objectives of Auschwitz were not communicated to the intended victims and hundreds of thousands were smoothly being deported to Auschwitz. It is of interest to know that Eichmann's cronies from Budapest, SS officers Krumey and Hunsche, were protected from prosecution after the war because Dr. Kasztner, in the name of the World Zionist Congress, issued them protective affidavits.[58] Krumey and Hunsche were in fact brought to trial only after 1969, i.e., twenty-five years later.[59] Dr. Kasztner also issued a "whitewashing note" to SS-Obersturmbannführer Kurt Becher,[60] and to my knowledge the latter was still a happy millionaire in Hamburg in the late 1980s.[61] Wisliceny was arrested by the British, delivered to Czechoslovakia, and hanged in Bratislava.[62] Kasztner enjoyed a distinguished career after the war in the new State of Israel but after a complex libel trial he was shot dead on the street in Tel Aviv in 1958 and rehabilitated posthumously.[63] Weissmandel became a much admired rabbi in New York and died there in 1958.[64]

---

58   Karla Muller-Tupath, *Reichsführers gehorsamster Becher*. Eine deutsche Karriere (Fulda: Konkret Literature Verlag, 1982).
59   Krumey and Hunsche were tried in Frankfurt in 1969–70. Krumey received five years in prison and Hunsche was found not guilty. An appeal by the public prosecutor led to a second trial, which found both guilty. Krumey was sentenced to twelve years and Hunsche to five years. In both cases, I was a witness for the prosecution.
60   Bauer, *American Jewry*, p. 432.
61   See note 58.
62   Reitlinger, p. 567.
63   Braham, *The Politics*, p. 721.
64   Reb Moshe Shonfeld, *The Holocaust Victims Accuse. Documents and Testimony on Jewish War Criminals* (Brooklyn, NY: Neturei Karta, 1977), p. 12.

FIGURE 1

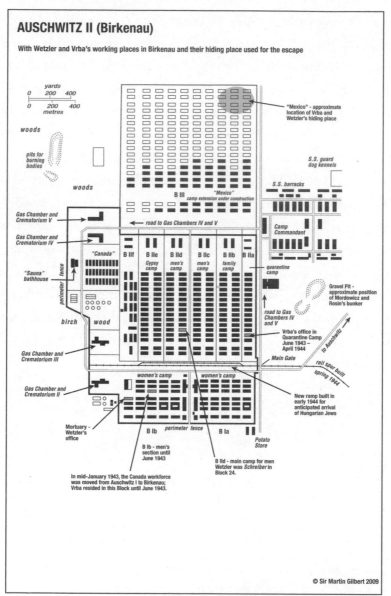

AUSCHWITZ II (Birkenau)

With Wetzler and Vrba's working places in Birkenau and their hiding place used for the escape

yards
0   200   400

0   200   400
metres

woods

pits for
burning
bodies

woods

B III   "Mexico"
camp extension under construction

"Mexico" - approximate
location of Vrba and
Wetzler's hiding place

S.S. guard
dog kennels

S.S. barracks

Gas Chamber and
Crematorium V

Gas Chamber and
Crematorium IV

← road to Gas Chambers IV and V

Camp
Commandant

"Canada"   B IIf   B IIe   B IId   B IIc   B IIb   B IIa

Gypsy   men's   men's   family
camp   camp   camp   camp

quarantine
camp

"Sauna"
bathhouse

perimeter fence

birch   wood

Gravel Pit -
approximate position
of Mordowicz and
Rosin's bunker

road to Gas
Chambers IV
and V

Vrba's office in
Quarantine Camp
June 1943 –
April 1944

Gas Chamber and
Crematorium III

Main Gate

to Auschwitz

rail spur built
spring 1944

women's camp   women's camp

Gas Chamber and
Crematorium II

New ramp built in
early 1944 for
anticipated arrival
of Hungarian Jews

Mortuary -
Wetzler's
office

B Ib   perimeter fence   B Ia

Potato
Store

B Ib - men's
section until
June 1943

B IId - main camp for men
Wetzler was *Schreiber* in
Block 24.

In mid-January 1943, the Canada workforce
was moved from Auschwitz I to Birkenau;
Vrba resided in this Block until June 1943.

FIGURE 2

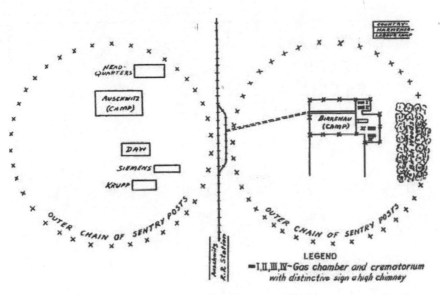

Approximate situation sketch of Auschwitz and Birkenau camp districts.

This sketch shows the relative positions of Auschwitz I and Auschwitz II (Birkenau) to the "old" ramp. Auschwitz I (on the left side of the sketch) includes the building of DAW (Deutsche Ausrüstungsworke), Siemens and Krupp factories. The "Canada stores" were situated next to DAW. On the right side of the sketch, the map of Birkenau is shown including the four gas chambers and crematoria. The railway line with the branch serving the ramp was situated between the outer chains of sentry posts of Auschwitz I and Auschwitz II (Birkenau), as shown above.

This sketch was prepared by myself (Rudolf Vrba) in Žilina on April 25, 1944, shortly after my escape from Auschwitz (Birkenau).

FIGURE 3

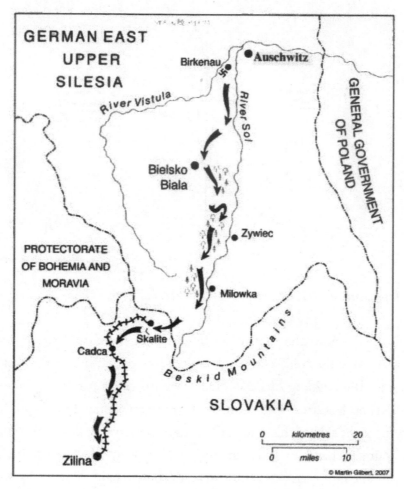

Escape route of Rudolf Vrba and Alfred Wetzler from Birkenau to Slovakia.
April 1944, showing the main deportation railway from Slovakia,
Austria, and Hungary to Auschwitz (through Žilina), and their own
route southward (indicated by arrows). From Auschwitz and the Allies,
by Martin Gilbert (Holt, Rinehart and Winston, New York, 1981).
Reproduced with permission of Martin Gilbert.